EARLY CHILDHOOD EDUCATION 86/87

Editor

Judy Spitler McKee
Eastern Michigan University

Judy Spitler McKee received a B.A. in elementary education and social sciences from Central Michigan University, an M.A. in developmental psychology and an Ed.D. in curriculum and teaching from Teachers College, Columbia University. She is a professor of Early Childhood Education and Educational Psychology at Eastern Michigan University. She is actively involved with teaching and conducting workshops on play, Piaget, assessment, and stress-reduction for children on local, state, and national levels.

Editorial Contributor

Karen Menke Paciorek
Eastern Michigan University

Karen Menke Paciorek teaches at Eastern Michigan University and supervises student teachers. All of her professional training is in Early Childhood Education, with a B.S. from the University of Pittsburgh, an M.A. from the George Washington University, and a Ph.D. from Peabody College of Vanderbilt University. She is active in the state and local Association for the Education of Young Children.

Cover illustration by Mike Eagle

Annual Editions
A Library of Information from the Public Press

The Dushkin Publishing Group, Inc.
Sluice Dock, Guilford, Connecticut 06437

The Annual Editions Series

Annual Editions is a series of over forty volumes designed to provide the reader with convenient, low-cost access to a wide range of current, carefully selected articles from some of the most important magazines, newspapers, and journals published today. Annual Editions are updated on an annual basis through a continuous monitoring of over 200 periodical sources. All Annual Editions have a number of features designed to make them particularly useful, including topic guides, annotated tables of contents, unit overviews, and indexes. For the teacher using Annual Editions in the classroom, an Instructor's Resource Guide with test questions is available for each volume.

PUBLISHED

Africa
Aging
American Government
American History, Pre-Civil War
American History, Post-Civil War
Anthropology
Biology
Business/Management
China
Comparative Politics
Computers in Education
Computers in Business
Computers in Society
Criminal Justice
Drugs and Society
Early Childhood Education
Economics
Educating Exceptional Children
Education
Educational Psychology
Environment
Geography

Global Issues
Health
Human Development
Human Sexuality
Latin America
Macroeconomics
Marketing
Marriage and Family
Middle East and the Islamic World
Personal Growth and Behavior
Psychology
Social Problems
Sociology
Soviet Union and Eastern Europe
State and Local Government
Urban Society
Western Civilization, Pre-Reformation
Western Civilization, Post-Reformation
World Politics

FUTURE VOLUMES

Abnormal Psychology
Death and Dying
Congress
Energy
Ethnic Studies
Foreign Policy
Judiciary
Law and Society
Nutrition
Parenting
Philosophy

Political Science
Presidency
Religion
South Asia
Third World
Twentieth Century American History
Western Europe
Women's Studies
World History

Library of Congress Cataloging in Publication Data
Main entry under title:
Annual Editions: Early Childhood Education
    1. Child development—Periodicals.   2. Child welfare—Periodicals.   3. Domestic Education—Periodicals.   4. Education, Preschool—1965—Periodicals.   5. Children—Management—Periodicals.   I. Title: Early Childhood Education.
HQ777.A7A   649'.1'05   77-640114
ISBN 0-87967-628-0

Eighth Edition

Manufactured by The Banta Company, Menasha, Wisconsin 54952

To The Reader

In publishing ANNUAL EDITIONS we recognize the enormous role played by the magazines, newspapers, and journals of the *public press* in providing current, first-rate educational information in a broad spectrum of interest areas. Within the articles, the best scientists, practitioners, researchers, and commentators draw issues into new perspective as accepted theories and viewpoints are called into account by new events, recent discoveries change old facts, and fresh debate breaks out over important controversies.

Many of the articles resulting from this enormous editorial effort are appropriate for students, researchers, and professionals seeking accurate, current material to help bridge the gap between principles and theories and the real world. These articles, however, become more useful for study when those of lasting value are carefully *collected, organized, indexed,* and *reproduced* in a *low-cost format,* which provides easy and permanent access when the material is needed. That is the role played by *Annual Editions.* Under the direction of each volume's *Editor,* who is an expert in the subject area, and with the guidance of an *Advisory Board,* we seek each year to provide in each *ANNUAL EDITION* a current, well-balanced, carefully selected collection of the best of the public press for your study and enjoyment. We think you'll find this volume useful, and we hope you'll take a moment to let us know what you think.

Americans are very ambivalent about their commitment to young children and their families. Many divide their loyalties and support and are able to care deeply about and provide for children they know personally, but are unable to extend that caring or action to children in their communities or nation whom they do not know. Many taxpayers and legislators who focus solely on inflation and taxation philosophies vote to slash millages, programs, and services for Early Childhood Education. Beginning in 1980, federal programs for child health, nutrition, child-care subsidies, and other social programs were drastically reduced, resulting in an increase in millions of parents and children living below the poverty level. The nation lacks a coherent national policy guaranteeing the physical and social well-being of families, and children remain the *poorest of all age groups* in America.

Professionals in the field can cite the results of several longitudinal research studies that incontrovertibly show that investment in quality preschool compensatory education in the 1960s during the Great Society era has been cost-beneficial (i.e., initial outlay returns greater benefits) in the 1970s and 1980s for children, parents, and communities. Investment in quality knowledge-based child-care programs has been scientifically demonstrated to reduce later expenditures for special education programs, grade retentions, teenage pregnancies, school drop-outs, and juvenile delinquency (Lazar, et al, 1977, 1979; Weikart, et al., 1982, 1984). However, while these research reports have been circulated by professional organizations to their members, press coverage and dissemination of these critical findings on the financial, social, and human payoffs have been minimal. Clearly, Early Childhood Education, historically linked with social reform efforts to improve the quality of life, is good for children and families and saves taxpayer money in the long run. Today's educational investments will continue to pay off in dividends of developed human potential, personal fulfillment, and societal contributions. The lack of investment will continue to reap its harvest of lost human capital and resources, personal suffering, and societal disruption and disorder.

A major purpose of this eighth edition of *Annual Editions: Early Childhood Education 86/87* is to capture the dynamic spirit of this heightened interest, while bringing to light the contradictory tapestry of attitudes and actions regarding young children and their families by sampling both professional and lay sources. A second purpose is to stimulate awareness, interest, and inquiry into the historical trends, issues, controversies, and realities of the field.

Given the diversity of topics included in the volume, it may be used in many ways: with undergraduate or graduate students; as an anthology of primary and secondary sources; as supplementary readings correlated with textbooks in developmental or child psychology, human development or special education, home economics, family life, pediatrics, and child care; for individual term papers, oral presentations, and projects; or for class discussions, group work, panel discussions, and debates.

The selection of articles has been a cooperative venture involving input from readers of previous editions, professionals in the field, reviewers, and members of the *Annual Editions* Advisory Board. Your comments on this eighth edition are invited and will serve to modify future anthologies. Please fill out and return the article rating form on the last page. Speak out for this edition, and then speak out for young children and their families. Our future depends on them, but they depend on us *now.*

Judy Spitler McKee

Editor

Contents

Unit 1

Perspectives

Five selections provide a brief history on the development of Early Childhood Education and assess the human value and cost-effectiveness of programs for young children.

Unit 2

Childhood and Society

Five selections present the interrelationship between young children and society and the role of the teacher in helping them develop their abilities to cope and evolve into effective citizens.

The concepts in italics are developed in the article. For further expansion please refer to the Topic Guide and the Index.

Unit 3

Development and Educational Opportunities

Fifteen selections, in six subsections, examine the development of children within their educational environment. Also considered is the responsibility of the early childhood educator to provide growth-enhancing educational opportunities.

The concepts in italics are developed in the article. For further expansion please refer to the Topic Guide and the Index.

The concepts in italics are developed in the article. For further expansion please refer to the Topic Guide and the Index.

Unit 4

Families, Child Rearing, and Parent Education

Six selections consider the effects of family life on the growing child and the importance of parent education.

The concepts in italics are developed in the article. For further expansion please refer to the Topic Guide and the Index.

Unit 5

Behavior, Stressors, and Guidance

Four selections examine the importance of classroom disciplinary guidance and consider the effects of stressors and stress-reduction on behavior.

Unit 6

Children with Special Needs

Three selections consider the benefits of a young child's educational experience in a common classroom, where all levels of abilities are present.

The concepts in italics are developed in the article. For further expansion please refer to the Topic Guide and the Index.

Unit 7

Curricular
Applications

Four selections consider the philosophy and practice of
curricular choices.

Unit 8

Teaching and
Evaluation

Seven selections, in three subsections, discuss teaching
as an art and the importance of environmental
planning and program evaluation for the effective
professional.

The concepts in italics are developed in the article. For further expansion please refer to the Topic Guide and the Index.

The concepts in italics are developed in the article. For further expansion please refer to the Topic Guide and the Index.

Topic Guide

This topic guide suggests how the selections in this book relate to topics of traditional concern to students and professionals involved with Early Childhood Education. It is very useful in locating articles which relate to each other for reading and research. The guide is arranged alphabetically according to topic. Articles may, of course, treat topics that do not appear in the topic guide. In turn, entries in the topic guide do not necessarily constitute a comprehensive listing of all the contents of each selection.

TOPIC AREA	TREATED AS AN ISSUE IN:	TOPIC AREA	TREATED AS AN ISSUE IN:
Abuse and Neglect	6. Childhood Through the Ages 9. Wednesday's Child 45. Can Teacher's Touch Children Anymore?	Divorce/Death	13. Why, Mommy, Why? 27. The Teacher's Role in Facilitating a Child's Adjustment to Divorce
Academics	22. Readiness 23. The 5s and 6s Go to School 24. When Parents of Kindergarteners Ask ''Why?'' 41. Encouraging Dramatic Play in Early Childhood 42. Piaget: The Six-Year-Old and Modern Math	Elementary Grades	42. Piaget: The Six-Year-Old and Modern Math 49. Testing Testing Testing Testing Testing
		Equipment and Materials	15. How to Choose a Good Early Childhood Program 40. Choosing Good Toys for Young Children 41. Encouraging Dramatic Play in Early Childhood
Advocacy	1. The Best Day Care There Ever Was 3. Who Are We in the Lives of Children?	Excellence	25. Nebraska State Board of Education, Position Statement on Kindergarten 39. Leading Primary Education Toward Excellence
Affective Development	2. What Is Basic for Young Children? 4. The Hurried Child 11. Your Child—From Birth to Twelve 14. Is Seven the Perfect Age? 34. The Name of the Game Is Confidence	Fine Arts	4. The Hurried Child
		Future Projections	5. The Statistical Trends
Basics of Education	2. What Is Basic for Young Children? 3. Who Are We in the Lives of Children?	Gifted	36. Meeting the Needs of Gifted Preschoolers
Cognitive Development	11. Your Child—From Birth to Twelve 14. Is Seven the Perfect Age? 17. The Real World of Teaching Two-Year-Old Children 30. Practical Parenting with Piaget 39. Leading Primary Education Toward Excellence	Head Start	8. Head Start 29. Changing Family Trends
		Health and Safety	26. Developmental Effects on Children of Pregnant Adolescents 38. The Medically Special Child 45. Can Teachers Touch Children Anymore?
Curiosity and Creativity	12. What Do Young Children Teach Themselves? 13. Why, Mommy, Why? 46. 15 Ways to Cultivate Creativity in Your Classroom 47. Thoughts on Creativity	History	1. The Best Day Care There Ever Was 6. Childhood Through the Ages 23. The 5s and 6s Go to School
		Infancy and Infant Programs	16. Meeting the Needs of Infants 18. Very Early Childhood Education for Infants and Toddlers 26. Developmental Effects on Children of Pregnant Adolescents
Day Care	1. The Best Day Care There Ever Was 19. Day Care in America 20. The Day-Care Child 44. Overworked and Underpaid 45. Can Teachers Touch Children Anymore?	Kindergarten	23. The 5s and 6s Go to School 24. When Parents of Kindergarteners Ask ''Why?'' 25. Nebraska State Board of Education, Position Statement on Kindergarten
Discipline	32. Classroom Discipline Problems? 33. Building Self-Control 35. Stress	Latchkey Children	10. Latchkey Children

Perspectives

The field of Early Childhood Education has a humane legacy dating back to the 1800s and a recent history of measured cost benefits to children, parents, and communities (Weikart, et al., 1984). Today's researchers are relating in scientific terms what yesterday's teachers and social workers have been saying all along: As a result of quality, knowledge-based intervention before the age of six years (1) young children's lives are changed for the better; (2) taxpayers save money; and (3) communities benefit. Yet, Early Childhood Education, despite its resounding successes and cost-saving effects, remains a concept not universally understood or accepted as either necessary or desirable. The field is embedded within a social, political, economic, and technological matrix of macrosystems that govern its funding, form, and functions, and shape its policies and practices.

During World War II, when the United States faced international and national crises, the talented staff of the Kaiser Centers in Portland, Oregon responded to the needs of thousands of working mothers by providing efficient and innovative twenty-four hour programs that served their children from eighteen months through school-age. This comprehensive day-care program was exceptionally high in quality, due to the dedication and education of a staff who provided physical and medical care, education, nutritional programs, precooked and packaged take-home meals, and shopping services for parents—all so the working mothers would be spared time, energy, and worry. Today, millions of working mothers again need quality child-care programs that are comprehensive in nature and operated by a dedicated and educated staff of specialists so they can be more competent parents.

The difference between the 1940s and the 1980s is due to the urgency posed by the wartime emergency. Those centers were seen as vital to America's security and were federally supported through the aegis of industry. Today, although national legislation for child-care support has been proposed several times during the last decade by a few members of Congress, most child-care centers struggle to be self-supporting, receive only a fraction of their operating budget from outside sources, pay low wages to their staff, and cannot provide comprehensive services to either children or parents who need them. Consequently, millions of young children under six years of age are inadequately cared for by untrained persons, are transported to the homes of relatives, friends, or to two different programs in a single day, or are left to fend for themselves without any direct adult supervision. This patchwork of alternative child-care arrangements will work its developmental effects in significant ways on young children. What personal and societal legacy of attitudes and actions are these young children receiving in the process as they grow and learn during the 1980s?

Projections from the National Center for Education Statistics and the United States Census Bureau indicate that with a baby boomlet under way since the 1980s, the numbers of children three to six years of age will continue to increase substantially until at least the early 1990s. Thus, a greater demand for quality programs for children in these age ranges will occur as more mothers work outside the home. This urgent need for programs must be linked with professional and public concern about what constitutes "quality" or "appropriate" or "basic educational opportunities" for young, vulnerable children. The persistent topics of "what is basic?" "what is quality programming?" and "who are we in the lives of young children?" have been addressed in many discussions and publications over the generations.

Inextricably tied to these recurring questions about quality programming and the basics are issues concerning the varied, often conflicting responsibilities caregivers and teachers of young children can, are expected to, or should assume. Part of the dilemma is related to the fact that today's young children will inhabit the twenty-first century—a time when problems and possibilities may be very similar, vastly different, or more urgent from the ones facing people today. What will be basic, then? Clearly, although individual biases and experiences separate both professionals and the public served, early childhood educators must continue to look to the individual child and the family, as they have done for generations, and exhibit humane, caring attitudes and knowledge-based actions as professionals and public search together for more adequate answers to these persistent questions.

An accelerated tempo of life, changes in family patterns, sizes, and income, viewing of adult media forms, and parental demands for earlier instruction have all greatly affected young children's development. As the pace of life quickens and fears about the future produce greater insecurities, expectations for individual achievement increase. Consequently, many young children are being subjected to a greater quantity of pressures (stressors). The more-sooner-faster syndrome, or the "hurrying" of children to grow up, to succeed, to act like adults, and to meet adult expectations is having dispiriting effects on children's affective, cognitive, and motivational development. Childhood seems to be less often a protected, fun-filled, innocent time of wonder. This section involves the reader in issues of historical and contemporary concern and offers projections for future enrollments in programs. The unit includes sections on the basics, educators' multiple roles, and pressures for a shortened, hurried childhood.

Looking Ahead: Challenge Questions

What combination of national events precipitated the urgency, enthusiasm, and dedication that resulted in "The Best Day Care There Ever Was"? What are the parallels between the needs of working mothers during World War II and the late 1980s? What is the role of industry and government in funding "deficit-producing" programs of high quality?

What are the projections for the enrollment of three-through six-year-old children from 1986 to 1992? What do these figures mean for Early Childhood Education?

In the daily lives of young children, what constitutes the basics for growing and learning? What types of basics could be provided by knowledgeable, humane educators?

Look at the multiple life-styles and problems faced by today's young children and determine "who are we" as professional educators? How can professionals more adequately look at the child and manifest active, helpful caring?

What special stressors are affecting the development of children growing up today? How do parents, schools, and the media produce pressures for a shortened childhood? How are play and the arts the antidotes for these "hurried" children?

THE BEST DAY CARE
There Ever Was

CAROLINE ZINSSER

Caroline Zinsser is an educational consultant and former school director who writes and lectures on childhood in America.

In 1943, in Portland, Oregon, two massive shipyards had begun to build a "bridge of ships"—tankers and cargo ships to carry the men, ammunition and supplies that were desperately needed in the war in Asia. It was possible to build the vessels, from keel-laying to launching, in an unbelievable four days. To help accomplish this miracle of production, 25,000 women—5,000 of them mothers—worked not only as secretaries and clerks, but as welders, chippers and burners in the yards and at the ways. Women worked the day shift, the swing shift and the graveyard shift, for the shipyards operated day and night, seven days a week, racing against time to turn the tide of war.

It was in this atmosphere of wartime emergency that Edgar Kaiser, general manager of the yards, launched a plan for the world's largest day care centers. To help mothers on their jobs, he planned two centers to serve 1,125 children each, open 24 hours a day, 364 days a year. He enlisted the backing of his good friend Eleanor Roosevelt and set about building the finest facilities for child care that this country has ever known.

As the word went out that anybody who wanted to work at the Kaiser Shipyards could have a job, women from all parts of the country flooded into Portland. They rented every spare room, they jammed the buses, they depleted the stores, and they looked for places to leave their children. Many of the women, from farms and small towns, had never seen the ocean, had never left home before, had never been on their own. To the conservative Portland residents, these newcomers, unwanted and unwelcomed, often appeared to be "riffraff."

In the midst of this uncertainty and upheaval, Kaiser moved his plans forward with the same urgency and efficiency that characterized his production line. Used to cutting through delays by finding top people who would get the job done, he hired leading Portland architects to design the children's centers. The architects produced two buildings unlike anything anyone had seen before, huge, round wheel-plans with 15 large rooms in the spokes and a protected playground at the central hub. Instead of being separated from the shipyards, the centers were placed at the plant entrances so that every worker passed by and mothers could drop their children off in the most convenient way.

To find a director, Kaiser asked government agencies to name the best-qualified people in the country. Using this advice, he hired Lois Meek Stolz, a pioneer in child-development theory, and today a still-lively 93-year-old, as consulting director and James Hymes, Jr., as on-site manager. Kaiser gave Stolz and Hymes only two months to find staff, get equipment, set policy and begin operation. They still remember those days with awe. "Things happened so quickly," recalls Hymes, "we had no time to be apprehensive. We were plunged into implementing the plan."

The most important job was to recruit staff. Only the best professionals would do—teachers with degrees in child development and with three or more years of experience. The directors sent two-page telegrams to every major teacher-training institution, describing the urgent need for teachers and the dramatic location and huge size of the nurseries. The telegrams caused great excitement (some were kept and framed) as nursery-school teachers found themselves in the unaccustomed spotlight of a wartime emergency. One hundred adventurous teachers responded to the call.

An additional lure, as it was for all war-workers, was pay. Stolz and Hymes had assumed they would pay teachers the going rate for nursery-school work. "But," recalls Stolz, "when Kaiser heard how low the figure was, he nearly exploded. 'You can't pay college graduates that,' he said. 'You won't hold them a week. All the administrative offices in the yards will steal them away from you!' "

Salaries were raised to compete with those of other Kaiser workers. Ruth Berkman, one of the teachers who responded to the recruiting telegram, remembers, "I had earned two hundred dollars a year as a teaching apprentice. As a head teacher, I was earning sixty dollars a month. At Kaiser the salary was *five thousand dollars* a year. I had never even had a Social Security number before! They made us feel like treasured members of the profession."

Equipping the centers was another challenge. Materials were scarce and wartime transportation nearly impossible. But once again the Kaiser Company used its expertise. Accustomed to speeding up shipments of steel to meet production schedules, the company now pushed and urged carloads of children's play equipment westward across the country. The numbers were staggering: For a planned 2,000 or more children, 30 rooms were equipped with nonbreakable juice glasses and self-feed bibs, with cots, sheets, blocks, puzzles, easels and everything else needed for round-the-clock care. Because metal was scarce, children made do with awkward wooden scooters constructed in the shipyards, and teachers scrounged scrap material from the docks.

The buildings were a teacher's delight. Classrooms were large and each had storage space and a bathroom with child-size sinks and toilets. Windows on two sides gave the children views of the shipyards. Covered porches provided a place to play outdoors on rainy days. At Stolz's suggestion, two bathtubs were added, built high enough so that adults did not have to bend over, and big enough so

that children could splash and play in the water. Many children who arrived tired, hot and dirty from their cross-country trip were to receive their first bath in days in these famous bathtubs.

The full staff of 100 teachers, six group supervisors, 10 nurses, five nutritionists and two family consultants formed an astonishing concentration of experts in child care. Here was an unprecedented opportunity for pooling ideas to produce the finest facilities possible, and out of excited discussions came many more innovations.

Like other nursery schools of the time, the Kaiser Centers had a policy of having each child go through a health test every morning before being admitted to class. Instead of asking mothers to take mildly sick children home, Lois Stolz suggested converting a room in each center into an infirmary. Nurses and a consulting pediatrician who made a daily visit took care of the children in isolated glass cubicles, and teachers working in the infirmary developed forms of quiet bed play with the children.

Since not all the mothers who worked at the yards enrolled their children in the center, a Special Service Room was set up to care for children on a temporary emergency basis. Fathers could also use the service when they would otherwise have had to stay home to care for their children. Because working parents weren't able to take their children to public-health clinics during the day, the nursing staff offered to immunize children; 3,606 immunizations were given in the first year.

The centers' kitchens provided the children with breakfast, a midmorning snack, a hot meal at noon, an afternoon sandwich with milk, and supper in the evening. The aim was to supply two thirds of each child's daily nutritional requirements. The chief nutritionist sent parents a weekly list of meals served and suggestions for additional food to complete an adequate day's diet. Free booklets, *Recipes for Food Children Like* and *Good Meals for Children on the Swing Shift,* were distributed.

Perhaps most helpful of all was Home Service Food. Eleanor Roosevelt, on a trip to England, had seen women war-workers buy precooked food for their families right at the factory. She persuaded Kaiser to set up a similar service. By selecting from a weekly menu, a mother could order her family's evening meal, to be picked up—precooked and

packaged—at the center's kitchen when she collected her child at the end of the day shift. The kitchen specialized in food that required long cooking, such as a fresh salmon loaf, which came with an avocado-and-lemon gelatin salad and sold for 50 cents a serving.

As the centers began operation, it became clear that mothers needed group care for infants as well as for preschoolers. Group infant care was almost unknown at the time, and the center's decision to admit children as young as 18 months became one of its most closely studied activities. The teachers, who had no training or experience with younger children, worried about the possible traumatic effects of separating infants from their working mothers. However, the teachers found that children adjusted "happily and comfortably."

Elizabeth Oleson Garvais, who kept a journal, wrote of her experiences as a "babies teacher" on the swing shift, which began at 2:30 p.m. and ended near midnight: "At 11:30 the yard whistle gives a long blast. At 11:45 the first parents come in, walking quietly in their heavy shoes, lowering their voices as they collect their children's belongings. Big men in metal helmets gently pick up sleeping babies. Mothers help wrap them in blankets. Many children manage a sleepy smile and hug. Some, wide awake, are carried from the room looking back over Dad's broad shoulders. Some go out still sleeping soundly. Finally the last helmet and the last lunch pail have gone along with the last child, Ruthie, who blinks at me like a sleepy owl. I turn on the overhead lights. The room is a mess of unmade beds, wet sheets, and screens at crazy angles. Ronny's panda lies on the floor beside his cot. The graveyard-shift housekeepers come in. It is 12:05. It is a new day."

In addition to caring on a daily basis for children from 18 months to six years, the centers expanded their services: They cared for school-age children after school, on Saturdays (which were working days at the yards) and during summer vacations. A commissary provided small but necessary items like toothbrushes and shoelaces. For a short while, a Mending Service was in operation. The centers also sent home a biweekly newsletter describing the children's activities; free booklets on child care, written by the staff, suggested toys, holiday activities and shopping ideas and advised parents on how to talk to children about the war.

In addition, parents could borrow children's books from the center's library.

Some ideas were discussed but never fully developed: a dormitory for mothers and infants with a community kitchen and a nursery, a shopping service where parents could leave their orders in the morning for food and household items and pick up the packages after work, a barber service and a photographer who would take informal pictures of the children to send to their fathers overseas. As James Hymes puts it, "We thought that anything that saved the working mother time and energy meant she would have more to give to her child."

The Kaiser Centers were in operation for only two years. They closed in 1945, as the war in the Pacific was winding down, having served 3,811 children, provided 249,268 child care days and freed 1,931,827 woman-work-hours. When the staff was disbanded, the members hoped their work would provide a model for an ongoing effort toward excellent day care. Portland women, as well as those in other cities where wartime day care centers had been established, deluged Congress and the President with protests against closings.

But the Kaiser Centers were never to be replicated. When James Hymes prepared a report to be distributed to other industries, he made a crucial point: "All education is deficit-producing. Child Service Centers are no exception. The greater the number of children served, the greater the deficit." Parents at the centers paid a fee of five dollars for six days of child care, but this covered only a small part of the cost. The deficit was paid by Kaiser, who in turn passed the cost on to the government. In effect, the centers were federally supported through industry.

The Kaiser Centers demonstrated that day care can be good for children and mothers. But it took a special set of circumstances to bring about full support for working mothers. Only the urgency of wartime, with every woman needed on a job, broke down the traditional barriers against caring for children on a large-scale basis.

The centers stand on record as a reminder of what can be done when the need is great. The many people who worked together in Portland over 40 years ago, in the midst of war, brought about a level of excellence in day care that has not been matched. Eleanor Roosevelt was one of those most instrumental in backing the plan, and it is particularly fitting to remember this month, on the centennial celebration of her birth, that the Kaiser Centers would never have been possible without her deep and intelligent commitment to the welfare of women and children.

What Is Basic for Young Children?

Lilian G. Katz

Lilian G. Katz is Professor of Early Childhood Education and Director of the ERIC/ECE Clearinghouse (Educational Resources Information Center for Early Childhood Education) at the University of Illinois, Urbana-Champaign.

ALL OF US who teach young children often express disappointment over not having had time to do all we had planned to in any given week, or month, or year. We cannot introduce all the topics of potential interest, all the activities that might stimulate learning, all the materials that might help develop skills. Teaching always involves choices. From among the virtually infinite variety of possible topics, ideas, skills and activities, we can only address a few.

On what bases are our choices made? Probably *tradition* accounts for a large proportion of our selections: traditional topics, materials, holidays, games and activities. To some extent the *availability of resources* determines what activities we select. Often choices are made for us by school district mandates or by central office officials, state or federal funding agencies, or boards of directors of day care centers.

Busy teachers have all too little time to reexamine the bases upon which they select the components of their programs. Most of us do well to cope with the day-to-day demands of our roles. Recently I had an experience with

This paper is an adaptation of Dr. Katz's keynote address to the Fourteenth National Congress, Australian Preschool Association, held at the University of Melbourne May 15-21, 1976. (Proceedings were published by the Association in a publication, *The Young Child in Focus*, edited by Forbes Miller.) Reprinted with permission.

a group of students that caused me to step back and reflect on the underlying assumptions upon which early childhood programing might be based. I hope these reflections will help your own thinking as you look for the bases on which you make the choices in your program.

The occasion that stimulated my thinking was a seminar with a group of young, zealous students who were discussing their reactions and impressions from working in day care centers. One young woman, Susan, spoke of her experience in deeply disappointed tones. Among the complaints against the program she listed was that the director refused to let the children have small animals in the day care center. I listened appreciatively for a while to Susan's righteous indignation, and then asked her as gently as I could: "Let's speculate! What do you think are the chances that a child could develop into a wholesome adult without having had animals to play with in the day care center?"

After a few moments' thought, Susan indicated that the chances were fairly good. "What about finger paint? Block play? Can a child grow into normal adulthood without them in the day care center?" I asked. A lively discussion followed these questions, leading all of us to search for answers to the question, "What does each child have to have for wholesome development?" I want here to share with you my own answers to this question by offering seven interrelated propositions. I hope these propositions will be helpful to you as you consider how you might have responded.

The seven propositions below are built upon an assumed first principle I have dis-

It is basic in the development of young children for them to make sense of their own experiences. This verification process has to come from adults or older children.

cussed elsewhere (Katz, 1975); namely, that whatever is good for children is only good for them in the "right" or optimum proportions. Another way of stating this principle is that just because something is good for children, more of it is not necessarily better for them. This applies to so many influences on children's development that it could be called the "Law of Optimum Effects." Among the many examples of influences that should be experienced in optimum amounts are: attention, affection, stimulation, independence, novelty, choices of activities, etc. All of the latter can be thought to be "good" for children, but only in optimum amounts, frequencies or intensities.

Taking the first principle of optimum effects as fundamental, we can return to the question of what children have to have for wholesome development.

Proposition One: *The young child has to have a deep sense of safety.*

I am referring here to psychological safety, which we usually speak of as a sense of "security." Over the last twenty years or so the term "security" has come to be used as a cliché. By psychological safety I refer to the subjective feeling of being connected and attached to one or more others. Experiencing oneself as attached, connected—or safe—comes not just from being loved, but from *feeling* loved, *feeling* wanted, *feeling* significant, etc., to an optimum (not maximum) degree. Note that the emphasis here is more on *feeling* loved and wanted than on *being* loved and wanted.

As I understand early development, feeling strongly bonded or attached comes not just from the warmth and kindness of caretakers. The feelings are a consequence of the child perceiving that what he (or she) does, or does not do, *really matters* to others—matters so much that they will pick him up, comfort him, get angry and even scold him. (After all, we do not become angry with someone we are indifferent to.) Safety, then, grows out of being able to trust people to respond not just warmly but *really*.

This proposition seems to apply to all children, whether they are wealthy or poor, at home or at school; whether they are handicapped or normal, at whatever their ages, until perhaps young adulthood.

Proposition Two: *Every child has to have adequate—not excessive—self-esteem.*

At first glance this proposition seems to be quite simple. But a few comments are in order. It is useful to remember that one does not acquire self-esteem at a certain moment in childhood and then have it forever. Self-esteem is nurtured by and responsive to the significant others—adults, siblings and other children—throughout the growing years.

Even more important to keep in mind is that one cannot have self-esteem in a vacuum. Our self-esteem results from evaluations of ourselves against criteria. We evaluate ourselves as having high or low esteem against criteria we acquire very early in life. We acquire them in our families, neighborhoods, ethnic groups and later on from peer groups and the larger community. Early in life these criteria against which we come to evaluate ourselves as acceptable, worthwhile—against which we judge or experience ourselves as lovable—vary from family to family. In some families beauty is a criterion; in others, neatness, or athletic ability, or toughness is a criterion. Consider that such characteristics as being dainty, or quiet, or talkative, or pious, or well-mannered, or academically precocious, etc., might constitute the criteria against which young children are judged lovable, worthy and acceptable.

Each family has of course the right, if not the duty, to establish what it considers to be the criteria against which esteem is accorded. The process and the patterns by which such criteria are implemented are most likely un-self-conscious in formulation as well as expression. One of our responsibilities as educators is to be sensitive to the family's *own* criteria. We may not agree with a family's definition of the "good boy" or the "good girl." But we would be very unwise to downgrade, undermine, or in other ways violate the self-esteem values the children bring with them, even though we must help children acquire criteria that serve to protect the welfare of the whole group in our care. I cannot think of any way it could help a child to have his respect for his family and his family's criteria of the "good person" undermined.

I suggest that children have to have optimum self-esteem wherever they are, whether they are wealthy or poor, handicapped or normal, throughout their growing years.

Proposition Three: *Every child has to feel, or experience his/her life as worth living, reasonably satisfying, interesting and authentic.*

I have in mind here the potential hazard inherent in modern industrialized societies of creating environments and experiences for young children that are superficial, phony, shallow and trivial.

This proposition suggests that we involve children in activities, and interactions about activities, that are real to them, significant and intriguing to them. It suggests also that we resist the temptation to settle just for what amuses them. I would suggest as a criterion of appropriateness for children's activities that they give children opportunities to operate on their own experiences, to reconstruct their own environments and give us opportunities to help children to learn what meanings to assign to their experiences.

As I visit early childhood programs in both developed and developing countries, I wonder whether people have taken our long-standing emphasis on warmth and kindness, acceptance and love to mean: "Let's be nice to children!" As I watch adults being "nice" and "kind" and "gentle," I often speculate as to whether if I were a child in such a pleasant environment I would look at the adults and say to myself—everybody is kind and sweet, but inside them is there anybody home (Katz, 1977)?

It seems to me that children should be able to feel that their lives are real, authentic, worth living and satisfying whether they are at home, in schools or day care centers throughout their growing years.

Proposition Four: *Young children need adults or older children who help them to* *make sense of their own experiences.*

By the time we meet the young children in our care, they have already acquired some understandings or constructions of their experiences. Their understandings or constructions may be incorrect or inaccurate although developmentally appropriate. As I see it, our major responsibility is to help the young to improve, extend, refine, develop and deepen their own understandings or constructions of their own worlds. As they grow older and reach primary school age, we may help them with their understandings of other people's worlds. Indeed, increasing refinement and deepening of understandings is a lifelong process.

What do young children need or want to make sense of? Certainly people, what they do, what they will do next, how they feel; how things around them are made and how they work; how they themselves and other living things grow; where people and things come from. The list is endless.

If we are to help young children to improve and develop their understandings of their experiences, we must *uncover* what those understandings are. The uncovering that we do, or that occurs as children engage in the activities we provide, helps us to make good decisions about what to *cover,* or what subsequent activities to plan.

Youngsters need help in making sense of their experiences wherever they are: at home or in programs, whatever their backgrounds, throughout their growing years.

Proposition Five: *Young children have to have adults who accept the authority that is theirs by virtue of their greater experience, knowledge and wisdom.*

This proposition is based on the assumption that neither as parents nor as educators are we caught between the extremes of authoritarianism or permissiveness. Authoritarianism may be defined as the exercise of power without warmth, encouragement or explanation. Permissiveness may be seen as the abdication of power but offers children warmth, encouragement and support as they seem to need it. I am suggesting that young children have to have, instead of these extremes, adults who are *authoritative;* i.e., adults who exercise their very considerable power over the lives of young children *with* warmth, support, encouragement and ade-

quate explanations. The concept of authoritativeness also includes treating children with respect; i.e., treating their opinions, feelings, wishes and ideas, etc., as valid even when we disagree with them. To respect people we agree with is no great problem; respecting those whose ideas, wishes and feelings are different from ours may be a mark of wisdom in parents and genuine professionalism in teachers.

The combination of the exercise of optimum power and optimum warmth implied in authoritativeness is helpful for children wherever they are, whatever their background, throughout their youth.

Proposition Six: *Young children need optimum association with adults and older children who exemplify the personal qualities we want them to acquire.*

Make your own list of the qualities you want the young children in your care to acquire. There may be some differences among us. But it is likely that there are some qualities we all want all children to have; e.g., the capacity to care for and about others, honesty, kindness, acceptance of those who are different from themselves, the love of learning, and so forth.

This proposition suggests that we look around the children's environments and ask to what extent do our children have contact with people who exhibit these qualities? We might ask also: To what extent do our children observe people who are attractive and glamorous counter-examples of the qualities we want to foster? It seems to me that children need communities or societies that take the necessary steps to protect them from excessive exposure to violence and crime while their characters are still in formation.

The role and significance of adequate adult models seems valid for all children wherever they are, wherever they come from, throughout their developing years.

Proposition Seven: *Children need relationships or experiences with adults who are willing to take a stand on what is worth doing, worth having, worth knowing, and worth caring about.*

This proposition seems to belabor the obvious. But in an age of increasing emphasis on pluralism, multi-culturalism, and community participation, professionals are increasingly hesitant and apologetic about their own values. Such hesitancy in taking a stand on what is worthwhile causes us to give our children unclear signals about what is expected, and what is worth knowing and doing. When we do take a stand, we cannot guarantee that our children will accept or agree with our version of the good life. Nor do we imply that we reject others' versions of the good life. We must, in fact, cultivate our capacities to respect alternative definitions of the worthwhile life. But when we take a stand, with quiet courage and conviction, we help the young in that they can more easily see us as thinking and caring individuals who have enough self-respect to respect our own values as well as others'. Such thinking and caring adults seem to be important to children wherever they are, wherever they come from, throughout development.

In summary, all seven propositions hang together on the central question of our responsibilities for the quality of the daily lives of all of our children—wherever they spend those days, throughout the long years of growth and development.

References

Katz, Lilian G. "Psychological Development and Education in Early Childhood." In *Second Collection of Papers for Teachers*, L. G. Katz. Urbana, IL: ERIC Clearinghouse on Early Childhood Education, 1975.

———. "Teachers in Preschools: Problems and Prospects." *International Journal of Early Childhood* 9,1 (1977): 111-23.

Who Are We in the Lives of Children?

Shirley C. Raines

Shirley C. Raines, Ed.D., is Field Services Coordinator, Northeastern State University, Tahlequah, Oklahoma. This viewpoint is adapted from her keynote address to the Spring Conference of the Knoxville Area Association on Young Children, April 1983.

When Sally Struthers stares at me from the pages of a magazine and asks for $18.00 a month to feed a hungry child through the Christian Children's Fund, I ask myself, "Who am I in the lives of children?"

When Marian Wright Edelman, President of the Children's Defense Fund, implores me with horrendous statistics to defend the needs of children to my legislators, I ask myself, "Who am I in the lives of children?"

When David Elkind (1981) in his best selling book urges me not to hurry the child and Neil Postman (1982) in his best selling book accuses me of removing the innocence from childhood, I ask myself, "Who am I in the lives of children?"

When NAEYC President Bettye Caldwell (1983) urges me to accept the challenge of educating the American public about the profession of early childhood education and child care, I ask myself, "Who am I in the lives of children?"

Collectively, NAEYC members must ask themselves, "Who are we in the lives of children?" just as Stephanie Feeney and Doris Christensen (1979) ask *Who Am I in the Lives of Children?*

When we attend conferences, we quickly learn that our colleagues already are committed to many just and worthy causes. We have families, teach Sunday School, lead volunteer efforts—we are the pillars of the community. The Sally Struthers ad for the Christian Children's Fund, the statistics from Marian Wright Edelman and the Children's Defense Fund, the best sellers about children and childhood, and the appeals from NAEYC strike responsive chords in us because we are committed to many just and worthy causes—we do care.

"But I am convinced if we are ever to attain those lofty ideals shouted from conference and convention podiums, if we are ever to reach those treasured goals written in Greek and Latin on the emblems of our learned societies, we must follow our concerns with action" (Raines 1983). We must follow our declaration of how much we care about children and about our profession with action in which we share the responsibility of the messages we hear about children with our own message.

WHAT IS OUR MESSAGE?

The following three examples illustrate the caring and basic principles of child development which are the messages we must carry for children and for our profession.

As many of you who teach kindergarten know, tying shoes is a big deal in kindergarten. The children practice tying each other's shoes, work with lacing frames, and even have adult shoes to tie. Tying shoes even had a place to be checked under fine motor skills on the developmental checklist I used when I taught. We had a list on our bulletin board of all those five-year-olds who knew how to tie shoes. We applauded and cheered each child's accomplishment and made a ceremony of adding each name to the list, but Randy's name was not there. I mentioned to his parents Randy's adequate development of fine motor control with puzzles, Tinkertoys, and drawing, but that he had not learned to tie his shoes yet. They said they would have him practice at home, but the end of the school year came and Randy still had not learned to tie his shoes.

In September, on one rainy muddy Monday morning, I arrived at school early and rushed to my classroom to prepare those extra activities I knew would be needed for a rainy day. Suddenly I saw two wet, dripping, muddy tennis shoes plopped down right in front of me on top of the red construction paper. Just as I turned to say, "What do you mean splattering my paper and blouse with those awful shoes" I saw two big brown eyes and the widest smile and heard Randy say, "I did it! I tied my shoes!" And there they were, wet, muddy, dripping, and tied.

As educators and child development professionals, we often are guilty of overemphasizing some small tasks while overlooking the whole-

Reprinted by permission from *Young Children,* Vol. 39, No. 3 (March 1984) pp. 9-12. ©1984 by the National Association for the Education of Young Children, 1834 Connecticut Ave., N.W., Washington, DC 20009.

ness of the child. We often expect all the spaces to be checked on the developmental profile and all the names added to the board, but we must be certain to convey the message to parents, to children, to administrators, and to program designers, that we follow the basic principle of child development:

"Development is continuous, gradual, and orderly."

(Lay-Dopyera and Dopyera 1982)

Our message doesn't stop the day we give the Metropolitan or the California Achievement Test, or check the spaces on the local developmental checklist. Realizing this, we must be quite concerned about programs, teachers, principals, and parents who make decisions about program and grade placement for September on the basis of a test given in March. That practice is adverse to what we know about the development of young children.

Another principle of child development which we must carry as our message is that:

"Development proceeds from the general to the specific. Throughout the life span, human beings' responses become more detailed and specific."

(Lay-Dopyera and Dopyera 1982)

This principle must be recalled when we absurdly ask young children to remember each letter sound and expect them to string all those sounds together to read words and sentences on topics of which they have no understanding. Children must have meaningful material to learn to read, as in the language experience approach, before we can move to the specific parts of the process.

Another principle of child development which we must proclaim as our message is that:

"Growth and development vary among individuals. While general patterns of development are predictable, each person has an idiosyncratic pattern."

(Lay-Dopyera and Dopyera 1982)

We seem to have lost sight of this basic principle when we want all the spaces on the developmental checklist checked by March or all the scores of all the children reaching 1.5 grade level on the reading test.

WHAT CAN WE DO?

As teachers we can enjoy these delightful stories of children, but there are also times when we cry with parents. Yet, the tears are not enough. We must communicate our sympathy and empathy and then follow them with information. As a Head Start director, I recall teachers who cried with families at the news of another surgical operation for a handicapped child. Then they proceeded to give information about services and assisted with arrangements, referrals, transportation to rehabilitation centers, and counseling.

I also recall fondly those role models and mentors who gently guided me in my first year of teaching children, in my first year as a program director, and in my first year of college teaching. We have a message to share as mentors, as role models, as gentle guides to other professionals through the anxieties of those first experiences. The message to the novices in our profession is that of information we share from our real life experiences, from research, and from plowing deeply into the writings of great thinkers and educators who have influenced our profession. The message that we care is written with information—practical, theoretical, and applied—which helps in the struggles of new jobs.

We are the writers of the message that we care. We are the writers of the message of the principles of child development, of information, of role models and mentors. But we are more. To other concerned citizens, we volunteer to join together to advocate for children because we know the statistics. To parents, we offer our expertise because we want parents to recognize and select good quality programs for their children. We show them high quality. The mark of excellence is evident in our centers, schools, programs, and services. To the new members of our profession we show by example what it means to believe in staff development and continuing education. We attend conferences, enroll in courses, complete degrees, and design and execute research. We convey the message that there is more to learn, that growth and development are gradual and continuous for the child, but also for the adult.

As we continue to learn, as we lead our profession, we need a source to guide us. An incident that Mario Montessori, Maria Montessori's son, once told illustrates the need for a source to guide us (Canady 1983). When Maria Montessori was quite old, in fact just before her death, a worldwide assembly of Montessori educators met in India. After many days of conferencing and listening to long speeches filled with numerous accolades, the finale for the assembly was an address by Dr. Montessori. As she approached the podium walking very slowly, a hush fell over the crowd. Near the end of her speech in which she traced the development of Montessori education throughout the world, Maria Montessori stepped from behind the podium and pointed her finger at the absolutely silent audience and after a long pause said, "For many years I have been pointing to the child, and you have been looking at the end of my finger."

As professionals, as leaders, as role models for those people beginning their careers, we must be careful that in our search for new methods, new products, new software, that we look to the child, not at the end of our fingers.

When asked, "Who are we in the lives of children?" we must answer. We are the people who respond to the Sally Struthers' pictures of low-income children because we do want the basic needs of all children met— for we are pointing to the child. We are the documenters of needs, the collectors of statistics for Marian Wright Edelman and the Children's Defense Fund and for legislators— for we are pointing to the child. We are the researchers who seek answers, who replicate and validate new and old information—for we are pointing to the child. We are the interpreters of the Elkind, Postman, and Caldwell positions on the child, childhood, and the profession—for we are pointing to the child.

"Who are we in the lives of children?" We are the bearers of the message: "We care." But our declarations of caring are followed by actions, for we are more than celebrators of muddy tied shoes and all the other small triumphs of a child's learning. We are more than empathizers with parents for all the anguish children and parents suffer in their struggles.

1. PERSPECTIVES

We are more than providers of guidance for those who enter our profession. We must share the messages of our profession.

REFERENCES

Caldwell, B.M. "Week of the Young Child: Increasing Its Effectiveness." *Young Children* 38, no. 2 (January 1983): 39.

Canady, R.J. "Reading and Writing: The Natural Connections." Paper presented at the Catskills Reading Conference, Oneonta, New York, August 1982.

Edelman, M.W. *A Children's Defense Budget: An Analysis of the President's FY 1984 Budget and Children.* Washington, D.C.: Children's Defense Fund, 1983.

Elkind, D. *The Hurried Child: Growing Up Too Fast Too Soon.* Reading, Mass.: Addison-Wesley, 1981.

Feeney, S., and Christensen, D. *Who Am I in the Lives of Children?* Columbus, Ohio, Merrill, 1979.

Lay-Dopyera, M., and Dopyera, J. *Becoming a Teacher of Young Children.* Lexington, Mass.: D.C. Heath, 1982.

Postman, N. *The Disappearance of Childhood.* New York: Delacorte, 1982.

Raines, S.C. "Developing Professionalism: Shared Responsibility." *Childhood Education* 59 (January/February 1983): 151-153.

The Hurried CHILD

David Elkind

David Elkind, a well-known and highly respected child psychologist and chairman of the Eliot-Pearson School of Child Development at Tufts University, is a member of INSTRUCTOR's Editorial Advisory Board. He expands on this article in his new book, *The Hurried Child: Growing Up Too Fast, Too Soon* (copyright 1982 Addison-Wesley Publishing Company, Inc.).

Pressure to succeed at all costs . . . pressure to cope . . . pressure to survive! Sound like the beginning of a list of adult stressors? It probably is, but add to it pressure to achieve before one is ready to achieve . . . pressure to grow up and quit acting like a child when one is still a child . . . pressure to struggle to the top when one is only four, six, or eight years old. Combine those pressures, and others, and you have the stressors we are applying on our children as we hurry them into premature adulthood.

We even want them to *look* like adults. Take, for example, the mid-teens sex symbol who sensually gyrates her hips as she models designer jeans appealing to the very young. As a matter of fact, today even preschoolers wear miniature versions of adult clothing. From LaCoste shirts to scaled down designer fashions, a whole range of adult costumes is available to children.

Three or four decades ago boys wore short pants and knickers until they began to shave—getting a pair of long pants was a true rite of passage. Girls were not permitted to wear makeup or sheer stockings until they were in their teens. Clothing signaled adults that children were to be treated differently, perhaps indulgently; it made it easier for them to act as children. But no longer. And clothing is just one of the more obvious examples of how we hurry today's children into adulthood, pushing them toward many different types of achievement and exposing them to experiences that tax their adaptive capacity.

Look at the media, for example. Music, books, films, and television increasingly portray young people as precocious and present them in more or less explicit sexual or manipulative situations, reinforcing the pressure on children to grow up fast in their language, thinking, and behavior. But can they be hurried into growing up fast emotionally as well? The answer is no. Feelings and emotions have their own timing and rhythm and cannot be hurried. Young teenagers may look and behave like adults but they usually don't feel like adults. Growing up emotionally is complicated and difficult under any circumstances, but may be especially so when children's behavior and appearance speak "adult" while their feelings cry "child."

Academic achievement is another example of the many pressures adults place on children to grow up fast, to succeed at all costs at any age. There is no room for the "late bloomers," the children who come into their own later in life rather than earlier. Children have to be successful early or they are regarded as flops. It has gone so far that many parents refuse to have their children repeat or be retained in kindergarten—despite all evidence that this is the best possible time to retain a child. "But," the parents say, "how can we tell our friends that our son failed kindergarten?"

A recent study of children who have been held back or who repeated kindergarten found that almost all of the parents involved were pleased with the result. They felt that it had given their children, who were socially or intellectually below the norm at that time, a chance to catch up at their own speed. Many of these children were able to join their own age group later and, far from being handicapped, were helped by the opportunity to move at their own pace.

When should a child read?

As teachers know all too well, parents hurry children when they insist that they acquire academic skills, such as reading, at an early age. (Indeed, some programs now promise parents that they can teach their children to read as infants and toddlers.) This pressure by parents reflects parental need, not the children's needs or inclinations. While it is certainly true that some children gravitate to reading early, seeking out books and adults to read to them, such children seem to learn to read on their own and with little fuss or bother. But they are in the minority. Studies by my colleagues and me, and by other investigators, find that only 1 to 3 children in 100 read proficiently (at second grade level) on entrance to kindergarten. If learning to read was as easy as learning to talk, as some people claim, many more children would learn to read on their own. The fact that they do not, despite being surrounded by print, suggests that learning to read is not a spontaneous or simple skill. The majority of children can, however, learn to read with ease if they are not hurried into it.

Other studies suggest that children confronted with the task of learning to read before they have the requisite mental abilities can develop long-term learning difficulties. In one high school, for example, we compared the grades of students who had fall birthdays (September, October, November, and December) and had entered kindergarten before they were five, with those with spring birthdays (April, May, June, even July) and who had entered school after they were five. For boys in particular, there was an advantage, in terms of grades, to entering kindergarten after age five rather than before.

Children should be challenged intellectually, but the challenge should be constructive, not debilitating. Forcing a child to read early, just as forcing an adolescent to take algebra when simple arithmetic is still a problem, can be a devastating experience for a young person who is not prepared intellectually for the task.

The abuse of the factory system

Schools today hurry children because administrators are pressured to produce better "products." This leads them to treat students like empty bottles on an assembly line, getting a little fuller at each grade level. When the bottles don't get full enough, management puts pressure on the operator (the teacher, who is now held accountable for filling his or her share of the bottles) and on quality control (making sure the information is valid and the bottle is not defective). This factory emphasis hurries children because it ignores individual differences in mental abilities and learning rates. The child who cannot keep up in this system, even if only temporarily, is often regarded as a defective vessel and is labeled learning disabled or minimally brain damaged or hyperactive.

The factory mentality of our schools has been reinforced by machine-scored group testing probably more than any other single factor. Dependence on such testing has grown dramatically over the last 10 years as dissatisfaction with the schools and with children's attainments has become more virulent on the part of both parents and legislators. Whether blame is placed on television, single-parent homes, mothers working, or the decline of authority, academic performance has been declining, and efforts to remedy the situation rely heavily on testing and teacher accountability. The problem with this system is

that it pushes children too much, forcing them into a uniform mold. Children are being pressured to produce for the sake of teachers and administrators.

Management programs, accountability, and test scores are what schools are all about today and children know it. They have to produce or else. This pressure may be good for many students, but it is bound to be bad for those who can't keep up. Their failure is more public and therefore more humiliating than ever before. Worse, students who fail to achieve are letting down their peers, their teachers, the principal, the superintendent, and the school board. This is a heavy burden for many children to bear. Therefore, children become much more concerned with grades than with what they know. So it isn't surprising that when these young people go out into the work world, they are less concerned with the job than with the pay and the perquisites of the job. What schools have to realize—and parents ought to—is that the attitudes they inculcate in young people are carried over into the occupational world.

Schooling and education are thought of in narrow terms—of attaining basic concepts and skills. But education—true education—is coincident with life and is not limited to special skills or concepts and particularly not to test scores. Education should not come packaged or sequenced. Much of it is spontaneous, an outgrowth of openness and curiosity that needs to be imparted to children. Pressuring them to get certain marks on tests that at best measure rote knowledge is hardly the way to improve their education. What good is it if children can read but not understand what they read or if they know how to compute but not where, when, or what to compute?

Kids are hurried, because we are hurried

What is the first expensive, utilitarian gift we usually give our children? A watch! We hurry our children basically because we hurry ourselves. For all our technological finesse and sophisticated systems, we are a people who cannot—will not—wait. We are, in short, a hurried people, and only in the context of a society that is hell-bent on doing jobs more quickly and better and is impatient with waiting and inefficiency can we really understand the phenomenon of hurried children and hope to help them. And first of all, it is important to recognize what we cannot do. We cannot change the basic thrust of American society for which hurrying is

the accepted and valued way of life. When hurrying reflects cultural values like being punctual, then urging children to be on time has social justification. But the *abuse of hurrying* harms children—that is, when hurrying serves parental or institutional needs at the expense of children without imbuing them with redeeming social values.

Young children two to eight years old tend to perceive hurrying as a rejection, as evidence that their parents do not really care about them. Children are emotionally astute in this regard and tune in to what is a partial truth. To a certain extent, hurrying children from one caretaker to another each day, or into academic achievement, or into making decisions they are not really able to make *is* a rejection. It is a rejection of children as they see themselves, of what they are capable of coping with and doing. Children find such rejection very threatening and often develop stress symptoms as a result.

Accordingly, when parents have to hurry young children, when they have to be at a day-care center or with a babysitter, they need to appreciate children's feelings about the matter. Giving children a rational explanation, "I have to work so we can eat, buy clothes," and so on, helps but it isn't enough to deal with the child's implicit thought—"If they really love me, they wouldn't go off and leave me." We need to respond to the child's feelings more than to his or her intellect. One might say, for instance: "I'm really going to miss you today and wish you could be with me." The exact words are less important than the message that the separation is painful but necessary for the parents, too.

School-age children are more independent and more self-reliant than younger children. Consequently, they often seem to welcome hurrying in the sense that they are eager to take on adult chores and responsibilities, particularly in single-parent homes where they may try intuitively to fill the role of the absent parent. The danger with this age group is that too often parents take this display of maturity for true maturity rather than for what it is—a kind of game. The image to keep in mind for this age group is Peter Pan, who wanted to assume adult responsibilities but did not really want to grow up and take on some of the negative qualities that children perceive as characteristic of adults. Children want to play at being grown up but they really don't want adults to take them too seriously.

There are ways to fight hurrying

One effective tool against the onslaught of hurrying is play. Unfortunately, both the value and the meaning of play are poorly understood in our hurried society. Indeed, that which happened to adults in our society has now happened to children—play has been transformed into work. What was once recreational—sports, summer camp, musical training—is now professionalized and competitive. In schools, when budgets are tight, the first areas to be cut are art, music, and drama. And the media, suffused with the new realism, offer little in the way of truly imaginative fantasy. Perhaps the best evidence of the extent to which children are hurried is the lack of opportunities for genuine play available to them.

Certainly, children need to do more than play. At every turn they are learning social rules—how to behave in a restaurant, on a plane, at a friend's house; how to put clothes on and take them off; how to eat with utensils; how to wash behind their ears, to wipe oneself with a towel, and so on. Children can also be taught basic concepts about space, time, number, color, and so on. But they need to be given an opportunity for pure play as well as for work. If adults feel that each spontaneous interest of a child is an opportunity for a lesson, the child's opportunities for pure play are foreclosed.

Basically, play is nature's way of dealing with stress for children as well as adults. Parents can help by investing in toys and playthings that give the greatest scope to a child's imagination—a good set of blocks, for example, that give children leeway to create and that can be used for years; and crayons, paints, clay, and chalk. These are all creative playthings because they allow for a child's personal expression.

Along the way, all of us—parents, teachers, and citizens—need to assert the value of the arts in the schools. The overemphasis on the basics in contemporary education without a balancing emphasis on personal expression through the arts hurries children by destroying the necessary balance between work and play. The need for workers to have modes of personal expression at work is just beginning to be realized and appreciated by American industry. Schools need to recognize that children also work better, learn better, and yes, grow better, if time spent in social adaptation—learning the basics—is alternated with healthy periods given over to avenues for self-expression. Far from being a luxury, time and money spent on the arts enhance learning and development by reducing the stress of personal adaptation and giving children an aesthetic perspective to balance the workaday one.

It is important to see childhood as a stage of life, not just as the anteroom to life. Hurrying children into adulthood violates the sanctity of life by giving one period priority over another. But if we really value human life, we will value each period equally and give unto each stage of life what is appropriate to that stage.

We should appreciate the values of childhood with its own special joys, sorrows, worries, and concerns. But valuing childhood does not mean seeing it as a happy innocent period, but rather as an important period of life to which children are entitled. It is their right to be children, to enjoy the pleasures, to suffer the trials, of childhood that is infringed upon by hurrying. In the end childhood is the most basic human right of children.

THE STATISTICAL TRENDS

Preschool Enrollment Rate by Age: 1970 to 1982

	3 and 4 years old	5 years old	Total
1970	20.5%	69.3%	37.5%
1972	24.4	76.1	41.6
1974	28.8	78.6	45.2
1976	31.3	81.4	49.2
1978	34.2	82.1	50.3
1980	36.7	84.7	52.5
1982	36.4	83.4	52.1

Comparisons of School Enrollments: 1970, 1980, and 1990

Nursery and Kindergarten enrollment

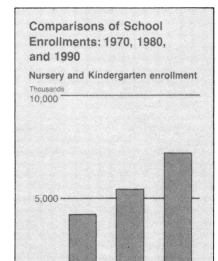

K-12 enrollment

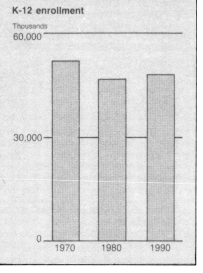

Past and Projected Annual Births: U.S., 1940 to 1990

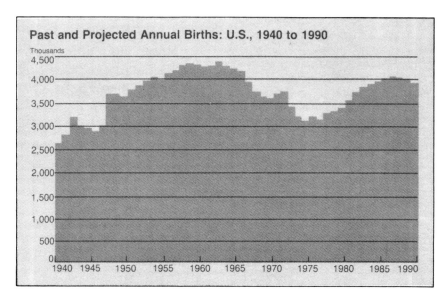

Projected Trends in Preschool Enrollment by Age: 1985 to 1993

(in thousands)

Year	Public Schools (Age)					Private Schools (Age)				
	Total	3 Years	4 Years	5 Years	6 Years	Total	3 Years	4 Years	5 Years	6 Years
1985	3,865	352	728	2,490	295	2,339	721	1,069	508	41
1986	3,931	364	754	2,514	299	2,404	745	1,106	510	43
1987	4,007	376	779	2,550	302	2,468	770	1,142	512	44
1988	4,079	388	805	2,580	306	2,533	794	1,180	515	44
1989	4,152	399	830	2,614	309	2,599	816	1,217	522	44
1990	4,220	409	853	2,644	314	2,664	838	1,251	529	46
1991	4,279	419	875	2,667	318	2,719	857	1,283	533	46
1992	4,324	426	894	2,683	321	2,766	872	1,311	537	46
1993	4,358	432	910	2,693	323	2,803	884	1,335	538	46

Labor Force Participation of Women by Age Group: 1970-80

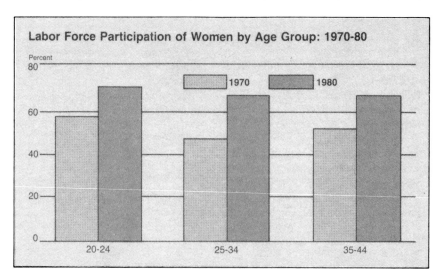

Preschool Enrollment by Age and Program: 1970 to 1983

(All numbers in thousands)

Age and Program	1970 Number	1970 Pct.	1975 Number	1975 Pct.	1980 Number	1980 Pct.	1983 Number	1983 Pct.
3 years	454	100.0	683	100.0	857	100.0	1,005	100.0
Full-day	142	31.3	259	37.9	321	37.5	357	35.5
Nursery	127	28.0	246	36.0	313	36.5	319	31.7
Kindergarten	15	3.3	13	1.9	8	0.9	38	3.8
Part-day	312	68.7	423	61.9	535	62.4	648	64.5
Nursery	305	67.2	407	59.6	512	59.7	626	62.3
Kindergarten	7	1.5	16	2.3	24	2.8	22	2.2
4 years	1,007	100.0	1,418	100.0	1,423	100.0	1,619	100.0
Full-day	230	22.8	411	29.0	467	32.8	441	27.2
Nursery	135	13.4	305	21.5	336	23.6	317	19.6
Kindergarten	95	9.4	106	7.5	131	9.2	124	7.7
Part-day	776	77.1	1,008	71.1	956	67.2	1,178	72.8
Nursery	436	43.3	671	47.3	728	51.2	898	55.5
Kindergarten	340	33.8	337	23.8	228	16.0	280	17.3
5 years	2,643	100.0	2,854	100.0	2,598	100.0	2,762	100.0
Full-day	325	12.3	625	22.0	763	29.4	888	32.2
Nursery	28	1.1	40	1.4	32	1.2	57	2.1
Kindergarten	297	11.2	585	20.5	731	28.1	831	30.1
Part-day	2,317	87.7	2,228	78.1	1,836	70.7	1,873	67.8
Nursery	62	2.3	75	2.6	61	2.3	130	4.7
Kindergarten	2,255	85.3	2,153	75.4	1,774	68.3	1,743	63.1
Total Enrollment	4,104	100.0	4,955	100.0	4,878	100.0	5,385	100.0
Full-day	698	17.0	1,295	26.1	1,551	31.8	1,686	31.3
Nursery	291	7.1	591	11.9	681	14.0	693	12.9
Kindergarten	407	9.9	704	14.2	870	17.8	993	18.4
Part-day	3,406	83.0	3,660	73.9	3,327	68.2	3,699	68.7
Nursery	803	19.6	1,154	23.3	1,300	26.7	1,654	30.7
Kindergarten	2,603	63.4	2,506	50.6	2,027	41.6	2,045	38.0

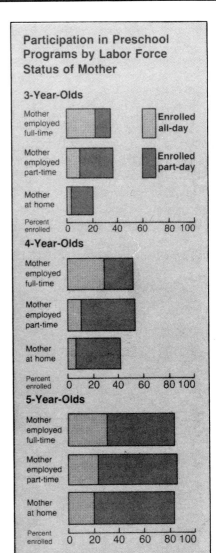

Participation in Preschool Programs by Labor Force Status of Mother

3-Year-Olds

Enrolled all-day / Enrolled part-day

4-Year-Olds

5-Year-Olds

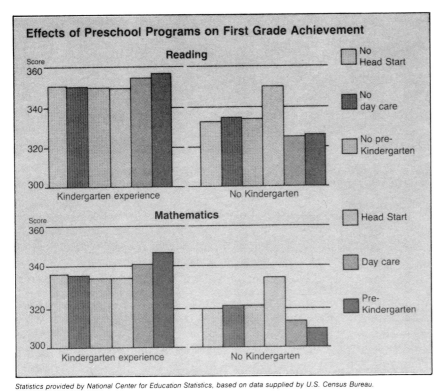

Effects of Preschool Programs on First Grade Achievement

Reading

No Head Start / No day care / No pre-Kindergarten / Head Start / Day care / Pre-Kindergarten

Mathematics

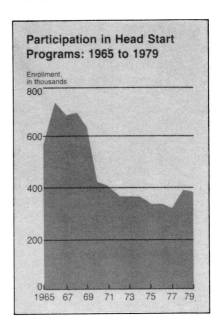

Participation in Head Start Programs: 1965 to 1979

Statistics provided by National Center for Education Statistics, based on data supplied by U.S. Census Bureau.

Childhood and Society

The transformational processes of learning and development cannot be fully understood in all their unity, diversity, and complexity without referring to the larger historical environmental contexts in which they are embedded. Accordingly, many social scientists have begun to look at molar, or overarching, forces that directly and indirectly affect the growth and functioning of human beings. The overarching contexts of American society are manifested in social, political, economic, and technological systems.

Fluctuations in these contexts produce ripple effects on all people, but exact their greatest influence on the young and vulnerable.

Family historians report that a study of child rearing and childhood of the past 2,500 years can reveal much regarding so-called "modern day" trends of single-parent families, working mothers, child neglect and abuse, and permissiveness. An analysis of the prevailing religious, social, economic, and technological values, beliefs, and practices of a societal era reveals how these macrosystems affected the way children were viewed and treated, or devalued and mistreated.

For too many young children, television has become the "second family," "the first curriculum" of socialization, a "plug-in-drug" that dominates their waking hours, shapes their values, and determines their development (or lack of it). The major aversive effects for children are that television viewing too readily becomes "a child amuser" and an addictive habit which replaces invaluable life experiences essential for the development of motor, language, social, and cognitive skills. Despite the repeated pleas of various groups to change the content of television for both children and adults, the major themes continue to be crass materialism, violence, exploitation of others, anti-social behavior, expressed sexuality, and sexism. Parents and educators can cooperate in trying to control its insidious and pervasive effects on impressionable children.

Violence against children is gradually being recognized by adults as an appalling and hideous fact of everyday life affecting millions of children from every economic group. There is greater awareness of the extent of child abuse and neglect and their crippling, dehumanizing effects. The majority of children who die are under five years of age, those who survive may be hurt so severely that they are deprived of trust, security, and nourishment, and their future coping and learning skills are altered. Educators are taking more action in recognizing the signs of child abuse and neglect, of reporting suspected cases, and of developing strategies and programs to help these damaged children.

For at least seven million "latchkey children," television viewing coupled with fears about safety, loneliness, and boredom are a weekly occurrence. The working mothers of these latchkey children experience guilt, anxieties, and worries about their children who are left without any direct adult supervision, and must care for themselves and sometimes their younger siblings. Again, educators are being asked to develop and staff additional programs for these children to accommodate the schedules of working parents.

This section contains articles on molar influences on children's lives—conditions and contexts that are not easily assessed but are highly potent in their overt and covert impact. By comparing recollections of childhood to the ways in which childhood is portrayed by the respective authors, the reader is given the opportunity to decide on an optimistic or pessimistic view of the future destiny of today's young children. Selected solutions are offered to a myriad of complex, interrelated problems facing the United States and its citizens of all ages.

Looking Ahead: Challenge Questions

What can a study of earlier historical periods reveal about changes in family life and childhood?

What are the interrelated effects of television viewing on children's achievements, aggression, and sex role identification? How does television viewing affect family life?

What has twenty years of research on Head Start shown about the ways in which intervention can alter the cycle of poverty? How has that research changed public policy since 1965?

What are the signs of child abuse and/or neglect, and what can educators be reasonably expected to do about suspected cases? What does research indicate about the possibility of helping these wounded children?

What are the daily fears faced by growing numbers of latchkey children?

Childhood Through the Ages

Elin McCoy

Elin McCoy is the author of "The Incredible Year-Round Playbook" (Random House).

A gentleman-in-waiting and the nurse of little Comte de Marle often amused themselves tossing the swaddled infant back and forth across the sill of an open window. One day one of them failed to catch him, and the infant landed on a stone step and died.

The surgeon of the newborn Louis XIII cut the "fiber" under his tongue a few days after he was born, believing that if it remained uncut, Louis would be unable to suck properly and would eventually stutter.

These aren't atypical examples of child rearing in the past. Recent historical research indicates that for most of the past 2,500 years, childhood was a brief, grim period in most people's lives, especially when judged against contemporary views of child rearing.

A new field—family history.

Through a new field of historical research, known as family history, we now know that family life and childhood in the previous centuries were startlingly different from what most people, including historians, had imagined them to be. Scores of historians are currently probing such questions as: How were children treated in the past? What concept of childhood did people have in different centuries? How important were children to their parents? Is there such a thing as "instinctual" parental behavior? What do the prevailing child-rearing beliefs and practices of the past tell us about the political, social, and psychological ideals of society? And

what kind of adults resulted from such child-rearing practices?

"Family history is the most explosive field of history today," says Professor Lawrence Stone—director of Princeton University's Shelby Cullom Davis Center for Historical Studies—whose 1977 book, *The Family, Sex and Marriage in England 1500–1800*, came out in an abridged paperback last year. "In the 1930s only about 10 scholarly books and articles on the family and childhood in history were published each year, but, incredibly, between 1971 and 1976 over 900 important books and articles were published on that subject, just covering America, England, and France." Two scholarly journals devoted to the subject were also started in the 1970s.

Why, suddenly, have so many historians focused on the family? "A whole series of contemporary anxieties has contributed to this new interest," explains Professor Stone. "General anxiety about the state of the family and whether it's breaking down, concern about the rising divorce rate, anxieties about current permissiveness in raising children, and concern about what effects women's liberation will have on children, the family, and society. And underlying all of these anxieties are two questions: Are we really doing so badly? Was it better in the past?"

In addition, two other trends in historical research have focused attention on childhood and the family. The first is social historians' growing interest in the daily lives of ordinary people in history, which has meant a greater concern with children, parenting, marriage, disease, death, and aging. The second is historians' recent efforts to employ psychological concepts as

a research tool in order to understand human motivations and experiences in the past.

Although all family historians agree that child-rearing patterns influence what happens in history, they disagree about how much and in what precise ways the treatment of children shapes history. Some researchers in the field, like Lloyd deMause, founder of *The Journal of Psychohistory: A Quarterly Journal of Childhood and Psychohistory,* go so far as to say that, in deMause's words, "child-rearing practices have been *the* central force for change in history." Along with some other psychohistorians, deMause believes that "if you want to understand the causes of historical events like the growth of Nazism, you have to look at how the children who became Nazis as adults were treated as children." But many scholars have reservations about attributing the character of a society solely to the relations between parents and children, pointing out that these relations must be understood in the context of the society as a whole and that such factors as economics must also be taken into account.

Surprising discoveries.

Family historians have recently exploded many long-standing myths about childhood and the nature of the family throughout history. It's now clear that the functions and structure of the family have changed continuously over the years and that a variety of family types coexisted in each historical period in different regions and classes. Scholars have found, surprisingly, that the prevailing family mode in America today (the small nuclear family of parents and children living apart from other relatives)—a structure that is under much attack—is not as new to our culture as they had previously thought. Even as long ago as thirteenth-century England, as many as half of all families consisted of only a mother and/or father and two to three children. In fact, the large, loving extended families we tend to picture, with eight to ten children and several generations of relatives living under the same roof, were more the exception than the rule, even in Colonial America.

According to Professor Tamara Hareven—founder and head of the first History of the Family program in the country, at Clark University in Worcester, Massachusetts, and founding editor of the *Journal of Family History*—one of the great surprises for today's historians was "finding out that in the past, the concept of childhood and children was not the same in all centuries, classes, and countries. While the middle classes were 'discovering' childhood and becoming interested in children," she explains, "the working classes still regarded children as small adults with the same responsibilities. And in the past, childhood as we know it lasted for a much shorter time." In medieval England, for example, children as young as seven were sent to live in other households as apprentices, and for peasant children, childhood was even briefer—they joined their parents to work in the fields as soon as they could.

Infants were regarded in medieval times as unimportant, unformed animals, in the sixteenth century as "exasperating parasites," and even as late as the seventeenth century they were not seen as individuals with their own identities. Children were considered interchangeable, and frequently were given the same name as an older sibling who had died. Small children were not even viewed as interesting; Montaigne, the French essayist, summed up the prevailing attitudes of a few hundred years ago when he dismissed infants as having "neither movement in the soul, nor recognizable form in the body by which they could render themselves lovable."

Scholars tell us that infants and small children were important only insofar as they could benefit their parents. Considered possessions with no individual rights, they were used to further adult aims, and they ended up as security for debts, as ways of increasing property holdings through arranged marriages, as political hostages, and even as slaves sold for profit.

Infancy in the past.

Throughout history, parents' treatment of infants and very small children has been characterized by psychological coldness and physical brutality that horrify most of us today. But this behavior becomes at least comprehensible when we realize some of the conditions of people's lives. The physical realities of life were oppressive. And there were severe parental limitations as well: in addition to being influenced by unscientific medical knowledge and religious views about the nature of man, most adults had to concentrate so much of their energy on mere survival that they had little time to care for or worry about infants and small children. Abusive and violent behavior was common among adults and, therefore, not looked on with disapproval when it appeared in the treatment of children.

In view of the following facts, consider what your experience as a parent and your child's experience as an infant would have been if you had lived prior to the eighteenth century.

Your child probably wouldn't have been wanted. Lack of birth control meant that having children was not a choice. For poverty-stricken peasants, an infant meant another mouth to feed—and food was precious—as well as interference with the mother's role as a worker whose contribution was necessary to the family's ability to survive. In all classes, the high risk of maternal mortality made the birth of a child a traumatic event. Even in the relatively healthy conditions enjoyed by the inhabitants of Plymouth Colony, 20 percent of women died from causes related to childbirth (compared with under 1 percent today), and in seventeenth-century England and France, the rates were much higher. It's no wonder that most children were probably unwanted. In fact, Professor Stone suggests that the availability of birth control was probably one of the necessary conditions for the increase in affection for children that began in England and America in the eighteenth century.

Your infant would have had a good chance of dying before his or her first birthday. In medieval England and seventeenth-century France, for example, between 20 and 50 percent of all infants died

within the first year after birth. Complications of childbirth, prematurity, diseases such as smallpox and the plague, and generally unsanitary living conditions, as well as such customs as baptism in icy water in freezing churches, took a heavy toll among vulnerable newborns. America was healthier for infants—in Plymouth Colony, infant mortality was only 10 to 15 percent (which is still ten times higher than it is in America today). The likelihood that one's infants would die discouraged parents from investing much affection or interest in them and from regarding them as special, unique individuals until it appeared more certain that they might live to adulthood.

Illegitimate infants and infants of poverty-stricken parents (and parents who felt they already had enough children) were often the victims of infanticide through deliberate murder, abandonment, or neglect. In ancient Greece, for example, infants who seemed sickly or didn't have a perfect shape or cried too much or too little were "exposed," or abandoned to die, a decision that was made by the father shortly after birth. In mid-eighteenth-century England, so many babies—both legitimate and illegitimate—were abandoned to die in the streets of cities and towns that the first foundling home established in London received several thousand babies a year. In early America, infanticide seems to have affected only illegitimate children.

If you were well-off, your baby probably would have been breast-fed by someone else. In spite of the fact that all medical advice since Roman times had stressed that babies breast-fed by their own mothers had a better chance of survival, for eighteen centuries any woman who could afford it sent her infant to a wet nurse.

Recuperation from a difficult childbirth prevented some women from breast-feeding, but many others thought it too demanding, especially since it was customary for infants to breast-feed for as long as two years. Also, many husbands would not allow their wives to breast-feed, partly because medical opinion held that women who were breast-feeding should not engage in sexual intercourse.

Underlying these reasons may have been parents' desire to distance themselves emotionally from their infants.

25

2. CHILDHOOD AND SOCIETY

In Renaissance Italy, middle-class infants were delivered to the *bália*, or wet nurse, immediately after baptism—two or three days after birth—and, if they survived, remained there for two years. Rarely did mothers visit their infants, and thus a baby was returned home at the end of that time to a stranger.

Although some wet nurses moved in with the family, most women left their babies at the wet nurse's home, where the child was often neglected and starved because wet nurses commonly took on too many babies in order to make more money. Frequently wet nurses ran out of milk, and infants had to be sent to a series of different nurses and thus were deprived even of a single surrogate mother.

The first groups of middle-class women to change this 1,800-year-old pattern on a large scale were the Puritans in the seventeenth century. Eventually, in the eighteenth century, there was a widespread cult of maternal breast-feeding in both America and England. Scholars have suggested that this shift may have contributed substantially to the shift in parental feelings for infants that began in the eighteenth century; certainly it reduced infant mortality.

Your infant would have spent little time with you. In the past, parents spent much less time with their children than even working parents do today and clearly did not feel the need to arrange supervision for them. Peasant women commonly left their infants and toddlers alone all day at home while they worked elsewhere. In one area of England during the thirteenth century, for example, half the infant deaths involved infants in cradles being burned while no one was home. Unsupervised toddlers frequently wandered off and drowned. In the middle and upper classes, parental neglect took the form of turning toddlers over to the servants to raise.

Your infant would have been swaddled in tightly bound cloths from birth to as old as eight months. Emotional distancing, economic necessity, and faulty medical knowledge are also evident in another common practice—swaddling. In England this practice continued up to the eighteenth century; in France, the nineteenth century; and in Russia, into the twentieth century. Kept in tightly bound bandages, swaddled infants were totally isolated from their surroundings for the first four months or so. After that, only their legs were bound. They couldn't turn their heads, suck their own thumbs for comfort, or crawl. Swaddling that was too tight occasionally caused suffocation. Although doctors advocated changing the infant two or three times a day, this apparently was uncommon, and even Louis XIII developed severe rashes because of his swaddling bands.

Medical reasons for the practice included the beliefs that if free, the infant might tear off his ears or scratch out his eyes, that swaddling was necessary to keep infants warm in cold, draughty cottages, houses, and castles, and that it ensured that the infant's pliable limbs would grow straight so he would be able to stand erect. Even when the swaddling bands were removed from their legs, children were not allowed to crawl "like an animal," but were forced to stand with the help

Mother's helper: The "roundabout" was a 19th-century gadget designed to keep baby out of mother's way. But it sacrificed a freedom of movement that today we know is crucial to a child's development.

of bizarre contraptions. Convenience was another reason for swaddling: it caused infants to sleep more and cry less, so they could be left for long periods of time while mothers worked. Also, swaddled infants were easier to carry and could even be hung on a peg on the wall out of the way.

Your infant or child would probably have received harsh beatings regularly—from you or a servant—even for such "normal" behavior as crying or wanting to play. For many centuries, discipline and teaching of the infant and young child concentrated on "breaking the child's will," which meant crushing all assertiveness and instilling complete obedience. This was accomplished through physical and psychological maltreatment that today we would consider "child abuse." Susanna Wesley, mother of John Wesley, the founder of the Methodist Church, records her treatment of her children: "When turned a year old, and some before, they were taught to fear the rod and cry softly." Louis XIII was whipped every morning, starting at the age of two, simply for being "obstinate," and was even whipped on the day of his coronation at the age of nine. The Puritans believed that "the newborn babe is full of the stains and pollutions of sin" and saw the first strivings of a one- and two-year-old to independence—which we now recognize as essential to a child's growing mastery of himself and understanding of the world—as a clear manifestation of that original sin. It was considered the duty of parents to use physical harshness and psychological terrorization—locking children in dark closets for an entire day or frightening them with tales of death and hellfire, for example—to wipe this sin out.

These child-rearing practices, as well as the difficult realities of life in the past, had important psychological effects on children's development. According to Professor Stone, the isolation, sensory deprivation, and lack of physical closeness that resulted from swaddling; the absence of a mother because of death in childbirth or the practice of wet-nursing; the common experience for small children of losing parents and siblings; and the suppression of self-assertion through whipping and other fear-producing techniques all resulted in an "adult world of emotional cripples."

A change for the better.

In the late seventeenth and eighteenth centuries, many of these child-rearing practices began to change among wealthy merchants and other groups in the upper middle classes of England and America. Some changes can be traced to the Puritans, who, even though they advocated harsh disciplinary measures, focused a new attention on children and the importance of their upbringing. By the late eighteenth century, among some groups, methods of contraception were available, swaddling had been abandoned, maternal breast-feeding had become the fashion, and "breaking the will" had given way to affection and a degree of permissiveness that seems extraordinary even by today's standards. In England the indulgent Lord Holland, for example, intent on gratifying his little son Charles's every whim, allowed him to jump and splash in the large bowl of cream intended for dessert at a grand dinner while the guests, a group of foreign ministers, looked on. Many adults feared the effect on society when these spoiled children reached maturity. And in fact, many of them did spend their lives in lifelong dissipation and often became followers of evangelical religions. While the Victorian era varied from harsh to permissive in the treatment of children, by the end of the nineteenth century the child-oriented family became a reality for all classes in Western society.

What it all means for us.

Were childhood and family life better in the past? The answer—obviously—is a resounding no. One is tempted to agree with Lloyd deMause that "the history of childhood is a nightmare from which we have only recently begun to awaken."

Nevertheless, Professor Hareven feels that there *were* some good aspects to childhood in the past, which we can learn from today. "Children were not so segregated from adults and responsibility," she points out. "The historical record shows children grew up in households that included servants, other workers employed by the family, lodgers, visiting relatives, and siblings of widely differing ages, as well as parents. They were exposed to a greater variety of adult roles than children usually are today and they interacted with a greater variety of people of all ages. They also knew more about their parents' work. And unlike today, children were working, contributing members of families and the society from an early age—as they are in contemporary China. Today's child-oriented family and the postponement of responsibility and work limit children's experience. The models are there in history for us to borrow and shape to today's ideals."

Historical research on childhood helps us view our own ideas about parenthood from a perspective in which it is clear that there are no absolutes. The new facts that are available to us show that assumptions behind child rearing change and that what we think of as parents' "instincts" actually depend on the beliefs and experiences of their society. The possessiveness and affection toward infants, which we take for granted, is a recent development. Even the "maternal instinct" to breast-feed one's own child was not instinctive for many women for over 1,800 years.

Family history also gives us an informative view of family structure. Those who are worried about the high divorce rate and the effect of parental separation on children, for example, should realize that in the past, approximately the same percentage of families were separated—only it was by the death of one of the parents instead of by divorce.

Although problems with child rearing will probably always be with us,

"**The Human Comedy**": That's the name of this 19th-century sketch—but the partially-swaddled child, left alone hanging on a wall, isn't finding anything in his situation to laugh about.

the very existence of family history means that we have come to the point where we are much more self-conscious about how we raise children, and, in turn, this may help us to be more thoughtful about the way we treat them. By examining childhood in the past, we become aware that our own attempts to do things differently—"nonsexist" child rearing, co-parenting, and different mixes of permissiveness and discipline—may have profound effects on society. If we can avoid the mistakes of the past, borrow what was good, and continue to examine our own aims and practices, the society our children make may be a better one than ours.

Television and Young Children

Alice Sterling Honig

Alice Sterling Honig, Ph.D., Professor,
Department of Child and Family Studies, Syracuse
University, Syracuse, New York.

"Pow. Pow. I'm gonna kill you. You're dead!" a five-year-old yelled definitively while he cocked a long wooden building block as if it were a gun in the direction of his playmate.

"There was a guy and he raped this girl on the TV last night," cheerfully reported Matt, four years old, to his day care teacher. She murmured, "How terrible! That must have hurt the girl and scared her awfully." "Oh, no," assured Matt, "My sister's boyfriend was watching with us and he said that girls love rape. You just don't know about that," the four-year-old responded in superior tones. Television is the not-silent companion and teacher of today's child. TV is the always available babysitter, friend, and handy substitute for skipping rope, marble shooting, ball bouncing, and a wealth of other activities into which children could throw all their budding physical and intellectual energies in pre-TV days. What are the effects of television watching on young children? To assess more effectively the role of television in the lives of young children we need to look at the research evidence.

In 1946, television was a nonexistent luxury in most homes, yet by 1973 99 percent of homes owned a set (Liebert and Spravkin 1977). Young children watch TV 25 to 54 hours per week. Before they reach the age of 18 years, children spend approximately 22,000 hours watching television. First graders watch for an average of 3 hours per day. In one study, about one-fourth of fifth graders were still watching television at 11:30 p.m. on a school day (Lyle and Hoffman 1972). By high school age, most children will have spent more time viewing television than in any other activity except sleeping (Kalba 1975). Nursery and kindergarten teachers often observe that characters and actions, fears, and horrors from TV shows invade the classroom in art work and in dramatic play. Children seem more dependent on TV show characters to imitate in play, and less apt to invent plots of their own.

Even young babies have become early television watchers. Hollenbeck and Slaby (1979) found that 72 babies, ranging in age from 21 to 31 weeks, looked longer at the television set during a sound-plus-picture condition than just-picture or empty-screen conditions. They vocalized more to picture-only than to sound-only TV presentations in the home. It is important for infants to use looking and vocalizing to elicit responses from adults (Honig 1982a). Yet infants have no control over a TV set that is on. This may be a hazard for infant emotional development. Martin (1981) has found that boy babies require maternal contingent responsiveness which makes it possible for them to develop an emotionally satisfactory balance of power and control. Television does not respond to a child's actions, coos, or calls.

Television viewing and child development

This review will look at various aspects of child functioning in relation to TV. First, there is a concern with how well a young child learns about the world if the major mode of learning is through passive viewing rather than through active participation. Second, caregivers and teachers have worried over the possibility of a lowered attention span as a result of the quick shifts in scene and character of

Reprinted by permission from *Young Children*, Vol. 38, No. 4 (May 1983), pp. 63-76. ©1983 by the National Association for the Education of Young Children, 11141 Georgia Ave., Suite 200, Whealen, MD 20902.

most programs, and the basic nature of commercial programming, which is geared toward entertainment rather than toward enhancing learning or encouraging persistent in-depth involvement with ideas. Some researchers have focused their studies, therefore, on the potential effects of educational television on school achievement and reading. Third, caregivers have worried about the impact of TV violence on children's aggression. A fourth area of interest has been the effect of television characters on sex-role stereotyping among children. Fifth, researchers have studied the effects of some television programs in promoting more prosocial behaviors among children.

Passive versus active learning activities

Children in what Piaget called the preoperational stage, from about two to seven years of age, have difficulty distinguishing between their wishes and the feelings and desires of others. They confuse fantasy and reality. They may well believe that what adults on a screen do to hurt each other is the way adults ought to behave or typically act in the real world.

Children struggle through to a more mature understanding of people's motives and feelings as they *interact* with others. And that is one of the difficult and crucial deficits of TV as teacher. As Cohen (1979) has succinctly phrased this issue:

> All during childhood there is sensory outreach for feedback which results in a construction of reality which grows out of an individual's action and experience. The insatiable search for feedback around which to construct an image of the world . . . has, until our era, encountered clearly nonhuman environments which young children had to disentangle. Never before was that task confused by long hours of contact with a nonhuman environment that simulates humanness as it does in our time. And therein lies the problem of television and the young child. (p. 221)

For Piaget, social interaction with family members, caregivers, teachers, and peers is essential for developing an understanding of our own and others' points of view. Interpersonal disagreements lead to cognitive struggles. Through such adjustments, children learn to understand the point of view of others and learn to coordinate their thoughts and desires with those of others. TV watching is a one-way

process. It does not allow a child to act upon, stop and think about, or compromise with the ideas of people who are viewed. As the noted pediatrician T. Berry Brazelton has observed: "What bothers me most about television is the passivity it forces on children—the passivity that requires all activity to be produced for them, not by them" (Kaye 1974, p. xiii). Children learn about the physical and chemical composition of the world as they play with toys, pour sand or water, dig in earth, climb, slide, roll objects, make pancakes, or mix paints. Can social interaction skills be learned as well under conditions of passive viewing for hours at a time?

Since preschoolers watch television for so many hours per day, concern has justly arisen as to whether or not their verbal skills are affected by passive viewing. Winn (1977) has argued that when young children could be playing and talking actively with parents or peers or reading, they are watching TV instead. Television, she suggests, may stimulate the development of the right hemisphere of the brain, which is involved with visual-spatial processes. She reasons that excessive stimulation of the right hemisphere may result in delayed or inhibited development of the brain's left hemisphere, which is involved in verbal-analytic information processing.

Murray (1980) has cited studies linking TV watching to children's vocabulary, visual-spatial ability, and creativity. No effect on children's word knowledge or spatial abilities was found. But creative verbal fluency was lower for children who watched TV more. The possibility that TV watching is tied to inhibition of some verbal skills should alert caregivers to ensure that sufficient verbal interaction times in play and conversation are always provided for young children. Such concerns also serve as a stimulus for parents to monitor and limit the amount of passive time a young child is permitted in front of a TV set.

Television and child achievement

One of the questions parents and educators ask most frequently is whether television boosts school achievement by increasing a child's knowledge, or interferes with school learning by taking time away from reading and active explorative play and by encouraging a shorter attention span.

Educational television. The most well-known and important of young children's educational television programs is "Sesame Street." This program was primarily developed to provide information and cognitive skills for "disadvantaged" preschoolers. The focus of intellective content is on numbers, letters, shapes, relational terms of time and place, body parts, sorting into classes, and ordering.

Evaluation of the effectiveness of the program in increasing preacademic achievements of preschoolers used tests of recognition and naming, as well as performance of tasks requiring information in each of the above areas (Ball and Bogatz 1972). Children's gains were found to be higher the longer time they spent watching the program. Children were reported to learn best the skills that were most prominently emphasized: numbers, letters, and classification. Gains were reported for children of different socioeconomic levels and for both sexes. Three-year-olds made the greatest gains in specific knowledge. Whether the children assessed would actually do better in elementary school than children who had not been exposed to "Sesame Street" was, however, not tested.

Looking and learning: Do they go together? Animation, movement, repetition, adult female voice, auditory change, and other characteristics used on TV have been found to enhance the attention of children from one to four years of age (Anderson and Levin 1976). Yet we still do not know whether holding the attention of young children means also that they are learning. Certainly, "Sesame Street" programmers have tried to ensure that many of the attention-getting attributes are present in their program. But do children learn just because, or while, they are looking? Often, a small child needs more time to digest a concept, or to understand an idea than the few seconds that a TV image may provide.

Indeed, some studies have found that a child's attention may not be entirely correlated with learning. Singer and Singer (1981) reported that during a viewing of "Mister Rogers' Neighborhood" many of the children did not continuously attend to the TV set, while children viewing a "Sesame Street" program did give their complete visual attention. When tested for recall of materials from the programs, both groups of children did equally well. Singer and Singer hypothesize that the slower pace and repetition of words on "Mister Rogers' Neighborhood" allowed children to process material even though they did not give their complete attention to the set during the showing. Even more significant was the finding that brighter girls were able to learn more of the material viewed on "Sesame Street," while less intelligent boys learned somewhat better with the slower-paced "Mister Rogers' Neighborhood" program. Is it possible that the technique of presenting quick, entertaining, brief bits of learning material, which was designed particularly to secure the attention of "disadvantaged" preschoolers, may actually decrease the effective learning of materials so presented to them?

An inquiry into the effectiveness of "Sesame Street" lessons in enhancing the cognitive performance of children in first grade has been reported by Sprigle (1972). Two dozen low-income children in an experimental kindergarten were exposed daily to the "Sesame Street" curriculum as the educational component of their daily program. Teachers followed up with activities suggested by the producers, the Children's Television Workshop. Matched control children were not exposed to "Sesame Street." Instead, each day they were provided with learning experiences in a game format along with equal emphasis on social and emotional development in the classroom. Results indicated that the educational TV program did not prepare the children for success at first grade work, nor could the program narrow the achievement gap between low-income and middle-income children.

Sprigle (1972) reported that "Sesame Street" graduates and the matched control group showed no differences on Metropolitan Readiness Tests after three weeks in first grade. Indeed, first grade classmates from working-class families did better on word meaning, listening, alphabet, numbers, and copying tasks than did the experimental children from low-income families who had had the benefit of the television experience. At the end of first grade, these differences between the children were more marked. Classmates from working-class families achieved significantly higher word reading, paragraph meaning, vocabulary, spelling, word study skills, and arithmetic scores on the Stanford Achievement Test than "Sesame Street" viewers from low-income families. Further study by Sprigle on length of viewing time did not show any increased benefit for four-year-olds from low-income families who viewed "Sesame Street" for two years rather than one year. Particularly impressive was the finding that low-income children in a control group provided with a special interactive curriculum focusing on academic preparation and with strong emphasis on social skills did increase their scores and chances for academic success. Sprigle wondered whether such television programming may not be sacrificing education for entertainment. "The mere manipulation of alphabet letters and numbers does not make a program educational" (p. 108).

He emphasized that there are no shortcuts through the problems of educating low-income children. Caring, interacting, teaching, in-the-flesh adults may be far more important than fancy format, fine pacing, and attractive TV characters. Of course, when an educational program such as "Sesame Street" is used in conjunction with a participating, caring adult who actively builds on the numbers, letters, and other concepts introduced by puppets or human characters, then the cognitive boost provided by this educational television program may indeed be more far reaching than the effects of passive viewing by a young child alone.

IQ and TV: Do brighter children watch TV less? Research data linking increased TV watching to lower school achievement are tricky to interpret. For example, Scott (1956) reported that children who watched more TV were inferior in arithmetic and reading achievement. Yet, children who were of lower socioeconomic status (SES) and lower IQ in this study watched TV the most. Thus, perhaps low-SES and IQ variables account more reasonably for lowered achievement findings than does the television watching per se. There may not be a simple relationship between reading scores and number of television hours logged per week.

Thompson (1964) also found lowered achievement by children who watched TV more. When he carefully controlled for mental age, however, the lower achievement scores were found not to be caused by TV watching but by the fact that children at lower intellectual levels preferred to watch more television. Teachers and parents need to be alert to the possibility that watching TV is an easier and preferred activity compared to the struggle and challenge of book reading for children who are slower in development.

Violent television and child aggression

"Violence defined as the 'overt expression of physical force against others or self, or the compelling of action against one's will on pain of being hurt or killed' is the dominant theme of television," states child development specialist Lefrancois (1980). More than 98 percent of all cartoon programs contain violent episodes, and the frequency of violence in children's programs is six times greater than that in adult programs (Gerbner 1972). Young children tend to prefer cartoons.

How does such a dosage of violence affect young children's behaviors? Many (about one-fourth of boys and one-third of girls interviewed) report being frightened by TV violence, but differences in maladjustment or delinquency between viewers and nonviewers have not been found. Bandura and his colleagues have demonstrated over and over that children will show an increase in aggressive behavior as a result of exposure to aggressive models (Bandura 1973). This effect occurs whether or not the model is a live person or a person dressed as a cartoon character in a film, or a filmed human model (Bandura, Ross, and Ross 1963). Children who have been exposed to these aggressive models behave more aggressively when placed later in a situation with objects the models have used violently. Typically, control children who have had prior exposure to a nonaggressive model, particularly a male nonaggressive model, show nonaggressive play or decreased aggression afterward. How realistic are such laboratory studies? Do they represent situations typical in children's lives? If children will smash a Bo-Bo doll with a mallet or sock Bo-Bo after watching an adult male model do so, does that mean they would be more likely to hurt real people? Recent studies have sought to link more naturalistic measures of television viewing and of children's interactions with others.

Short-term effects of TV violence. Brief exposure to violent TV over a short period of time rather than years of such viewing may have different effects. Also, measuring behavior right after such viewing rather than long after the violence was viewed may yield different results among children. Friedrich and Stein (1973) carried out a short-term experiment over nine weeks in a summer nursery school. They provided either antisocial, neutral, or prosocial TV programs daily for four weeks to three groups of preschoolers attending the preschool.

Intelligence tests and baseline observations of free play were carried out during the three weeks prior to the experimental television viewing. In the two-week postviewing period, the children were again observed at play and their mothers were interviewed. Batman and Superman cartoons containing instances of physical violence and verbal aggression comprised the antisocial TV fare. Children in this experimental condition notably declined in rule obedience, persistence, and tolerance for delay when observed at play. But not all children who had seen these films showed higher aggression levels. Only those who had been rated initially as above average in aggression responded to aggressive television programs by later exhibiting higher levels of aggression in play.

Violence on television may not affect all children the same way. Gouze (1979) too reports differential results with children divided into high- and low-aggressive groups based on their ideas about how social conflicts should be resolved. Before viewing a television program, children in each group heard stories in which different solutions to social conflicts were provided. Children in the low-aggressive group who had heard stories with negative consequences for aggression decreased in aggression after watching an aggressive TV show. In marked contrast, children in the high-aggressive group heard the same stories and watched the same TV show, but instead they showed

an increase in aggression after the program.

We must be cautious in assuming that watching violent films will automatically enhance violent behaviors. When children are more prone to act out aggressively with others, then adults beware! Watching violent TV may well enhance such a child's aggressive proclivities.

Understanding motives and consequences of TV violence. Educators have puzzled over whether young children's *understanding* of *why* people behaved aggressively (whether to rob someone or to catch a crook), or *what happened* because someone was violent (such as having to go to jail) would make a difference in the effects of viewing violence. Leifer and Roberts (cited in Liebert and Baron 1971) showed children from kindergarten through twelfth grade TV programs that varied systematically in the amount of violent content. Later, each child was presented with a series of real-life situations. For example: "You are standing in line for a drink of water. A kid comes along and just pushes you out of line." Children were asked to choose between a pair of alternative responses, one of which was typically aggressive: "Push them back," and one was not: "Go away." Children who had viewed the more violent programs responded with higher levels of aggression than those viewing the less violent programs. An important finding was that no change in children's aggression level was found whether they understood the reasons for the TV violence or understood what had happened to the story characters who acted aggressively. That is, even if "good guys" roughed up a criminal or "bad guys" got their just desserts, the kinds of *motives* or *consequences* associated with the violent programs did not affect the child's level of aggressive responding afterward. Only the presence of TV violence itself affected the later levels of aggressive responding.

Imitation and/or disinhibition: Are both involved? Although there is extensive evidence for imitation of aggressive acts against toy victims, those who downplay the effects of violent TV do not believe that such experiments have proved that children would actually harm *people*, even if they would beat up Bo-Bo dolls. Theorists have had contradictory views. Some have held that watching TV violence provides catharsis for aggressive feelings and should lead to decreased impulse to hurt others. Some suppose that watching violence will have a *disinhibitory* effect so that children do not need to imitate a model. After seeing violence they will be more apt to act out and accept a variety of aggressive actions against others. Liebert and Baron (1972) investigated the effects of exposure to short (three-and-one-half minutes) excerpts from either "The Untouchables" or a highly active videotaped sports sequence. "The Untouchables" sequence contained a chase, two fist-fights, two shootings, and a knifing. The 136 children who participated were five- and six-year-olds and eight- and nine-year-olds from varied social backgrounds.

After the brief viewing, the children were given an opportunity either to help or hurt a peer supposedly playing in the next room. The children were told that when a light came on,

> if you push this green button, that will make the handle next door easier to turn and will help the child to win the game. If you push this red button, that will make the handle next door feel hot. That will hurt the child. . . . Remember, this is the *help* button, and this is the *hurt* button. (p. 471)

Despite how short "The Untouchables" sequence was, children who had seen it made hurting responses more often and significantly longer than those who saw the highly active, yet nonaggressive sports program. The children had been told that a brief red button push would cause only minimum discomfort. Yet they pushed longer! They were more willing to shock another person after observing filmed aggressiveness. The authors urge consideration of the significance of their findings that "emerged despite the brevity of the aggression sequences (less than four minutes), the absence of a strong prior instigation to aggression, the clear availability of an alternative helping response, and the use of nationally broadcast materials rather than specially prepared laboratory films" (p. 474). Disinhibition as well as imitation may make aggressive responses more probable after children watch violent TV.

Long-term effects of violent TV viewing. The most thorough inquiry into the long-range effects of viewing early television violence has been carried out by Eron and his colleagues. In the original study (Eron et al. 1972), television viewing habits and levels of aggression were assessed in 875 8-year-old children in upstate New York. Ten years later, 475 of these subjects were reinterviewed. To their surprise, the researchers found that the correlation between viewing violent TV programs in third grade and being characterized as aggressive at age 18 was much higher for boys than the contemporaneous correlation in late teens of watching violent TV and being aggressive. Eron (1982) concluded that there might be a sensitive period that begins somewhere before age 8 when a child is especially susceptible to the effect of continued violence viewing.

Huesmann and Eron (in press) therefore decided to look at 750 children from six to ten years of age in the Chicago area. During a three-year period, they interviewed parents and tested children in classrooms. Measures taken at three different times included peer-nominated aggression and popularity, self-ratings of aggression, fantasy, and preference for sex-typed behaviors. Also obtained were various measures of television habits including frequency of viewing, violence of favorite programs, and identification with aggressive male and female television characters. The parent variables included rejection, nurturance, physical punishment for aggression, self-ratings of aggression, social mobility, and the violence of the TV programs that the parents themselves watched. This study was also carried out in three other countries.

In general, the correlations in all four countries indicated that viewing of television violence is associated with higher levels of aggression, not only for boys but also for girls. Over time, aggressive children continued to watch an increased amount of violence. For boys, low reading achievement is associated with increased observation of violence. For both boys and girls, the lower the intellectual ability as indexed by scores on a reading achievement test, the more a child believes that television violence is real:

> Less achieving children watch television more often, identify more strongly with aggressive television characters and are more apt to believe aggressive television content is real. Thus, they are more likely

to be influenced by the behaviors they observe on the screen. In addition, they are likely to be frustrated more often. (Eron 1982, p. 202)

Lowered intelligence, with its attendant frustrations, seems to exacerbate the relation between television violence and aggressive behavior. Of the parent variables, rejection and physical punishment were significantly associated with aggressive behaviors of sons. Parental viewing of violent programs showed no relation with child aggression.

In an effort to counteract the effects of TV violence, Eron and colleagues asked some of the high violence viewers in this Chicago study to write an essay on "Why TV violence is unrealistic and why viewing too much of it is bad." During the course of two sessions, children wrote the paragraph, rewrote it, were taped reading it, and watched a TV tape of themselves and their classmates reading the paragraphs. Four months later, it was found that the mean peer-nominated aggression scores for these children had decreased significantly from ratings a year earlier. One pitfall was that the more that children identified with TV characters, the *less* likely they were to change as a result of the intervention procedure. Those who watched violent TV and identified with the aggressive characters were the most aggressive of all subjects.

Another significant predictor was the extent to which children had read fairy tales or had fairy tales read to them. The more extensive the reading of fairy tales, the more the children's attitudes toward television changed as a result of the intervention.

Educators need to be alert to several important implications from these studies. Harsh punitive parenting and/or violent TV watching may increase aggression. Children who are aggressive are not liked as playmates. They may then be driven to watch more violent TV. Thus there is a *circular* relation between parental use of harsh physical punishment, children's low social interaction skills, rejection by other young children, and a tendency then to watch more violent TV, which will provide more models for aggression and more loosening of inhibitions to aggress.

In addition, strong belief in the reality of TV characters increases violent viewing and peer ratings of a child's aggressiveness. Low reading achievement is associated with more viewing of violence. As Bettelheim (1976) has so cogently argued, a fairy tale allows children to face their angry, bad feelings and gives tangible form and substance to children's anxieties. The frightening symbols of monsters can be gotten rid of in the fairy tale (the dragon is slain, the wicked witch is burned up). Singer and Singer (1981) have also found that training in fantasy can affect the relation between TV violence viewing and child behavior.

Children need adult positive role models and guidance in order to learn to master life crises without recourse to violence. Teachers who boost young children's prereading and reading skills help break the cycle that involves poor intellective achievement, viewing violent TV, and aggressive behaviors.

Sex role socialization and television

How true a picture of the world of real men and women does television paint for children? In 1974 Sternglanz and Serbin chose ten of the most popular children's programs at that time, which featured males and females and scored them for sex of character, importance of character, goodness or badness of each character, and kind of behavior the character exhibited, such as achievement, dominance, nurturance, magic, and activity. In their sample, 67 percent of the characters were male and 33 percent were female. Indeed, they could not include about half of the most popular children's programs due to total absence of female characters.

Almost all evil characters were male (67 good males, 25 bad males, 43 good females, and 2 bad females). Females were significantly more likely to be shown as deferent. Males were significantly more likely to be shown as aggressive, constructive, and succorant (seeking aid, protection, or information to help carry out a project). Four of the five title-role females were witches of one kind or another—hardly a realistic work role model for later life! Females were punished more for high levels of activity. Males were more often rewarded than females, who were more often ignored. Preschool teachers, in fact, *are* more likely to respond to boys' activities (Serbin et al. 1973), and more frequently respond to boys' noncompliance even when boys comply as often as girls (Honig and Wittmer 1981). Thus, some TV sex roles may well mirror the real world. Yet is this what we wish for our children to learn about sex roles?

Girls who watched these shows and identified with female characters would have learned that it is inappropriate for them to make plans and carry them out and that they will be punished if they abandon a sedate female style and move rapidly. Boys who watched and identified with the male characters would have learned that it is inappropriate for males to defer to another's plan or suggestion or to express admiration of others. Incidentally, the girls may also have learned that "almost the only way to be a successful human being if you are female is through the use of magic" (Sternglanz and Serbin 1974, p. 714)!

New evidence, based on more than 2500 studies (Pearl and Bouthilet 1982) provides an update on the original 1972 Surgeon General's Report on Television and Social Behavior. In the earlier report, women were found to play fewer noteworthy roles on TV than men. They tended to appear in a more derogatory light, in a sexual context, or in romantic or family roles predominantly. They were seldom portrayed as aggressors, and when they were, they were usually punished (Gerbner 1972).

What about the new findings? Rubenstein, a member of the original panel and the update task force, has been quoted as concluding that "there is a causal relationship between televised violence and later aggression . . . (but) the newer research shows influences of television on the viewer much beyond the issue of violence" ("Violence in TV" 1981, p. 151). The report, for example, also finds that television does a poor job depicting health care issues such as portraying people using seat belts. In the report, a census of characters and their occupations on prime time and children's television programs revealed that three times as many men as women appear on TV. The most common jobs portrayed are in traditionally male areas—law, medicine, and policework. Will children's ideas about the value of women's mothering roles and outside work roles be distorted by such lopsided representation? These are difficult questions to answer.

Prosocial television: Can it make a difference?

Some TV programs emphasize consideration, gentleness, and trying to take the point of view of others different from ourselves. For young children, "Captain Kangaroo" is one such program. It made its debut on October 3, 1955, and is the longest running children's TV program. In 1978, Bob Keeshan, creator of the Captain Kangaroo character, introduced "Picturepages" to the show. Shape, size, sensory, and other concepts which enhance learning in preschoolers were then added to the program. Research is lacking to examine the effects of viewing "Captain Kangaroo" on children's positive social-emotional adjustment on early learning.

Happily, there are data that point to positive effects of another prosocially oriented children's television program, "Mister Rogers' Neighborhood." Friedrich and Stein (1973) chose episodes from this program with themes of cooperation, sharing, sympathy, affection, friendship, verbalizing, and understanding one's own and others' feelings, persistence, and competence at tasks, control of aggression, delay of gratification, and adaptive coping with frustration. In their research (mentioned earlier in this review) they showed a 10- to 15-minute prosocial film from "Mister Rogers' Neighborhood" daily for four weeks to one-third of the preschoolers participating in a nine-week summer program, where the other children received either antisocial or neutral films.

Overall, prosocial TV exposure was followed by increased task persistence, self-control, and tolerance for delay (particularly for children of above-average IQ) in comparison with the trends in these scores for children who had viewed either antisocial or neutral films.

Increases in prosocial interpersonal behaviors were most evident in *low-income* children who had viewed the prosocial films. Across social class, those children most familiar in their own homes with "Mister Rogers' Neighborhood" showed more increases in task persistence and rule obedience compared to all the other children in the experimental nursery school.

The implications are clear. Adults need to arrange for children to watch prosocial programs such as "Mister Rogers' Neighborhood." Of special importance is the finding that increased cooperative play, nurturance, and verbalization of feeling were significantly greater among low-income children who viewed this program.

TV: Help or hindrance to family life?

Many parents find TV a boon. They can send a child to the TV set and be free to do other things besides child care. Yet television may not be an unmixed blessing in relation to family life. Commercials, for example, may arouse appetites for advertised products which parents cannot or do not wish to purchase.

Effects of commercials. Children are attentive to TV commercials, which are brief, colorful, rhythmic, and emotionally exciting. Most food commercials that children view are for sugary foods. The Federal Trade Commission suggested banning sugary-product advertising as detrimental to children's dental and general health (1978). How carefully children attend to such messages may be testified to by weary parents nagged by young children to purchase commercial products whose TV allure is strong.

The FTC report was also concerned that television advertisements may increase the amount of strife between parents and children. With strong TV product appeal, children and parents may find themselves more often in opposition. Parents may wish to reject a child's request for the product, and may use more firm or even negative control methods. Atkin (1975) asked children to report the frequency of mother-child conflict following the children's request to purchase a cereal or toy. Children heavily exposed to TV commercials reported more parent-child conflict than did children who seldom viewed commercial television. Whether the directionality of effect was from the viewing to the conflict, or whether more oppositional parent-child relationships impel a child to view more commercial TV, however, is impossible to determine in this study.

Goldbert and Gorn (1978) showed young children advertisements for a new toy. Then the children were asked to role play how a child would feel who wanted the toy but was denied it by a parent. The children projected more feelings of rejection from parents than positive affect to parents.

When a group of children and their mothers separately watched a cartoon with frequent sugary-food commercials, and another group watched the cartoon without commercials, then shopping habits of mothers and children differed significantly later (Stoneman and Brody 1981). Children exposed to the food commercials made many more attempts to influence parental buying. They also made significantly more attempts to influence the parent to purchase advertised products. The mothers who had seen the TV with commercials used power assertion techniques more, such as saying, "No," or "Put it back," than did mothers of children in the noncommercial condition. We need to be more aware of the pervasive impact of TV. Television may not only directly affect child behaviors, but indirectly affect parent-child relationships in families by increasing child demands followed by increasing parent attempts to control a child. What is the long-term impact of a cumulation of such negative interactions?

TV and family intimacy. There is current concern that parents are interacting less with children and that undue peer influence and pressure exists in socializing the young. What role does TV play in absorbing the time of family members and diluting the intimate quality of family relationships?

Brody, Stoneman, and Sanders (1980) observed 27 families of three- to five-year-old children in a living room setting. Families were assigned randomly to either a TV session or play with magazines and toy sessions. Each family spent ten minutes in each condition. The TV program was chosen by the child.

In this laboratory setting, both parents were more likely to touch their child under the TV condition. Fathers interacted quite differently under the TV condition. They smiled less, talked less, and looked less at the child. These results suggest that parents may need to look at non-TV time to see whether they cannot provide closeness and communicative interactions at the same time.

During the TV time, children oriented toward their parents less, talked less, and were less active. Parents may need to analyze their conflicting goals for children. They may value TV as a babysitter to keep children quiet. That it did in this study! But are other goals for our children being shortchanged as young children watch more and more TV quietly and passively, and perhaps tune out their parents? Also, if TV is used frequently as a babysitter, then it is unlikely that the increased closeness seen in the laboratory condition of this study would occur in real life.

How parents and teachers can take charge

Television is the most powerful communication tool we have. It is here to stay. TV can be used for violence, for crass commercialism, for instruction, and for enhancing and enriching lives. Its influence will depend on many factors, not the least of which is vigorous lobbying by citizens for quality children's programming.

Parents and teachers need to start early to develop good viewing habits in children. *Parents are the gatekeepers to the TV world.* They must choose good programs for children and develop a *plan* and a daily time limit for children's viewing.

Adults need to balance a child's television needs against other needs—for play, reading, exploring, socializing, studying. When parents allowed infants and toddlers unlimited TV viewing and also used harsh methods of discipline, the children by three years of age turned out to be less competent and had lower IQs than three-year-olds whose families restricted TV to one hour of high-quality children's programs per day (Carew, Chan, and Halfar 1978).

Staff at the Federal Trade Commission determined that children view 20,000 TV commercials per year based on a daily average of three hours of TV viewing. Adults need to expose deception in TV advertising to their children. They need to make sure that children understand that the glamorous or famous or goodnatured screen character urging them to buy a product is being paid to do so.

Parents and teachers can read the *Sesame Street Parents' Newsletter* and contribute their own experiences, insights, and concerns with young children and TV to help other adults in a network of concerned caregivers. Many books have helpful ideas for families and curricula for teachers to enhance the usefulness of TV as a teaching tool (Rubenstein 1979; Singer, Singer, and Zuckerman 1981a; 1981b).

Distinguishing between make-believe and real life is hard for preschoolers. Adults need to help children differentiate between fantasy and fact by *talking with children about TV* plots and characters. Suppose a TV hero kills or maims someone. Adults can talk about the grief and sorrow of hurt, and the tragedy of loss for a family. Express your own disapproval if violence is done to people on a screen. Children need to know that their special adults do not like violence nor approve of causing pain. If a TV episode downgrades members of a societal group, an adult can bring up a personal and positive episode that involves members of that group.

Children learn best from educational TV shows if adults who watch TV with them go on to explain difficult words and ideas and build on concepts introduced. Talk about what has happened, what could have happened, what may happen. TV researchers Corder-Bolz and O'Bryant explain:

> An adult can dramatically influence the information a child *learns* and *retains* from watching TV. Thus, a young child, whose optimal level of cognitive ability has not yet been reached, will gain far more knowledge if the parent or an older sibling [or teacher] will re-phrase television dialogue, define difficult words and make further explanation of the events that are portrayed during the TV program. Missing a few minutes of television's continuous verbalization is not nearly as important as establishing enlightened dialogue within the family. (1978, p. 22)

Adults can enlarge young children's awareness of educational TV concepts through reading daily with them and through household and neighborhood activities that enhance the scope of a child's understanding (Honig 1982b).

We can work together with other concerned adults in Action for Children's Television (ACT). This group started in

1968 as a grassroots movement to help improve children's television programs.

Let us be in charge of TV rather than letting TV control our lives. Let us plan and choose with and for our young children so that TV becomes an ally in promoting cognitive and prosocial learning.

References

Anderson, D., and Levin, S. "Young Children's Attention to 'Sesame Street.'" *Child Development* 47 (1976): 806–811.

Atkin, C. "Effects of Television Advertising-Survey of Children's and Mothers' Responses to Television Commercials." *Technical Report*, Michigan State University, 1975.

Ball, S., and Bogatz, G. "A Summative Research of 'Sesame Street': Implications for the Study of Preschool Children." In *Minnesota Symposium on Child Development*, Vol. 6, ed. A. Pick. Minneapolis: University of Minnesota Press, 1972.

Bandura, A. *Aggression: Social Learning Analysis*. Englewood Cliffs, N.J.: Prentice-Hall, 1973.

Bandura, A.; Ross, D.; and Ross, S. A. "Imitation of Film-Mediated Aggressive Models." *Journal of Abnormal and Social Psychology* 67 (1963): 601–607.

Bettelheim, B. *The Uses of Enchantment*. New York: Knopf, 1976.

Brody, G. H.; Stoneman, Z.; and Sanders, A. K. "Effects of Television Viewing on Family Interactions: An Observational Study." *Family Relations* 29 (1980): 216–220.

Carew, J.; Chan, I.; and Halfar, C. *Observing Intelligence in Young Children*. Englewood Cliffs, N.J.: Prentice-Hall, 1976.

Cohen, D. "Television and the Child under Six." In *Television Awareness Training: The Viewer's Guide for Family and Community*, ed. B. Logan and K. Moody. New York: Media Action Research Center, 1979.

Corder-Bolz, C. R., and O'Bryant, S. L. "Tackling 'the Tube' with Family Teamwork." *Children Today* 7, no. 3 (1978): 21–24.

Eron, L. D. "Parent-Child Interaction, Television Violence, and Aggression of Children." *American Psychologist* 37 (1982): 197–211.

Eron, L. D.; Huesmann, L. R.; Lefkowitz, M. H.; and Walder, L. O. "Does Television Violence Cause Aggression?" *American Psychologist* 27 (1972): 253–262.

Federal Trade Commission. *Staff Report on Television Advertising to Children*. Washington, D.C.: U.S. Government Printing Office, 1978.

Friedrich, L. K., and Stein, A. H. "Aggressive and Prosocial Television Programs and the Natural Behavior of Preschool Children." *Monographs of the Society for Research in Child Development*, Serial No. 151. 38, no. 4 (1973).

Gerbner, G. "Violence in Television Drama: Trends and Symbolic Functions." In *Television and Social Behavior*, Vol. 1, ed. G. A. Comstock and E. A. Rubenstein. Washington, D.C.: U.S. Government Printing Office, 1972.

Goldbert, M., and Gorn, G. "Some Unintended Consequences of TV Advertising to Children." *Journal of Consumer Research* 5 (1978): 22–29.

Gouze, K. "Does Aggressive Television Affect All Children the Same Way?" *Early Report* 6, no. 3 (1979): 2.

Hollenbeck, A. H., and Slaby, R. G. "Infant Visual and Vocal Responses to Television." *Child Development* 50 (1979): 41–45.

Honig, A. S. "Research in Review. Infant-Mother Communication." *Young Children* 37, no. 3 (March 1982a): 52–62.

Honig, A. S. *Playtime Learning Games for Young Children*. Syracuse, N.Y.: Syracuse University Press, 1982b.

Honig, A. S., and Wittmer, D. S. "Caregiver Techniques and Sex of Toddlers." Paper presented at the biennial meetings of the Society for Research in Child Development, Boston, April, 1981.

Huesmann, L. R., and Eron, L. D. "Factors Influencing the Effect of Television Violence on Children." In *Learning from Television: Psychological and Educational Research*, ed. M. J. A. Howe. London: Academic Press, in press.

Kalba, K. "The Electric Community." In *Television as a Social Force: New Approaches to T.V. Criticism*, ed. D. Cater and R. Adler. New York: Praeger, 1975.

Kaye, E. *The Family Guide to Children's Television*. New York: Random House, 1974.

Lefrancois, G. R. *Of Children: An Introduction to Child Development*, 3rd ed. Belmont, Calif.: Wadsworth, 1980.

Liebert, R. M., and Baron, R. A. "Short-Run Effects of Televised Aggression on Children's Aggressive Behaviors." Paper presented at the symposium "The Early Window: The Role of Television in Childhood." American Psychological Association Convention, Washington, D.C., September, 1971.

Liebert, R. M., and Baron, R. A. "Some Immediate Effects of Televised Violence on Children's Behavior." *Developmental Psychology* 6 (1972): 469–475.

Liebert, R. M., and Spravkin, J. "Impact of Television on Children's Social Development." *School Media Quarterly* 5, no. 3 (1977): 163–170.

Lyle, J., and Hoffman, H. "Explorations in Patterns of Television Viewing by Preschool-Age Children." In *Television and Social Behavior: Television in Day-To-Day Life: Patterns of Use*, Vol. 4, ed. E. A. Rubenstein, G. A. Comstock, and J. P. Murray. Washington, D.C.: U.S. Government Printing Office, 1972.

Martin, J. A. "A Longitudinal Study of the Consequences of Early Mother-Infant Interaction: A Microanalytic Approach." *Monographs of the Society for Research in Child Development* 46, no. 3 (1981).

Murray, J. P. *Television and Youth.* Boys Town, Neb.: The Boys Town Center for the Study of Youth Development, 1980.

Pearl, D., and Bouthilet, L., eds. *Television and Behavior: Ten Years of Scientific Progress and Implications for the 80's.* Washington, D.C.: U.S. Government Printing Office, 1982.

Rubenstein, E. "Television and the Young Viewer." In *Television Awareness Training: The Viewer's Guide for Family and Community,* ed. B. Logan and K. Moody. New York: Media Action Research Center, 1979.

Scott, L. F. "Television and School Achievement." *Phi Delta Kappan* 38 (1956): 25–28.

Serbin, L. A.; O'Leary, D. K.; Kent, R. N.; and Tonick, I. J. "A Comparison of Teacher Response to the Problem and Preacademic Behavior of Boys and Girls." *Child Development* 44 (1973): 796–804.

Singer, J. L., and Singer, D. G. *Television, Imagination and Aggression: A Study of Preschoolers' Play.* Hillsdale, N.J.: Erlbaum, 1981.

Singer, D. G.; Singer, J. L.; and Zuckerman, D. M. *Getting the Most Out of Television. Resource Book for Teachers—A Curriculum about Television.* Santa Monica, Calif.: Goodyear, 1981a.

Singer, D. G.; Singer, J. L.; and Zuckerman, D. M. *Teaching Television: How to Use Television to Your Child's Advantage.* New York: Dial, 1981b.

Sprigle, H. A. "Who Wants to Live on Sesame Street?" *Young Children* 28, no. 2 (December 1972): 91–109.

Sternglanz, S. H., and Serbin, L. A. "Sex Role Stereotyping in Children's Television Programs." *Developmental Psychology* 10 (1974): 710–715.

Stoneman, Z., and Brody, G. H. "The Indirect Impact of Child-Oriented Advertisements on Mother-Child Interactions." *Journal of Applied Developmental Psychology* 2 (1981): 369–376.

Thompson, G. W. "Children's Acceptance of Television Advertising and the Relation of Televiewing to School Achievement." *The Journal of Educational Research* 58, no. 4 (1964): 171–174.

"Violence on TV: A Ten-Year Update." *Science News* 120 (September 1981): 151.

Winn, M. *The Plug-In Drug.* New York: Viking, 1977.

Resources

Action for Children's Television. 46 Austin, Newtonville, MA 02160. 617-527-7870.

Sesame Street Parents' Newsletter. One Lincoln Plaza, New York, NY 10023. 212-595-3456.

HEAD START

How Research Changed Public Policy

Bernard Brown

Bernard Brown, *Ph.D., is a Social Science Analyst with the Administration for Children, Youth and Families of the Department of Health and Human Services, Washington, D.C.*

The story of Head Start research is a thrilling adventure about how new ideas can change the future for millions of children and their families. Twenty years ago Head Start began as a comprehensive early intervention program for low income parents and their young children. But from its inception Head Start has been the center of a national debate on early intervention programs.

Now reaching more than 400,000 3- to 5-year-old children each year, Head Start continues to provide education, opportunities for healthy social and emotional development, nutrition, and medical and dental care so that children can develop and learn at their best throughout their lives. Head Start has now served more than 9 million families.

The influence of Head Start extends far beyond the children and parents involved in the program. Head Start models continue to affect child care, the public schools, health care, and social services. Therefore, the debate about the future of Head Start—the role of the government, federal fiscal policy, the

Head Start provides education, opportunities for healthy social and emotional development, nutrition, and medical and dental care so that children can develop and learn at their best throughout their lives.

needs of children, and the conditions of minorities and low income families—is in a larger sense a debate about the care of all of America's children.

In 1967, the Office of Economic Opportunity Research Advisory Council for Head Start was organized. This Advisory Council included Edward Zigler, Urie Bronfenbrenner, Boyd McCandless, and Edmund Gordon, four distinguished experts. The Council urged more longitudinal and comprehensive research on Head Start that would include multiple comparison groups. This research

 Reprinted by permission from *Young Children*, Vol. 40, No. 5 (July 1985), pp. 9-13. © 1985 by the National Association for the Education of Young Children, 1834 Connecticut Ave., N.W., Washington, DC 20009.

would document families and children's experiences before, during, and after Head Start. The Dismal Period of Head Start research began when the Council's advice was ignored.

The Dismal Period

In response to demands for the evaluation of Head Start by the Johnson administration, the Evaluation Division of the Office of Economic Opportunity, then the federal agency in charge of Head Start, proposed a study of former Head Start children. The Westinghouse Learning Corportion and Ohio University were awarded a contract to evaluate those children, then in grades 1 to 3. In 1969 the Westinghouse Report (Cicirelli, Evans, & Schiller), as it came to be known, was published.

The design of this study did not meet the criteria established by the Research Council in four important ways:

• The research was conducted only *after* the children completed Head Start.
• The comparison group was not selected until the time of the post-test by matching characterstics with the children who had been in Head Start.
• The children were tested mainly with cognitive measures.
• The primary method of analysis used a constructed index of socioeconomic status as the single covariate in a covariance analysis.

This study concluded that the Summer Head Start program was totally ineffective and even had a negative impact, while the full-year program was only marginally effective. Moreover, the report stated that results from the summer program were so negative that it was doubtful any change in design would reverse the findings.

The Westinghouse Report was immediately the subject of a widely publicized controversy. "Shortly after the results were released, Robert Finch, then Secretary of Health, Education and Welfare, announced that the study contained insufficient facts and the data was sloppy. Dr. William Madow, the chief statistical consultant to the study, publicly withdrew his name from the report; the White House defended the results and the directors of the Summer Head Start programs (involving over a million children) were given the option

to shift their funds to full-year programs" (Smith & Bissell, 1970, p. 52).

In the years that followed, many analysts (Campbell & Erlebacher, 1970; Smith & Bissell, 1970; Barnow, 1973) reanalyzed the data and pointed out other deficiencies in the analysis. Ten years later, Magidson (1977) demonstrated that the study actually showed that Head Start was effective. But by then the damage had been done.

In 1971 a 3-year plan was drawn up to phase out Head Start. While the plan was averted by a narrow margin of supporters, many remained convinced by the single flawed study that Head Start was a failure. Nevertheless, the impact of the Westinghouse Report was devastating. Morale was shattered, and good staff left the program. Summer programs were abandoned and the program budget was held constant for many years. But Head Start survived, largely because of a grass roots constituency led by Head Start parents and staff.

The Latency Period

The early 1970s were dark days for Head Start, but just as the Dark Ages were a period of creative change, constructive forces were at work reshaping Head Start and improving its evaluation. Under the leadership of Edward Zigler, then Director of the Office of Child Development (OCD), a series of experimental Head Start programs was launched. Administration, training, and service programs were improved. Performance standards were developed.

Evaluation techniques were also improving. Esther Kresh, the Federal Evaluation Project Officer, and Ann O'Keefe, the Federal Program Director, worked together to build a pure experimental design into the evaluation of Home Start, an experimental home-based intervention program. A study by High/Scope showed positive effects (Deloria, Coelen, & Roupp, 1974). Other evaluations of Head Start components and experimental programs, such as the MIDCO Parent Involvement Study (1972) were also starting to reveal positive results.

Despite the setbacks, the comprehensive early intervention model established by Head Start increased during this period. Child development workers, who had always been convinced of its value, remained strong and convincing

advocates for children and families. As a result of these and many other factors, the demand increased for early intervention programs in public schools. Child care programs were expanding to meet the growing demands of working parents.

Head Start's experimental and training programs continued, and health services were improved. The federal government began to upgrade the quality of Head Start evaluations.

Meanwhile, the child development research community was learning more about children's growth. Studies were under way on parent-oriented and home-based intervention programs. Several well-designed studies, although conducted with small numbers of children in a short time period, nevertheless seemed to indicate the value of early intervention programs (Brown, 1978).

Bronfenbrenner's review of longitudinal studies up to 1972 showed only short-term gains which faded out and indicated that there were no long-term effects except in those programs that worked closely with parents (1974).

Despite the progress in early childhood research, by the mid-1970s the Office of Management and Budget called for gradually cutting the Head Start budget and eliminating the program altogether in 1980. The rationale was based on the Westinghouse Report. Although researchers were convinced that their findings had been misread, Head Start's budget was held constant and hope was dim.

It was during this bleak time that a major breakthrough began. Irving Lazar met with Edith Grotberg at OCD to propose an idea for a research project. The problem with the studies on early intervention projects was that there were too few children enrolled in any one program to identify statistically significant trends and effects which extended over time. Could the data from the major studies be pooled and perhaps combined with a new round of data collection using the same set of measures?

The idea was offered to principal investigators of major studies at the 1975 meeting of the Society for Research in Child Development. It met with skepticism. Some of the original Head Start children were now in high school. The approach might not be technically feasible. No such project had ever been attempted. The researchers, who were

> Head Start research is a victory for a compassionate and caring nation which has given the world a new standard of social progress.

competitors for ideas and scarce research funds, would have to cooperate closely. In essence, the project asked researchers to risk their life's work by opening their files to public scrutiny.

Despite such misgivings, all but one of the principal investigators agreed to collaborate. The project would clearly contribute to child development research, and it would provide follow-up data for their own studies. And so the Consortium for Longitudinal Studies began.

A proposal was submitted to OCD and a grant was awarded. Lazar set up an independent analysis group at Cornell University where the researchers were to send their old and new data. Each project would administer common IQ tests, collect parent and child interviews, and obtain school records.

The membership of the Consortium included many renowned child devel-

opment researchers: Kuno Beller of Temple University, Ira Gordon of the University of Florida, Martin and Cynthia Deutsch of New York University, Susan Gray of George Peabody College, Merle Karnes of the University of Illinois, Phyllis Levenstein of the Verbal Interaction Project, Louise Miller of the University of Louisville, Francis Palmer of SUNY-Stony Brook, David Weikart of the High/Scope Foundation, Myron Wolman of the Institute for Education Research, and Edward Zigler of Yale University. Altogether, the staff and consultants working on the project numbered about 40. I was Technical Consultant and later Federal Project Officer.

The Consortium studies were well-run early intervention programs but few were Head Start programs. Some programs had begun before Head Start. The studies were carefully controlled experiments, usually in university settings. Nevertheless, if these early intervention programs were shown to be successful, it was reasoned, other high quality programs for young children, such as Head Start, could also work.

As the Consortium's data accumu-

lated, the investigators began to realize the study was far more important than they had anticipated. Experienced researchers, like detectives, are quick to sense new clues and patterns. The excitement of the search was building momentum. By the spring of 1976 every week brought news of additional findings.

The Watershed Period

The first indication that a new period in Head Start research was emerging came at the 1976 meeting of the American Psychological Association. Six months later, at the 1977 meeting of the American Association for the Advancement of Science, a symposium was chaired by John Meier, then Director of OCD. Robert Hess, Frank Palmer, Victoria Seitz, and Virginia Shipman presented their longitudinal study findings, and I reviewed the literature (Brown 1978).

By then I had information on two new variables which were later to assume enormous importance: the number of children retained in grade in school and the number of children assigned to special education classes. These variables do not necessarily involve IQ, but they are important in gauging program benefit. At that time, although the Consortium analysis was not yet complete, I cited 96 valid studies, including the just-completed reevaluation of the Westinghouse Report by Magidson, which showed positive effects of early intervention. None of these studies demonstrated with significance and statistical power that the programs were ineffective (Brown, 1978).

After the symposium, the participants held a press conference. The next day we were shocked to find positive newspaper reports published across the country for the first time in 10 years. We were deluged with requests for papers and interviews. There was a stunning impact on early childhood workers who, after 10 years of criticism, felt their life's work was vindicated. I recall the tears in then Head Start Director Jim Robinson's eyes as I related some of the first results to him.

Events began to move at a quicker pace. It became increasingly clear that the Consortium data was leading toward strong and consistent findings that early intervention programs work. As caring human beings and educators, we were delighted with the direction in which our work seemed to be heading, but we were first of all scientists committed to objectivity and truth. Findings were checked and rechecked. From the beginning we deliberately invited the participation of researchers. We met on research methods before the work began and eventually presented our findings at the meetings of every major research society in the country, always seeking criticism.

This open approach paid great dividends because the early and careful methodological criticism of researchers directed the course of the analysis. The Consortium's meticulous research, directed by Richard Darlington, has never been substantively criticized. Credit also belongs to the outstanding graduate students recruited by Lazar—Ruth Hubbel, Harry Murray, Marilyn Rosche, Jacqueline Royce, and Dan Koretz.

These careful, deliberate analysts took into account the human and political dimensions of their work.

Findings of the Consortium

What were the findings of the Consortium for Longitudinal Studies on the long-term effects of early intervention? Basically, the Consortium found that high quality infant and preschool services improve the ability of low income children to meet the minimal requirements of further schooling (Consortium, 1979, 1983; Lazar, Hubbell, Murray, Rosche, & Royce, 1977; Lazar, Darlington, Murray, Royce, & Snipper, 1982).

1. Early education programs significantly reduce the number of children assigned to special education classes. This benefit extends to all participants, regardless of their initial abilities or early home backgrounds.

2. Early education programs significantly reduce the number of children retained in grade.

3. Preschool programs produce a significant increase in the IQ and school achievement of low income children through at least the critical early primary years.

4. Children who attend preschool are more likely to give achievement-related reasons for being proud of themselves. Their mothers also have high vocational aspirations for them.

A recent study on one of the Consortium programs, the High/Scope Perry Preschool Project, found that this early intervention program has benefits that last into early adulthood (Berrueta-Clement, Schweinhart, Barnett, Epstein, & Weikart, 1984). In addition to improving school success and achievement, the program helped prevent delinquency and teenage pregnancy and improved the likelihood of employment. A cost-benefit analysis determined the net benefit to society to be $28,933 for a year of preschool, a 7 to 1 return on investment!

It is apparent that the evaluators of the 60s were wrong both in their conclusions and their methods. The recommendations for Head Start research by the experts—Bronfenbrenner, Gordon, McCandless, and Zigler—should have been followed in the first place.

Influence of research on public policy

How has the research on early intervention programs influenced public policy? We know that four events took place politically:

● Head Start's budget was increased by $150 million dollars as a result of the Congressional appropriation hearings in 1977, the first money for program expansion in a decade.

● A budget increase of $55 million dollars in a period of decreasing welfare funding was approved in 1978.

● In 1978 a major campaign to transfer Head Start from the Department of Health, Education and Welfare to the new Department of Education, a move opposed by the Head Start Association and many child advocacy groups, was blocked.

● On February 9, 1981, newly elected President Reagan announced that Head Start would be placed in his safety net, despite his intention to cut social programs. At that time Head Start served 387,300 children and had a budget of $819 million. The projected enrollment for 1985 is 452,250 children with a budget of $1,075 million.

The Head Start research reports made a difference. At the 1977 appropriation hearings, Senator Magnuson and Representative Flood cited the reports. At the hearings about the proposed transfer to the Department of Education, Senator Brooke and Representative Chisholm were especially impressed by the Consortium findings.

Head Start research has had a critical influence on public policy, but that is not the whole story. The politicians who voted for the program were ready to hear good news. Their attitudes were positive because they knew how many voters liked the program. They only needed evidence to move ahead. Perhaps the major influence was that the Head Start community became sophisticated lobbyists.

A victory for children

The debate over early intervention is not, and indeed may never be, over. It is inevitable that these findings will someday be challenged—no research can stand forever. The Consortium's findings should continue to be studied and new data accumulated. But until other data contradicts these findings, the scientific evidence supports early intervention.

One thing will not change: the story of the brilliant and heroic group of social scientists who set out upon a quest for a better life for children; a story of the miracles of so much devotion, intelligence, and energy focussed on a common objective, and of the child development profession persevering through a 12-year struggle to win a glorious victory for children.

This victory was not only for the 12 researchers who started longitudinal studies so many years ago, but also for the children, families, and staff of Head Start. It was a different kind of victory for the child development profession. When the work of the Consortium started, we were hesitant and cautious. But when in the future a battle is in the offing—and the fight for children never ends—we will trust ourselves to find the truth and communicate it.

But even more, the Head Start research is a victory for a compassionate and caring nation which has given the world a new standard of social progress. It stands as a tribute to a nation which is socially creative, optimistic, and dares to solve its problems.

References

Barnow, B. S. (1973). *The effects of Head Start and socio-economic status on cognitive development of disadvantaged children.* Unpublished doctoral dissertation, University of Wisconsin, Madison.

Berrueta-Clement, J. R., Schweinhart, L. J., Barnett, W. S., Epstein, A. S., & Weikart, D. P. (1984). Changed lives: The effects of the Perry Preschool Program on youths through age 19. *Monographs of the High/Scope Education Research Foundation, 8.*

Bronfenbrenner, U. (Ed.). (1974). *A report on longitudinal evaluations of preschool programs, Vol. II: Is early intervention effective?* Washington, DC: U.S. Department of Health and Human Services, Administration for Children, Youth and Families.

Brown, B. (Ed.). (1978). *Found: Long-term gains from early intervention.* Boulder, CO: Westview Press.

Campbell, D. T., & Erlebacher, A. (1970). How regression artifacts in quasi-experimental evaluations can mistakenly make compensatory education look harmful. In J. Hellmuth (Ed.), *The disadvantaged child. Compensatory education: A national debate* (Vol. 3, pp. 185–210). New York: Brunner/Mazel.

Cicirelli, V. G., Evans, J. W., & Schiller, J. S. (1969). *The impact of Head Start: An evaluation of the effects of Head Start on children's cognitive and affective development* (Vols. 1–2). Athens, OH: Westinghouse Learning Corporation and Ohio University.

Consortium for Longitudinal Studies. (1979). *Lasting effects after preschool, summary report.* Washington, DC: U.S. Department of Health and Human Services, Administration for Children, Youth and Families.

Consortium for Longitudinal Studies. (1983). *As the twig is bent—lasting effects of preschool programs.* Hillsdale, NJ: Erlbaum.

Deloria, D., Coelen, C., & Ruopp, R. (1974). National home start evaluation: Interim report 5, executive summary. High/Scope Educational Research Foundation, Abt Associates: Ypsilanti, MI.

Lazar, I., Darlington, R., Murray, H., Royce, J., & Snipper, A. (1982). Lasting effects of early education. *Monographs of the Society for Research in Child Development, 47* (1, 2, Serial No. 194).

Lazar, I., Hubbel, V. R., Murray, H., Rosche, M., & Royce, J. (1977). *The persistence of preschool effects: A long-term follow-up of fourteen infant and preschool experiments, summary.* Washington, DC: U.S. Department of Health and Human Services, Administration for Children, Youth and Families.

Magidson, J. (1977). Toward a causal model for adjusting for preexisting differences in the nonequivalent control group situation: A general alternative to ANCOVA. *Evaluation Quarterly, 1* (3), 399–414.

Midco Parent Associates, Denver. (1972). Investigation of the effects of parent participation in Head Start: Final technical report. Washington, DC: Office of Child Development, U.S. Department of Health, Education and Welfare.

Smith, M. S., & Bissell, J. S. (1970). Report analysis: The impact of Head Start. *Harvard Educational Review, 40,* 51–104.

Wednesday's Child

IN THE OUTCRY OVER PHYSICAL AND SEXUAL ABUSE, THE PLIGHT OF MORE THAN A MILLION NEGLECTED CHILDREN HAS BEEN VIRTUALLY IGNORED.

AVIS BRENNER

Avis Brenner, a professor emeritus of education at Lesley College in Cambridge, Massachusetts, is the author of Helping Children Cope with Stress *(Lexington Books).*

This cold Wednesday morning, John wears the same thin, dirty shirt he wore yesterday and the day before. As he draws lines in his spelling workbook, he pushes his bare feet back into torn shoes and begins rocking back and forth. When classmate Kevin tells a joke that breaks up the other children, John remains silent. Nothing that happens in the classroom makes him laugh or cry. Sometimes he falls asleep, wakes with a scream and then rocks silently in his seat. During recess he stands alone, skinny shoulders hunched under his light jacket.

John is a victim of parental neglect, one of an estimated million and a half children who, in the furor fueled by public attention to physical and sexual abuse, have been virtually ignored.

While abusive parents may simultaneously love and hate their children, neglectful parents have little or no feeling for them. Unwilling or unable to become involved with their children, these mothers and fathers are emotionally absent. They don't talk to their sons and daughters or teach them the simplest life skills. They stay away from home for days at a time and make no provision for their youngsters' care and safety. They neither see nor hear distress, however loudly it is expressed, even when in the same room with their children.

Neglected children's lives are so unpredictable that many never learn to trust adults. Infants' and toddlers' own natural impulses to express love are turned away with indifference by mothers and fathers who do not hold or cuddle them. Social workers find neglected babies lying silently in their cribs, covered with feces, with bottles of soured milk beside them. They see 3- and 4-year-olds who have never been outside to play or to go to a store, children who sleep on bare mattresses amidst garbage, who go hungry and lack appropriate clothing.

The National Center on Child Abuse and Neglect (NCCAN) identified 329,000 neglected children in the United States in 1981. Experts believe that this figure underestimates the scope of the problem: NCCAN limited its reports to cases in which there was proof of extreme neglect resulting in serious impairment or injury. When less extreme cases like John's are added, practitioners believe that the total comes to at least 1.5 million.

Researchers find both immediate and long-lasting deficits in physical, intellectual and emotional development among neglected children. Norman A. Polansky, a professor emeritus of social work at the University of Georgia, and his associates studied neglected children in Appalachia from 1965 to 1970 and in urban Philadelphia from 1975 to 1977. They found that neglected preschoolers had lower IQ's and were more inept socially. They were unsure of themselves, withdrawn and unable to express emotion.

While most neglected children survive into adulthood, they do so at a tremendous cost to society. By late adolescence a disproportionate number are mentally ill or have serious emotional and physical handicaps that make them dependent on mental-health and welfare agencies.

Even when cases of neglect come to the attention of social agencies, there's no guarantee the children will get all the help they need. As sociologist Isabel Wolock at Rutgers University and educational psychologist Bernard Horowitz of Welfare Research Inc. point out in their study of attitudes toward neglected children, social workers sometimes omit them from caseloads when scarce funds are barely enough to save the lives of youngsters who might otherwise be murdered by their abusive caretakers. Yet the long-term effects of neglect threaten to overwhelm our schools, courts, welfare programs and mental-health facilities in the coming years if nothing is done to alleviate suffering.

The first effects of parental neglect

are evident shortly after birth. Neglected babies are likely to be malnourished. Inadequate feeding takes its toll in reduced physical stamina and stunted intellectual development. Psychologists Marvin A. Koski and Eben M. Ingram studied neglected infants and toddlers at Denver General Hospital and found them to be less able than their normal peers in both mental and motor functioning. The older the children, the poorer their motor skills, and in the case of boys, the poorer their intellectual abilities.

Malnourishment can be countered with early intervention. The Child Neglect Project, which operated in Dallas from 1979 through 1982, focused on health care, relying on home visits to all newborn babies in a low-income area in West Dallas to identify cases needing help. When parents skipped their infants' scheduled clinic appointments, staff members persisted in reaching them and working to keep the children in good health. Simultaneously, they sought to improve the adults' parenting practices. Sometimes a mother was referred to a neighborhood center for two daily meals. In the process, staff members taught her to recognize and respond to her baby's needs, and ways to make mealtimes pleasant for herself and the baby.

For school-aged children, lunch programs are another potential health support for the neglected. Though servings are typically ample and nourishing, my experience is that most lunch programs are of limited value even for children who suffer from malnutrition. Too many lunchrooms are large, noisy spaces where crowds of children are rushed to clear their trays in 20 minutes. Consequently, little food is actually consumed.

Regardless of family income, neglected children need special lunch programs. They need to eat in small groups, preferably with classmates, in quiet and pleasant surroundings. They need the guidance of adults willing to sit at the table and help them interact with the other children so that they can learn to enjoy their food and gradually develop everyday social skills.

Many neglected children develop feelings of worthlessness by the time they are 3 or 4 years old. In one study, University of Rochester researcher Judith G. Smetana and her colleagues read stories about typical nursery school misbehavior to both normal and neglected preschoolers. When asked how they would feel if they faced the same punishment as the child in the story, normal youngsters were certain that they would deserve less punishment than other children, no matter what the transgression. Neglected children did not make this distinction, implying that they believe that they are not entitled to any special privileges or protection.

These feelings usually translate into poor performance in school. Teachers find that even in first grade, most neglected youngsters firmly believe that they cannot succeed in their schoolwork and that classmates will never like them. The usual school remedy—brief visits to a resource room for remedial lessons—is not enough to restore self-esteem and improve academic standing. Neglected children need lengthy one-on-one tutoring by a caring teacher or an aide to help them learn to trust adults.

In most cases, however, the emotional consequences of being neglected are so great that children specifically must be taught how to make friends, understand others' feelings and express affection, anger and other normal emotions in normal ways. Since their parents do not hear or respond to their words, they expect no better from teachers or peers and use fists to get what they want.

Karen Gail Lewis, a Cincinnati family therapist who practices group therapy with children from "chaotic" homes, finds that for them, physical contact is an important method of communication. Fistfights and wrestling express feelings and affirm that brothers and sisters are alive. Children

THE PARENTS

Most efforts to help neglected children focus on their parents, finding ways to make them more attentive to their boys and girls, to improve their homemaking practices and the like. Unfortunately, these efforts are largely unsuccessful.

Many neglectful parents are resistant to change. Typically they are lonely, yet hostile and mistrustful of all outsiders. Many live in poverty or have unpredictable incomes. A significant number try to escape through alcohol or drugs or by sleeping away long hours of each day. Mental illness, especially chronic depression, and borderline intellectual functioning are common. Frequently they are outcasts in their communities, isolated even from their own relatives, with no support from family or friends. Many had troubled childhoods, marked by delinquency, failure in school and parental divorce.

Marilyn Hall, a social worker at Hope Cottage, a multiservice counseling agency, observes that these families "drain agency resources and staff time and energy." While some work has been done with neglecting parents, progress toward better child rearing is slow and must be preceded by weeks or months of careful attention to the adults' own need for nurturance. Change, if it takes hold, is usually limited to one aspect of parenting at a time. A mother may begin to send her children to school every day, for example, but forget to shop for food. Change may come too slowly to counteract the stunting of a child's physical, intellectual and social development.

A more feasible alternative is to work directly with neglected children as soon as they are identified. Youngsters can overcome the effects of neglect when there are caring adults to guide them, even if the situation at home does not improve. The earlier in a child's life that such intervention begins, the greater the probability of success.

Norman A. Polansky, a professor emeritus of social work at the University of Georgia, and his colleagues interviewed men and women who had been neglected. Of those who appeared to have adjusted well to adult life, many credited their achievements to social workers and teachers who had helped them when they were young.

from such homes value noise and movement, she says, as proof that they are not alone.

Teachers, counselors and researchers have produced quite a number of packaged programs in social-skills training. Designed to be completed in a few weeks' time, the programs cover how to make friends, manage conflict, join a group, be assertive, empathize and solve interpersonal problems. While none of them have been tested yet with neglected children, the programs have been used to help emotionally disturbed and withdrawn children.

Solid friendships with children their own age can help draw out neglected children by providing them with a source of affection outside the family. Deep involvements with peers in hobbies, sports or academic interests can provide encouragement, fun and satisfaction, which make up, in part, for the lack of warmth at home.

Experiments in which socially competent children are taught to help their less able peers suggest another promising way to assist neglected children. Educators Samuel L. Odom and Phillip S. Strain at the University of Pittsburgh reviewed studies of existing peer-training projects and found that withdrawn youngsters seem to respond best to the socializing efforts of children who are a year or so younger than themselves. Perhaps their

SIGNS OF NEGLECT

Leontine Young, a social worker and formerly a board member of the New Jersey chapter of the National Committee for Prevention of Child Abuse, describes victims of extreme neglect in these terms: They must search for food when they are hungry and often go without; they fall asleep wherever they are when exhausted; they appear to wander aimlessly in homes that are disorganized, "without warmth [and] without meaning."

When neglect is moderate, Young says, the children usually have a supportive relationship with at least one relative whom they see from time to time. Their home, though dirty, is organized enough so that youngsters get to school regularly. Cooked food is available, although mealtimes are haphazard. Chronic illnesses are ignored, but children who are dangerously sick or injured are taken to hospital emergency rooms.

Some neglected children are physically well cared for, but have parents who give no love or attention, no moral guidance, no praise or punishment. According to the National Center on Child Abuse and Neglect, these emotionally neglectful parents encourage antisocial behavior, including drug and alcohol abuse, by refusing to know or care what happens to their children.

Presented below are the warning signs of neglect. No one child will exhibit all of these symptoms, nor is the presence of one or two proof of neglect.

PHYSICAL SYMPTOMS

Clothing and Grooming
Dirty skin, offensive body odor
Unwashed, uncombed hair
Inappropriate dress for weather
  or situation
Outgrown, worn-out, ragged
  clothing

Health
Chronic cold, runny nose
Easily tired
Frequent diarrhea
Medical problems ignored by parents
Untreated bruises and cuts that
  become infected

Preoccupation with Food
Often hungry
May beg for or steal food
Hoards food
Rummages through garbage cans

BEHAVIOR IN INFANTS AND TODDLERS

Unresponsive, listless
Disinterested, lacks curiosity
Seldom smiles, laughs, cries or plays
Excessive self-stimulation: rocks, bangs head, sucks
  hair, scratches body
Doesn't turn to parents for comfort or help

If hospitalized for failure to thrive, regresses after return home
Unable to concentrate
Seeks attention from any nearby adult
Is sometimes frenetically active to no apparent
  purpose

BEHAVIOR IN ELEMENTARY SCHOOL CHILDREN

Is rejected by classmates, makes no friends
Comes to school early and doesn't want to leave
Falls asleep in school
Destroys toys and teaching materials
Is withdrawn and depressed, or overactive and
  aggressive
When hurt, doesn't cry

Sees self as failure, refuses to try, tears up completed
  work
Older children may defy the teacher, rebel, be cruel to
  classmates, lie, steal
Parents refuse help, don't follow through on requests,
  fail to keep appointments

Adapted from Helping Children Cope with Stress (Lexington Books)

smaller size and younger age make them less threatening and thus easier to trust.

Lewis identifies another way in which neglected children buffer themselves against the chill of parental disinterest: Often one brother or sister will become a "parental child." Lewis tries to enhance this by teaching such youngsters constructive ways to impose discipline and show affection and finds that this often leads to improved self-esteem as siblings respond with warmth and respect. At the same time, she makes sure parental children develop friends outside of their families and have opportunities to express their legitimate anger at being thrust into the grownup's role.

Identifying neglected children is relatively easy when there is severe physical neglect. But even the subtle

*F*OR CHILDREN FROM CHAOTIC HOMES, FISTFIGHTS AND OTHER PHYSICAL CONTACT ARE IMPORTANT METHODS OF COMMUNICATION.

signs of parents' failure to provide emotional care can be spotted by the attentive observer. (See "Signs of Neglect.") And once neglected children

are identified, research suggests that active intervention often can compensate for inadequate parents. Michael Rutter, head of the department of child and adolescent psychiatry at the University of London, has studied children who grew up in exceptionally disruptive homes yet became well-adjusted adults. Rutter found that positive school experiences and good relationships with teachers healed many of the wounds of childhood. (See "Resilient Children," *Psychology Today*, March 1984.)

So there is hope. But we need a major, immediate effort to identify and help a million and a half neglected children while there is still time to change their lives. We must not wait until our courts and welfare and mental-health agencies are inundated with cases that could have been prevented.

Latchkey Children: The Fastest-Growing Special Interest Group in the Schools

Deborah Burnett Strother

DEBORAH BURNETT STROTHER is managing editor in the Phi Delta Kappa Center on Evaluation, Development, and Research, Bloomington, Ind.

Latch•key child (lach'-ke child) *n., pl.* latchkey children. **1.** A phrase coined during World War II to describe a child who is regularly left without direct adult supervision before or after school.

THERE WERE seven million "latchkey children" in 1983, according to *Editorial Research Reports.*[1] Meanwhile, the Children's Defense Fund, a child advocacy group, estimated that almost half of the 13 million children aged 13 and under whose parents are employed will get along without direct supervision during some portion of the working day.[2]

Sharp growth in the number of double-income families in the U.S. during the past quarter-century has raised some important questions. Should parents be solely responsible for the before- and after-school care of their children? What role might the schools play in providing this supervision for youngsters of working parents? How does self-care before and after school affect children's school performance? How can teachers help latchkey children and their parents?

Ellen Gray, director of research for the National Committee for Prevention of Child Abuse, notes that, along with increased interest in the problems of latchkey children, there is now some competition over who "owns" the issue. Day-care specialists would like to see available resources going for the provision of high-quality child-care programs for all families who need them, and they have been lobbying toward this end. In the main, day-care specialists advocate the establishment of school-based child-care programs for latchkey children; the schools or other organizations in partnership with the schools should administer these programs, they suggest.

Just as day-care specialists see latchkey children as an issue in which they should have some say, so do organizations devoted to child welfare or to the prevention of child abuse. A number of such organizations have developed "survival skills" curricula to better prepare children to take care of themselves. Critics — who sometimes represent other groups organized to fight child abuse — charge that such curricula condone self-care for children, and advocates of child-care programs fear that these curricula will dilute the strength of their position as lobbyists.

Feminists have also gotten into the act, arguing that a choice of child-care arrangements should be made available to working parents who are unable to provide before- and after-school supervision for their children. Many feminists fear that the issue of latchkey children will be used to argue against the employment of women outside the home.

Some researchers have also entered the debate with more vigor than is customary among academicians. In some cases, using inadequate data, these researchers have made matters worse.

THE ROLE OF THE SCHOOL

About three-fourths of the parents surveyed in a national study of child-care consumers in 1975 said that every community should have "supervised recreational programs" available to children during after-school hours. Nearly 60% of the respondents felt that the public schools should provide these programs.[3]

There are both pros and cons regarding the involvement of public schools in child care, however. School-based programs for latchkey children can help build parental support, attract students to or retain them in the public schools, put empty classrooms to use, and reduce the incidence of acts of school vandalism and juvenile delinquency committed by youngsters who "hang around" school after hours for want of something better to do. Some school-based child-care programs may also function, formally or informally, as magnet programs that will foster school desegregation.

But many administrators and teachers are confused about the limits of the schools' responsibility to children and their parents. These educators worry about such issues as heavier professional workloads, tax increases to pay for the new school-based programs, and the problems and conflicts that these new programs seem certain to generate.

At the federal level, late last October President Reagan signed into law a bill authorizing a two-year, $24 million program of federal aid for school-based child care. The new child-care block grant to the states was included in S. 2565, which extends the federal Head Start program for two years. Under the block grant, nonprofit groups can get help to set up before- and after-school child-care programs for children of working parents.

Several states — California, New York, Maine, Massachusetts, and Florida among them — have already begun to act on the problem of latchkey children.

From *Phi Delta Kappan*, December 1984, pp. 290-293. © 1985 Phi Delta Kappan, Center on Development, Evaluation and Research.

2. CHILDHOOD AND SOCIETY

State-level actions have included studies of the problem, reports to state governors, and the establishment of incentive grants for starting child-care programs.

Schools that wish to provide before- and after-school child-care programs will have to deal with legal and policy issues related to such things as licensing and liability. The School-Age Child Care Project has just released a new publication on legal issues. For information about purchasing this document, contact the Wellesley College Center for Research on Women, Wellesley, MA 02181.

PARENTAL PREFERENCE AND PRACTICE

The data now at hand — and reports by the mass media based on these data — confirm the growing need for child-care programs. But our information on the *availability* of child-care programs for school-age children remains incomplete and often confusing. For example, surveys of parental preferences in child care often reveal only the options that are available — not the kinds of child-care services that parents really need or want. Many studies also fail to differentiate between methods of care for different age groups, to define the age range covered by the phrase "school-age child," or to make a distinction between parents who work outside the home and those who do not. Some parents who hold full-time jobs even list themselves, in responses to surveys, as the major care-givers for their children.

Small-scale local studies often provide more accurate information about child-care practices and preferences than do larger studies. In 1982, for example, three employers in the Washington, D.C., area took part in a study that examined the parental responsibilities shouldered by their 953 employees and the day-care arrangements that these employees had made. The researchers found that single parents tended to miss work because of child-care responsibilities more often than married parents, that employed parents frequently expected children to care for themselves before or after school (24% of these youngsters were 11 years old or younger), and that one-third of the parents were ambivalent about this practice but had been unable to find acceptable care-givers outside the home.[4] Thomas Long and Lynette Long found that 30% to 35% of the children whom they interviewed in 1979 and 1980 in Washington, D.C., were caring for themselves before or after school.[5] In a more recent study (1983) conducted for the Department of Family Resources in Montgomery County, Maryland, the Longs interviewed 2,180 families; they found that 21% of all households in their sample that included children under age 14 used self-

care as the primary form of nonparental child care.[6]

Similar studies in other urban areas have confirmed the fact that some 15% to 30% of all children under age 14 take care of themselves or are cared for by siblings during nonschool hours. Such arrangements constitute the second-most-common child-care situation for children under age 14; only child care by parents is used more frequently.

Certain characteristics of parents play a role in determining the kind of child care that they provide for their children. Parents with higher-than-average incomes are more likely than others to care for their children themselves. Parents with very high levels of educational attainment, parents with lower-than-average incomes, and white parents all tend more often than others to expect children to take care of themselves or to be cared for by siblings.

Local needs assessments and small-scale surveys may not accurately predict the number of children who will use proposed child-care programs, and they certainly cannot guarantee that such programs, once begun, will be fully used. But such studies do provide data on which to base decisions about program development.

EFFECTS OF SELF-CARE

Few researchers have studied the long-term effects of self-care on children's self-esteem, social adjustment, and school performance. Even fewer researchers have studied the impact on these variables of participation in supervised after-school activities. Moreover, although many studies have focused on how mothers' employment outside the home affects their children's development, most of these studies have failed to consider the direct or indirect impact of child-care provisions on children's development. And no longitudinal study of school-age children has been conducted to compare the effects of self-care with those of various kinds of adult supervision during nonschool hours. In other words, researchers have paid little attention to the possibility that before- and after-school programs may be preventive services.

Studies of latchkey children during the past 15 years have concentrated on measuring the effects of self-care on children's academic and social activities, on their fears, and on rates of accidents and child abuse. In 1970 Merilyn Woods studied 108 black fifth-graders from low-income families in Philadelphia whose mothers worked outside the home. She found that the children who were left to care for themselves during nonschool hours had more academic and social problems than their peers who received adult supervision.[7] But she also found that the full-time employ-

ment of mothers exerted a positive influence on their children's academic and social performance and that a mother's relationship with her child and attitude toward her job are important factors in a child's adjustment.

Dolores Gold and David Andres studied the sex-role concepts, personality adjustment, and academic achievement of 223 10-year-olds from working-class or middle-class families, some of whose mothers were employed full time and some of whose mothers did not work outside the home.[8] They found that these children's academic achievement was related to the employment status of their

---

RESOURCE PANEL

The individuals listed below provided the ideas and information from which this column was developed. For further information, readers may contact panel members directly.

James Garbarino
Associate Professor of Human Development
Pennsylvania State University
S-110 Henderson Human Development Building
University Park, PA 16802

Ellen Gray
Director of Research
National Committee for Prevention of Child Abuse
332 S. Michigan Ave., Suite 1250
Chicago, IL 60604-4357

Louise F. Guerney
Associate Professor of Human Development
Department of Individual and Family Studies
Pennsylvania State University
Catharine Beecher House
University Park, PA 16802

Thomas J. Long and Lynette Long
National Institute for Latchkey Children and Youth
P.O. Box 682
Glen Echo, MD 20812

Hyman Rodman, Director
Family Research Center
University of North Carolina
Greensboro, NC 27412

Michelle Seligson, Director
School-Age Child Care Project
Wellesley College
Center for Research on Women
Wellesley, MA 02181

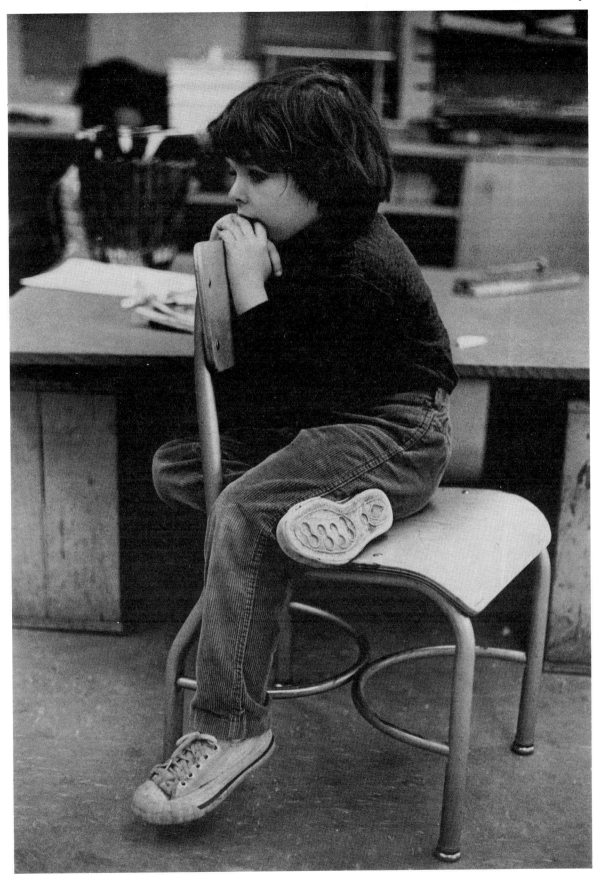

With the ever-increasing number of two income families, latchkey children have become a fact of life. Each community must develop responses to the problem that are tailored to local needs.

mothers, their own gender, the socio-economic status of their families, and the behavior of their parents toward them. When Gold and Andres divided the sons of employed mothers into two groups — those who received adult supervision and those who took care of themselves during nonschool hours — they found those boys who took care of themselves consistently lower than the others on all measures of social adjustment and academic achievement. However, the differences between the two groups were not statistically significant.

A recent study by Alan Ginsburg, Ann Milne, David Myers, and Fran Ellman also found lower academic achievement among children from one-parent or two-parent families in which the adults were employed full time.[9]

Meanwhile, several researchers have found that children who routinely care for themselves seem to be more fearful than those who receive adult supervision. In a sample of 2,258 children who ranged in age from 7 to 11 (part of the National Survey of Children conducted by researchers at Temple University in 1976), 32% of the boys and 41% of the girls said that they worried when they had to stay home without an adult. Fifteen percent of these youngsters said they worried "a lot," and 13% reported that they were frequently scared.[10] Their fears tended to focus on the possibility of intruders. Indeed, 30% of the girls and 20% of the boys said that they were afraid to go outside to play.

A 1981 study by Thomas Long and Lynette Long produced similar findings.[11] The Longs interviewed 53 latchkey children and 32 children who received adult supervision. Forty percent of the children who cared for themselves said that they were not allowed to go outside or to invite friends into their homes while their parents were away. The youngsters who cared for themselves expressed more fear than those who received adult supervision, but they were also better informed on procedures for dealing with their own physical well-being.

More recent research by the Longs found that children who cared for themselves experienced more fear, loneliness, and boredom than did children who were regularly supervised by adults.[12] Moreover, the frequency of fear reported by children who were left all alone was three times greater than the frequency of fear reported by children who were left with other siblings and 20 times greater than the frequency of fear reported by children who were left with adult caretakers.

The primary fear of these children was that someone would break into their homes while they were alone and hurt them, according to the Longs. A significant number of children left in the care of older siblings also feared being harmed by their sibling caretakers.

The research on self-care and fear suggests that fear levels differ markedly, depending on the location of a child's home. Urban settings produce the most fear; rural settings, the least. The Longs, who studied children in the most threatening environments (urban apartments), found high levels of fear among youngsters who cared for themselves. But Nancy Galambos and James Garbarino, using teacher ratings of supervised and unsupervised fifth- and seventh-graders in a rural setting, found no significant differences between the groups in academic achievement, classroom orientation, fear level, or school adjustment.[13]

Hyman Rodman, director of the Family Research Center at the University of North Carolina, Greensboro, compared the levels of fear and distress reported by matched groups of 48 children who cared for themselves and 48 children who received adult supervision.[14] He found no significant differences between the two groups. But he offers three suggestions to researchers who wish to continue this line of investigation:

• control the variables of parent attitude and the parent/child relationship;

• examine the interaction between these variables and the child-care arrangement; and

• determine whether the parents voluntarily or involuntarily opted for self-care and what part the child or children played in this decision.

Despite scant research, many people agree with David Elkind, author of *The Hurried Child*, who has argued that latchkey children are expected to assume too much responsibility too early in life. Elkind suggests that these youngsters may experience a higher incidence of depression and a greater number of personality problems during adolescence and in later years.

Other researchers contend that we simply don't know enough about children who look after themselves and that we ought not to generalize from the few small-sample studies that have been conducted. Implicit in this position is the view that, for many children, self-care experiences have not been all bad — and, indeed, that such experiences have often fostered such positive outcomes as increased self-confidence and greater independence.

PROGRAMS, PROJECTS, AND PRACTICAL ADVICE

Day-care programs and home-based support services both respond to the needs of latchkey children. The School-Age Child Care (SACC) Project at Wellesley College, directed by Michelle Seligson, is a leading promoter of day care. The SACC Project has been conducting research since 1979 on the types of child-care services for school-age children that are available nationally. Project staff members also provide information and technical assistance on the design and implementation of day-care programs that young schoolchildren can attend before school, after school, and during intervals when school is not in session but when parents must work.

Public school participation in the provision of before- and after-school programs for young schoolchildren is increasing, according to Seligson. In 1980 the SACC Project identified approximately 170 day-care programs for school-age children; more than half of these programs involved public schools or were sponsored by them.

Seligson adds that, although her staff has no accurate data on the number of schools involved in child-care programs, the number of inquiries from schools that are arriving at the SACC Project offices and the rate of participation of school staff members in special workshops conducted by the SACC Project staff suggest that the number is constantly growing. School involvement sometimes entails only the provision of space and other resources to private groups and agencies in the nonprofit sector that administer the school-based child-care programs. In other instances, however, the schools administer the child-care programs themselves. Among the many other options for involvement in child care that schools can select are: busing children to after-school programs located elsewhere, offering seminars for parents on self-care practices, and surveying parents in the school district regarding their child-care needs.

Home-based support services for parents who work are also increasing. Some parents ask a neighbor to check on their children after school, or they tell their children to check in with the neighbor, either in person or by telephone.

The telephone serves as a lifeline for many children who care for themselves during nonschool hours. One innovative program that makes use of this lifeline is Project PhoneFriend, a hot line established by a local branch of the American Association of University Women in State College, Pennsylvania. Through Project PhoneFriend, from 2:30 p.m. to 5:30 p.m. each weekday, adult volunteers dispense warm, parental advice to children who are lonely, frightened, or just plain bored. This free service is aimed at the more than 4,500 elementary students who attend schools near Penn State University.

Some communities provide support to latchkey children in the form of training in coping skills that will improve their safety and well-being. Last March, for example, Parents Anonymous of Connecticut, a nonprofit organization that helps to educate the public about child abuse and neglect, presented four 90-minute sessions on child care for employees of the Phoenix Mutual Life Insurance Company and their latchkey children. In Houston, the public school system and the Houston Committee for Private Sector Initiatives, a business group, have teamed up to sponsor a program on coping skills for 30 latchkey children at one school. Meanwhile, many companies have hired educators and social workers to conduct free seminars for employees on how to handle child-care problems.

Several service organizations have also stepped forward to help latchkey children, including Camp Fire (with "I Can Do It," a program to teach self-reliance), the Boy Scouts (with "Prepared for Today"), and the National Committee for the Prevention of Child Abuse (with "I'm in Charge," a self-care course for parents and children). "I'm in Charge" is probably the most fully developed of these efforts. This program emphasizes experiences that build such concrete survival skills as dealing with emergencies, strangers, and boredom. "I'm in Charge" also opens lines of communication between children and parents that result in the negotiation of contracts spelling out the rules, responsibilities, rewards, and schedules of self-care arrangements.

Many educators stress the need for such programs to focus on the developmental needs of school-age children. The programs, they say, should give children opportunities to gain self-respect, to mature as fully as possible, to become integral parts of the community, to choose their friends and activities, and to pursue their individual interests.

Meanwhile, educators can help latchkey children in several ways. First, they should concentrate on structuring homework carefully, since many children no longer have adults around to help them complete assignments correctly. School systems could also consider starting telephone hot lines for homework, staffed by teachers or by parent volunteers.

Second, educators should allow time

during the school day for children to discuss personal concerns. Latchkey children, in particular, need time each day to talk with adults.

Third, school officials should establish better procedures for contacting working parents in an emergency. They could also help those parents work out better strategies for responding to such situations as a child becoming ill at school.

Fourth, educators should develop extended day-care programs for children, and educational researchers should study the effects of such programs on participants. Available data on the short-term effects of before- and after-school child-care programs suggest that children do better with continuous adult supervision in school-based programs than they do when left on their own. But we need more information about the impact on children of spending long hours in school buildings.

N O ONE DOUBTS that there are risks for latchkey children — particularly young children left to care for themselves in urban areas. According to Garbarino, these risks include bad feelings (rejection, fear, loneliness), negative behaviors (victimizing younger siblings, engaging in destructive behavior in and outside the home), developmental problems (poor school adjustment, negative feelings about self and parents), and mistreatment (accidents, sexual abuse). All of these risks are real threats for many youngsters.

An informed national attitude toward latchkey children must go beyond decrying these risks — a reaction that serves only to increase the guilt and worry that many working parents already feel. Each community must instead develop responses to the problem that are tailored to local needs. Schools should, and inevitably will, have an important voice in the development of programs to respond to this problem.

1. Michelle Seligson, Andrea Genser, Ellen Gannett, and Wendy Gray, *School-Age Child Care: A Policy Report* (Wellesley, Mass.: School-Age Child Care

Project, Wellesley College Center for Research on Women, December 1983), p. 7.
2. Ibid.
3. Ibid., p. 9.
4. Arthur C. Emlen, *When Parents Are at Work: A Three-Company Survey of How Employed Parents Arrange Child Care* (Washington, D.C.: Greater Washington Research Center, 1982).
5. Thomas J. Long and Lynette Long, *Latchkey Children* (Urbana, Ill.: ERIC Clearinghouse on Elementary and Early Childhood Education, ED 226 836, 1983).
6. Ibid.
7. Merilyn B. Woods, "The Unsupervised Child of the Working Mother," *Developmental Psychology*, vol. 6, 1972, pp. 14-25.
8. Dolores Gold and David Andres, "Developmental Comparisons Between Ten-Year-Old Children with Employed and Nonemployed Mothers," *Child Development*, vol. 49, 1978, pp. 75-84.
9. Alan Ginsburg, Ann M. Milne, David Myers, and Fran M. Ellman, "Single Parents, Working Mothers, and the Educational Achievement of Elementary School Age Children," paper presented at the annual meeting of the American Educational Research Association, New York City, March 1982 (rev. June 1983).
10. Nicholas Zill, Gunnar Gruvaeus, and Karen Woyshner, *Kids, Parents, and Interviewers: Three Points of View on a National Sample of Children* (New York: Foundation for Child Development, 1977), as cited in Seligson et al., p. 17.
11. Thomas J. Long and Lynette Long, *Latchkey Children: The Child's View of Self Care* (Urbana, Ill.: ERIC Clearinghouse on Elementary and Early Childhood Education, ED 211 229, 1982).
12. Thomas J. Long and Lynette Long, *The Handbook for Latchkey Children and Their Parents* (New York: Berkley Books, 1984).
13. Nancy L. Galambos and James Garbarino, "Identifying the Missing Links in the Study of Latchkey Children," *Children Today*, July/August 1983, pp. 2-4, 40.
14. Hyman Rodman, David J. Pratto, and Rosemary Smith Nelson, "Child Care Arrangements and Children's Functioning: A Comparison of Self-Care and Adult-Care Children," *Developmental Psychology*, in press.

This issue of PAR identifies a problem to be solved: how best to deal with latchkey children. Empirical research provides few guidelines; thus we have relied on opinionnaire data. We have also tried to identify projects and practices that meet the needs of latchkey children.

Identifying exemplary practices is a new direction for the Phi Delta Kappa Center on Evaluation, Development, and Research. We look forward in coming years to making descriptions of exemplary practices an important part of the Center's mission.

Development and Educational Opportunities

- Development: Patterns and Variations (Articles 11-14)
- Choosing Quality Programs for Young Children (Article 15)
- Infant and Toddler Programs (Articles 16-18)
- Day-Care Programs (Articles 19-20)
- Readiness: Issues and Programs (Articles 21-22)
- Kindergarten (Articles 23-25)

The scientific study of child development began in the 1920s. Due to the complexity of the human being, no one discipline or approach identifies children or childhood as its exclusive domain of study. Efforts to chart the course of child development have attracted teams of investigators representing medicine, nutrition, genetics, psychology, sociology, and anthropology, as well as family life and education.

Basic organizing concepts in the study of child development include nature and nurture relationships, orderly development, ages and stages, and individual variation.

A contemporary version of the nature-nurture controversy identifies that heredity (maturation, temperament, and nature) and environment (nurture, including learning) interact resulting in the organization of growth, behavior, and adaptation over time.

When observing young children, one can see that a second concept—development—follows a sequential order. Although the age for walking varies by several months, every child goes through a number of predictable steps such as rolling over, moving on hands and knees, and pulling up to a standing position before finally walking.

The ages and stages concept recognizes unique periods of development when certain abilities are most observable. Stages refer to predictable, sequential, developmental periods that are qualitatively different from each other. They serve to describe what can be reasonably expected of children and what is beyond their abilities during a time period. Educators need to be keen observers of young children to determine at what stages they are operating.

The concept of individual variation indicates there are general developmental patterns and stages, but the time for their emergence varies widely for individuals. There is ample evidence that children follow the genetic principles of orderly development through stages, but variation within a wide spectrum of individual differences is the norm (e.g., children's loss of baby teeth and understanding of concepts vary widely among children of the same ages).

Researchers and educators agree on the importance of caregivers and teachers having a strong background in child development. Being knowledgeable about the developmental abilities of young children allows teachers to observe stages and plan quality learning opportunities appropriate for them.

As more and more children attend preschool programs, the issue of readiness will receive more attention. Educators are under increasing pressure from parents and the public to have children achieve earlier and faster. Some of the articles in this section address the issue of developmental abilities and educational responsibilities. The critical issue of appropriate programs for children from birth through six years of age is explored.

Looking Ahead: Challenge Questions

What advice do child developmental experts offer parents and teachers?

When a child asks a difficult question, what is the best way to respond?

What are some of the special considerations necessary when caring for and teaching infants and toddlers?

How has child care changed to keep pace with the changing American family? What do parents, employers, and caregivers need to do to meet future challenges?

When looking for child care, what are some of the important points parents should consider?

Why is kindergarten so different from first grade? Do five-year-olds really learn by playing?

How and what do young children discover by themselves? In what ways does the environment foster this development?

What can public school officials do to help families with preschool age children?

How much preparation should children receive in preschool prior to entering kindergarten and first grade?

Are children cared for at home by a relative different from those children cared for outside the home environment? If so, do the differences affect later academic performance?

Unit 3

YOUR CHILD—FROM BIRTH TO 12

LOUISE BATES AMES, with ELLEN SWITZER

Dr. Louise Bates Ames, author of many books of child development and a former contributing editor of Family Circle, is the Associate Director of the Gesell Institute of Human Behavior. The Institute, founded by Dr. Arnold Gesell in 1911, is a leading center for the study of child development.

There is not now, never was and never will be another child exactly like yours. Parents know this and take pride in their children's special qualities. But they also want to compare their children with others of the same age to make sure that their youngsters are developing normally, or even better than normally.

Statisticians have supplied enough data on children's physical growth patterns to enable physicians to reassure parents about their youngsters' height and weight. But *intellectual* and *emotional* growth has been harder to measure and evaluate. Now, however, this development *can* be examined scientifically, thanks to research conducted over many decades by the late pediatrician and psychologist Dr. Arnold Gesell and his associates at the Gesell Institute of Human Behavior in New Haven, Conn. This research, constantly being refined and updated, shows that, in a normal child, behavior patterns are predictable in the same way that physical growth is. Knowing about behavior patterns and stages can be of tremendous help to parents, for then Mom and Dad can measure their youngster's progress guided by a set of objective and scientific standards.

Everyone at the Gesell Institute emphasizes, however, that *normal children vary considerably in their emotional and intellectual development.* One child may walk at 11 months but not talk until age two. Another child may know a lot of words at 16 months but refuse to get off his diapered bottom until several months later. Knowing that much of what a baby does and does not do is dictated by inborn qualities can be very helpful to worried parents who have been told for too long that *everything* that happens with their children is their responsibility.

But even when taking into consideration all of the genetic and environmental factors that go into a child's development, it is still possible to give a general outline of what a youngster may or may not be expected to do at a given age.

In the following report, we tell you what you can expect your child to do from birth until age 12 and how you can provide the best care for him or her emotionally and physically.

WHAT TO EXPECT FROM BIRTH TO 24 MONTHS

BIRTH TO THREE MONTHS

How children develop: From birth on, most infants assume what might be called a fencing position when lying on their backs: one arm flexed, the other extended toward the side they face. When lying on their stomachs, they can lift their heads slightly. A short time after birth, they may close their fingers on objects placed inside their palm (like Mom's pinkie).

At the age of three months they begin to coo and smile, to look at people, to stop crying—unless bothered by colic or diaper rash—when soothed.

What parents can do: This is definitely not the time to worry about the baby's mind or disposition. At this early age it's impossible to "teach" young infants much of anything, and you can't spoil a baby by picking him up if he cries.

It's important, however, to consider the baby's eating and sleeping habits in relation to your own routine and lifestyle. If the infant won't sleep through the night, Mom should try to get extra rest during the day, especially if her nights are interrupted by breast-feeding. But whether the baby is breast- or bottle-fed, hold and cuddle him a lot. In this way babies develop trust in the world.

THREE TO SIX MONTHS

How children develop: Big changes occur. Lying on her back, the baby probably looks at and grasps objects above her head. Lying on her stomach, she may adopt a swimming position. One day, she rolls over, and at six months she may even sit unaided. She follows objects with her eyes, smiles at people (including strangers) and begins to show different emotions: joy, contentment, fear, anger.

What parents can do: Help the baby's developing interest in the outside world: Hang a mobile over the crib or move the crib or playpen around to give the baby different things to look at. And when the baby acquires a new skill, show that you enjoy the accomplishment, but don't worry about "teaching" anything. The six-month-old, still too young to remember events from one minute to the next, is unable to learn in the accepted sense.

This may also be a good time to start leaving the baby with a reliable sitter. A baby who has never seen anyone but family may object vehemently when left with a stranger, unless this has become a natural part of life.

SIX TO NINE MONTHS

How children develop: During this period many babies learn new skills almost daily. One day they roll over; a few weeks later they pull themselves up to a standing position in the playpen. At the end of this period, many sit steadily without support.

Next, babies usually start crawling. On toward nine months, they may even get up on their hands and knees. They can usually hold their own bottle and feed themselves crackers or bananas—getting more food in the immediate vicinity than into their mouths. Nine-month-olds start saying "Mama" and "Dada," and most are on a reasonable schedule, even sleeping through the night.

What parents can do: Most parents really begin to enjoy playing with the babies now. You roll a ball toward the baby, he returns it. You hold a mirror up to the baby's face, she laughs at it. Babies at this age may be afraid of strangers for a brief time—even Mom if she is wearing dark glasses or looks "different." Don't worry. That's a natural part of development.

It's very important now to keep babies out of harm's way. They've developed minds of their own and therefore are more work than they were earlier. Don't place them in the middle of a large bed and expect them to stay there. And if a baby is allowed to crawl around, baby-proof the house: get rid of sharp objects, disconnect electric cords and cover sockets.

NINE TO 12 MONTHS
How children develop: Most babies in this age bracket can creep, pull themselves up to a standing position and sit down again, cruise around crib or playpen holding onto a rail, stand unsupported. At 12 months, they may be able to walk with one hand held. They can drive parents to distraction by such activities as repeatedly throwing toys out of playpens and then wailing until they are retrieved.

They have learned some skills that are helpful: they can feed themselves finger foods and drink from a cup. With a word or two besides "Mama" and "Dada," they may be able, in a general way, to let Mom know what they want and need. Unfortunately, teething begins now and babies are occasionally cranky and uncomfortable.

What parents can do: Spend as much time as possible playing with the baby; by now babies need companionship. Rock them, sing to them, mention their name in songs.

Babies notice their surroundings at this time, thoroughly enjoying carriage rides, for instance. They also begin to appreciate playthings, not necessarily "educational." Unbreakable cups and saucers, spoons, anything that rattles will do just fine. (A little later, the baby may enjoy round and square blocks that stack, water toys and large, soft animals.) By now, your home should be thoroughly baby-proof.

12 TO 18 MONTHS
How children develop: Children now assume the upright posture much of the time and by 14 months or so usually walk with ease. They can probably climb stairs, though getting down them is a skill they learn later.

Babies become really curious: they poke and pry. They also begin to play with real toys and to look at printed pictures with interest.

Many now combine words into short phrases, making their wants known, but some babies still prefer gestures. For example, they hold out their arms when they want to be picked up.

What parents can do: If you wish, begin to "teach" your child. Provide paper and crayons, blocks that fit together, untearable books, pull-and-push toys, stuffed animals. Do things

your child can imitate, such as scribbling with a crayon on paper. Point out objects to the child on carriage rides.

Babies 18 months old are aware of property rights, so don't feel rebuffed if they slap your hand away from something they've claimed. They are turning into individuals and letting you know it.

Safety reminder: Put protective gates on stairs.

18 TO 24 MONTHS
How children develop: Children can now walk, run, climb stairs (some awkwardly). They can kick a large ball, build a tower out of more than two blocks, take apart and reassemble toys with simple separate parts. They particularly love a toy or blanket and may insist on having it around for security. They combine two or three words and ask for food or toys. Unfortunately, they don't ask politely. They want what they want *now*. They refuse the blue bib if they have the yellow one in mind. This is the age for tantrums, thumb sucking and other activities that indicate displeasure with the world in general—and parents in particular.

What parents can do: If you expect tears, tantrums and other kinds of negative behavior, you won't worry that your lovable, cuddly baby is changing into a tyrant. By the time children are two years old, they have usually left this difficult stage behind.

Appreciate that children now want their own way—usually opposite from the one you would choose—and don't expect to control them with words alone. For example, if it's bedtime, pick babies up and put them to bed, protests notwithstanding.

Keeping children busy, and taking advantage of their love of motion, will probably cut down on tantrums. Expect frustration and don't think you are a bad parent or that you have an impossible child. Everything will look a lot brighter at age two.

WHAT TO EXPECT FROM TWO YEARS TO FIVE YEARS
TWO YEARS
How children develop: A growth spurt around this age brings happier times. Children walk and run securely, falling down much less frequently; improved language skills enable them to make their wants known; many even feed themselves with good control of the spoon, pull on a simple garment, and, much to parents' delight, perhaps become aware of toilet training. They suddenly are loving and friendly again.

Their interests expand somewhat. They like other children more, and many two-year-olds enjoy looking at pictures and naming various objects in books and magazines.

What parents can do: You have always been the most important people in your child's life, but now the child often *shows* how much he or she loves and needs you. While this can be very gratifying, it may bring some problems

too. At bedtime the children don't want to give up your company. They may object loudly to being left with a sitter.

Children are also ready for new experiences and activities: slides, climbing apparatuses, rocking boats and sandboxes will delight them, either at home or in the nearest park. Both boys and girls love dolls, doll clothes, doll furniture and toy dishes at this age. Give them opportunities to widen their horizons.

TWO-AND-A-HALF
How children develop: There are great strides in some directions. Children can line up two or three blocks for a pretend train. Drawing, they make vertical and horizontal strokes. They correctly insert differently shaped blocks into formboard holes.

Verbally children mature too, speaking some sentences. They feed themselves less messily than before, don most of their own clothes and are probably toilet trained.

But emotionally, two-and-a-half-year-olds can be a problem to themselves and their parents. Some return to all the old, difficult ways, with the tears, temper tantrums and generally negative attitudes they exhibited at 18 months.

What parents can do: It's possible to avoid some fights and tantrums if you're tolerant of two-and-a-half-year-olds' need for ritual. They want things done just so: You put the peas on one side of the plate, meat on the other. Go along with some of their whims and bossiness. By the time children turn three, they are a lot more flexible.

Youngsters now find it difficult to choose and, having chosen, suddenly want the opposite. If you have both cheese and frankfurters in the refrigerator for lunch, decide which to serve. If you ask, the answer is likely to be "cheese," only to have a demand for hot dogs the minute the cheese sandwich appears.

• Instead of giving direct orders, try "How about . . ." or "Let's . . ."
• Don't put your child in a position in which he must share toys or food. He won't be prepared to.
• Never, as "punishment," take away security blankets and other items that make the child feel comfortable.

THREE YEARS
How children develop: With any luck, you'll find this an easy, happy time, as the three-year-olds seem to turn into real persons with whom easy communication is possible. They talk to parents, nursery-school teachers and other children, share toys and other possessions. They dress themselves (even putting on shoes and socks) and feed themselves. Nearly all three-year-olds are completely toilet trained. Most can recite a few rhymes; some may be able to carry a tune, and they can draw their versions of a circle and a cross. They love to "help out" with such tasks as dusting and drying dishes. And if

there are shelves and toy boxes within easy reach, it's time for them to learn to pick up after themselves.

What parents can do: Your three-year-old can fool you—one minute almost adult, the next minute a baby again.

Encourage creative activities involving clay, crayons and wooden jigsaw puzzles. Other especially good toys for this age would include tricycles, toy cars, soap-bubble pipes and games like Lotto. Also encourage any interest in letters and numbers—but don't push! If you insist on "teaching" such skills, they become a chore.

If Susie wants to help set the table or rake leaves, let her. If Johnny wants to help wash the car or mix cookie dough, let him. If they get into a pattern of being helpful at age three, when tasks are games to be enjoyed, they may continue the pattern later on when they can really be of great assistance.

Don't worry about baby talk, but don't use it yourself or allow others to do so. Children learn by imitating, and it's important that they hear language spoken correctly.

Supervise television watching. Don't let the TV set become a constant baby-sitter for you.

THREE-AND-A-HALF

How children develop: These children become more responsible with every passing day. They may even wash their hands before eating—without a fuss. As their intellectual curiosity increases, they ask lots of "how" questions. Girls seem to be slightly better coordinated than boys. For instance, many girls can hop on one foot, many boys can't.

While both boys and girls at this age play cooperatively with friends, they may take all parental reprimands to heart and may be extremely stubborn or uncooperative at times. It's often difficult to decide whether to scold the child or ignore what might be considered undesirable behavior.

What parents can do: Children of this age, when playing, learn how to behave, cope and relate to others. So encourage active, imaginative play whenever possible. Parents' participation isn't always a good idea, since children need to learn independence in play as well as in other areas.

Don't worry if your child has imaginary playmates now. Experts find that such playmates may be a sign of superior intelligence rather than loneliness or some emotional problem. Don't worry, either, about stuttering or stumbling over words, or about hands that seem less steady than earlier. These are normal parts of growth at this age.

It's an excellent time to enroll your child in a good nursery school if one is available. You might also consider the Sunday School classes that some churches have for three-year-olds. Most children begin to enjoy the company of other boys and girls at this age.

FOUR YEARS

How children develop: Four-year-olds can print one or more recognizable letters or numbers, tell you how many apples are in that picture book and recognize a few letters. They wash their hands and faces at the sink and are relatively competent to bathe themselves. Thank you, but *they* can button their coats and tie their shoelaces without your help.

Most speak clearly in sentences, and in this TV-viewing era, you'll probably be amazed at their vocabulary. They may also use swear words they've heard, without realizing what they mean. They are also developing a set of values: they are beginning to learn that running off with Mike's toy is wrong.

What parents can do: Don't worry about exaggerations, boasting or an imaginary playmate who emptied the cookie jar. The child is not being deliberately untruthful. However, parents should discourage the child from blaming someone else (including an imaginary being) for disobedience or other untoward behavior.

If you take children's swearing with a certain calm, explaining that some people don't like to hear those kinds of words, they will probably stop being profane in due course. But if you overreact, the youngster may decide that this is a great way to annoy you.

You can expect some silly talk, giggling and play on words. Take advantage of this by being a little silly yourself and by starting to read humorous books to your youngster. (Ask the local librarian for advice.)

Children at this age are becoming much more mobile and independent. Stress street safety; children are too young to cross a street on their own. They can go alone on a short errand to a neighbor's house on a safe street, but any attempt to go visiting alone, outside of hailing distance, should be firmly discouraged. It's too easy for a four-year-old to forget even the most careful instructions about never crossing a street or talking to a stranger.

WHAT TO EXPECT FROM FIVE YEARS TO 12 YEARS

FIVE YEARS

How children develop: To many parents looking back on a youngster's early years, five may seem like a golden age at which, for a short time, the tides of physical, intellectual and emotional development seemed to flow smoothly.

Mom is the center of the world for the five-year-old. Susie wants to be just like her. Johnny wants to marry her. Both like being with her, helping her, watching her, playing alongside her. What five-year-olds seem to fear most is that Mom might leave or not be there when they need her.

By now, children are usually great talkers. They are also beginning to appreciate the difference between fact and fiction. Although the world seems full of sunshine, especially during the

day, it has its shadows and terrors too. Thunder or sirens may awaken dread; darkness and solitude may cause fear. Nightmares often disturb sleep.

What parents can do: The five-year-old's universe has a clear center—the parents. It's important, then, for parents to show their love and their enthusiasm about what children *can* do rather than their worry about what they *can't* do. Mom and Dad must be careful, too, not to be fooled by their youngster's seeming competence. A child, for instance, may love to hold and otherwise take care of a younger brother or sister, but this should be permitted only when there is competent adult supervision.

If more than one child is in the home, each youngster probably needs some special attention, some time that's all her or his own with Mom and Dad. A chat with Mom after supper, a walk to the drugstore for ice cream with Dad, can be an important event in a five-year-old's life.

Most U.S. children are in kindergarten by this time. Academic interests should be supported by parents, but not pushed.

SIX YEARS

How children develop: "What's gotten into him?" "She's a changed child." Puzzled parents often ask such questions about the six-year-old offspring, at war with everybody—and especially parents. Instead of wanting to please, thee children seem intent upon getting their parents as angry and puzzled as possible. Worst of all, they don't seem able to make up their minds about anything: Today's best friend is tomorrow's worst enemy.

There are tantrums and fights with almost everyone, about—it seems to parents—everything or nothing. Besides being aggressive and combative, the six-year-old may at times also be fearful, shy and insecure. It's a confusing and difficult time for children—and therefore for parents as well.

By now the child is in school. In a way, this makes the situation more complicated because all the youngster's natural inclinations are for *physical* activity. Boys especially find it very hard to sit for any length of time. And that's exactly what school expects of them.

Six-year-olds tend to become very interested in sex, asking all kinds of questions. They may decide to "play doctor" with younger brothers, sisters or friends. Many take advantage of learning to read, and for hours entertain themselves with books. They love records and games like Chinese checkers, and they have a stronger sense of right and wrong than ever before, although they find it difficult to do what they agree is right.

What parents can do: Again say, "How about..." and "Let's..." instead of issuing orders. If head-on collisions can be avoided by reasonable compromises, use them. For example, give children several chances to do something right ("Guess you're going to need three chances to get that school bag packed").

This is a time when many people expect a great deal from children and when children have an especially hard time meeting expectations. Don't worry too much about academic accomplishments, when the child has to go through all kinds of physical and emotional changes.

Realize, too, that your child now faces all kinds of new temptations. If you suspect that your youngster might be taking things, lock them up. If there are fights with younger siblings, keep the children out of each other's way whenever possible. Avoid taxing, competitive games and letting the child become overtired. Above all, don't let the child get a rise out of you. If he says, "I hate you," say something like, "I'm sorry about that, but I *love* you."

SEVEN YEARS

How children develop: Sometime around the latter half of age six, children generally quiet down a lot. Some even seem melancholy or downright unhappy. They may decide that others—friends, neighbors, teachers, parents—don't like them and are picking on them. This is normal seven-year-old behavior.

At this age, children begin to worry about whether their peers like them. They tend to idolize their teachers, scoutmasters and other adults—but not their parents.

Boys and girls in this age bracket are acquiring more and more academic skills. Although they seem to take learning in stride, they need lots of praise. Most show new evidence of critical capacity, thinking things over and considering various possibilities.

Other notable traits?
- The youngster's attention span is growing.
- They like to organize their days and get upset if plans don't work out.
- They are developing a sense of humor and an active imagination—and by now know what's real and what's imagined.
- They enjoy reading by themselves.

What parents can do: Recognize and respect a child's minor moods at this time but don't be thrown by them. Sympathize when they say the teacher is picking on them but take such complaints with a grain of salt.

Take advantage of the new thoughtfulness and maturity; read with and to children, and discuss things they have read or have seen on television. Remember it's hard for them to stop what they are doing: reading, watching television, and so on. Allow them to finish the chapter or stay up to the end of the program. If an interest in a musical instrument is shown, make lessons available. But, again, don't push!

In situations involving right and wrong, appeal to their consciences. They are developing a sense of values, and this sense, like their muscles and brains, must be used in order to grow.

EIGHT YEARS

How children develop: Eight-year-olds typically cover a lot of ground, both intellectually and physically. But they can be quite self-critical and are often unhappy with what they have accomplished. They criticize others as well as themselves. (This is when children tell their parents they don't practice what they preach.) Many eight-year-olds become very attached to their mothers again. This doesn't mean they're reverting to babyhood. It simply means that they need at least one close relationship they can rely on.

Children of this age like variety and dislike being alone or playing by themselves. Physically, they can learn to do almost anything they want: ride a two-wheel bicycle, roller skate, ski, swim, play tennis or baseball. They enjoy organized sports but should not be pushed into intense competition. Generally they are naturally competitive.

What parents can do: Since a child now wants all of the parents' (especially the mother's) attention, spend some time concentrating fully on the child, then going about other duties.

Children want praise at this age, but have learned the difference between sincere and insincere words. Suddenly they develop a sense of what's false and what's natural in a relationship.

Since the company of other children is so important, plan after-school activities. Children of this age can go short distances in safe neighborhoods on their own. They're old enough to take some responsibility for themselves, but be sure to discuss pedestrian (and bike) safety with them.

NINE YEARS

How children develop: Suddenly, Mom seems to recede into the background while teachers and peers take on a new importance. However, self-motivation is the cardinal characteristic of this age and the key to understanding the youngsters and their progress toward maturity. They have a growing capacity to put their minds to a task on their own initiative, which gives them a preoccupied, businesslike air. Hating interruptions, they can work for hours at a stretch.

Their sense of what is and is not fair is very important at age nine. "That's not fair" becomes the favorite complaint about almost anything.

Boys generally become exceedingly disdainful of girls. Girls, for the most part, don't feel quite the same way, and the little girl next door with whom Johnny has played for years may feel rejected when he suddenly decides that she's not worth bothering with.

What parents can do: Appreciate the fact that your child needs to become freer of Mom. Nine-year-olds need to

assert themselves, and can do so more easily by relating to people not as close as yourself.

Avoid too many petty instructions, or you may have a rebellion on your hands. Try not to interrupt children when they are preoccupied, and give them plenty of warning before stopping whatever they are doing. And show, in every way, that you are willing to help with projects and to discuss problems—but don't intrude. Respect your child's developing sense of privacy.

10 TO 12 YEARS

How children develop: Ten can be a golden year. Typical 10-year-olds admire their mothers, worship their fathers, want to participate in family activities, strive to be cooperative. Often they love school and regard their teachers as heroes.

Then around age 11 comes a change so drastic that parents think their child has turned into a premature terrible teen. Eleven-year-olds turn into exceedingly demanding critics, with Mom especially coming in for negative comment. If she has a job, her child tells her she ought to be at home. If she's at home, the youngster compares her to a friend's mother who has a glamorous job. Even teachers are given a hard time, with complaints about unfairness and too much homework.

Then at age 12, there is often another turnabout. Many children seem well adjusted, outgoing, cooperative and, wonder of wonders, very accepting of adult foibles, including those of their moms and dads. All in all, they tend to have a very positive attitude toward themselves, their parents and life in general. Enjoy it. The teens are next.

What parents can do: During these years children undergo drastic changes in emotions and behavior. But this is a time to enjoy what's good and coast with what's difficult.

Generally, allow children to make more decisions on their own. Let them, pick out their own clothes (within reason, of course), decide what elective courses they want to take at school and so on. This is the time for practicing decision-making. But a child still needs order, discipline and some rules. Too much freedom may just confuse.

Consult with other parents about neighborhood customs in such areas as dress, bedtime, TV watching, movies and such. Children during this period are wont to protest that *their* parents are the only tyrants in town.

Don't worry if your child admires a rock star or a sports figure whom you consider less than admirable. Hero worship is fickle at this age. That awful record you've heard all day for a month may be forgotten the next week.

And understand that your child needs to grow away from you gradually to become an independent adult. If you can accept this fact, the preteen years won't seem nearly as trying. For at every age a child can be difficult and delightful, challenging and lovable.

What Do Young Children Teach Themselves?

Nancy Balaban

Faculty, Graduate Programs, Bank Street College of Education, New York

What is it that young children teach themselves, and how do they do it? Current knowledge points to a strong relationship between how infants learn and how later, as children in school, they come to read, write and do mathematics.

A selective review of some findings about infant development, in conjunction with some research into reading and arithmetic learning, points to a profound link between babies as explorers and young school children as learners.

Intrinsic Motivation and Learning

It is easy to forget that only 48 to 60 months earlier preschool children were neonates, barely hatched. Within this dramatically short period of time, children have used and coordinated their physical, intellectual and sensory equipment with remarkable results. They have, in fact, played a major role in teaching themselves, among a host of achievements, to talk, to walk, to differentiate the strange from the familiar and to distinguish cause from effect.

The work of Piaget and other more recent research show that intrinsic motivation in young infants and children is a powerful force. Hours-old babies have been shown to have a preference for bold patterns (Fantz, 1965, p. 624). Babies seem to choose these patterns because the interesting sight is reward in and of itself. Piaget's well-known records of his own infant children (Piaget, 1963, obs.* 102, p. 166; obs. 103, p. 167) reveal that the baby's movements, which cause a rattle to shake overhead, change from random to intentional as the baby actively seeks environmental stimulation for its own sake. A mountain of studies now

*observation

make it evident that the effort "to make interesting spectacles last" (Piaget, obs. 111, p. 198) comes from within the infant and no other reward is required but that of internal satisfaction.

The old notion of the child as an empty vessel that requires filling has not stood the test of time. The vessel has long since cracked and been discarded. From these shards and ashes a new phoenix has arisen—competent infants who, from the moment of birth, display a range of sensory capabilities. Their talents include following a moving object (Greenman, 1973, p. 323), staring into mother's eyes (Klaus & Kennell, 1976, p. 70), reacting to sound and light (Brazelton, 1969, p. 27-28). Through continual interaction with things and people in the environment—pushing here, poking there; pulling here, smelling there; grasping here, mouthing there—infants begin to unravel the chaos that is their world, mainly because it's there and because they want to know it (Wolff, 1973, pp. 484-93). "The neonate," wrote William Kessen quoting André-Thomas, "is no neophyte" (Kessen, 1968, p. 52).

Perception and Learning

If we follow these self-activated infant learners into early childhood, we will get a glimpse of some of the other things they have taught themselves.

☐ *Learning Math.* Consider arithmetic. What have babies and children taught themselves about arithmetic? Incredibly, they have learned about quantity. They lie in cribs with a particular number of bars. Their parents go in and out of the room many times. And, it is hoped, they have more than one toy (Ginsburg, 1977, pp. 30-1). Quantity is everywhere. In fact, the concern for quantity is reflected in one of the first words that children utter—"more." "More milk," "more cookie," "more kitty." Number, repetition, equivalence, differences in magnitude, all are deeply rooted in the naturally occurring experiences babies and children have with their world.

Herbert Ginsburg (1977) writes that most young children understand the concepts *more* or *less*, percep-

From *Childhood Education*, April/May 1980, pp. 296-303. Reprinted by permission of Nancy Balaban and the Association for Childhood Education International, 3615 Wisconsin Avenue, N.W., Washington, D.C. Copyright ©1980 by the Association.

tually, even though they may be unable to count. Between the ages of 2 and 6, he states, children's math knowledge is intuitive and based on appearances (Ginsburg, pp. 41-42). It is self-directed, self-regulated and passionate. A child sorting and counting pebbles, flip cards, bottle tops or a Hallowe'en "take" illustrates that mathematics is not only magnetic for the young, but is everywhere—and the opportunity for practice is unlimited.

□ *Learning Reading.* What of learning in the area of language, reading and writing? By the time most children are 5, they have perceptual, cognitive and language capabilities that will serve their budding ability to read. According to Eleanor Gibson and Harry Levin (1975), it is also "perceptual learning" that lies at the base of learning to read.

What is meant by "perceptual learning"? Gibson and Levin describe it as a highly active process by which persons extract relevant information from the multitude of animate and inanimate objects that inhabit their world. By means of perception, a person "takes out" from the environment information about things as well as events (Gibson & Levin, p. 13). Meaning is rooted in such learning much before a child is even able to talk (Gibson & Levin, p. 20).

Here is a stunning personal example of perceptual learning. My son, at 9 months, began to sit on a stool at the kitchen counter to eat his meals. Since he no longer required the confines of the highchair, it was put in a storage room and forgotten. Some 12 to 14 months later when he was about 22 months old, he asked to my astonishment, "Where's my highchair?" Quite clearly, he had learned perceptually that his highchair had disappeared but was not able to frame the question until many months later when language was becoming more firm.

It is from this sort of learning that children acquire the ability to familiarize themselves with the distinctive features of things and people. From perception they know, for example, in what ways mom's face is different from Aunt Jane's face. They know which features of a chair invite sitting or climbing or define it as a chair at all, even though they cannot say the words.

□ *Apprehending Order in Relation of Things.* It is also by means of perception that children begin to make sense out of the chain of events that flow by them continually, to understand that things happen in a particular order and that a certain outcome may be predicted. For example, the door opens, a parent walks in with a bottle and gives it to the baby. When this happens many times, the baby experiences anticipation and satisfaction based in great measure on the functioning of perception. This is the baby's way of making some order out of the confusion and chaos "out there." "There is a long road," Gibson and Levin remind the reader, "from perception of the meaning of an ongoing event to perception of meaning in words printed on a page that one is reading, but the beginning is here" (p. 20).

□ *Drawing, Writing and Reading.* That poling, prodding baby who was learning math from the bars of the crib is also learning to read. Consider this observed example: a baby manipulates a foam rubber cube, rotates it in her hands, chews on it, squeezes it and temporarily transforms its shape, turns it many times as she explores these reversals and rotations with her eyes. Amazingly, this process is akin to the reversal of letters seen in many 5- and 6-year-olds, a reversal that is not so much an error as it is a continuing search on the child's part for perceptual meaning that began with the manipulation of three-dimensional objects. The child is *used* to looking at things from many views (Gibson & Levin, p. 240). Therefore, it is not surprising when she does it to letters.

Another aspect of language arts learning is writing. Research shows that children as young as 3 can not only differentiate between drawing, or pictures, and writing (Lavine, 1972, in Gibson & Levin, p. 237), but in their own drawings they make the "writing" smaller (Brittain, 1973, p. 13). This study by Brittain revealed that children who were making closed forms in drawing were also found to be making closed forms in writing (pp. 12-13). Furthermore, children who were making recognizable objects in drawing were also making recognizable letters. A profound connection exists between experience and ability in drawing and interest in and ability to write. Brittain contends that, contrary to popular belief it is not muscle control or coordination that is the prime factor in writing, but rather the ability to form concepts and to portray recognizable objects that appear to be most basic to this skill (p. 13). "The use of art materials," he writes, "is serious business. . . apparently satisfaction comes from the accomplishment and resulted from the process itself" (p. 11). He refers to the use of materials and to the creation of forms as "self-learning experiences" (p. 12)

Another study, described by Gibson & Levin (Ginsburg, Wheeler & Tulis, 1970, p. 233) and a follow-up (Wheeler, 1971, p. 233) extend this drawing-writing marriage and raise implications for direct classroom practice. In this situation, kindergarten children were given notebooks and told to do their writing in them. No formal instruction was given and no teacher intervened in any way with the children's entries in their notebooks. However, letter charts and a variety of attractive written materials were hung about the room, available to the children at their eye level. In analyzing the contents of the notebooks over several time periods, there seemed to be a progression noted. It went like this: scribbling occurred most frequently in the beginning of the year, giving way to designs, pictures, letters, words in isolation, word phrases and words in sentences.

While a wide variety was detected in the number of letters produced, all the children in this group, mixed in terms of IQ and family background, produced some letters. Errors were seen to spontaneously decrease as time went on. Children progressed naturally in writing, although they could apparently read little of what they wrote.

As a pre-reading activity, however, it provided opportunities for learning the visual characteristics of letters and the features that distinguish them. It was an activity that tapped the deep well of the children's own passion to be readers and writers. It is fascinating, in this connection, to be reminded of another study by Dolores Durkin (1969). The study found that one of the features common to all the children who read early—and continued to hold their lead in reading achievement as they progressed through the grades—was that their parents reported them to be "pencil-and-paper kids" for whom "Almost without exception the starting point of curiosity about written language was an interest in scribbling and drawing" (Durkin, 1969, p. 108). Clearly, a connection seems to exist between early and continued experience with drawing and scribbling and later reading and writing competence.

☐ *Understanding Language.* Deeply rooted within the complex network that lies beneath the skill of reading is the importance of language development. Talking is the handmaiden of reading. Regard again the 5- or 6-year-old as baby. In the context of a warm and loving relationship with a significant, nurturing adult, the infant is engaged, and engages in, face-to-face conversations. With a "speaking social partner" (Provence, 1970, p. 31), infants and children attend to the sounds of words, the rhythms and inflections of speech.

In *Reading and Loving* (1977), Leila Berg reveals her belief that the enjoyment of books and the acquisition of reading and writing are not primarily academic or technical skills, but grow from a warmly physical and emotional base of shared enjoyment with another human being (Berg, p. 11). Through this intimacy, the magical door to the symbolic world inhabited only by human beings swings open.

So this child, this pre-reading miracle, can at age 5 or 6—by virtue of development, of interaction with the environment—perceive the distinctive features of objects; apprehend order in the relations of things; exhibit a developed language; and be capable of such cognitive strategies as focusing attention, searching for a hidden object, problem-solving, remembering, selecting pertinent information from a variety of stimuli.

The lubricant for this whole, wonderful thinking machine called *child* is that powerful, electric, compelling passion *to find out for oneself.* "I do it myself" rings across the generations in an affirmation of Robert White's classic theory that human motivation springs from an innate desire to have an effect on one's environment and to cause something to happen (White, 1959, WITE-1A).

Implications for Practice

The implications for practice are here. Keep alive those vigorous capabilities in arithmetic, reading and language, that mammoth push toward thinking which children naturally bring to school with them. Encourage scribbles! Provide unlimited access to paper, pencils, crayons, magic markers, paints, chalk, all those things by means of which children can make their marks upon the world. Let children draw in damp sand, paint the outside fence with water, use sticks to make marks in the yielding earth. These are children's ways. Use and encourage them. Art is no frill. Art is a necessity.

Does this mean, then, that the teacher has nothing to do? It might seem that if a teacher just stands around, letting children scribble, they will learn to read and write. Of course, that is nonsense. Brittain's study (1973) showed that when the teacher was present and nearby as children drew, they spoke more, explained what they were drawing and engaged the teacher in direct conversation about their drawing. Clearly, teachers have not become obsolete.

Before examining ways of developing further those intrinsic abilities of children, attend to what the math and reading experts have to say about "readiness activities" and formal academic training for 5-year-olds. Ginsburg describes formal written math work and training as nonproductive for kindergarten children. He found, for example, that in working out an addition problem with 5-year-olds, in which one mark on the paper corresponded with one object in the collection, the children became unable to complete the task. It was too difficult for them to use the simplest and most elementary math recording device, the tally. It was easier for them to calculate on their fingers or even in their heads than to mark tallies on paper (Ginsburg, p. 58).

As for reading, Gibson and Levin state that there is no evidence that workbooks, basal readers or formal instruction in the kindergarten are the way to teach all children to read. On the contrary, there is no one way in which all children learn to read at all. Reading, according to their definition, is not a collection of skills taught to children. It is a process of extracting information from a text. Texts take many forms; they contain pictures and/or words or the most abstract symbols used in physics and mathematics. As such, reading requires a multitude of skills and many life experiences; it rests on a base of rich human interpersonal relationships. There is no one direct line to learning to read (Gibson & Levin, p. 5).

Clearly, young children's spontaneous math and reading capabilities need to be nurtured in school. Formal, adult-imposed methods tend to be rigid in their expectations, narrow in their definition and out of sync with children's native styles of learning. Formality and the adult concept of "product" hinder rather than foster this burgeoning self-directed learning.

Informal math activities are a comfortable, natural way for young children to learn—as they plow their way through the day, counting fingers, silverware, plates, pegs, people, and as they arrange and classify objects in their classroom environment. Children do not need to be made ready for elementary arithmetic. They are already interested by the time they arrive at school. It is up to the teacher to provide further opportunities and materials for the continued development of these abilities.

In classrooms that encourage natural, spontaneous, lively, intense curiosity in an environment of interesting and challenging materials, children will gain experiences needed for developing both linguistic and mathematical concepts. For example, by using dough, they may experience that which is *alike* (one dough ball is like another); in using sand, they can understand things that are *not alike* (wet sand is not like dry sand). The environment can yield other experiences: objects that are *patterned* (a brick wall is patterned, children's chants are patterned); events that follow a *sequence* (story comes after snack); *parts and wholes* (cutting apples, oranges and bananas for salad); things that have *direction* (a pulley lifts the pail up); objects that have *size, weight, textures.*

Informality can also predominate in the language arts. It has been found that awareness of the parts and sounds of words is a necessity in learning to read and that such awareness is difficult for 5- to 6-year-olds. It is not surprising to learn that rhyming is highly correlated with reading achievement (Gibson & Levin, p. 229). Playing rhyming games like "stinky-pinky," making up real and nonsense rhymes with children, playing games that demand attention to the beginning and ending sound of words (like "I packed my trunk and in it I put . . .") are all enjoyable activities that foster the kinds of skills that 5- and 6-year-olds need.

In addition, teachers must continue to read stories and more stories; poetry and more poetry; books for information, for fun; books for laughter, for tears; books for holidays, for birthdays; books for snow, for rain, for spring and fall; books for the endless list of things that children want to understand. Teachers must continue to talk with children and encourage them to talk with each other. Such teaching activity has been shown to be effective. A study by Dorothy Cohen (1971) revealed that the single variable that influenced children's reading ability in two otherwise similar public school classrooms was a daily story read aloud by the teacher.

Acknowledging the role of perception and of children's innate motivation to learn is a first step toward encouraging children to continue their teaching of themselves. Implicit in this is the need for a rich environment to support the flowering of young and natural curiosity.

In classrooms that have structure but not chaos, materials in great variety but not disorder, time sequences that are predictable but not stifling, and peers who are outgoing but not out of bounds, children thrive as self-motivated learners and grow prepared for the academic skills to come.

References

Berg, Leila. *Reading and Loving.* London, Henley & Boston: Routledge & Kegan Paul, 1977.

Brazelton, T. Berry, M.D. *Infants and Mothers: Differences in Development.* New York: Dell Publishing Co., 1969.

Brittain, W. Lambert. "Analysis of Artistic Behavior in Young Children." Final report. Mar. 1973. Cornell University, Ithaca, NY, Research Program in Early Childhood Education. ERIC document no., ED 128 091. ERIC Document Reproduction Service, P.O. Box 190, Arlington, VA. 22210.

Cohen, Dorothy H. *Criteria for Evaluation of Language Arts Materials in Early Childhood.* New York: E.C.E.C. of New York, 1971.

Durkin, Dolores. *Children Who Read Early.* New York: Teachers College Press, 1969.

Fantz, Robert L. "Visual Perception from Birth as Shown by Pattern Selectivity." In *The Competent Infant,* edited by J.L. Stone, H.T. Smith & L.B. Murphy. New York: Basic Books, 1973. Pp. 622-30.

Gibson, Eleanor J., & Harry Levin. *The Psychology of Reading.* Cambridge, MA & London: MIT Press, 1975.

Ginsburg, Herbert. *Children's Arithmetic: The Learning Process.* New York: D. Van Nostrand, 1977.

Ginsburg, H.; M.E. Wheeler & E.A. Tulis. *The Natural Development of Printing and Related Graphic Activities.* Mimeographed. Dept. of Human Development, Cornell University, 1970.

Greenman, George W. "Visual Behavior of Newborn Infants." In *The Competent Infant,* edited by J.L. Stone, H.T. Smith & L.B. Murphy. New York: Basic Books, 1973. Pp. 323-26.

Kessen, William. "Research in the Psychological Development of the Infant: An Overview." In *Contemporary Issues in Developmental Psychology,* edited by N. Endler, L. Boutler & H. Osser. New York: Holt, Rinehart & Winston, 1968. Pp. 49-58.

Klaus, Marshall H., & John H. Kennell. *Maternal-Infant Bonding.* St. Louis: C.V. Mosby Co., 1976.

Lavine, L.O. "The Development of Perception in Writing in Pre-reading Children: A Crosscultural Study." Unpublished doctoral dissertation. Dept. of Human Development, Cornell University, 1972.

Piaget, Jean. *The Origins of Intelligence in Children.* New York: W.W. Norton & Co., 1963.

Provence, Sally, M.D. "The First Year of Life: The Infant." In *Early Child Care: The New Perspectives,* edited by Laura L. Dittmann. New York: Atherton Press, 1968. Pp. 27-39.

Wheeler, M.E. "Untutored Acquisition of Writing Skill." Unpublished doctoral dissertation. Dept. of Human Development, Cornell University, 1971.

White, Robert W. "Motivation Reconsidered: The Concept of Competence." In *Early Childhood Play,* edited by Milly Almy. New York: Selected Academic Readings, 1968. WITE IA-37A.

Wolff, Peter H. "Developmental and Motivational Concepts in Piaget's Sensorimotor Theory of Intelligence." In *The Competent Infant,* edited by J.L. Stone, H.T. Smith & L.B. Murphy. New York: Basic Books, 1973. Pp. 484-93.

Why, Mommy, Why?

Ruth Formanek and Anita Gurian

Do boy babies get born from fathers?
Daddy, when you were little, were you a boy or a girl?
When I was born, how did I know I was Jason?

Real children asked these real questions. Every day bewildered parents are faced with the job of answering dozens like them. It isn't easy. Children will not hesitate to touch upon things very personal to parents—their values, their fears, their loves. But answering is important. Children explore their world by asking questions about it. It is a way they develop confidence in their own abilities; honest answers give a child a sense of self-respect. Not all of their questions, however, are asked in the same way, nor do they all have the same significance. Here, for example, are seven types they often use.

1. *The nonverbal question,* such as an unspoken "Can you help me?" in a child's tugging at her parent's arms.

2. *The practice question.* For the toddler, questions may simply be a test flight, a trying-out of the process. For example, Ruth Weir, a linguist, tape-recorded her two-and-a-half-year-old son as he was falling asleep alone in his room: "What color blanket? What color hat? What color glass? Not the yellow blanket, the white."

3. *The classification question.* Preschoolers ask questions to organize their impressions and to make comparisons. A table may be red and a block may be red—why aren't all the same things the same color? One way of getting categories straight is by asking questions until the differences click into place. "Bird?" "No, Janie, it flies, but it isn't a bird, it's a kite."

4. *The information question.* "How do computers work?" "How come the sound and the picture on the television come out together?"

5. *The security question,* arising out of children's fears and worries about the continued presence of their parents. "Will you be around when I'm big?" "Will you still be my mother when I'm grown up?" "Why can't I go to the movies with you?"

6. *The pseudo-question* that seeks neither information nor reassurance. "Why do I have to go to bed?" is more likely to be an attempt to get some rules changed than a quest for information.

7. *The hidden-agenda question.* Often a seemingly straightforward query such as "What time are you going out tonight?" may have a hidden meaning. The child may hesitate to say straight out that she wishes her parents wouldn't leave her with a baby-sitter.

The secret of success in responding to children, whatever their age, is to try to tell them what they want to know at the time. These steps may be helpful:

● Try to find out the meaning of the question to the child. Say, "Tell me what you think, and then we'll try and figure this out together." Don't distort the truth, but do remember the level the child is at—don't go over his head.

● Think of what the question means to you. It is important to examine your own feelings on sensitive issues—sex, divorce, adoption, death. Your answer will reveal attitudes and feelings as well as facts.

● Don't tell children more than they can handle at the moment. In the desire to explain, parents often overwhelm youngsters with information. There was a three-year-old, for example, who asked his mother about the workings of a telephone. "Mommy, when you talk to me on the telephone, how do you get in there?" His mother undertook to explain the structure of the telephone. The boy waited patiently and then asked the question that, according to him, logically followed the first one: "But when you are finished, how do you crawl out again?" A complicated answer glances off a child's mind without making any noticeable impression.

There are five subjects that, above all others, require sensitive treatment and a genuine understanding of the child's *needs* when he asks them and the limitations of his age. Here they are:

1. BIRTH AND SEX

What follows are some commonly asked questions and suggestions for answers. Don't use these answers verbatim—find the style that suits you best.

"Why, Mommy, Why?" *Woman's Day,* September 2, 1980, pp. 56-60, 108. Adapted from WHY? CHILDREN'S QUESTIONS: WHAT THEY MEAN AND HOW TO ANSWER THEM by Anita Gurian and Ruth Formanek. Copyright ©1980 by Anita Gurian and Ruth Formanek. Reprinted by permission of Houghton Mifflin Company.

Ages three to five:
Why is that lady so fat?
"There's a baby inside her."
You mean she swallowed a baby?
"No, she didn't swallow it. It's growing inside her."
Will the baby stay in there?
"No, it will come out."
How will the baby get out?
"The baby comes through a special opening in the mother's body."

Ages six to nine:
Children at this age are ready for more detailed information and often are curious about the role of the father.

How does a baby get inside the mother?
"When a woman wants to have a baby, one of the little eggs inside her starts to grow in a special place called a uterus. The baby needs to grow inside the mother for a long time before it's ready to be born."

How come the baby gets bigger inside the mother? How does it eat?
"The baby grows because it gets its food from the mother. There's a special cord called the umbilical cord that connects the baby and the mother. The baby gets its food and air through the cord."

How does the sperm join the egg?
"The man's body fits with the woman's body. His penis makes the sperm and he puts his penis near the entrance to the uterus so the sperm can join with the egg. A fluid called semen comes out of the penis and carries the sperm into the uterus. One sperm cell joins an egg cell. The joining of the two cells starts the baby growing."

How do you do it?
"The mother and the father lie close together and feel loving toward each other. The father's penis fits into the mother's vagina." (Children at this age cannot understand the idea of pleasure in intercourse. Actually the process sounds rather odd to them. They need to be reassured that it is a pleasurable, not a peculiar experience.)

Ages ten to twelve:
Children at this age are apt to be concerned about bodily changes.

At what age do boys get sperm? When can girls get pregnant?
"A boy's body is ready when he is about twelve years old. A girl can become pregnant after her menstrual periods begin if she has intercourse with a boy whose body has begun to make sperm cells."

2. DIVORCE

"When are you and Daddy getting divorced?" five-year-old Roy asked his happily married parents. His assumption that divorce is the automatic sequel to marriage makes sense in the light of current statistics. Young children cannot understand the real causes of the separation or the arrangements for custody and visitation. Underlying their questions are the fears that one or both parents no longer love them, that they will be alone, that no one will take care of them, and that, in fact, they might be responsible for the trouble. Calm, rational responses aren't always possible. Parents, embroiled in their own conflicts, often find it difficult to respond to their children's basic needs, let alone to their questions. Your answers should be simple; stress the immediate rather than the remote, the practical effects rather than the causes of the divorce.

Why are you getting a divorce?
"We're not happy with each other."
"You've seen us fight and have arguments. Sometimes we get angry with each other. Remember, we're not angry with you. We think it will be better for all of us, and we'll be happier, if Dad and I live in separate houses."

Are you going to divorce me?
"No, You're not getting a divorce. Mom and I are getting a divorce. We're not happy with each other, but we're happy with you. You're one of the good parts of our lives."

What will happen to me?
"You're our child. You always will be. Daddy will always be your Daddy, and I will always be your Mom. You'll always have us to take care of you."

If Daddy loves me, why is he going away?
"Because he and I aren't happy with each other and we want to live apart. You'll live here, but both of us will still take care of you. That's what loving you means; it means taking care of you and being with you."

If I'm good will he stay? Is he going because I was bad?
"He's not going because you were bad. It's not your fault that we're getting a divorce. Sometimes you're bad. All children are bad sometimes. That's not why Daddy's going. He's going because he and I aren't getting along with each other, and we've decided to live in separate houses. I know you feel mixed up about it, but whenever you're wondering about it, you ask me, and we'll talk about it."

Why didn't you do something to make her stay? It's your fault!
"There's nothing I can do to stop what's happening. It's not the fault of just one of us. The trouble has been caused by both of us."
"Grownups make mistakes too. We're not perfect. Nobody is."

What's the use of getting married, if you're going to get divorced anyway? Why did you get married in the first place?
"We once loved each other but now we disagree more than we agree. We've thought it over very carefully, and we think it will be best for all of us, for the whole family. We've stayed together for a long time because we love you. But now we think we'll be better off if we separate."

Did you ever love each other?
"We loved each other very much when we decided to get married. We were very happy and we wanted

children. Part of loving each other was having you, and you're still at the top of our list. But over the years we've grown in different ways, and things have changed. We feel we don't love each other anymore. That doesn't mean that we don't love you. We still do and we always will. We've tried to work things out to stay together, but there doesn't seem to be anyway to do that. We feel it's better for all of us if we separate."

3. REMARRIAGE

"Will she take my father from me? Will I be able to see my real mother? Will he love her more than me? Will they have a baby?"

A remarriage dashes a child's hopes for a parental reconciliation, and for some children a conflict of loyalties ensues. They may feel they're betraying the still single parent if they like the new partner of the remarrying one. They have to make room in their emotional lives for another person—not an easy task for anyone.

Why does he have to be part of the family? I've already got a father.

"Yes, you're right; you do. Bill isn't going to take his place and doesn't want to. He just wants to have a good relationship with you and to be a special kind of relative to you. He doesn't ever want to stop you from being with your father. He's going to be part of the family because he and I love each other and we want to live together.

You're not my mother, so why should I do what you say?

"I know I'm not your mother; I'm your father's wife. No one will replace your mother. I don't want to take her place. I'm acting like a mother to you now. I can tell you what to do in our house. I'm telling you what I believe is best for you."

For some children, it would be helpful to add some additional reassurance that it's not unusual to feel the way they do.

"I know you feel angry, and that's okay. If you don't like what I say, you can tell me about it and let me know what you think. If I still think I'm right, you'll have to go along with it."

4. ADOPTION

Questions about adoption, more than any other sensitive topic, seem to raise the parental anxiety level. Most adoptive parents are highly self-conscious about the whole procedure. They've been analyzed, interviewed, processed and computerized. They've had to face a lot of hard issues before the adoption could actually take place. They've been influenced by the attitudes of their community; they've been flooded with material about the joys, sorrows and hazards of adoption. Here are some specific questions they should be prepared for from their adopted children.

Where did I come from? How did I get born? Whose body did I come from?

A three- to-five-year-old is probably not looking for the story of her adoption, although her parents may think she is because they've been waiting for this question from the beginning. At this point, the most appropriate explanation is that all babies grow in a special place in a woman's body before they are born. Questions such as *Did I drink from a bottle? Was I born in a hospital? Did I eat baby food? Was I cute? Did I cry?* can all be answered with a simple yes. As the child begins to build a sense of time past and to perceive of herself as growing and changing, she wants to know what she was like as a baby.

What's "adopted"?

That's one way a child comes into a family."

Often specific questions are likely to arise if there is a birth of a sibling. One adopted child recalls that he thought his parents were dissatisfied with him and were trying out a new baby. Specific statements that he would always be a part of the family reassured him of his continued safe place. Tell the story of adoption gradually, in tune with the child's ability to understand.

How did you pick me out? How did you get me? What if you picked wrong? Could you give me back?

"The doctor (or agency, or home) took very good care of you. We came and saw you, and we loved you and took you home. We're all very lucky to be together, and we'll always be a family."

Why did my mother give me away? Where is she now? Didn't she like me? Why should I care about her if she didn't care about me?

Many adoptive parents are very uncomfortable with these questions. Some feel threatened. Usually they don't arise before the age of seven or eight unless the parents have overemphasized the adoption. With the younger child, misconceptions may arise no matter what the adoptive parent says. For example, there is the comment made by one little girl, "After I was borned, my mother didn't like my hair so she gave me to the baby store."

The child over six understands that someone can be born to one person and raised by another. Naturally, the answers about that will vary from child to child, but the following may be appropriate.

"Another woman gave birth to you. She and your birth father wanted you but they could not take care of you because they were too young (or too poor, or had to separate, depending on the circumstances). The doctor (or agency) helped us take you home and become your parents."

"Your birth mother was young when you were born. She was still in school and didn't have a job. She cared about you and wanted you to have a home and a family. She talked to your father. They went to an adoption agency. The agency knew we wanted a baby so you came to our house. Now we're a family and we always will be."

Who is my real family? You can't tell me what to do! You're not my real mother!

"Yes, I am. We are your real family. We've taken care of you, and that's why we are and why we can tell you what to do. I know you get angry with us sometimes, but that happens in every family."

5. DEATH

In our culture death has replaced sex as the most taboo subject. Even the most sophisticated parents usually retreat when the subject arises, and children who are quite knowledgeable about the facts of life have been shielded from the facts of death. Parents often need special help when answering questions about it. It may be useful to remember these principles:

Tell the truth. When there is a death in the family, tell the children the facts according to their age and emotional needs. Recognize the need for protection against grief and fear of death, but don't lie.

Be simple and direct. For young children the best explanations are those that draw on concrete experiences. They learn that flowers die, they see a dead bird or pet. Dying and death have been shown in movies and on television shows.

Don't hide your grief. Even children who can't grasp the actual facts can grasp emotional reality. This may be the first time they have seen adults cry; explain to them that all people cry when they feel sad.

Keep the child with the family if at all possible. Familar surroundings and routines provide security and a sense that life will go on. Children over five or six can usually attend a funeral. This helps them know in the most concrete way possible what is happening. "What I want to know is how will he get out of that box?" asked one incredulous little boy. The simple act of placing a flower or throwing a handful of dirt into the grave enables children to participate with the family in a meaningful ritual and to sense the importance of the event.

Try to explore your own feelings about death. How do you reconcile your own emotions? There's no one way and there is no single way to answer the questions of a child, either. Your explanation may be religious; it may be scientific; it may focus on the values of life and death in general. Don't use a religious explanation if you don't believe in it yourself—it won't ring true and your child will know it. The most important thing is to let children know that you are there and you understand what is happening to them. They may wish to talk about times they have shared with the dead person or about their own anxious feelings now. Talking about familiar things is a way of reinforcing the stability and continuity of life's routines. Let them express their sadness, and listen to them. Hold them and hug them, letting them know they can count on your support.

Ages three to five:

During these years children ask questions mainly about the concrete details of the funeral, the coffin, the cemetery and so forth. They are too young to understand the abstract idea of death itself.

Do you keep growing in heaven? What does a person say when he dies? How do you go to the bathroom when you're dead?

"A dead person can't talk and can't see and can't hear and can't go to the bathroom."

Are you going to die too?

"I'm probably going to live until you're old. I take good care of myself. When I'm sick I go to the doctor so he can help me get well. But there will always be somebody to take care of you, and we hope we will all live together for a very long time."

Can little children die too?

"Most children live until they are old. Once in a while a child may die, but hardly ever—only when he is very, very sick or is in an accident.

If you're sleeping, can somebody think you're dead and bury you by accident?

"No. Sleeping is not dying. Nobody gets buried by accident."

Ages six to nine:

About the age of six many children become fascinated with killing. "I'll kill you dead!" "I'll chop you to pieces!" Some six-year-olds may also become interested in rituals and be disturbed by pictures and stories of dying and dead animals, but they still don't believe that everyone must die. Around eight they become interested in what happens after death and ask numerous questions about the disposition of the body, a subject that many adults would prefer not to talk about.

By nine or ten, children understand that death is universal, inevitable, final and personal. They begin to realize that their parents will die one day and so will they.

What happens to the body?

"Dead people are buried in special places called cemeteries. Stones are put on each grave to tell the names of the people. The place is kept beautiful with flowers and trees. It's a pleasant place to visit, and it helps us to remember the person who died. Before people are buried, there is often a funeral. This is a way that people can say good-bye to someone they care about."

Why did he die?

The older child should be told the facts: the person was old, had a serious illness, was hurt in an automobile accident, whatever the case may be.

Could I have stopped him from dying?

"We all took the very best care of him that we could. There's nothing anyone could have done that would have stopped him from dying."

Research shows that some preschoolers ask more than three hundred questions in one day. This is a far cry from the number of questions allotted to children by Lewis Carroll:

" I have answered three questions,
   and that is enough"
Said his father. "Don't give
   yourself airs!
Do you think I can listen all day
   to such stuff?
Be off, or I'll kick you downstairs!"

Wise parents don't do that. Instead they patiently answer the questions as they come along.

Is Seven the Perfect Age?

Well, no, but for many children it marks a major milestone on the road to maturity.

Joanna Cole

Joanna Cole, the author of "Parents Book of Toilet Teaching" (Ballantine), writes for and about children.

It's the age when medieval children were hired out as apprentices; when children begin formal schooling in many countries; when first Communion is given in the Roman Catholic Church. It's the age seven, also known as "the age of reason," a year that has been recognized through the ages as the start of a new era in a child's development.

Certainly parents notice a big change as seven unfolds. Suddenly their children seem more cooperative and willing, more independent and thoughtful. Temper tantrums are much rarer than they were in the past, as are the struggles over daily routines that were commonplace only a year or two before. The boy who often needed a parent to negotiate arguments with playmates now handles most differences smoothly himself. The girl who hated to play alone spends time on her own, coloring, organizing her toys, and making signs, lists, and endless collections of objects. And both children seem to have a new self-awareness, apologizing spontaneously for transgressions, and saying after an argument, "I really got madder than I ought to" or "I didn't mean to hurt her feelings."

These developments, of course, come on gradually and at different times for different children. Some six-year-olds are considerate, while some eight-year-olds are just beginning to mature. And every child seems to grow in fits and starts—acting grown-up one day and babyish another. Still, there do seem to be real changes in children as they leave the preschool years and enter middle childhood, the years from about seven to the beginning of adolescence at eleven or twelve.

Freud called this period "latency" and postulated that the calming down seen at this time was due to an abatement of children's sexual curiosity. Today, many child-development experts note that interest in sex does not disappear during these years, but is under more control and may be overshadowed by children's expanding interest in the world outside themselves—in their schoolwork, hobbies, and friendships with other children.

The brain at seven: the physiology of maturity.

New traits and abilities no doubt come in part from the experience of living for seven years, but there are also physical changes in children that underlie their new maturity. The brain itself shows some dramatic growth. For one thing, the sheer size and weight of the brain increases: by seven, the brain has 90 percent of its total weight, compared to 25 percent at birth. And there are also other more specific changes in the brain that psychologists believe may be the basis of children's new capacities.

Dr. Sheldon White, professor of psychology at Harvard and the author of major research in development from ages five to seven, says that several important areas of the brain grow dramatically before seven. Among them is the area of the brain associated with foresightful activity and planned sequences of behavior—the kind of behavior children show when they construct things or engage in games played by the rules. In addition, the right and left sides of the brain are bridged by neural connections at around six or seven. This new linkage may bring language and thought into a closer relation and explain why older children are able to learn so much more effectively.

Another area of the brain that grows around this time is the one associated with muscle control. According to Dr. White, this development probably has a lot to do with the new physical abilities of school-age children. "In the preschool years, kids are clumsy," says Dr. White. "They throw a ball funny, they stagger a bit when they walk, but they start to get graceful when they enter the school years." This increased coordination may explain not only why middle childhood is a time of preoccupation with sports and physical games but also why older children are able to do things like pour milk without spilling, build models, and even read and write with much less frustration than in earlier years.

Changes in the brain may also underlie many changes in children's thinking that begin to appear around age six and are consolidated for most children at seven. The Swiss philosopher and developmental psychologist Jean Piaget has shown that very young children do not think the same way adults do at all. A three-year-old girl may believe that she could become a boy if she dressed like one. Similarly, she may cry if her father shaves off his beard, thinking he has become someone else. And if juice is poured from a short, wide glass into a tall, narrow one, the child will insist that there is more in the tall glass, no matter how many times her mother explains that it has to be the same amount. The very young child cannot seem to notice transformation—that is, the process of dressing, shaving, and pouring in the examples just given. Instead, she focuses on the *results* of the changes.

Between the ages of five and seven, most children pass from this early level of thought to one that is closer to the adult mode. They now laugh at the idea that someone could alter his sex by changing clothes or his identity by shaving off whiskers. In the juice experiment, they realize that the amount in the glass remains constant, often saying, "You didn't add anything or take anything away, so it must be the same. It only *looks* like more because it is higher." Not tied anymore to the physical appearance of things, they are able to use reason to solve the problem. They can focus on transformations and on more than one quality at a time, recognizing that the second glass is not only taller but also narrower, which must affect the level to which the liquid will rise.

At the same time, older children become capable of reversing a process in their mind; for instance, they can be aware that if one plus two is three, then reversing the process to take two away from three will leave one again. Being able to reverse a thought process gives school-age children a new power and

flexibility in thinking and understanding.

Looking outward, looking inward.

All these cognitive developments herald the beginning of middle childhood, the years when children profit most from formal instruction in school. At this stage, children also change socially, as they begin to realize that their own point of view is not the only one in the world. They recognize that others may have feelings and opinions that are different from theirs. A very small child often believes that everyone else knows the same things he does. I recall two-year-old Saskia coming to her day-care center after a holiday and saying enthusiastically to the director, "Grandma came. 'Member Grandma?" The director had never met the lady, but she was in tune with Saskia's cognitive level, so she nodded yes. At other times, a preschooler will ask someone to look at something without realizing that the other person can't see it from his vantage point. My child at five and six would often point out a word to me on a page, unaware that I couldn't see it if her finger was covering it!

As they enter the next cognitive level, children lose this kind of egocentrism. They are now able to put themselves in another's shoes. When my daughter was almost seven, I chided her one evening by saying, "Honey, you're being a pain." She responded, "I am not. I'm being a pest." Her description was indeed more accurate than mine, and I remember doing a double take, for it was a first—the first time she'd seen herself and her behavior from my point of view.

This ability allows children to take others into account much more. I recall overhearing a mother telling about the change in her

daughter from six to seven. At seven, the girl called her mother from a pay phone to say that the school bus had left her off late. "I'm standing on the corner, but I'm all right. I knew you would be worried, so I called," she said. Remembering the situation, the mother exclaimed, "I was astounded. She knew I would be worried! This was a different child."

While seven-year-olds are still children and do not always display such thoughtfulness, they are capable of it at times. And this new mode shows itself not only in their relations with parents, but also with siblings and friends. The mother of an almost-seven-year-old reports, "She comes and asks me to help her decide how to approach a friend in school. She wants to be frank about something, but then she adds, 'I don't want to hurt Marsha's feelings. She's very sensitive, you know.'" Another parent comments that her son will now remark after an argument with his little brother, "I really got madder than I ought to. He didn't do anything that bad," and resolve to do better in the future at self-control.

Along with control comes an increased self-awareness. Indeed, psychologists have long identified the age of seven, or thereabouts, as a time when children are forming a true self-concept. Young children are self-involved, but that is quite different from having an intellectual awareness of themselves as separate people with special qualities. A child will begin to see herself as someone who is, for instance, a good reader, a fast runner, an animal lover. She will also be sensitive to the reactions of others to her: whether teachers find her pleasant or annoying, whether strangers are

friendly or dismissive, whether other children are accepting or rejecting.

Dr. Sheldon White says, "Seven-year-old children begin to drape themselves in adjectives. You take any dimension on which adults divide themselves—such as race, religion, income, appearance, popularity, intelligence—and that dimension begins to show up in the early years of school, and values, both positive and negative, begin to appear. The child begins to place people in a social landscape, and at the same time he places himself and his family in that landscape."

School-age children become introspective, or able to analyze themselves and their feelings, for the first time. Seven-year-olds have been described as "sad" and "pensive" by some child-development experts, and, according to Dr. White, this quality may be related to the fact that they are thinking about themselves and where they stand in relation to others.

The age of industry.

Psychologist Erik Erikson has labeled middle childhood as the age of industry, when, under favorable conditions, children are acquiring a view of themselves as basically competent. At seven, parents will see the beginnings of a preoccupation with making, doing, collecting. School-age children want to practice physical skills, create, and learn; they become almost obsessive about mastering sports like playing ball, swimming, and jumping rope. They throw themselves into projects like woodworking, clay modeling, making collections. Parents will report that a child has "developed very strong interests," or that "he really sticks to something until he masters it, without becoming quite so frustrated as he used to." The same boy will "look up sports scores in the newspaper, even though he still can't read very well."

Most children become intensely involved in artwork, spending hours drawing pictures of the day's activities, people, cars, planes, even Smurfs, Pac-Man, and GI Joe. At this age, they want their drawings to be realistic and will spend a tremendous amount of effort trying to achieve that end. Parents may look back fondly to the spontaneity of their children's preschool creations, but the artwork of middle childhood is no less creative. Children are using their expressive abilities to organize their experience, which is as good a definition of the artist's task as any.

The seven-year-old's new capacity to look inward is brought to bear on these new abilities. Like toddlers, older children have an expansive desire to do, a compulsion to master their environment. But unlike toddlers, school-age children can assess their abilities with a good amount of accuracy, and they often worry about success or failure.

At times, their anxiety about performance will lead to a self-critical stance: "I can't do anything," or, when wielding an eraser, "Stupid, stupid, stupid!" Sometimes a child appears confident to the point of boastfulness, but her anxieties may be revealed when they are projected onto others. Then parents may find their school-age child scornfully characterizing a classmate as the "dumbest," or saying of a younger sibling, "She can't even tie a bow!" We may be upset when we see a previously sunny preschooler showing these new insecurities and negative values. We can help by setting limits by imposing a "time-out" peri-

od whenever an older child is abusive to a younger sibling. And we can also give a child room in private to talk about the "dumb" classmate, while making it clear that we expect her to refrain from name-calling or bullying in school. It may help us as parents to realize that these attitudes are natural, given the child's new concern about her ability to achieve, and she will grow out of them if she is given a chance to become more competent and sure of herself.

Whether a child ultimately develops a healthy sense of industry, or instead begins to see herself as incompetent and inferior, depends a lot on what happens at home and in school during middle childhood. In his book *The Hurried Child*, psychologist David Elkind says school-age children need someone who "senses their capabilities, gives them opportunities to work and reinforces their achievements." This would mean giving a child household jobs to do—without finding fault with the results when less than perfect; encouraging a nonathletic child to join a computer club, rather than insisting on Little League; and showing up at parents' day at school despite competing commitments elsewhere.

It also means supporting children when they want to try something new, or when they express an interest in pursuing an activity. Within the limits of the family budget, parents should provide the opportunity for gymnastic lessons when a child says, "Gee, that looks like fun." When a child wants to plan and execute a project, parents should try to make the necessary materials and tools available, and offer adult help when it is needed. If a project is too expensive, they can suggest an alternative using less costly materials.

Support means not insinuating your own standards into a child's project, and communicating pleasure in the results, while keeping evaluation to a minimum. For instance, a parent might say, "I really enjoy using that letter opener you made. It's a big help," rather than, "That's a great letter opener."

Similarly, if a project doesn't turn out to a child's liking, or if he finds he absolutely *hates* gymnastics, a supportive parent can say. "It's too bad it didn't work out, but I'm proud of you for trying anyway."

Such parental guidance can be undermined, according to David Elkind, by a school that is too intent on hurrying children into academics. Elkind recommends that schools acknowledge children's individual differences and avoid pressing them to acquire skills before they have the requisite mental abilities to do so.

Friendships, chumships, and childhood gangs.

If middle childhood is a time when children develop a sense of competence, it is also a time when they find their place among peers. Forming friendships with other kids becomes a top-priority issue, and seven-year-olds are just at the brink of a social revolution when peers become as important or more important than parents. Indeed, it seems fair to say that, developmentally speaking, children have as much need for their peers during middle childhood as they had for their parents during infancy and toddlerhood. In the third to sixth grades, children will be forming what developmental psychologists call "chumships," close friendships with another child or two—usually of the same sex. At this time "childhood gangs" also ap-

pear; these do not involve motorcycles or street fights, but are organized mainly for play. Seven-year-olds usually have a few years before the passionate attachments of the middle grades appear, but first friendships will start to form. Increasingly, a child's friends will be chosen for their personal characteristics, rather than simply for their availability to play, as playmates were during the preschool years.

It is just as important for parents to support their children's friendships as it is to give them after-school lessons or to encourage them to do their homework. This means making sure a middle-grades child has time to play with friends in an unstructured setting (taking a violin lesson at the same time as a friend probably doesn't give the kids a chance to play anything but the violin). Depending on where you live, you may need to make an extra effort to arrange play dates, providing whatever transportation is needed.

Differences in development.

All along, we've been making fairly broad generalizations in order to make understandable what parents may be seeing in their growing children. It's important, however, to say that every child is unique. You may see these traits very clearly in your child, or you may not. Or the time frame may be a little different for your child. Your six-year-old may fit the description here to a T. Or your seven-year-old may not show any of the changes I've described until eight or older. In either case, you can chalk it up to individual differences, which often make for a variation of plus or minus one year. And if your seven has a tantrum, is inconsiderate, or refuses to perform her household chores, keep in mind that in development there are no rigid boundaries or points of no return.

In general, however, the changes do seem to be very real for most children as they pass from early to middle childhood. In addition, there are some traits that seem peculiar to the age seven—traits that will gradually be replaced by others as the child matures.

Many of the characteristics of seven have been reported in meticulous detail by the Gesell Institute at Yale University, where children were studied in depth at various ages. If seven-year-olds have a fault, it seems, it lies in the very introspection parents appreciate so much. For this pensive quality can make children seem sad and moody, and their self-absorption means seven-year-olds resent being interrupted for such mundane matters as dressing and getting off to school. Less likely than at six to lash out at parents in anger, seven-year-olds may withdraw in a huff to sulk, and their recently acquired ethical sense is focused for the time being on themselves; that is, they often proclaim in a loud voice, "That's not fair!" when they perceive a real or imagined injustice committed against themselves.

While these traits are easier to manage than the more volatile resistances of six-year-olds, they do require some patience, and parents may become upset by them, for we all worry if our children seem unhappy. The Gesell researchers advise parents to relax and wait for eight, when, they say, children become expansive again.

Meanwhile, there is plenty to enjoy at seven. One mother, when asked, "What's it like to live with a seven-year-old?" answered without missing a beat, "It's heaven! Just heaven!"

How to Choose a Good Early Childhood Program

What should parents look for in selecting a good early childhood program? NAEYC's most popular public information brochure has just been rewritten to reflect current research and theory about what is best for young children in group programs. Teachers and program directors also have found it useful for evaluation and staff development. "How to Choose a Good Early Childhood Program" is reprinted in this issue of Young Children *so that all NAEYC members will know how valuable this information is for parents, the media, decision makers, and our profession.*

A good early childhood program can benefit your child, your family, and your community. Your child's educational, physical, personal, and social development will be nurtured in a well-planned program. As a parent, you will feel more confident when your child is enrolled in a suitable program, and the time your family spends together will be more satisfying as a result. Early childhood education plays an important role in supporting families, and strong families are the basis of a thriving community.

If you are thinking about enrolling your child in an early childhood program, you probably have already decided upon some of your basic priorities, such as location, number of hours, cost, and type of care that best suits your child. If you feel that a group program is appropriate, you can obtain a list of licensed programs for young children from your local licensing agency. Then you can call several programs for further information, and arrange to visit the programs that seem best for you and your child so you can talk with teachers, directors, and other parents.

What should you look for in a good early childhood program? Professionals in early childhood education and child development have found several indicators of good quality care for preschool children. You will especially want to meet the adults who will care for your child—they are responsible for every aspect of the program's operation.

Who will care for your child?

1. The adults enjoy and understand how young children learn and grow.

Are the staff members friendly and considerate to each child?

Do adult expectations vary appropriately for children of differing ages and interests?

Do the staff members consider themselves to be professionals? Do they read or attend meetings to continue to learn more about how young children grow and develop?

Do the staff work toward improving the quality of the program, obtaining better equipment, and making better use of the space?

2. The staff view themselves positively and therefore can continually foster children's emotional and social development.

Do the staff help children feel good

Reprinted by permission from *Young Children*, Vol. 39, No. 1 (November 1983), pp. 28-32. ©1983 by the National Association for the Education of Young Children, 11141 Georgia Ave., Suite 200, Whealen, MD 20902.

Michaelyn Straub

A good center provides appropriate and sufficient equipment and play materials and makes them readily available.

about themselves, their activities, and other people?

Do the adults listen to children and talk with them?

Are the adults gentle while being firm, consistent, and yet flexible in their guidance of children?

Do the staff members help children learn gradually how to consider others' rights and feelings, to take turns and share, yet also to stand up for personal rights when necessary?

When children are angry or fearful are they helped to deal with their feelings constructively?

3. There are enough adults to work with a group and to care for the individual needs of children.

Are there at least one teacher and an assistant with every group of children?

Are infants in groups of no more than 8 children?

Are two- and three-year-old children in groups of no more than 16?

Are four- and five-year-olds in groups of no more than 22 children?

4. All staff members work together cooperatively.

Do the staff meet regularly to plan and evaluate the program?

Are they willing to adjust the daily activities for children's individual needs and interests?

5. Staff observe and record each child's progress and development.

Do the staff stress children's strengths and show pride in their accomplishments?

Are records used to help parents and staff better understand the child?

Are the staff responsive to parents' concerns about their child's development?

What program activities and equipment are offered?

1. The environment fosters the growth and development of young children working and playing together.

Does the center have realistic goals for children?

Are activities balanced between vigorous outdoor play and quiet indoor play? Are children given opportunities to select activities of interest to them?

Are children encouraged to work alone as well as in small groups?

Are self-help skills such as dressing, toileting, resting, washing, and eating encouraged as children are ready?

Are transition times approached as pleasant learning opportunities?

2. A good center provides appropriate and sufficient equipment and play materials and makes them readily available.

Is there large climbing equipment? Is there an ample supply of blocks of all sizes, wheel toys, balls, and dramatic play props to foster physical development as well as imaginative play?

Are there ample tools and hands-on materials such as sand, clay, water, wood, and paint to stimulate creativity?

Is there a variety of sturdy puzzles, construction sets, and other small manipulative items available to children?

Are children's picture books age-appropriate, attractive, and of good literary quality?

Are there plants, animals, or other natural science objects for children to care for or observe?

Are there opportunities for music and movement experiences?

3. Children are helped to increase their language skills and to expand their understanding of the world.

Do the children freely talk with each other and the adults?

Do the adults provide positive language models in describing objects, feelings, and experiences?

Does the center plan for visitors or trips to broaden children's understandings through firsthand contacts with people and places?

Activities are balanced between vigorous outdoor play and quiet indoor play in a good center. Children are given opportunities to select activities of interest to them.

Are the children encouraged to solve their own problems, to think independently, and to respond to open-ended questions?

How does the staff relate to your family and the community?

1. A good program considers and supports the needs of the entire family.

Are parents welcome to observe, discuss policies, make suggestions, and participate in the work of the center?

Do staff members share with parents the highlights of their child's experiences?

Are the staff alert to matters affecting any member of the family which may also affect the child?

Do the staff respect families from varying cultures or backgrounds?

Does the center have written policies about fees, hours, holidays, illness, and other considerations?

2. A good center is aware of and contributes to community resources.

Do the staff share information about community recreational and learning opportunities with families?

Do the staff refer family members to a suitable agency when the need arises?

Are volunteers from the community encouraged to participate in the center's activities?

Does the center collaborate with other professional groups to provide the best care possible for children in the community?

Are the facility and program designed to meet the varied demands of young children, their families, and the staff?

1. The health of children, staff, and parents is protected and promoted.

Are the staff alert to the health and safety of each child and of themselves?

Are meals and snacks nutritious, varied, attractive, and served at appropriate times?

Do the staff wash hands with soap and water before handling food and after changing diapers? Are children's hands washed before eating and after toileting?

Are surfaces, equipment, and toys cleaned daily? Are they in good repair?

Does each child have an individual cot, mat, or crib?

Are current medical records and emergency information maintained for each child and staff member? Is adequate sick leave provided for staff so they can remain at home when they are ill?

Is at least one staff member trained in first aid? Does the center have a health consultant?

Is the building comfortably warm in cold weather? Are the rooms ventilated with fresh air daily?

2. The facility is safe for children and adults.

Are the building and grounds well lighted and free of hazards?

Are furnishings, sinks, and toilets safely accessible to children?

Are toxic materials stored in a locked cabinet?

Are smoke detectors installed in appropriate locations?

Are indoor and outdoor surfaces cushioned with materials such as carpet or wood chips in areas with climbers, slides, or swings?

Does every staff member know what to do in an emergency? Are emergency numbers posted by the telephone?

3. The environment is spacious enough to accommodate a variety of activities and equipment.

Are there at least 35 square feet of usable playroom floor space indoors per child and 75 square feet of play space outdoors per child?

Is there a place for each child's personal belongings such as a change of clothes?

Is there enough space so that adults can walk between sleeping children's cots?

For further information

If you have remaining questions about how to select a good program, consult an NAEYC Affiliate Group, the early childhood department of a local college, your state licensing agency, the resources listed here, or others knowledgeable about early childhood education.

Choosing Child Care: A Guide for Parents, by S. Auerbach. Institute for Childhood Resources, 1169 Howard St., San Francisco, CA 94103, or from E.P. Dutton through any bookstore. Paper $7.25; hardcover $15.00. 1982.

The Day Care Book: A Guide for Working Parents to Help Them Find the Best Possible Day Care for Their Children, by G. Mitchell. Stein and Day, Scarborough House, Briarcliff Manor, NY 10510. $10.00. 1979.

A Parent's Guide to Day Care, U.S. Department of Health and Human Services, Administration for Children, Youth and Families, Day Care Division. Gryphon House, 3706 Otis St., P.O. Box 217, Mt. Rainier, MD 20712. Paper $4.45. 1981.

Quality Day Care: A Handbook of Choices for Parents and Caregivers, by R. C. Endsley and M. R. Bradbard. Prentice-Hall, General Book Marketing, Special Sales Division, Englewood Cliffs, NJ 07632. $5.95. 1981.

Meeting the Needs of Infants

ALICE STERLING HONIG

Alice Sterling Honig, Ph.D., is Associate Professor of Child Development in the College for Human Development, Syracuse University, Syracuse, New York. She has written numerous books and articles on infant care and has also presented a variety of workshops on this topic throughout the country.

What are the most important ingredients that day care providers will need in order to meet the needs of infants they serve? First and foremost, babies need dominion over a warm, loving responsive body. Babies need a caregiver's body for comfort, for play, for feeding, for companionship and for reassurance. Caregivers need to think carefully about how comfortable they feel about their bodies serving as a security base, a place of tenderness and refuge for babies.

Cuddling and Carrying Nourish a Sense of Good Self

Some babies need much carrying. Indeed, they sometimes seem to be habitually draped on a shoulder as one goes about daily household or center tasks. How the adult nurtures these needs for body contact will make an important difference in the emotional well-being of infants. Cuddling, nuzzling and lap snuggling give babies the courage to go forth and tackle some of the more difficult early adventures of learning such as eating solids with a spoon, learning to explore while creeping or toddling and yet learning to comply with caregiver rules about what is safe or dangerous to do. Caring and confidence in a baby's learning ability are gifts of the sensitive caregiver. Courage-to-try, compliance and affection are the treasures infants give to adults in return.

Loving Looks

Infants need admiring glances, looks of pleasure and adult eyes with calmness that signal all is well, or will soon be well. A baby laboriously hoists herself upright, holding on to a sturdy chair. She is not too certain how to get down again. The way up was adventure enough. Her eyes turn to the caregiver. "Yes, you got up all by yourself. You pulled up to standing by the chair so well, I am proud of you." This and much more is the message the provider's eyes and words send forth. Reassured, the baby senses that her wobbly stance, her brave tries, are O.K. Even if she plops down to the floor, all will be well. The provider's eyes have lovingly validated her venturing, validated the essential goodness of her strivings and activities.

Babies who feel that they are essentially good can grow up to be good human beings. They have fortunately not caught the sad message sent all too often by some adults that babies are "bad," or will "get into trouble" or are expected to be a burden.

Positive Voice Tones

Voice tones are a powerful tool in meeting the needs of infants. Sharp, suspicious and impatient tones can shrivel courage. Cold annoyed tones can lead to a feeling of "I am bad. I am unlovable." Seated on a potty, a toddler heard interesting noises of blocks tumbling down. Since the noises came from an adjoining room to the bathroom, the toddler shuffled, with panties down around her ankles, toward the door in order to investigate. "Sit down! Didn't I tell you to sit there till you make!" ordered the caregiver sharply.

We need to listen to our voice tones. Good feelings about the self are nourished with gentle voices that can be firm yet caring when rules may have to be restated and explained.

From *Dimensions,* January 1983, pp. 4-7. Reprinted with permission of Dimensions, a Journal of the Southern Association on Children Under Six.

Knowledge of Developmental Norms: Necessary for Curriculum Planning

To meet the needs of babies we need to become familiar with developmental tasks and gains for each period of infant development. If we know that most babies have moved from earlier whole-hand raking swipes and scissor-like attempts to pick up items then we can plan experiences to boost more precise thumb-and-forefinger coordinations for a baby nearing the end of the first year of life. Safe, nutritious finger foods, such as cooked carrot slices, bits of grated apple or cooked peas on a tray will help boost pincer-prehension skills and at the same time boost the self-confidence of babies that they can indeed feed themselves.

Piagetian developmental stages should be recognized by a caregiver (Honig, 1974). If we know that a five-month-old is able to coordinate looking and batting at toys, we can hang mobiles where baby can practice swiping at and grabbing suspended toys that she tracks with her eyes. If we know that an eight- to 12-month-old is in that stage of sensorimotor development where actions-as-means have begun to be separated from actions-as-goals, then we can more ably provide toy-on-a-string games or pull-the-diaper-to-get-the-toy-on-top games (Honig & Lally, 1981).

Erikson's stages of development give us good ideas for promoting infant mental health. For example, Erikson explains well the toddler's seesawing between a growing need to assert herself and feelings of doubt that it is indeed O.K. to be unique, even sometimes to have different desires from the caregiver. Adults need to realize that a two-year-old may not know how to express a separate sense of self except by saying "No" occasionally to adult requests. Skills are in short supply. A sense of will in struggling to become a separate individual with legitimate wants and wishes is strong in toddlers.

For example, a provider announces that lunch is ready, and expects the toddler to move toward the eating area. The toddler may run off in the other direction with that dauntless "No-no" that asserts his will to be separate and to be different. Knowing the importance of the Eriksonian "autonomy" stage, the provider sniffs the air appreciatively and remarks "Mmmm. That hamburger sure smells good!" Toddler gallops past the adult on his eager way to eat lunch.

Interpreting Behaviors and Misbehaviors

How we handle what may appear to be misbehaviors often depends crucially on our knowledge and expectations of when developmental tasks occur. A caregiver may well understand that 12-18 months is a developmental prime time for "trial-and-error" behaviors. Then, when a toddler attempts to pull a toilet paper roll to see what is at the end or a toddler experiments to see where toys fall as they are dropped or flung different distances from a highchair or play pen, these actions can be seen not as predominant desires to annoy an adult, but as expressions of passionate curiosity to find out "what will happen if." A provider with foresight baby-proofs an environment where toddlers in this stage will be sure to try out new actions to see just what might happen. Often, when seemingly "naughty," the toddler is just as surprised as the adult at the results of her actions. She drops a potato on the floor to see it bounce as balls do. And the potato may split open and not bounce at all.

Babies Are Budding Scientists

Providing safe opportunities for such experimentations with toys and with items the adult approves of can boost children's thinking skills and attempts to make sense of the physical world. The physics of liquids and solids are learned early on in the nursery years. How do different toys behave in the bath tub? What happens when you squeeze or throw down hard or bouncy or soft items? How come milk pours out when a container is turned upside down, but oatmeal sticks to the bowl? Early scientific puzzles are explored energetically by toddlers.

Meeting Needs Promptly Leads to Less Crying and More Compliance

Dealing effectively with baby moods also depends on developmental knowledge. Ministering to a crying baby becomes easier if caregivers remember that a healthy young baby cries because he or she needs something. Feeding, diaper changes, being talked to and amused, having a toy to swipe at or bang with, being put into a new position with further opportunities to explore with eyes and hands—these are some of the needs that prompt the cry. Research shows that the more promptly the cry is responded to in the first months of life, the more appropriately the baby's needs are met, then the less a baby uses crying as a communication mode by the last months of the first year (Ainsworth, 1977).

Babies will use other signals, such as coos and calls and tugs and arm movements. They have learned to trust their caregivers. If they cried, someone cared and came and helped. Such securely attached babies have been found to be more compliant with adult requests to toddlers. Meeting babies' needs helps them learn to meet adult needs. Giving to babies supports their long-time learning to become more generous in meeting adult requirements in living together.

Be Alert to Task Difficulty: Increase Baby's Chances for Successful Learning

Knowledge of developmental norms helps a provider become more aware of how hard or how easy a task may be for each baby. A baby who has trouble banging two blocks together in pat-a-cake play will find a shape-sorter box or a tower-building task impossibly difficult to handle. A baby who can put several blocks in a large cup without taking each one out right after putting it in may well be ready for a pegboard game where she can put several pegs in a peg-board.

Hand-release skills are still shaky toward the end of the first year. A 10-month-old baby may put a hand holding a block down into a plastic margarine container for his caregiver on request. But that same fist may come right back up still clutching the block. Defiance? No! Hand-release skills still need time and practice to improve. Knowledge of developmental norms helps us to change our attitudes in relating to the troubles babies have while learning the tasks we set for them. Control of the anal sphincter muscles may still be poor. Such a baby will still have many toileting accidents. Toilet-training should wait until voluntary-control skills over those muscles is in better supply. Babies are not out to misbehave or aggravate caregivers. They are indeed struggling to gain mastery over their bodies and understanding of the world they live in. A secure, loving relationship with a calm, unharried, understanding provider is the best prescription for the development of the baby's ability to feel that he is successful.

Feeling Well-loved Lets Babies Give Energy to Learning

The learning careers of infants are launched in an aura of certainty of loving care and with the provision of opportunities to practice emerging skills. The emotionally anxious baby must give too much energy to the struggle to feel loved. There may not be enough energy left over for optimal learning and the growth of mastery.

Babies Need Games with Responsive Toys and Responsive People

The learning tasks of infants in the first years of life are awesome. Infants must learn that objects out of sight still exist and can be searched for. Peek-a-boo games often initiate this search for the hidden object—the beloved face of the caregiver. Babies must also learn that sometimes they cannot carry out their well-practiced actions such as banging or waving or mouthing a toy without first using another action as a means to obtain the toy. First the baby may have to stretch or lean around a provider's body to retrieve a toy that has been moved a bit away. Or, the baby may have to pull a string to get a toy within her reach for play. Later, babies learn to search for the causal mechanisms that make toys work. They need toys that require a button to press, a handle to turn, or a key to wind to make the toy go. These learnings of causal relationships, of means to goals, require that caregivers provide a rich assortment of toys and interactions that give feedback to the baby (Honig, 1981). If the baby acts, then the toy or the person reacts. To meet the needs of infants, caregivers have to become creative arrangers of learning experi-

ences with people and with objects (Willis & Ricciuti, 1975).

Interaction games, such as cooing back and forth with baby, or playing "so big" foster mutual satisfaction, learning the rules of games and taking turns. Giving a baby floor freedom provides the space and the furniture obstacles that will facilitate navigational skills and the ability to make sense of spatial arrangements. Safe opportunities for tumbling, sliding, climbing and running will help babies develop competence and grace in their large muscle skills.

Babies are sensuous creatures. They need to taste, stroke and explore with lips, mouth and hands. Water play and self-feeding experiences, as well as soft blankets and cuddly animals, will satisfy some of these sensory needs.

Appreciate Early Signs of Learning

Noticing skills help providers forestall boredom or frustration. A clear understanding of the components of tasks and the capabilities of each baby aids a provider in appreciating the earliest signs of success at a new and relatively difficult task. An infant at 11 months may not be able to bring a block up to, then over and down onto another block to build a two block tower. Yet the good noticer is aware when baby clearly approaches one block toward another in attempting this task. Appreciating such beginnings allows the provider to enjoy the first fruits of baby's struggles to master a new task. Adults need to take joy in infants' beginnings. For some babies, discouragement comes easily unless the provider encourages the earliest steps in new learnings. Caregiver approval and delight gives the baby confidence to continue to progress.

Good Matchmaking Boosts a Child's Chance for Learning

Babies need encouragement to become problem solvers. When caregivers sharpen their noticing skills they can boost the baby's problem solving efforts such as when they provide a steadying hand on a pegboard as baby pushes a peg onto a board that is sliding around too much to allow success. Good noticing gives the adult clues as to whether to make a game a bit easier or a bit more challenging. Matchmaking involves the ability to adjust the task difficulty to the present level of child ability. The adult must lure the baby forward just a step at a time toward new and more difficult accomplishments. Matchmaking skills are a precious adult resource. They ensure that developmental tasks will not be too easy or too frustrating, but mostly stimulating, to a baby's curiosity and need to gain competence.

Matchmaking skills are the truly creative contribution of caregivers. Suppose a toddler needs practice in sorting objects (classifying skills) or in lining items up in order (seriating skills). Sorting and matching doll clothes or stacking or nesting cardboard boxes of different sizes are good activities that promote the intellectual development of toddlers.

Knowledge of the individual strengths and developmental level of each baby is important. Chronological age does not always give good clues. A baby's ability clues in the wise caregiver. Then the challenge presented to each baby can be adjusted to match the individual readiness level. Fewer tantrums or sullen angers or unhappiness will result as caregivers set goals and tasks that each baby can succeed at with a bit of trying rather than an overload of frustration.

Recipes for Quality Caregiving

Let us sum up then, a caregiver's six secrets for supplying a nourishing environment in which the very young child can flourish:

1. Embed curriculum in daily routines whenever possible. Diapering and feeding give good opportunities for lots of talking and learning experiences.

2. Loving and learning are intertwined in infancy. A caring relationship is necessary to permit an infant to learn. Be sensitive to infant signals. Meet needs promptly. Exploration and competence flow from secure attachment.

3. Matchmaking skills boost the baby's chances for success, since tasks are geared to his or her developmental abilities.

4. Learning involves a struggle. Arrange opportunities sometimes for babies to learn on their own from encounters with materials at an appropriately challenging level. Toddlers see-saw between cooperation and a fierce desire to try to do things on their own and their own way. Be judicious in offering help. Empathize with the toddler's struggle between still needing intimate closeness and yet wanting to be big and bold and independent.

5. "Dance the developmental ladder." If a task is too hard, find a way to dance down and ease the baby's way. If the baby is bored, dance up the ladder. Challenge them with new problems they can work hard to solve.

6. Learn from each encounter. A caregiver who watches a baby's interactions with people and with events can sharpen noticing skills. Positive engagements with babies increase our abilities to become ever more harmonious and effective infant caregivers.

References

Ainsworth, M. Social Development in the first year of life: Maternal influences on infant-mother attachment. In J.M. Tanner, (Ed.) *Developments in Psychiatric Research.* London: Hodder & Stoughton, 1977.

Honig, A.S. Curriculum for infants in day care. *Child Welfare,* 1974, *53,* 633-643.

Honig, A.S. What are the needs of infants? *Young Children,* 1981.

Honig, A.S. & Lally, J.R. *Infant Caregiving: A Design for Training.* (2nd edition) Syracuse, New York: Syracuse University Press, 1981.

Willis, A. & Ricciuti, H.A. *A Good Beginning for Babies: Guidelines for Group Care.* Washington, D.C. National Association for the Education of Young Children, 1975.

The Real World of Teaching Two-Year-Old Children

Ida Santos Stewart

Ida Santos Stewart, Ph.D., is Associate Professor and Chairperson, Early Childhood Education Program, University of Houston, Texas.

The second year of life is perhaps the most neglected in programs for group care and education of young children. Although the exact number of toddlers enrolled in centers is unknown, a portion of the estimated 3,124,000 two-year-olds can be expected to need day care (U.S. Bureau of the Census 1977). As many parents have discovered, finding a center that can accommodate a two-year-old child is difficult.

Over the years much heat but little light has been generated in the development of curricula for two-year-old children. What can we expect of the two-year-old child in nursery school? What should toddlers be guided to do in group care? Anyone who has ever been responsible for a group of two-year-old children has felt as if she or he were in a tumultuous kaleidoscope of continuous crises. Teaching a group of toddlers is not easy.

The best word to describe two-year-old children is *busy*. Teachers of older children often spend time discussing ways of motivating their students, a problem about which teachers of two-year-old children seldom have to worry. Toddlers want to do everything at once. Try asking if any of them would like to hear a story. Before the announcement is completed, at least one child is already on your lap, impatiently waiting for the reading to begin. The ordinary limitations of space, time, and competency rarely dampen their enthusiasm.

It is generally more difficult to provide and implement a program for two-year-olds than for younger or older children.

Infants are less mobile and so much easier to handle; older children are more developmentally competent with the resultant increase in self-control and autonomy. A common descriptive term for toddlers is the Terrible Twos. The jump from difficult to terrible is unjustified; two-year-old children are not terrible. What child wants to be referred to as terrible? What teacher when approached by a director will willingly agree to teach the Terrible Twos? White and Watt (1973) more accurately describe toddlerhood. "The one year old is generally an agreeable child, as are most three year olds, but sometime during the second year of life, our subjects begin asserting themselves, rejecting suggestions, ignoring commands, testing limits, and generally flexing their muscles" (p. 236). Such attempts to become autonomous might better be described as energetic, impulsive, egocentric, but not terrible.

The child at two

If there is an overriding interest of toddlers, it is their desire to act grown up. The most degrading insult is the charge that their behavior is similar to that of babies. They want to do all the things that adults do—cook supper, mow the lawn, and drive a car. Infancy is behind them, and they look forward to meeting the world on their terms. Each uncertain step plunges them ahead, rejoicing unrestrained in small joys adults no longer understand, such as walking up and down stairs unassisted.

It is their physical ability that forms the basis of their cognitive and social-emotional development. "To a child, his body, and what he can do with it is his identity. Most of his activities . . . depend on physical motion" (1970 White House

Reprinted by permission from *Young Children*, Vol. 37, no. 5 (July 1982), pp. 3-13. Copyright © 1982 by National Association for the Education of Young Children, 1834 Connecticut Ave., N.W., Washington, DC 20009.

Conference on Children 1971, p. 44). Their primary mode of learning is through imitation and play with their thinking grounded in action and sensory experiences. Two-year-olds will actively seek sensory experiences. They will touch objects, carefully run their fingers over surfaces, and poke fingers through holes. Although they may have learned to keep things out of their mouths, it is not unusual for them to explore objects with their tongues.

Given a choice, most two-year-old children will select the floor rather than chairs and tables for their activities. The floor provides so much more space: for spreading out puzzle pieces, for looking at the hole at the top of a form box from several angles in order to ascertain which piece will fit, or for just cuddling up close to the teacher as she or he reads a favorite book. Tables and chairs just will not do!

At this stage, toddlers have a few basic words and can string these together. They learn language naturally by hearing it spoken in a concrete context of objects, events, and feelings that have meaning for them, not in structural, formal instruction (Stone and Church 1979). Because their limited verbal abilities cannot meet their linguistic needs, outbursts of crying remain an integral part of their communication. Their inability to adequately communicate their feelings, especially of anger, jealousy, or frustration quickly produces strident howls accompanied by tears. Such outbursts can frighten other toddlers who may join in the crying without understanding its origins.

Program objectives

When teachers understand the developmental needs of two-year-olds, they are ready for the next step in preparing to teach a class of toddlers. These four basic objectives provide the parameters within which a quality program for two-year-old children can be measured. In order to help toddlers become competent, the following objectives will need to be met:

1. The classroom will provide a safe, healthy, and stimulating environment that focuses on action-based sensory experiences.

2. The children will be encouraged and supported in their attempts to care for themselves and become autonomous, and to interact appropriately with other children.

3. A major focus will be on gross motor development.

4. Specific cognitive learning experiences, designed to enhance children's social-emotional and intellectual development, will be provided.

Prepare the physical environment

Set the scene. Nothing surpasses a large, cheerful, clean room for welcoming children. A room that meets licensing requirements for space, but is crowded with tables, chairs, and equipment, may communicate a stifling environment in which there is not enough area for needed movement and exploration. However, too large a room with too many open spaces may not provide the children with the security of limits essential at this stage.

Well-planned rooms show that teachers are in control through the careful organization of the physical environment for the children's safety and enjoyment. The environment should be not only predominantly supportive of individual activity, but should also provide for a few group activities. Materials and equipment, small enough and low enough to allow toddlers to use them comfortably and unassisted, are essential. When the children are seated, their feet should touch the floor, and clothes hooks must be at a height that enables children to hang up their jackets without adult help.

To expect two-year-old children to participate as a group in one activity at the same time for more than a few minutes is foolhardy. They function best on a one-to-one basis, less so in a small group, and even less so in a large group. One technique for providing different types of individual activities simultaneously is to arrange learning centers around the room. Learning centers allow toddlers to grasp new skills or to practice old skills in their own way at their own pace. These children require lots of floor space. Using learning centers makes possible wise use of floor space. The following suggestions might be helpful in setting up a room for two-year-old children:

1. To save time and energy, prepare a

room plan to scale on paper before setting up the room. Locate electrical outlets, doors, and windows. Place the listening center with its tape recorder or phonograph near an outlet. The plants in the science center will need to be near a light source. Clothes hooks should be near the door.

2. Separate noisy activities from quiet ones by using room dividers, shelves, or distance. However, arrange centers so that teacher supervision is always possible.

3. Organize clearly defined centers so that the children know where to find specific materials and what to do with them. Set up only a few centers, but enough to hold children's interest. Place all the materials needed for each activity within the center area.

4. Arrange centers to handle the traffic efficiently. The block area, for example, should be away from the flow of traffic.

5. Place the art center near the water source. Floors and tables should be washable.

6. Erect a permanent indoor gross motor center in which children may climb, slide, jump, etc.

7. Provide centers for individual activities rather than for small group participation. For example, have one table for stringing beads and another table for puzzle making.

8. Keep the dramatic play/housekeeping center very simple. Toddlers find it difficult to share and to play with others, so you will need three or four of each of the key accessories.

9. Provide a large area for music and creative movement involving the whole body.

10. Have a mirror above the wash basin so that children may see how they comb their hair, brush their teeth, etc.

Organize the materials. Materials that extend children's skills and conceptual learning, as well as toddlers' demand for independence, vary in such attributes as color, size (not too small), texture, shape, and complexity. In general, they are concrete and manipulative. Popular items include sets of building blocks with accessories such as vehicles, people, and animals; and interlocking, plain, and brightly colored cubes. Two-year-old children will surprise adults with their concentration on any activity that requires

fitting by twisting and turning. Stringing beads, putting together single-shape puzzles, ordering graduated cyclinders and table blocks, pouring water or sand from one container into another, transferring pebbles or buttons from one container to another with a scoop or large spoon, and manipulating pegs with knobs on pegboards are always inviting to two-year-olds. Miscellaneous nuts, bolts, and rods are enthusiastically sorted. Crayons for toddlers must be large and sturdy, and paper should be big enough to contain their freewheeling, whole-arm movements. Finger paint allows them to express themselves creatively without the restrictions of patterns, which most two-year-old children wisely ignore anyway. Additional materials are balls of varying size for throwing and catching; and clay, Plasticene, and dough clay for pounding and rolling.

A variety of materials arranged on low, open shelves will encourage toddlers to make decisions about what they want to do and to easily return materials after use. Enough materials should be available to provide an interesting and challenging room, but not so many as to overstimulate the children. It is also helpful to provide enough materials so that the need for sharing can be kept at a minimum because toddlers find it difficult to share. Repair or replace materials that break or pieces that are lost. Toddlers can only handle materials in good repair. Selection of sturdy, well-constructed items will prove to be a valuable investment.

Organize the school day. A daily schedule provides a framework for the best use of available time. It should reflect and balance the children's individual and group needs, the teacher's goals, and the school's policies. Such a schedule for a class of two-year-old children must be flexible, but with certain routines carried out at specific times. Within the parameters of center requirements, such as arrival and departure times, schedules should be developed mainly around the physical needs of the children. This means responding to individual patterns of eating, toileting, sleeping, and resting. These guidelines can assist teachers in developing schedules for their group:

1. Balance active and less active times.

2. Alternate quiet and noisy periods in the sequence of activities. For example, large muscle activities may follow naptime.

3. Allow individual activities to predominate, but select a few group activities.

4. Make realistic provisions for toileting.

5. Plan nutritious snack and lunch times, allowing ample time for children to eat in a relaxed, pleasant atmosphere.

6. Designate naptime and resttime. Depending on the length of the day, a resttime may be needed in the morning, and at least two hours should be set aside in the afternoon for sleeping.

7. Offer many opportunities for daily indoor and outdoor motor skill activities.

8. Schedule a short planning time with the children.

Behavior problems are most likely to occur during transitions (Davidson 1980). Toddlers do not like to be interrupted and find it difficult to wait, so unless transition periods are carefully planned, the move from one activity to another will rapidly degenerate into mass confusion. A prearranged plan in which the staff agrees on the procedure for moving the children from one activity or area to another will minimize behavioral problems. It helps if a teacher prepares the children for the move by saying, for example, "It's time to get ready for lunch. Will you please finish what you are doing?"

Whenever possible, it is best to help two-year-olds move to a new activity individually. When this is not possible, a teacher can lead two or three children at a time, while other staff supervise the remaining children. Occasionally it will be necessary for all the children to move simultaneously. A short, clear explanation of the procedures will ensure a reasonable chance of success. Sometimes, singing a song to gather the group will help. One teacher should lead; another should follow the last child. If conflicts arise, it is sometimes possible to offer an alternative, such as, "Let's you and I walk together." If a child poses a serious behavioral problem, a teacher should gently, but firmly, remove the child, accompanying the removal with a brief explanation of the reasons for this action.

Provide social learning activities

Two processes are at work in the teaching/learning environment of a roomful of two-year-old children. First is their awareness that grows out of action, of doing something. Squeals of excitement follow achievement of a new skill. Their feelings of competency are openly expressed and shared. The second process is the response of the adults to children's actions. What is the response of the teacher to that squeal? Annoyance? Delight? Embarrassment? Whether the adults view it as competent or not, good or ill-advised, their responses will influence the children's learning (Stone and Church 1979).

The relationship between a teacher and a group of toddlers is in a constant state of flux. Each time two-year-old children take a new step toward independence, there is a corresponding change in their relationship with the teacher. Flexibility and supportive informality are the most effective base for teacher/child interaction. This does not imply casual teacher behavior. With this age group, teachers must always be in control, tenderly but firmly orchestrating the socialization process.

Toddlers fight over materials with some regularity. Knowing this, teachers can prevent some of the fighting by carefully thinking about which rules are necessary for group living. Apply the cardinal rule of classroom management—the fewer regulations the better; eliminate all but the most basic rules. Child-proof the room so that some rules will not be necessary. For example, have enough favorite materials so that there is less need for constant sharing. Another strategy to prevent sharing problems would be to redirect children to centers where confrontations are unlikely. In a "go away" situation, such as in the housekeeping center in which a child will not accommodate a new player, sometimes the teacher can suggest a positive, face-saving solution, "You could be the mother, and Tom could be the father." Two-year-old children need the assurance that comes from knowing there is someone who can protect them from their own lack of adequate control.

Socialization skills that allow toddlers to live successfully with others in the classroom must be developed. Self-help socialization skills comprise approximately one-third to one-half of a program for toddlers.

In order for a program to function, as well as for two-year-old children to begin the road toward independence, they must be able to independently handle the tasks of dressing, toileting, eating, sleeping, and room cleanup. These skills are not ends in themselves, but rather the means to autonomy. These routine activities, such as hanging up sweaters upon arrival, should be automatic, not topics for daily discussion. Self-help tasks should occur without prompting, saving the children's energies for creative activities.

Dressing. The process of teaching a child to dress or undress can be broken down into several steps. First, the teacher demonstrates the process while explaining the steps involved for the child. Then, while the teacher observes, the child tries one part of the task. After this, the child can be encouraged to continue to be responsible for this aspect of dressing without supervision. As the child becomes ready, the teacher can demonstrate another step, until the child has mastered the entire process. The child is then able to assume full responsibility for dressing or undressing. The teacher's role is to make positive, concrete suggestions, to provide sufficient time for achievement, and to give only enough help to enable a two-year-old to complete the task unassisted. Toddlers can be expected to hang up their clothing as soon as they begin to learn to dress themselves.

Teachers should communicate to parents the necessity for simple, easy-to-manage clothing. In a roomful of two-year-old children who have to dress and undress themselves several times daily, the process should be planned to conserve time and energy and avoid unnecessary frustration. Overalls with attached straps are too cumbersome, as are one-piece suits which usually fit more snugly than separate tops and bottoms. Loose-fitting T-shirts with no buttons or snaps and elasticized pants are marvelous energy savers until the children have learned to button, snap, and zip on practice frames and on the clothing of friends. It is much easier to button a shirt on someone else than to button one's own shirt.

Toileting. One of the major socialization skills for two-year-olds is toileting control. Day control of the bladder can usually be established between the ages of two and two-and-one-half. Teachers should look for the following clues that children give that suggest that they are ready to be toilet trained:

- the ability to stay dry for several hours,
- self-awareness of when there is a need to urinate, indicated by facial expression or body stance (usually holding of genitals just before urination), and the ability to follow simple directions.

Children who are identified as physically ready then are given responsibility to acknowledge that they have control over their bodies and are in charge. Individual children may need to use the potty at different times during the day, but it is helpful to have regular times for toileting as well. Most teachers take the children to the bathroom before naptime, for instance.

To help two-year-olds take complete care of their toileting needs without any assistance, the teacher can divide the process into small, teachable steps. Children need to learn to recognize their internal warning signals, go to the potty chair, lift the lid, lower their pants, seat themselves, wait until elimination is achieved, wipe themselves, redress themselves, and flush the toilet or empty the pot. Urination training can generalize to defecation so that separate training is usually unnecessary. Azrin and Foxx (1974) suggest a demonstration of role-playing the procedure by having a doll that wets; the two-year-old can then toilet train the doll.

To avoid accidents, children need a readily accessible bathroom, easy-to-pull-down clothing, and potty chairs for those too short to sit on a larger toilet comfortably. Teachers can talk with the children about their internal warning signals, using the word for the need to urinate that the child's parents prefer. Some commonly used words are urinate, wet, tinkle, peepee, and potty. Once in the bathroom a few toys may give the child time to develop a sense of privacy. A timer can remind the busy teacher that a child is in the bathroom. Finally, each child's success must be followed with praise. The combination of children's physical and emotional readiness, and the parents' and teachers' consistency in attending to toileting generally will assure development of bladder and bowel control.

Eating. With few exceptions, two-year-old children love to feed themselves, but adult guidance is needed to limit the spills so their table behaviors do not repulse others. Enough adults are needed to assure careful supervision. Try serving family style with only three or four children and an adult at each table; seat the children so they are not within easy reach of each other. The size and placement of the tables and chairs should allow them to eat comfortably. Spoons and forks need to be small enough for toddlers to manipulate, with all dishes of nonbreakable materials. Snacks and meals should be scheduled at specific times. Having the children help prepare and serve class snacks makes food and eating more enjoyable, and it provides an opportunity for children to learn about a variety of foods and develop their fine muscles and eye-hand coordination.

Sleeping. Most two-year-old children nap from one to two hours daily. If a child does not sleep, a rest period is still essential in order to prevent fatigue. Naptime should be at the same time each day, usually after lunch. Allow enough time for the naptime preparations to be leisurely completed. A darkened room should be ready. As the children quietly enter their sleeping area, they can get their own mats or cots and place these in their assigned places. Within the constraints of the room, children should be as far apart from each other as possible. For those who need it, a favorite toy or blanket may help in preparing for sleep. Once down on a mat in a darkened room, most toddlers will fall asleep within minutes. For a few, sleep will come more quickly if an adult pats their backs rhythmically or sings a lullaby.

Room cleanup. With supervision, two-year-old children can help with simple cleanup chores. A few basic rules that are systematically enforced will generally assure that cleanup of a room goes smoothly. To maintain an orderly classroom, two-year-old children can learn to:

1. Keep their materials within the appropriate center or area. For example, if children want to build with blocks, they may do so only within the block area.

2. Carry materials on trays for easier handling.

3. Use both hands to hold trays, or other items.

4. Carry only one thing at a time.

5. Return each material to its storage place when they are finished and before getting anything else.

6. Pull out chairs safely and push chairs in after getting up.

As the children gradually become responsible for the materials in their room, they will learn to use language to communicate, engage in cooperative, responsible behaviors, and solve problems.

Provide physical development activities

Gross motor. A substantial portion of the day will be used for children's gross motor skill development, both indoors and outdoors. Such an emphasis on large muscle development will require large blocks of time for supervised free play. Outdoor equipment should include special equipment that will encourage children to climb, walk, ride, jump, push, slide, etc. For indoor gross motor activities, a rug will help to limit such active play to one area and to control the noise, as well as provide a safe, soft cushion for strenuous physical activities.

Watch a group of two-year-olds outdoors at play. The children seem to be in constant motion. The quiet intervals between activities are brief as they hurry to begin and to finish motor activities. Wheel toys that they can sit on and push are a favorite. Two-year-old children like to handle large objects; thus they enjoy rolling, tossing, or just walking about with large, light balls. Children will climb on climbing sets, crawl under and through them, and engage in lively dramatic play around them. Because of their need to develop physically at this time, children enjoy obstacle course equipment such as large tires and boxes or plastic figures to crawl on, climb through, or just to quietly sit on and watch the other children playing.

Fine motor. Only by having sensory experiences with materials such as pegs, puzzles, shapes, and blocks can two-year-old children develop control of their small muscles and eye-hand coordination. They need to be able to handle materials, move them about, and play with them.

One way to prevent loss of the many small pieces of manipulative materials is to place the materials for each activity on individual trays or rug samples. Plastic pet bowls placed on trays are difficult to tip and easy to clean. Plastic cutlery storage trays are ideal for sorting wooden cubes, washers, etc.

Two-year-olds enjoy puzzles that have easy-to-grasp knobs on single shapes, such as those with a discrete apple, banana, and strawberry. Self-help skills can be practiced with frames for zipping, buttoning, and snapping.

Provide cognitive learning activities

The thinking of two-year-old children is decidedly different from that of older children and adults. Until rather recently, very little was known about children's thinking. Today because of Piaget's interest in how children acquire knowledge, we understand much more about intellectual development. We know, for example, that the learning of two-year-old children is very concrete and that abstract thinking follows much later. Because toddlers are egocentric, they can best understand experiences in relation to themselves. Consequently, much of their learning occurs through physical activity in direct interaction with their surroundings. As concrete sensory experiences build upon each other, these young children gradually come to recognize likenesses and differences, to categorize, to learn colors and basic shapes, to understand relationships between actual objects and pictures of the objects, to increase their ability to reason, to solve problems, and to make comparisons.

The development of internal representation has begun, albeit falteringly, as two-year-old children begin to use symbols to represent objects.

> Between the age of about 1½ years and the age of 7 or 8 years when the concrete operations appear, the practical logic of sensory-motor intelligence goes through a period of being internalized, of taking shape in thought at the level of representation rather than taking place only in the actual carrying out of action. (Piaget 1970, p. 45)

Of all the skills toddlers develop, language is by far the most marvelous. Language maturity follows a sequence of emerging from concrete experiences that stimulate thinking, and in turn, foster language. Chukovsky (1968) has written, ". . . beginning with the age of two, every child becomes for a short period of time a linguistic genius" (p. 7). One-word utterances begin around 12 months of age; at about age 2 children are ready to put words together. From then on, toddlers' sentences steadily increase in length and accuracy. They enjoy repetition whether in language or games like Find Me. At this age the phenomenal growth of language is greatly influenced by adults who are available to talk with the children, listen to them, and elicit responses from them (see Cazden 1981).

There are many activities with which teachers can stimulate the intellectual capacities and language of two-year-old children. All the activities should be fun for the children and generate the far-reaching benefits of a positive attitude toward learning and problem solving.

Begin by surrounding the children with an environment that values reading and thinking and encourages problem solving and communication. Have lots of books and magazines available. Stories, told or read aloud, are a major instructional strategy. In storytelling, children hear rich and varied language. To get the attention of toddlers and keep it, it is important to choose stories that are of interest to them and that will further their development. Stories about families, animals, nursery rhymes, and make believe are favorites. Once the child is sitting as close to you as possible, probably on your lap, begin with a succinct introduction in which the child is prepared for the story. Following the storytelling, give the child a chance to comment upon the characters or relate some aspect of the story to personal experiences. Once the story is familiar, the child can turn the pages and read the pictures.

Gordon (1970) and Gordon, Guinagh, and Jester (1972) suggest many activities that children will enjoy and that prepare them for reading. Recommended is a variation of the game in which an object is hidden in one of three cans with the size of the can in which the object is hidden the significant cue. Occasionally put the object under the can at the far left and shuffle the cans, making sure the object ends up at the left. Repeat shuffling until the toddler always selects the can on the far left. While playing, the adult can introduce the words, *left, right,* and *middle.* Another way to play is to select cans with labels the children will recognize.

Cooking is a basic experience that can be used to teach mathematical concepts such as one-to-one correspondence, more than, less than, and measurement. It is impossible to cook without talking about food names and mentioning sifting, pouring, stirring, etc. Cooking is a superb occasion to teach children what foods are good for them and how to prepare them.

Another activity that supports language and intellectual development is classroom telephone communication. Children can hold make-believe conversations with the teacher and with one another. Many other activities also fascinate them. Simple jigsaw puzzles are challenging and self-correcting so toddlers will not get bored. Try having the children name and classify familiar objects by placing those that belong on one tray and the remaining ones on another tray. Guide the children to explain their reasons for doing so. Classification activities are almost limitless— fruits, vegetables, shapes, colors, sizes, etc. (see Spitzer 1977). Although two-year-old children will not be able to learn to sing many complete songs, they delight in filling in familiar words and phrases to their favorites.

The real world of teaching toddlers centers on the socialization of the children in a safe and stimulating environment as the basis for extending their cognitive abilities. It is much more than routinely caring for children's physical needs of sleeping, eating, eliminating, or playing. What can two-year-old children do in nursery school? They can learn social skills, become autonomous, and through action and sensorimotor cognitive activities live as competent, happy toddlers.

References

Alschuler, R. H. *Two to Six: Suggestions for Parents of Young Children.* New York: William Morrow, 1933.

Azrin, N. H., and Foxx, R. M. *Toilet Training in Less Than a Day.* New York: Pocket Books, 1974.

Chukovsky, K. *From Two to Five.* Los Angeles, Calif.: University of California Press, 1968.

Cazden, C. B., ed. *Language in Early Childhood Education. Revised ed.* Washington, D.C.: National Association for the Education of Young Children, 1981.

Davidson, J. "Wasted Time: The Ignored Dilemma." *Young Children* 35, no. 4 (May 1980): 13-21.

Gordon, I. J. *Baby Learning Through Baby Play: A Parent's Guide for the First Two Years.* New York: St. Martin's Press, 1970.

Gordon, I. J.; Guinagh, B.; and Jester, R. E. *Child Learning Through Child Play.* New York: St. Martin's Press, 1972.

Piaget, J. *Genetic Epistemology.* New York: Columbia University Press, 1970.

Report to the President: White House Conference on Children. Washington, D.C.: U.S. Government Printing Office, 1971.

Spitzer, D. R. *Concept Formation and Learning in Early Childhood.* Columbus, Ohio: Merrill, 1977.

Stewart, I. *Introduction to Early Childhood Education.* Houston, Tex.: University of Houston Press, 1977.

Stone, L. J., and Church, J. *Childhood and Adolescence.* New York: Random House, 1979.

U.S. Bureau of the Census, Current Population Reports, Series P-25, No. 704. Washington, D.C.: U.S. Government Printing Office, 1977.

White, B. L., and Watt, J. C. *Experience and Environment.* Englewood Cliffs, N.J.: Prentice-Hall, 1973.

Very Early Childhood Education for Infants and Toddlers

Christine Z. Cataldo

Christine Z. Cataldo is Director, Early Childhood Research Center, and Assistant Professor of Early Childhood Education, State University of New York at Buffalo. She is the author of Infant and Toddler Programs: A Guide to Very Early Childhood Education *(Addison-Wesley, 1982).*

WHEN DISCUSSING the subject of infant programs, it is not unusual to be greeted with the comment, "But, what can you do with a baby?" Unlike the more familiar notion of good day care for the very young, education under 3 is a rather new concept. Yet, the infant or toddler who participates in a group situation gains something special, something that can be described as educational. When needed, infant programs can also serve a role in preventing and remediating developmental problems.

Part-time infant/toddler programs can be incorporated into many different types of preschool and child care settings. If babies are expected to gain from their participation in such an effort, the group must be small, the environment organized, and the adults alert and responsive. Once these basics are established, it is important to employ strategies that pinpoint and describe how education for infants and toddlers is actually carried out. These strategies will be discussed in the context of the overall purposes of infant and toddler programming.

Purposes of Infant and Toddler Education

Implementation of any effective program involves understanding of intended purposes and scope. Two major themes emerge from an examination of published material for teachers and caregivers who work with the very young. One is that programs should help the baby fully develop the sequence of specific skills and abilities thought to express and develop competence in growth and learning (Caldwell and Stedman, 1977; Cohen, 1977; Day and Parker, 1977; Fowler, 1980). Achievement of these "milestone" behaviors and skills enables the infant to become increasingly competent in such areas as motor control, experimentation and mastery with toys, communication and expression, and successful interactions with others.

When focusing upon these abilities, program staff members facilitate and monitor the baby's development by conscious attention to progress. Through play, stimulation and thoughtful caregiving, infants and toddlers are helped to learn and understand more about what they experience around them. Thus, skills are not usually taught in the didactic sense; they emerge with encouragement and improve with adult mediation and appropriate materials. The methods are informal but meaningful and educational in nature.

The second major purpose of infant programs, which has both historical tradition and contemporary validity, is to help

From *Childhood Education,* January/February 1982, pp. 149-154. Reprinted by permission of Christine Z. Cataldo and the Association for Childhood Education International, 3615 Wisconsin Avenue, N.W., Washington, D.C. Copyright ©1982 by the Association.

the baby develop a personal and social self. This includes the ability to manage feelings, maintain relationships and demonstrate individuality (Gonzalez-Mena and Eyer, 1980; Jones, 1980; Willis and Riccuiti, 1975). Babies are, in a sense, emergent people. Their temperament and personal style take on the dimensions of a personality during the first 4 years of life. From the time that infants begin to demonstrate food preferences, toy interests or special abilities, adults play a role in forming character. Professionals contribute to the child's developing personal-social style by the manner in which they handle the baby's feelings and needs. The attention and affection that are provided, the behaviors that are respected, the qualities that are valued—these grow into positive self-concepts and feelings of worth that help the baby grow up confident and capable.

Thus, these two overall goals of infant and toddler education reflect recent trends toward general competence and well-being in home and day care (Aston, 1971; Caplan and Caplan, 1977; Leach, 1976; White, 1975) and toward acquisition of developmental milestones such as in curriculum-style materials and early intervention (Karnes, 1979; Koch, 1976; Levy, 1973; Marzollo and Lloyd, 1972; Meier and Malone, 1979; Painter, 1971; Sparling and Lewis, 1981; Stein 1976; and Watrin and Furfey, 1978).

Differences in Infant Versus Preschool Programming

In establishing the value for the early years of social exchanges, play opportunities, experiential learning, a carefully planned environment, and supportive attention of adults, early childhood education has contributed greatly to the structure and form of infant and toddler programs. Yet there are some important priorities for infants and toddlers that create additional program qualities.

Babies have urgent physical, emotional and developmental needs. The interpersonal and environmental features of the program therefore become critical to effectiveness. With babies, more attention is focused upon one-to-one physical care, the adults' emotional availability, and the stimulation of, and response to, basic developmental growth. This makes infant education intensely personal in nature—a difference from the more distal, group-centered management of the social and physically skilled preschooler.

Also important at the infant level is an appropriate response to the very rapid pace at which development proceeds in the opening years of life. This requires that infant education focus upon developmental progessions in abilities as well as in personal development. Teachers and caregivers need to monitor and consciously enhance learning in these areas. This differs somewhat from the primary use of incidental and discovery learning and peer social learning that predominate at the preschool level.

Still other developmental qualities of infants and toddlers dictate program concerns. For example, infants are vulnerable to extremes in stimulation—too much can be distressing, too little can depress motivation and learning. Toddler's egocentrism and independence strivings are often misunderstood; the behavior is not as problematic when adults perceive its contribution to growth and the role of preventive planning in its control.

Finally, adults who work with babies need some special skills (Honig and Lally, 1981). They must be able to observe and meet specific needs in each individual child, against a backdrop of knowledge of overall developmental norms from birth to 3 and 4 years. They must also be emotionally responsive, enjoy the physical contact involved in the care of babies, and appreciate the give-and-take needed to manage the active toddler. In cases where developmental delays are apparent, the teacher/caregiver needs some competence in conducting specific exercises or providing experiences that focus on identified needs, especially in the motor and language domains.

To highlight these differences between infant and preschool programming is not to imply any discontinuity. Indeed, there may be more commonality than is often recognized. But it is important to clarify how the special qualities of infants and toddlers influence the roles of teachers, the design of environments and the implementation of educational policies and programs.

Infant Program Strategies

The process of education in childhood can be said to begin in the bassinet or, more appropriately, in the arms of a loving parent. Following this secure beginning, when the infant is stabilized in body functions (usually 3-4 months) and healthy enough to be exposed to others, he or she can most likely participate in a small group program. Of course, parents need to feel that program goals and strategies are complementary to the family experience. After completing a gradual introduction to the program setting and staff, the baby is usually able to play and respond to others without much stress associated with separation from the parent. Indeed, many mothers and fathers can serve as regularly scheduled participant/helpers—a valued program feature (Cataldo, 1980).

Basic good caregiving of babies is essential. An effective program also employs an assortment of educational strategies. Discussed below are a "basic dozen" such ingredients in this process, all of which apply to any type of part- or full-time, home- or center-based program for these very early years.

An educational infant/toddler program provides:

□ *Energetic teachers,* in adequate numbers, who talk to babies, encourage them to try new skills, watch for their needs, and mediate their experiences so that learning and personal growth are supported. The teacher/caregiver works with babies within the daily program, using many naturally occurring learning opportunities, responding quickly to needs and giving abundant affection and praise. This interpersonal aspect of the program is most critical in assuring a pleasant and personal experience for the child.

□ *A cheerful, secure environment* that provides both familiarity and variety, promotes good feelings in its atmosphere, and facilitates open, child-paced learning in its materials and arrangements. This environment contains playthings and equipment appropriate for the first 3 years of life. They are organized into relatively distinct "interest areas" that reflect a range of typical infant and toddler activities; i.e., an exercise area, block and vehicle area, small manipulative toy area, quiet area, potty/diaper area, etc. Toys are well-maintained (commercial and teacher-made) and available most of the day.

□ *Playmates* who model different approaches to people and playthings, who share and participate in discoveries and reflect comparable feelings and needs. Peers are a source of play and learning for babies; they help each other to develop language and social-interactional abilities. Even very young babies respond to the nearness of one another with smiles, vocalizations and touching. Toddlers learn important social rules and the rudiments of respect and concern for others.

□ *An abundance of available playthings* designed to encourage learning at many levels of difficulty and in all areas of development, including those emphasizing physical mastery, imagination and problem-solving. Small toys, a variety of sensory and art materials, and larger pieces of commercial equipment provide sensory, manipulative and peer experiences through play. With adult guidance, they are used by infants and toddlers in a way that builds intellectual, physical and social skills. Toys are an important part of the young child's world of daily play and exploration. Adults can observe toy uses to determine the child's developmental status and personal interests.

□ *Simple games* designed to stimulate good feelings and positive, play-oriented interactions with others. They also develop habits of attention and task persistence. Examples include games with balls, dolls, rubber animals, hidden objects, and surprise and peek-a-boo games. Such games help adults and children to attend and interact—then become familiar with one another in a play situation. Those which are easy to master also help babies to feel competent and involved.

□ *Daily routines* that help to organize the day and provide repeated contact with familiar people and events. Routines can assure that babies' needs are met with consistency. Often a good deal of the learning and emotional/social support provided to infants and toddlers is integrated into such daily routines as dressing, washing, diapering and eating. This is done informally, with conversation and affectionate game playing as routines are carried out. The child not only learns names for things and procedures for independent care of self but experiences a sense of security as well.

□ *Meaningful sensory and language experiences* that aid perception, self-expression, thinking and communication. Concrete, participatory activities with varying textures, sights and sounds help babies to grow in their abilities to observe and understand. Experiences with natural objects, music, fluid media (sand, water, clay), playhouses with role play props, and books and pictures enable children to feel, see, hear and talk throughout the program. These enriching activities provide an experiential base for present and later intellectual development.

□ *Planned and spontaneous task-oriented activities* that challenge and reinforce developing skills, reveal needs, and provide stimulation and opportunities to discover new competencies. Babies are urged to work with simple nesting toys, puzzles, take-apart games, assorted containers and climbing equipment. As they work with these materials, they grow in ability and reveal to their teachers special needs for further experience.

□ *Space and frequent opportunities* for independent exploration, discovery and practice that enable infants and toddlers to play at their own pace with activities of their own choosing. Unstructured time, open (but organized) physical space, and the appropriate withdrawal of teacher instruction are often necessary to development of the child's motivation to participate in learning as a self-satisfying activity. Even the youngest babies need some free time to express themselves and demonstrate some self-reliance, to try out skills and to look for interesting play situations. Through observation of this process of self-definition, teachers/caregivers receive help in understanding the child's needs and interests.

□ *Small and brief group times* in which babies can attend to others, participate with adults and share with their peers a specific activity. Simple participatory songs and stories, with gestures, help to develop social skills and the pleasure felt in joining a play group. Small infants enjoy watching others; older babies and toddlers can participate in ten minutes of a singing, puppetry or rhythmic activity. Often these times provide very special periods of lively amusement for everyone in the program.

□ *Quiet periods* alone or with relaxed, affectionate adults to permit a baby to be cuddled or be passive, to gather energy for other activities or quietly play with a favorite toy. Individual rest times are very important to the infant/toddler program. They not only protect children from overstimulation and exhaustion but also enable adults to provide the soothing physical contact, rocking, snuggling and stroking that are important aspects of babies' involvement with others.

□ *Opportunities for adults to observe and record* individual and group progress in accordance with developmental guidelines. These norms provide a starting point, but they also need to be weighted against each child's unique history and developmental-personal pattern of growth. The maintenance of accurate information about children's status and behavior is the responsibility of all educational programs. With appropriate adjustments of norms and standards, programs can support development yet allow the baby's own developmental clock to operate. The professional should watch closely to determine the significance of any signs of consistent difficulties or extended delays and to provide assistance as needed to bolster the child's progress.

Summary

This discussion of strategies used in conducting an effective educational program for infants and toddlers provides a snapshot of the world of very early childhood education—a skeletal overview of the special qualities of a good program for babies. If recent trends continue, the concept of infant and toddler education will become a permanent part of educational planning for preschool children in diverse settings, and definitions of quality will be more thoroughly understood.

Bibliography
Aston, A. *How To Play with Your Baby*. Larchmont, NY: Fountain, 1971.

3. DEVELOPMENT AND EDUCATIONAL OPPORTUNITIES: Infant and Toddler Programs

Brazelton, T. *Toddlers and Parents*. New York: Dell, 1974.

―――. *Infants and Mothers*. New York: Dell, 1969.

Caldwell, B., and Stedman. *Infant Education: A Guide for Helping the Handicapped in the First Three Years*. New York: Walker and Co. for TADS, NC, 1977.

Caplan, F., and T. Caplan. *The Parenting Advisor*. Garden City, NY: Anchor-Doubleday, 1977.

Cataldo, C. "The Parent as Learner: Early Childhood Parent Programs." *Educational Psychologist* 15 (1980): 172-186.

Cohen, M., ed. *Developing Programs for Infants and Toddlers*. Washington, DC: ACE1, 1977.

Day, M., and R. Parker. *The Preschool in Action: Exploring Early Childhood Programs* (2nd edition). Boston: Allyn and Bacon, 1977.

Evans, B., and G. Saia. *Day Care for Infants: The Case for Infant Day Care and a Practical Guide*. Boston: Beacon Press, 1972.

Fowler, W. *Infant and Child Care: A Guide to Education in Group Settings*. Boston: Allyn and Bacon, 1980.

Gonzalez-Mena, J., and D. Eyer. *Infancy and Caregiving*. Palo Alto, CA Mayfield, 1980.

Gordon, Ira. *The Infant Experience*. Columbus, OH: Charles E. Merrill Publishing Co., 1975.

Herbert-Jackson, E.; M. O'Brien; J. Porterfield and T. Risley. *The Infant Center*. Baltimore, MD: University Park Press, 1977.

Honig, A., and R. Lally. *Infant Caregiving: A Design for Training* (2nd edition). Syracuse, NY: University Press, 1981.

Jones, E., ed. *Supporting the Growth of Infants and Toddlers*. Pasadena, CA: Pacific Oaks College, 1980.

Karnes, M. *Small Wonder! Activities for Baby's First 18 Months*. Circle Pines, MN: American Guidance Service, 1979.

Koch, Jaroslav. *Total Baby Development*. New York: Wyden, 1976.

Leach, P. *Babyhood*. New York: Knopf, 1976.

Levy, J. *The Baby Exercise Book*. New York: Pantheon, 1973.

Marzolla, J., and J. Lloyd. *Learning Through Play*. New York: Harper Calaphon, 1972.

Meier, J., and P. Malone. *Facilitating Children's Development: A Systematic Guide for Open Learning*. Baltimore, MD: University Park Press, 1979.

Painter, G. *Teach Your Baby*. New York: Simon and Schuster, 1971.

Segal, M., and D. Adcock. *From Birth to One Year/From One to Two Years*. Rolling Hills Estates, CA: B. L. Winch and Associates, 1979.

Sparling, J., and I. Lewis. *Infant Learningames: Resources for a Parent-Child Partnership*. New York: Walker and Co., 1981.

Stein, S. *New Parents' Guide to Early Learning*. New York: Plume, 1976.

Watrin, R., and P. Furfey. *Learning Activities for the Young Preschool Child*. New York: D. Van Nostrand Co., 1978.

White, B. *The First Three Years of Life*. Princeton, NJ: Prentice-Hall, 1975.

Willemson, E. *Understanding Infancy*. San Francisco, CA: Freeman, 1979.

Willis, A., and H. Riccuiti. *A Good Beginning for Babies*. Washington, DC: NAEYC, 1975.

Day Care in America

*With the surge of working mothers and single-parent families,
millions of our children are being left alone each day, and millions
more entrusted to care that is haphazard, unregulated
and sometimes dangerous. Here's what must be done
to curb the growing chaos*

Carl T. Rowan and
David M. Mazie

Every weekday morning across America, millions of parents leave home with a briefcase or lunch box in one hand and a youngster or two clinging to the other, a touching sign of the times. Along the way, Mom or Dad will stop to deposit the children with someone who will care for them while the parents work. As they kiss their kids good-by, many of these mothers and fathers are nagged by doubts: Is my child in safe hands? Should I be staying home with him? Can we afford this?

Yet these parents are more at ease than those who must leave infants in the care of young brothers and sisters, hoping that an older relative will drop by. Or the women who sit home on welfare, unable to work because they have no one to take care of their children.

Growing Crisis. With the dramatic increase in single-parent households and those in which both parents work, America has truly plunged into the Age of Child Care. In 1984, over two-thirds of American women with school-age children worked outside their homes (compared with about one-half in 1975). In the future, even more of our children will take their first steps and learn their ABCs under the tutelage of people other than their parents.

What this means is that millions of children are subjected to social and emotional risks that no one fully understands. But if this troubles many parents and child psychologists, it is also increasingly accepted as a reality of life. A Massachusetts mother summarized her own situation: "Day care has given me the freedom to get an education so that I can find employment and someday get totally out of the welfare system."

The U.S. Commission on Civil Rights cites *lack* of adequate child care as a main obstacle preventing some disadvantaged mothers from escaping poverty. "Increasing the availability of good child care is one of the most pressing human-resource issues facing us today," declares Gov. Thomas Kean of New Jersey, speaking for the National Governors' Association. "The health and welfare of our children depend on it. And, increasingly, the success of American business depends on it."

Yet, it's often easier to find a good job than good child care. Waiting lists for child-care programs are enormous. By one count there are only about seven million day-care slots available in the United States. That means at least an equal number of children 13 and under are left alone without supervision for part of the day.

The stories you hear about them are troubling. Like the mother in Wichita, Kan., who took her youngsters to work and left them all day in her car at her factory's parking lot. Or the seven-year-old Cleveland "latchkey" boy who would come home to an empty house after school, lock himself in the bathroom and pray that no one would break in.

"We are facing a child-care crisis in this country," says Marian Wright Edelman, president of the Children's Defense Fund, a nonpartisan research and lobbying organization. And the crisis is growing as more mothers enter the work force.

Charges of Abuse. There was a time when working parents would have simply left these children at home with a grandmother. Today, that grandmother is unlikely to live in the same city, and even if she does, she may be working herself. So parents look elsewhere for help, and what they find is what one observer calls "child care-lessness," a bewildering, expensive hodge-podge of choices, ranging from terrific to terrible.

Basically, there are two types of child-care facilities: family day homes, in which a few youngsters are cared for by a woman in her own home, and day-care centers which provide care for larger numbers.

More than two-thirds of day-care kids are in family day homes; the Children's Defense Fund estimates there are over five million such slots. Family day homes are usually less expensive than centers and have more flexible hours. The care-giver is often a neighborhood mother, who can pay close attention to the kids and is almost a substitute parent. For this reason, the homes are especially popular for babies and toddlers.

Day-care centers come in all sizes and styles. They're found in churches, schools, meeting halls, office buildings and storefronts. They may be run by individuals, community groups, churches, schools and other public agencies, parent co-ops, employers or by nationally franchised chains. Some programs are much like the family day homes—games, story-telling, playtime, naps, meals. Others put more emphasis on educational activities and therefore resemble nursery schools.

Whichever form parents choose, many will have ambivalent feelings about turning their children over to someone else—especially after the news stories that broke last year. Seven teachers in a privately owned day-care center in Manhattan Beach, Calif., including the center's founder, were charged with 207 counts of sexual abuse on small children, allegedly occurring over the last nine years. This was followed by the indictment of three persons on charges ranging from sexual abuse to rape or sodomy at a city-financed child-care center in the Bronx, New York. Other reports of sexual abuse in child-care settings have come from Texas, Florida and South Carolina.

Kids or Jobs. The most serious problems of child care are staffing and regulation. The low salaries (two-thirds of care-givers earn less than poverty-level incomes) are bringing unqualified, and perhaps even dangerous, people into the field. Most states don't run a thorough background check on employees or inspect facilities often. The issue is especially severe in family day homes, of which up to 75 percent are unlicensed. But child-care professionals have tackled the question of quality, setting up a voluntary accreditation system for early-childhood programs and offering a training course that gives individuals credentials in child development.

How to Choose a Day-Care Program

IF YOU'RE THINKING of home care, talk at length with the person who will be providing it. Is she warm and understanding, experienced, attuned to your own philosophy of child-rearing? Look over the play area, kitchen, bathroom, napping space. Is the home clean and safe?

At day-care centers, while a spacious, pleasant setting and ample equipment are important, the critical factor is the general mood. Do the children seem happy and busy? Are the staff members friendly, relaxed, attentive? What is the ratio of staff to children?

How much experience and training does the staff have? How long have they worked there?

Check out the activities schedule. Is time allotted for outdoor as well as indoor play, with a good variety of activities?

Before making any decision, consult with parents who have children in the day-care home or center. Once you've chosen a place, drop in without warning now and then. Talk with your children regularly about how things are going, and listen to what they say. If you get any hint of trouble, ask questions and compare notes with other parents. Parental alertness is the key to safe child care.

Cutbacks in public assistance have increased the shortage of good, affordable day care. Direct federal subsidies for child care rose in the 1970s until about $650 million a year was paid to states to provide licensed care for some 750,000 children from low- and moderate-income families. But that funding was slashed by 14 percent in 1981, and related federal programs were reduced or eliminated. Although Congress restored some of this money in 1983, funding is still far below earlier levels.

The shortage of day care is especially acute for infants, who require more costly care. The average family can afford to spend about ten percent of its gross income on child care, but services for infants may cost as much as $50 to $150 a week. That is well beyond ten percent of the incomes of most single parents, working poor, and even many middle-class families.

When federal subsidies were slashed, further cutbacks by most states forced working families to pay more. "Thousands of parents are faced with excruciating choices," says Rep. George Miller (D., Calif.). "Either leave the kids alone, or leave their jobs."

Necessity, Not Luxury. To increase the supply of child care, improve its quality and make it more affordable, we need a cooperative effort that involves every segment of society.

Private Business. Around 11:30 each weekday morning, accountant Kathy Zweber leaves the Zale Corporation office in Irving, Texas, and walks across a parking lot to a modernistic one-story building. There, her son Zack is crawling on the floor with playmates in Zale's child-care center. "Ready for lunch?" Kathy asks. She sits in a chair and nurses him. Afterward, Kathy and Zack play a few minutes, and then she returns to work.

This is day care at its most convenient. Parents need not go out of their way to drop children off, and they're close by if a child gets sick.

"Corporate-sponsored day care is the fastest-growing employee benefit of the eighties," says Dana Friedman, a senior research fellow with the Conference Board, a non-profit business-research organization. She estimates that about 1850 American companies now provide some sort of child-care support, compared with only about 100 in 1978.

Some companies, in lieu of their own day-care center, pay for part or all of their workers' day-care costs. Some contract with child-care vendors for a certain number of spaces for employees; others offer referral services to match programs and parents. IBM has funded more than 200 community-based organizations or paid local consultants to provide information and guidance to IBM employees on selecting child care.

Employers generally find that their involvement with child care is good business. They report recruitment is easier, turnover down, absenteeism reduced and productivity increased. "When parents know children are being cared for nearby, they are less distracted by worries and stress," says Zale's Michael Romaine, a vice president of the company and head of its child-care association. He estimates that 40 percent of the employees using the Zale center came to work at the company because of it.

Still, only one percent of businesses offer any sort of child-care help. Dana Friedman reported that lack of knowledge is a principal reason: 49 of 50 company officials she spoke with had never even heard of child-care needs.

But the situation is likely to change. A new generation is moving into corporate management, and they know first-hand about conflicts of work and family. Government is also helping to spread the word; the White House has sponsored meetings to educate chief executives about child-care options and the tax benefits of support for private industry.

Community organizations. Churches are the largest provider of early-childhood programs, with more than 18,000 church-based centers, half operated by the congregations, half by others using church space.

Civic groups are also helping. Junior Leagues, for example, have projects throughout the country, including a demonstration childcare subsidy program, referral operations, and an after-school telephone support system for latchkey children. Many other groups, from labor unions to service clubs, sponsor one or two poor kids for a day-care "scholarship," or provide volunteers, or furnish space, materials and other help.

Government. Without federal support, says the House Select Committee on Children, Youth, and Families, "the supply of day care accessible to lower-income families will not keep pace with the increase in demand," with likely damage to the physical, emotional and educational needs of the children. At a minimum, Congress should restore the funds for direct aid and food programs that were cut in 1981. Washington should also develop national standards that states and localities could use as a guide for their facilities.

State and local governments can play key roles in promoting child care, and a number are doing so. California established a network of 61 agencies throughout the state to help educate parents regarding child care and to provide technical assistance to care-givers. New York City has made available approximately 500 day-care openings for the children of teen mothers, who then are able to go back to school. In Dallas, a mayor's task force was established to mobilize and coordinate childcare efforts. And elsewhere, a number of communities have begun programs of before- and after-school care in their public schools.

Parents. In the end, responsibility falls most heavily on parents themselves. They must exert political pressure on the government, let employers know their needs, enlist the aid of community organizations and, most important, become knowledgeable consumers of quality care for their children.

In Reston, Va., parents formed a cooperative nonprofit day-care center that now serves 300 children and is still owned by the parents. A California mother persuaded her employer, an electronics company, to set up a child-care center in a nearby vacant school building. In Des Moines, Iowa, Tiny Tot Child Care, Inc., has become a model of inner-city child care because its founder and director, Evelyn Davis, got parents involved from the start.

GOOD CHILD CARE is a necessity, not a luxury. It should be a vital concern for *everyone,* not just the parents of young children, because it touches so many aspects of our lives—productivity, poverty, education, women's rights, health. It is not meant to replace the family, but to strengthen and support it.

To be sure, there is no simple, quick, cheap solution to the problem of providing quality care to all who need it. But if every individual and every institution that is concerned about the needs of our children pitches in, the job can be done.

The Day-Care Child

Alison Clarke-Stewart

Alison Clarke-Stewart is an assistant professor in the departments of education and human development at the University of Chicago and the author of "Daycare" (Harvard University Press).

Today in families across the United States the mothers of 8 million preschool children will go out to work.

About half of these working mothers are able to arrange their work schedules so that their husbands or a relative can watch their children while they are at work. The rest must put their children in some kind of day care. Most of them would prefer a licensed day-care center or nursery school. But such centers are not always available or are too expensive for the family budget, so the majority use informal day-care arrangements: with a sitter or housekeeper in their own home, or with a neighbor, a friend, or a day-care home provider in her home.

In any of these care arrangements not involving relatives, the child spends a substantial amount of time under the supervision of people who are not "family." Quite appropriately, working mothers have been concerned about the effects that this care will have on their child's development. Will the child be disciplined in the way they like? Will he get enough attention from a caring adult? Will he get enough food and exercise? Will he be treated kindly? Will his mind be stimulated? Will he become detached and alienated from his family?

If the child is cared for outside his own home, what will be the effect of his spending so much time with other children? Will the other children pick on him or teach him bad habits? Will he become unruly, whiny, disobedient? Will he get too dependent on his peers? Will he become too aggressive or competitive? Will he become too submissive?

What will be the long-term effects of this day-care experience? Will he do as well in school as an entirely home-raised child? Will he be a successful, individualistic adult or a conformist weakling?

It is natural that mothers anxiously ask themselves such questions since, working or not, they are still responsible for their child's well-being. Unfortunately, many authorities on child development have not been of great help in allaying mothers' worries about fulltime day care. They have advised mothers simply to stay home, at least until their child is old enough to go to school, rather than run the risk of putting him in day care.

But most mothers who are working today do not have the option of staying home. They work because they *have* to in order to maintain or improve the family's standard of living or to pursue their own careers. They need to know if day care really is harmful for children, and, if so, what they can do about it.

The limitations of research.

Recently, researchers interested in child development—myself among them—have awakened to the fact that day care is a permanent necessity for modern mothers and have begun to investigate its effects on children's development, rather than just warning of potential dangers. They have observed and tested hundreds of children in scores of day-care facilities across the country and compared the children's performances on these tests with those of children being raised exclusively by their parents at home. To find out what effects day care has on children's development, however, is extremely difficult, and even though a significant number of studies have been done, the answers they have provided so far are very limited. Before reading the results of these studies, you should be aware of their limitations.

One important limitation is that the day-care settings studied have usually been well funded, well run, and designed to reflect what child development experts think is the best possible day care. Sometimes they have been set up for the sole purpose of studying the effects of day care. Even when the day-care settings studied have been selected from the community, it seems likely that the day-care directors and staff involved would agree to participate in a research project only if they were proud of the care they were providing. Consequently, the results of all these studies are likely to apply only to better-than-average day care. You should not assume that the findings from these studies will apply to below-average day care.

The way in which the effects of day care have been measured sets a second limitation. Researchers don't have thermometers or yardsticks, such as those for physical health and growth, that give accurate and reliable

"The Day-Care Child," Allison Clarke-Stewart, *Parents*, September 1982, pp. 72-75. Reprinted by permission.

measurements of children's intellectual and psychological development. They can only make rough estimates of the differences between day-care and home-care children. The instrument that they have used most often to assess these differences is the IQ test. For preschool children this test measures the child's abilities to use and understand language and to manipulate and organize objects, such as putting pegs in holes as quickly as possible or copying a complex design with different colored blocks. This test does tell us something important about how the child is progressing. It gives a reasonably good prediction of how well a child of three or four is likely to do when she begins school. But it does not indicate anything about children's social skills, emotional development, or practical competence. These aspects of development have been measured by observing day-care and home-care children in experimental situations set up by the researchers: playing with other children, being introduced to a stranger, or being left alone in an unfamiliar place, for example. It is quite possible that these tests and experimental situations have missed important differences between day-care and home-care children. You should not generalize beyond the results of these studies to all possible child-development outcomes.

Yet a third limitation of the research on day-care effects lies in the fact that the parents of children who are in day care are likely to be different in various ways from those whose children are not. When differences between the two groups of children have been found, they may reflect these parental differences rather than (or in addition to) the effects of day care itself. Ideally, to equalize these parental differences, a researcher would assign children to either day care or home care on a random basis. But this is difficult to accomplish, since most parents would be understandably unwilling to have their work status or their children's care arrangement determined by the random roll of a researcher's dice. Thus the results of the studies on daycare effects are limited to parents who themselves decided to put their child in day care and selected the day-care setting their child is in. Those who selected nursery school were likely to have been particularly interested in education for their child; those who selected day-care homes or babysitters may have been more concerned about cost, convenience, and a continuing homelike atmosphere for the child; while those who used no day care may have been especially committed to the belief that Mother's place is in the home and that this is best for the child. These parental differences may have accentuated the effects of day care that have been observed in studies. You should not assume that the results of these studies will apply to your situation unless your decision about day care is consistent with values like these.

The last limitation to be aware of is the unavoidable one in any research: no matter how many studies and how many tests are done, the results will inevitably be no more than probabilities. Research is based on the law of averages; it gives only the odds and does not guarantee the outcome in a particular case. When a difference between day-care and home-care children is found, it means that children in day care are more likely than children at home to behave this way. It does not mean that every child who goes to a day-care facility will behave this way. Therefore, you should not assume that the findings from these studies will apply to your own individual child.

Because of all these limitations, the results of research on day-care effects are not absolute truths or guarantees. They are only hints for you to use in making your own decisions about your child's care.

Day care and children's physical health and development.

Physical health and development are perhaps the most obvious indications of how well children in day care are doing. We can all at least agree on whether a child has a cold or can climb stairs. Numerous studies have shown that there are no negative consequences to the physical growth and development of children who attend day care. However, children in daycare centers, by and large, have more bouts with the flu, colds, coughs, rashes, and runny noses than those who are at home. They catch everything that's going around—even if they're from the best of families and go to the best of day-care centers.

Day care and intelligence

Wiping noses may be a price mothers are willing to pay to have their children in day care while they work—especially if most of the wiping is done by the day-care staff. But what about the child's intelligence? Is day care detrimental to intellectual development, as some have feared? This has been a question of much concern and the focus of more than 30 different studies in the last fifteen years.

The good news from all these studies is that care in a decent day-care center has no apparent detrimental effect on children's intellectual development (as measured by IQ or similar tests). Only one out of all these studies, a doctoral dissertation by M. V. Peaslee on day-care centers in Polk County, Florida, found test scores to be lower for children attending daycare centers than for children of comparable ages and family backgrounds being cared for at home. The twoyear-olds in Peaslee's study had been in day care since they were less than two months old, and the day-care centers they attended met only minimal standards for quality. There was only one day-care teacher for every 16 to 24 children in these centers, and care was custodial at best. With this one exception, studies have consistently shown that children in day-care centers or nursery school do at least as well as those at home. This has been found not only in the model day-care centers in Syracuse, New York; at Harvard University; and at the University of North Carolina in Chapel Hill, but also in community day-care centers in New York City, Chicago, Toronto, and Boston. Studies of the cognitive development of children in day care have usually concentrated on children from lower socioeconomic groups.

Such children have been shown to develop better cognitively in day care than their peers from the same groups, raised at home. They have been found to do better than home-care children in tests of verbal fluency, memory, language comprehension, and problem solving. They can copy designs with blocks, string beads, write their names, and draw circles and triangles earlier than children in home care. They manage on their own better, know more about the environment, and ask more questions.

The gains in intellectual performance increase the longer the child is in day care, throughout the preschool period. But soon after they start elementary school, most home-care children catch up with their classmates who have attended a day-care center or nursery school.

Day care and relations with Mother.

Over the course of the first year of life, infants being raised at home develop a strong emotional bond with the person who cares for them, plays with them, and loves them—usually their mother. The child wants to be near Mother, especially in times of stress, fatigue, or illness, "to have and to hold her," to keep her in view, or at least at beck and call. This relationship starts the child on the path of healthy emotional and social development. If this early relation with Mother is weak or disturbed, the individual may never be emotionally secure.

Will children in day care, who spend so much time away from their mothers, fail to form this close bond and suffer as a consequence?

Some two dozen studies have investigated this possibility by observing the behavior of day-care and home-care children with their mothers, noting particularly the children's reactions when their mothers leave them and then return. The findings from these studies clearly indicate that children in day care do form strong attachments to their mothers and that these attachments are not replaced by their relationships with other care-givers. They may also form an affectionate relationship with a care-giver at the day-care center who is involved in their care over several months, but they still overwhelmingly prefer their mothers. At the day-care center, they go to Mother more often, especially for help or when they are bored or distressed; they stay closer to her and interact with her more than with the care-giver.

But are their feelings for Mother as strong as the feelings of children who spend all day at home with their mothers? It is difficult to answer this question, because simply asking a two-year-old how he feels about Mom is likely to elicit an idiosyncratic, perhaps whimsical, response. Day-care children have been observed to be just as likely as home-care children to cry, protest, or follow when their mothers leave them in an unfamiliar place. But this is not necessarily a reliable index of how they feel about

their mother; it may just indicate that they don't like to be left alone.

There is one way in which day-care children have been observed by some researchers to act differently from home-care children. In an unfamiliar setting they were less likely to stay as physically close to their mother or to go to her or talk to her as often when she returned after a brief absence. This was especially true for children who began fulltime day care in the first year of life. Does this difference indicate that these children felt less close or securely attached to their mothers? Frankly, we don't know the answer to this question. But at this time it seems reasonable to assume that the "distancing" from their mother represents only a physical independence from her that is an adaptive and realistic reaction to their daily separations from her. Although day-care children maintain greater physical distance from their mothers, these studies have also shown the children to be just as affectionate and sociable with them. However, if their mothers are emotionally inaccessible and insensitive when day-care children are at home, this may push the child's independence to an unhealthy extreme. But otherwise, it seems unlikely that day care impairs the child's emotional development or relationship with his mother.

Day care and social relations.

During the preschool period, most children first learn to play with other children, progressing in the course of a few short years from simple stares and parallel play to complex games and shared activities. A number of studies have examined the social interactions with their peers of day-care or nursery-school children in contrast with those of home-care children to see if the additional experience with other children offered in day care or nursery school makes a difference in the development of social skills. I myself was involved in one such study, the Chicago Study of Child Care and Development, which looked at 150 children ages two through four in home care with parents, in home care with a sitter, in family day care, in nursery school, and in day-care centers. There was a range of socioeconomic backgrounds among the children, but none came from extremely disadvantaged homes. None had been in day care prior to the age of eighteen months. These children were extensively observed and tested.

On a wide variety of these assessments we found that although home-care and day-care children do not differ obviously in their interactions with friends or familiar playmates, children from day-care centers or nursery schools were more outgoing, helpful, and cooperative than were home-care children with children they had never met before. Their activities were more complex and mature. At the same time, however, their actions may also be more boisterous and aggressive than their home-reared agemates', and they may be less compliant. This may be worrisome for their parents. But since this kind of behavior, like the social skills of helpfulness and cooperation, increases over the preschool period as children get older, this difference, too, fits into a pattern of greater social maturity for day-care children. It has been found that such boisterous, aggressive behavior usually levels off during the elementary-school years, but so far there is not sufficient longitudinal research to allow us to conclude that it does or doesn't for day-care children.

The Chicago data demonstrated advanced social competence for day-care children, not only with their peers but with adults as well. Our findings suggest that children attending nursery schools and day-care centers are likely to be more self-confident, self-assured, and assertive with unfamiliar adults. In unfamiliar situations they are more independent and at ease. At home they make their own choices, dress themselves, and brush their own hair at younger ages. Though they are not always as polite or obedient as home-care children, they are more likely to be cooperative and helpful to parents or teachers when the situation requires it. When they start school they are better adjusted, more persistent at tasks, and more likely to be leaders.

Like the differences in intellectual competence, these differences in social competence have been observed primarily in children in day-care centers and nursery schools, not in day-care homes or with babysitters, and although they have been found to carry over into the first few school grades, parents should not conclude that they are necessarily permanent.

A Day-Care Checklist

You can assess the quality of various day-care settings by making observations using the following checklist. When you have visited a number of settings, use their relative scores as an indication of relative quality.

Health and Safety

Adults do not smoke when with children _____

Floors are clean _____

Children's eating area is clean and attractive _____

No children with soiled diapers or pants _____

At least one adult present is always with children _____

Detergents, medicines, and drugs are kept out of reach of children (high shelf or locked cabinet) _____

Electrical outlets covered with safety caps _____

First-aid supplies available _____

Toys and equipment in good repair (no sharp edges, splinters, paint chips, electrical wires, loose parts on toys) _____

Heavy pieces of furniture (e.g., lockers, bookcases) secure and stable, cannot tip over on children _____

Physical Space

Individual cubby space for each child _____

A space can be made dark and quiet for naps _____

Storage space is available for children to return toys and equipment to shelves when they have finished using them _____

Windows low enough for children to see out _____

Temperature and humidity are comfortable (approximately 68 to 70 degrees Fahrenheit) _____

A variety of pictures, posters, and mobiles _____

Toileting area is easy for children to get to _____

Children can walk directly into enclosed outdoor play area from the building _____

Outdoor play area has open space where children can play on sunny days _____

Outdoor play area has covered space where children can play on rainy days _____

Outdoor play area is easy to supervise (no hidden areas where children can go and not be seen) _____

Materials, Equipment, & Activities

Enough materials and equipment are available so that children do not have to wait more than a few minutes to use them _____

Children are given opportunities to run and climb both indoors and outdoors _____

Children are free to choose what they want to do from several activities much of the time _____

Both boys and girls are allowed the full range of activities _____

Each of the following kinds of materials or equipment is available for children's use:

story and picture books _____   riding/climbing equipment _____

manipulatable materials _____   academic games and puzzles _____

musical toys _____   social games _____

art supplies _____

building or construction materials _____

There is a play area indoors where no furniture or objects are off limits to children _____

Toys and play materials are accessible to children without their having to ask an adult to get them _____

Teachers, Adult Staff, & Care-givers

Enough adults are available so that children can be given individual attention if they need it _____

Adults explain clearly what they want children to do in words children can understand _____

Adults get children to do things by encouragement, suggestion, and praise rather than orders or reprimands _____

Adults respond to children's questions when asked _____

Adults are observed to *teach* children sometimes (but not *all* the time) _____

There is some sort of educational program _____

Adult does not spend *all* her time with one child while other children are at loose ends _____

Male as well as female adults are present _____

Punishment is not practiced _____

The adult in charge thinks of herself as a professional and has some training in child development _____

Children

Children appear happy (laughing, smiling, joking) _____

Children are busy and involved in whatever they are doing (not wandering aimlessly, just sitting and staring blankly, waiting for a long time) _____

Each child spends at least some of his or her time interacting with other children playing, talking, or working together _____

Fighting (hitting, pinching, kicking, grabbing toys) among the children is not allowed _____

Children are in relatively small classes or groups _____

Minimum staff-child ratio for day-care centers:

Age	Maximum Group Size	Staff-Child Ratio
Birth to 2 years	6 children	1 adult: 3 children
2 to 3 years	12 children	1 adult: 4 children
3 to 6 years	16 children	1 adult: 8 children

Minimum ratio for day-care homes:

Birth to 2 years	10 children	1 adult: 5 children
2 to 6 years	12 children	1 adult: 6 children

Parents

Day-care staff encourage parents to visit the day-care setting at any time the child is there _____

Staff are willing to answer parents' questions or talk about the program with parents _____

There are regular opportunities to meet with the staff to confer about the child's progress _____

—A.C.S. ◉

"A Day-Care Checklist" was developed by Marilyn Bradbard and Richard Endsley, originally appearing in a slightly different form in the *CHILD CARE QUARTERLY* (1978 vol. 7, pp. 279-302 and 1979 vol. 8, pp. 307-312).

Conclusions about day care.

What can a mother conclude from the findings of these studies? Keeping in mind that these studies deal with probabilities not certainties, the results nevertheless can allay at least some of the fears of both working and nonworking mothers. Mothers who must work can take heart in the fact that as far as researchers can tell, decent day care in a day-care center, day-care home, or with a babysitter does not impair children's development—physical, emotional, social, or intellectual. And, in fact, day care in a better-than-average day care or nursery school may accelerate children's development of social skills and intellectual competence. Mothers who choose to stay home with their children can be encouraged by the fact that not only are they able to share a greater physical closeness with their children but their children's chances for social and academic success will not be hurt by the fact that they have not attended a day-care center or nursery school, since after a few years of school these children will catch up with any possible advances their day-care agemates may have made.

The major effect of day care seems to be a speeding up of some children's development of social and intellectual skills during the preschool period. Studies suggest that this occurs when day care offers children organized educational activities and the opportunity to interact with a variety of other children under the guidance of a caregiver who can focus on the children's needs and interests without the distractions of daily household tasks. So far, research indicates that these opportunities are more likely to be found in day care centers than in day-care homes, but that does not rule out the possibility that the same advantages will be offered in a home by a babysitter, housekeeper, or day-care provider who sets aside the time to arrange and supervise them.

The real challenge is for each mother to find a day-care setting that offers her child the kind of care she values and opportunities from which he will benefit. As long as she can find this kind of day care, she need not feel that her child's development is being damaged as a result of her situation as a working mother.

Early Childhood and the Public Schools

An Essential Partnership

Helen Blank

Helen Blank, M.U.P., is Director of Child Care at the Children's Defense Fund, Washington, D.C.

What role should the public schools play in meeting the diverse child care needs of families? This question is surfacing again, this time as an outgrowth of increased interest in public school prekindergarten programs. As advocates for young children, we must not ignore the challenges and opportunities the question raises. Our involvement is essential to ensure that programs are appropriate for young children and their families. Early childhood educators can

- stay informed about new proposals and critically examine state and local early education initiatives
- pose more effective alternative strategies if needed
- aggressively participate in the expansion of early childhood programs within the educational system.

State and local initiatives

Several states have considered or passed legislation to increase the public school's role in serving young children. For example, the South Carolina Education Improvement Act of 1984 allows the state to reimburse local districts for one half the cost of programs for 4-year-olds who have "predicted significant readiness deficiencies." Funds will increase from $2.4 million in 1984 to $16 million by 1988–89.

Texas has enacted legislation that mandates most districts to provide a part-day program for 4-year-olds who cannot speak English or are from low-income families.

Missouri passed a bill to fund school districts to conduct developmental screening, parent education programs, and early childhood programs for developmentally delayed children.

Baltimore, Maryland has approved pilot programs for 4-year-olds in kindergarten. Maryland considered a bill to mandate a state-wide preschool program for 4-year-olds that would be partially funded by a $5 a week parent fee.

Other governors and legislators have expressed interest in lowering the age at which children are eligible to attend public programs. Vermont's former Governor Snelling proposed that pilot projects in local districts be set up to screen all 3- to 5-year-olds for developmental problems, and provide early intervention to ensure that children enter primary education "fully prepared to learn." Both New York and Connecticut's Commissioners of Education support starting school at the age of 4. These initiatives are spurred not only by the series of reports on the crisis in our education system but also by the research that demonstrates the significant positive effects of early intervention for the futures of low-income children.

The Perry Preschool Project, a comprehensive program started in the early 1960s by the High/Scope Educational Research Foundation, has identified the long-term effects of preschool on low-income children (Berrueta-Clement, Schweinhart, Barnett, Epstein, & Weikart, 1984). The project includes a follow-up study of 123 19-year-olds who had attended the Perry Preschool. The researchers found marked differences in school performance, employment rates, adolescent pregnancies, and crime rates when participants were compared to other low-income children who did not attend the program.

Almost twice as many preschool participants held jobs or went to college or vocational school after high school. Eighteen percent of the preschool group were on welfare, compared with 32% of those who did not attend the program. "Seventeen pregnancies or births were reported by the 25 women who had attended preschool; 28 pregnancies were reported by the 24 women who had not attended preschool" (p. 69). While 31% of the preschool group had been arrested or detained at some time, 51% of the nonpreschool group had been. The total economic savings of the investment in two years of preschool (as opposed to the expenses required by the nonpreschool group—special education classes, repeating a grade in school, etc.), was calculated to outweigh the costs by seven times!

While policymakers seem to quickly grasp the potential economic impact of early intervention, they are less likely to focus on the cost per child that is necessary to achieve the impressive results described by Berrueta-Clement, et al. The Perry Preschool Project cost

3. DEVELOPMENT AND EDUCATIONAL OPPORTUNITIES: Readiness

$4,818 per child in 1981 dollars, while the average cost of Head Start was $2,300 per child in 1984. The programs that are being organized today appear unlikely to be able to replicate the comprehensive Perry Preschool and Head Start model programs. For example, Texas plans a staff-child ratio of 1:22 for 4-year-olds for a part-day program. The early childhood community can play an important role by reminding legislators that by skimping in the short term they will likely not attain the scope of positive, long-term results achieved by High/Scope.

It is also important to see that these new programs will be coordinated with Head Start. It is conceivable that the interest in early childhood education could result in expanded Head Start services. For example, an initiative supported by the governor of Maine included a $1.7 million appropriation to expand Head Start. The program currently serves about 14% of the eligible children. The new funds will allow every county using a per child cost of $2,500 a year to reach 25% of those eligible. Although the concept was part of an education package, the Department of Community Services will distribute the Head Start monies.

Many other questions need to be raised as children's advocates work more closely with educators in the public schools who are considering services for 4-year-old children.

- What performance standards will guide programs toward long-term success?
- How will the curriculum be designed? What role will early childhood/child development specialists play?
- What will the staff:child ratios be? (In New York City's 3 o'clock kindergarten classes, they are 1:30 or 1:35.)
- What credentials will be required for teachers? Will adequate opportunities be provided for those skilled in working with children who do not have college degrees to work in the classroom?
- What policies will guarantee parent involvement?
- How will programs demonstrate sensitivity to minority families?
- Will existing early childhood programs have the opportunity to operate the new 4-year-old programs?

- What criteria will be used to grant entry into the programs? To determine readiness for kindergarten? Will inappropriate testing procedures and labeling of children be avoided (see Meisels, 1985)?
- What arrangements are being made for children of working parents? Can a full day be offered at the school site? Will transportation be provided to community child care facilities? Will school space be offered to community child care programs to provide child care for the remainder of the day? If schools run a part-time program, what considerations will be given to the economic impact on child care programs if they are asked to reduce the hours of their services?

Other questions should be asked which concern an expanded role for the schools in helping to meet a wide variety of child care needs. For working families and the child care community, the key question may not be whether to lower the school-entrance age. Rather, we must find ways to meet other child care needs.

Kindergarten expansions

Before children's advocates respond to proposals for early school entrance, we should step back and consider how such an expansion would fit into a community's child care needs.

Schools could first be asked to expand the roles they play in meeting the child care needs of the kindergarten children they now serve. Most public school kindergarten programs meet only half days. This policy means that young children are shifted between two or three caregivers in a single day. Continuity of care and stability could be increased with a longer kindergarten day in which children learn through play.

The definition of a full-day kindergarten must also be reconsidered. When New York City implemented an all-day kindergarten program, many automatically assumed *all day* was from 8 a.m. to 6 p.m. Instead, the children's school day ended at 3 p.m. Does a 3 o'clock closing for kindergarten encourage more working parents to leave their 5-year-olds home alone or with older siblings for the remainder of the day?

An all-day kindergarten operated by the schools, and a before- and after-

school program to supplement it, possibly operated by community child care organizations, is a logical extension of the schools' involvement with younger children.

After-school programs

While there has been considerable public attention on the millions of children left alone in the early morning or early evening hours, most public schools do not offer school-age child care programs. Now that more than one-half of the private schools provide these services, public schools may be more interested in school-age child care as a community support. Many parents prefer a school-based program that is less complicated because it alleviates mid-day transportation problems.

Several programs run by schools or contracted to community groups are available to serve as models from which to learn (see Baden, Genser, Levine, & Seligson, 1982). The School-Age Child Care Project offers technical assistance and publications for local communities.

Adolescent parent needs

Each year approximately 523,000 teenagers give birth, and more than half of these young mothers have not completed high school. Without education or training, they face the prospect of low-paying jobs at best, or welfare at worst.

Few programs provide them with parenting skills or enable teenage mothers to return to school. A significant unmet need for teenage mothers and their babies is the provision of facilities, funds, and staff for infant care. Child care is an absolutely essential service if young mothers are to be able to complete high school. Schools are a logical and convenient place in which to locate programs to meet the special child care needs of adolescent parents.

Become an equal partner

Early childhood professionals and advocates must become equal partners with schools and legislators when decisions are made affecting young children. Early childhood representatives can be included within the education bureaucracy at many levels.

- Serve as an early childhood representative to the State Board of Education Committee on Instruction and Curriculum.

Programs for young children in public schools?

Only if . . .

Many state legislatures are considering bills that could add local and state resources to child care and early education programs. However, this enhanced role for the school system will have positive effects only if certain conditions are spelled out in the legislation for these early childhood programs. Funds should be available for early education through the school system:

• only if this money adds to the total resources for child care and early education programs. *Not* if legislators simply shift or reduce funding from Head Start and the social service system to support school-based programs.

• only if schools can choose to institute such programs. *Not* if schools lacking interest in early childhood programs are mandated to start them.

• only if early childhood experts are involved in planning with the schools. *Not* if schools initiate early childhood programs without input from those in the community who know about child development and early education.

• only if the schools have the option to contract with an existing early childhood program or to offer vouchers to parents who can select their own programs. *Not* if community resources are ignored in favor of exclusively school-based programs.

• only if knowledge about early childhood development is required for all lead teachers in preprimary programs. *Not* if any teaching credential is the sole requirement for teachers of young children in these programs.

• only if standards are established, including minimum staff-child ratios and group sizes, to assure that the early childhood programs offer quality care and education. *Not* if schools are permitted to operate programs that fail to meet, at a minimum, the state licensing standards that apply to other programs serving 4-year-olds.

• only if the funding mechanism assures an adequate per child reimbursement based on the cost of providing quality care to 4-year-olds. *Not* if kindergarten and first grade costs are used to determine funding levels for the 4-year-old programs.

• only if the needs of kindergarten children are addressed as well. *Not* if schools with low quality kindergarten programs are required to add 4-year-old programs without simultaneously upgrading their kindergarten program.

• only if the schools are required to have a plan to make 4-year-old programs accessible to all children, with parent fees on a sliding scale, if necessary. *Not* if school-based programs serve only certain children based on income, social class, or race.

• only if provisions ensure that the needs of children of full-time employed parents are met by the addition of school-based early childhood programs. *Not* if these programs are likely to increase the number of latchkey children in the community.

• only if parents would be welcome and respected as partners in early childhood programs for their children. *Not* if the orientation is to ignore both parent input and children's family and cultural heritage.

—*Gwen Morgan*

Note: This list is derived from "Child Care and Early Education: What Legislators Can Do" by Gwen Morgan, which is available from NAEYC upon request for $2.00.

• Initiate an Early Childhood Development Advisory Committee appointed by the governor.
• Join the staff or Early Childhood Board from the state department of education to act as liaison with other departments responsible for child care.
• Establish Regional Early Childhood Specialists.
• Require local boards of education to have an early childhood department.
• Mandate early childhood training for administrators and principals.
• Demand a public hearing process to determine the 4-year-old curriculum and other child care policies.

While child advocates must continue to press for expanded federal and state dollars for child care, we cannot ignore the possibility of new partnerships with the public schools. Partnership means that early childhood educators will be involved in shaping programs and policies responsive to the special needs of younger children as well as improving child care for school-age children.

The education community will not necessarily seek our partnership. New state programs are being started without taking into account the valuable contributions early childhood educators can make. We can help others recognize the components of high quality, appropriate, and comprehensive programs for young children. If these new programs are to achieve the success of their predecessors, early childhood professionals must take the initiative to be involved.

References

Baden, R. K., Genser, A., Levine, J. A., & Seligson, M. (1982). *School-age child care: An action manual.* Dover, MA: Auburn House.
Berrueta-Clement, J. R., Schweinhart, L. J., Barnett, W. S., Epstein, A. S., & Weikart, D. P. (1984). *Changed lives.* Ypsilanti, MI: High/Scope Press.
Meisels, S. J. (1985). *Developmental screening in early childhood: A guide* (rev. ed.). Washington, DC: National Association for the Education of Young Children.
Resource
School-Age Child Care Project, Center for Research on Women, Wellesley College, Wellesley, MA 02181. 617-431-1453.

Readiness: Should We Make Them Ready or Let Them Bloom?

The current emphasis on achievement of minimum competencies, basic education, and the pressure for early maturity has surfaced in early childhood as pressure for teachers to get their students ready for the next level. As teachers and caregivers, it is important for each of us to evaluate our view of the concept of readiness. We need to reconsider our definitions of readiness and how we apply these definitions to practice.

Rosalind Charlesworth

Rosalind Charlesworth is Associate Professor at the College of Education, Louisiana State University in Baton Rouge.

The traditional developmental early childhood view of readiness is exemplified by Leo in the book *Leo the Late Bloomer* by Robert Krauss. Leo has everyone concerned because he hasn't learned to read, write, draw, eat neatly, or speak. When the pressure is taken off and Leo is allowed to "bloom" in his own good time he develops all those skills in a normal way. At the end of the story he says with relief, "I made it." This "let them bloom" view of readiness has traditionally dominated early education. However, in the surge to get children ready for the elementary grades are we neglecting to allow them time to bloom? There seems to be a movement toward a view which defines readiness as making children ready rather than helping them to "make it" when they are ready. Often, it seems that the term readiness is used in a way that is harmful to children, a way that makes it almost a crime to not be ready.

Several questions regarding readiness need to be answered. Where did the term readiness as applied to children come from? What determines our view of readiness? Should we throw out the term *readiness* or is it still useful? How do the "let them bloom" and "make them ready" approaches compare in the classroom? Can we defend the "let them bloom" view under today's pressures? The purpose of this article is to clarify and suggest answers to these questions and assist early childhood educators to support a developmental approach to readiness.

Where Did the Term Come From? Readiness as an idea began with some of the important figures from the past who influenced the directions that early childhood education has taken. These figures include Rousseau, Montessori, Piaget, and Gesell who all believed that children should have freedom to grow and construct their own knowledge through firsthand interaction with the environment. These scholars viewed readiness as developmental. Others began to define readiness as less developmental and less individual. It became popular to define readiness in relation to when the average group of individuals has the capacity/skills/knowledge to undertake some specific type or area of learning. However, the developmen-

tally oriented early childhood educators have tried to fight this trend. Some even see readiness as a vague, unclear, useless idea. They feel that programming for readiness has led to rigid instruction that leaves no room for flexibility and view the idea of teaching readiness as foolish. These differing points of view leave early childhood practitioners wondering what readiness might be and whether it is even a useful concept.

What Determines Our Basic View? Our basic view of readiness is formed to a great extent by the degree of faith we have in children's ability to control and regulate some of their own learning. In a presentation at the annual meeting of the Jean Piaget Society in 1980, Elkind presented himself as a Swiss clock salesman representing the clockmaker Piaget. Elkind developed an analogy of classroom clocks representing our view of how children function relative to time, maturation, and instruction. Several influential persons from the past were given roles as clockmakers for early childhood classrooms.

The philosopher Rousseau invented the "self winder," but schoolmasters liked manual winding better because they liked to feel resistance and over-

From *Day Care and Early Education*, Spring 1985, pp. 25-27. © 1985 by Human Sciences Press, Inc. Reprinted by permission.

come it with brute force if necessary. Pestalozzi invented the "grandmother clock," but this was too nurturant to be widely accepted. Montessori introduced the wristwatch as a means of doing away with regimentation. Each child could follow his or her own schedule. This approach didn't last long: a single wall clock was soon put up in each room. John Dewey introduced the calendar. Dewey saw time beyond hours and minutes to weeks, months, and years. He saw school time and life time as continuous. However, the "calendar clock" never seemed to work right in the classroom. John B. Watson came up with the idea of the "alarm clock." This type of clock would catch and hold the children's attention and insure efficient learning. Currently this clock has been replaced by bells that ring when the child is involved in something interesting. The "digital clock" was introduced by B.F. Skinner who felt this would be easier than translating the positions of the clock hands on the traditional clock in order to tell time. By making the task simpler we then think the children are brighter.

Piaget's unique contribution was the "biological clock" or the child himself. Observing the child is a guide to the maturity level and tells you what "time" it is. Rather than the child learning to tell time, the teacher learns to tell time. Nature provides each child with a "clock."

Elkind notes that somehow the alarm clocks and digital clocks won out over the self winders, the wristwatches, and the biological clocks. The former view corresponds to the perspective that we make the child ready; the latter to the view that the child becomes ready. We are all well-acquainted with the first view since it has long been the dominant one in America education. The second view has never seemed to go over very well or last very long except at the early childhood level. The first view puts the burden on the child to comprehend what the teacher has to say while the second puts the burden on the teacher to comprehend what the child has to say. The first view underlies the "make them ready" approach to readiness and the second the "let them bloom" approach.

How Do the Approaches Compare in the Classroom? The types of activities emphasized are in marked contrast in classrooms guided by the two different views of readiness. Looking at the so-called "basics" of reading, writing, and arithmetic, the following contrasts might be observed:

"Make them ready" classrooms tend to emphasize right and wrong responses while "let them bloom" classrooms recognize developmental stages and individual rates of growth and accept the children as they are. For ex-

ample, in the "make them ready" classroom there is an emphasis on writing the letters of the alphabet correctly. In the "let them bloom" classroom there is recognition that young children begin to acquire knowledge of written communication early, and if given the opportunity and full acceptance of their products they enjoy writing at their own level. They can operate at any stage: controlled scribbling, mock letter writing, mixtures of mock and real letters, or real letters. At each stage they can write labels, lists, messages, letters, and stories. The adults accept these products as the early steps in writing. In teaching

	Make Them Ready	Let Them Bloom
Reading	• Alphabet recognition • Sound/symbol association • Sound/symbol discrimination and matching • Vocabulary building • Workbooks, ditto sheets, and other paper-and-pencil activities	• Print is everywhere in the environment—books; labels on shelves and on learning centers; food packages, recipe books, telephone directories, and magazines in the housekeeping area; play traffic signs in the block area, etc. • There are opportunities and materials for story retelling and dramatization—flannel board figures, puppets, tapes • Stories are read and reread to groups and individuals • Children are encouraged to read
Writing	• Practice copying and tracing letters • Tracing lines, circles, and shapes • Workbooks and ditto sheets	• A writing center is located in a prominent place and contains an assortment of plain and lined paper, pencils, pens, markers, and crayons • There is a restaurant dramatic play center with real menus, note pads for writing down orders, recipes and shopping lists • There is an office dramatic play center with a typewriter, a microcomputer with word processing capability, paper, envelopes, pencils, pens, and other office materials • Many manipulative materials are available such as clay, clothespin games, building sets, tinkertoys, scissors and glue, and other materials that help to develop finger dexterity
Arithmetic	• Numeral recognition • Set/symbol matching • Workbooks and ditto sheets • Counting	• Exploration of materials: unit blocks, inch cubes, unifix cubes, sand and water—things which allow children to explore and construct concepts of size, volume, and number • Self-correcting materials which allow children to learn by trial and error and correct their own mistakes • Concrete materials are used for counting and set/symbol matching.

reading the "make them ready" teachers emphasize mastering the alphabet as the major readiness skill for reading. The "let them bloom" teachers know that the alphabet is most helpful for reading when used for writing and that writing (as described above) is the reading activity young children will choose most often if given the opportunity. Further, these teachers know that listening, retelling, reenacting, and dictating stories are foundations of print awareness and the early steps in reading. "Let them bloom" teachers realize that arithmetic for young children is more than counting, recognizing numerals, and matching symbols to sets. They know that arithmetic begins with the exploration of concrete materials accompanied by adult questions which make the child perform informal mathematical operations. For example, as a child pours water from a cup into a pitcher, the teacher asks, "How many cups of water will it take to fill the pitcher?" The "let them bloom" teacher provides an environment rich with stimulating concrete materials, guides the children to these materials, responds to their questions, asks questions that present realistic problems to solve, accepts whatever the children produce, and provides new challenges as needed. Such teachers believe that children can be responsible for some

of their own learning if given appropriate materials and adult guidance.

Which View? For this author, the "let them bloom" definition of readiness is the preferred one. This view respects the child's own biological clock, while at the same time it provides experiences which will enable him or her to learn at the fastest rate possible. Achieving success will motivate children to learn more.

Those who believe in letting the child bloom need to develop confidence and be prepared to clearly articulate this view of readiness. They need to look at their program and be able to explain to parents, other educators, and the public that the activities and experiences support emergent reading, writing, and arithmetic skills and concepts. For example, using clay, picking up small objects with tweezers, and experimenting freely with various writing implements are all activities that encourage the beginning levels of handwriting instruction. Matching, comparing, classifying, and counting objects are initial levels of arithmetic instruction. Reading is learned through developing print awareness while working with print in many forms.

The view that readiness is something that emerges from the child rather than something that is taught is positive and one that can guide

teachers away from the frustrations of teaching at levels the children are not ready for in order to make them ready. It allows children to bloom, much like Leo did.

References

Elkind, D. Action in the Classroom: The Swiss Movement. *Theory Into Practice*, 20 (2), p. 74–78, 1981.

Krauss, R. *Leo the Late Bloomer.* New York: Windmill Books, 1971.

For Further Reading

Ames, L.B. *Is Your Child in the Wrong Grade?* Lumberville, PA: Learning Press, 1978.

Carll, B. & Richard, N. *One Piece of the Puzzle: A Practical Guide for Schools Wishing to Implement a School Readiness Program.* Lumberville, PA: Learning Press.

Durkin, D. Reading Readiness. In W.B. Barbe, M.N. Milone, V.H. Lucas & J.W. Humphrey (eds.) *Basic Skills in Kindergarten: Foundations for Formal Learning.* Columbus, OH: Zaner-Bloser, 1980, pp. 64–70.

Jensen, A.R. *Understanding Readiness: An Occasional Paper.* Urbana, IL: ERIC Clearinghouse on Elementary and Early Childhood Education, 1969.

Lamme, L.L. Handwriting in an Early Childhood Curriculum. *Young Children* 35, pp. 20–27, 1979.

Ramsey, M.E. & Bayless, K.M. *Kindergarten: Programs and Practices.* St. Louis, MO: C.V. Mosby, 1980.

Read, K.H. & Patterson, J. *The Nursery School and Kindergarten.* New York: Holt, Reinhart and Winston, 1980.

Rudolf, M. & Cohen, D.H. *Kindergarten and Early Schooling,* 2nd ed. Englewood Cliffs, NJ: Prentice-Hall, 1984.

The 5s and 6s Go to School, Revisited

Nancy K. Webster

Nancy K. Webster is currently on a one-year Fulbright Exchange in Leicestershire, England. Before leaving the United States she was a kindergarten teacher for 14 years.

THE CHILDREN arrive, to be greeted by name at the door by their teacher. The room is spacious, colorful and warm: it calls to the kindergartners who come in and get started on their day. Blocks, woodworking, art projects, a child-size housekeeping corner and a wooden climber fill the room.

It is "activity time," and the children are eager to begin. As others arrive, the teacher observes the busy atmosphere. She guides Joey away from the overcrowded block corner to a new book she thinks might be of interest. As he settles into the book, Martha calls for help in copying her name "correctly." As the movement in the room ebbs and flows, the excited voices of Mark and Allison reach the teacher; she smiles at the "good noise" of constructive, involved children. She notes in her anecdotal record that Dorothy is listless and tired again; she watches her lying in the housekeeping corner and makes a mental note to speak to her mother after school.

Out of the corner of her eye she sees Oliver knock down Tim's garage, built out of small blocks. As she hurries over to inquire what is happening and sees Tim's anguished expression, she asks Oliver to remember their rule: "Use the room as you like, so long as you do not annoy others" (Sheehy, 1954, p. 9). When "activity time" ends, the group moves outside.

The pace flows and the 5s and 6s go to school for another day.

Background

When I was in college in the mid-'50s, majoring in Child Development and working in the lab school, one of the books that meant the most to me was Emma Sheehy's *The 5s and 6s Go to School* (1954). It was held up as a model in class, and we used it regularly. "The room must talk to children" (Sheehy, p.4). How hard I tried! As an assistant in the lab school and a helper at Fels Institute, it was easy to see the progression from nursery school to kindergarten. Sheehy's program ideas fit so well in our curriculum: it was almost as if the book came to life before one's eyes.

Ten years later as I began teaching kindergarten in the public school system, I came back to the book. Discuss with the children . . . learn from them . . . take their ideas and build the program around them . . . the structure should come from them. . . . Here was a woman with years of experience in teaching, whose book displayed a wonderful feeling for children and whose program was familiar to me from college. To use Sheehy's ideas in my classroom, I had the support of an understanding principal, time to plan and gather materials, and an aide for one hour each day.

From *Childhood Education*, Vol. 60, No. 5, (May/June 1984): pp. 325-330. Reprinted by permission of Nancy K. Webster and the Association for Childhood Education International, 11141 Georgia Avenue, Suite 200, Wheaton, MD 20902. Copyright © 1984 by the Association.

3. DEVELOPMENT AND EDUCATIONAL OPPORTUNITIES: Kindergarten

I am still a kindergarten teacher today, by preference, although it is in another public school system. As I have watched our program change through the years, I have often thought of Sheehy's book. To open the book again is to visit with an old friend. The time is fall 1983, and another group of 5s and 6s goes to school.

The 5s and 6s Go to School

Emma Sheehy asks teachers to provide children with a rich atmosphere in a room that will speak to them. She suggests initial conferencing with parents to build good community-school relations (Sheehy, p. 30). Since group living must be based on organization, she stresses preplanning (p. 22). It is that planning which will allow the teacher time to devote full attention to the children. Include in this whatever consultant help you can get (art, music, physical education), she reminds us (p. 33). Since children come to school expecting to be taught, "use any technique that will help the child to learn" (p. 250). The schoolroom should be a place where a child's interests can be developed, where genuine work can be done and where a child may grow naturally (p. 82).

The teacher's job is to observe, listen, help and most of all guide, contends Sheehy (p. 122). Each chapter of her book details a part of the curriculum (language arts, reading, science, etc.). She suggests that "children need space" and the teacher, an adequate budget (pp. 73-83). She urges a balanced program, with a good outdoor period and a relaxation time between periods of mental activity (p. 315). In short, the book stresses the need for children to learn in an enriched atmosphere that includes concern for each child's whole being and uniqueness. It is still exciting reading!

1960s

Early childhood was rediscovered in the 1960s and accepted by the public (as evidenced by the popular press) (Headley, 1965, p. 95). An infusion of government money, research, experimental programs, books and articles all generated interest in the young child's early learning and schooling. I do not think of the field as a sleepy backwater up to that time, but the importance of our mission with young children had certainly been a well-kept secret. This "quiet" period seemed to disappear in a wave of publicity after the Sputnik-generated question, "What *are* we teaching our children?" Who can forget the effect of Bruner's statement that any subject can be taught in some intellectually honest form to any child at any age (Bruner, 1960, p. 12)? Or the emergence of Piaget? Or the impact of "Sesame Street"? In kindergarten meetings across the United States, articles by Bloom (1964), Bereiter and Englemann (1966), Weikart (1967), and Robison and Spodek (1965) were discussed. How would all this affect us in the classroom? Looking back, it seems to have been a "golden period" for early childhood.

Photographs by Kay Pardee

1970s

Head Start . . . Follow Through . . . Infant Programs . . . Home Start . . . British Infant Schools . . . Open Classrooms . . . Nimnicht's Toy Library . . . Day Care . . . Children's Television . . . the list goes on. With the seemingly endless alternatives from the '60s carried over into the literature of the '70s, a bit of tightening occurred as some of the research results became less than glowing. Instructional objectives were "in," and the term "accountability" was heard for the first time. But more than instructional objectives, "mastery learning" was the key concept (Bloom, 1981, p. 167). The idea was that anyone could learn if the appropriate prior conditions for learning existed, and that meant not only systematic planning but a more comprehensive strategy (Pratt, 1980, p. 38). Goals had to be clearly stated in the kindergarten program. What were our objectives with the children day to day, week to week, month to month? It was not enough to demonstrate that one was an observant guide. The teacher had to show that he or she was really teaching something.

By 1973 every school in my district had a kindergarten unit as part of the total program (Dade County Public School System, 1969, p. 10). Class size rose, at least in my area, until it was not unusual to have 30+ in the classroom. The allocation in 1978 was based on a ratio of 1 to 27.5. As I personally struggled with 34 in my class in 1979, I rarely had enough time to wonder about the unique needs of each child.

But I was aware that sweeping curriculum changes were under way, as a Piaget-based Early Childhood Curriculum was introduced, and both math and reading systems were integrated into the program. By 1978 we had a written "balanced curriculum"; and I was left to ponder, "What had been unbalanced in the kindergarten classroom prior to this?"

1980s

We are "back to basics" now. In Florida we have new legislation, which mandates kindergarten for every child (the *first* in the nation) (Robinson, 1982), and PREP (Primary Education Program) legislation, which brings class size down to 22.5. Both of these innovative steps are excellent indicators for the future of early childhood. We have a kindergarten curriculum that lists approximately 200 objectives in every content area, to be met over the course of the year. Due to financial constraints, I no longer have an art and music consultant to work with the children weekly. "Back to basics" to me has meant "I do it all now."

A Kindergarten Classroom, 1983-84

The children arrive, to be greeted at the door by their teacher. The room is spacious, colorful and warm: it calls to the kindergartners who come in and get started on their day (Dade County Public School System, 1980):

Basic Skills

Math	30 minutes/day
Writing/Spelling	30 minutes/day
Reading	30 minutes/day

Interdisciplinary

Science	20 minutes/day
Health/Safety	20 minutes/day
Social Studies	20 minutes/day
Literature and Expressive Language	30 minutes/day

Fine Arts

Art	50 minutes/week
Music	20 minutes/every other day

Lunch
30 minutes/day

Physical Education
20 minutes/day

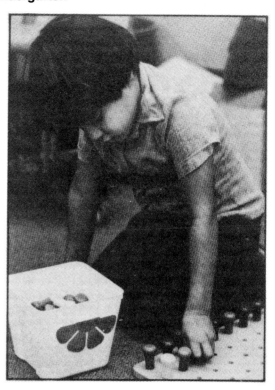

The preferred reading program is Houghton Mifflin, a series with workbooks, support materials and complete teacher's guide. The mathematics program is the newly implemented TMP (Total Math Program), a sequenced learning series of booklets with an initial placement test to assure individualized learning. From workbooks to kits to booklets to packaged units, the day passes, meeting program objectives in my lesson plans. We have a full complement of curriculum materials on our shelves for every part of the program.

An aide helps reduce the teacher-pupil ratio, which is over the 22.5 recommended size (I have 29). Parent volunteers are scheduled daily to provide program support. Our files bulge with work folders, homework folders, parent notes and behavior forms. Our walls display charts with math and reading skills.

There is still an "activity time" in the schedule of this particular classroom, although it is not provided for in the balanced curriculum. It has been reduced to 30 minutes a day, sandwiched between more identifiable cognitive areas. I still consider it one of the highlights of the day (and, interestingly enough, so do the children, who are questioned on their "likes" and "dislikes" at the end of every year). My program may differ somewhat in detail, scheduling and actual implementation from other full-day kindergartens, but the structure is basically the same. It is a day that moves along very quickly. Most children easily adapt to the pace. It is the '80s!

Introspection

As an early childhood educator teaching since the '50s, I have seen many changes through the years. Some have touched me more profoundly than others, depending on my location and employer. My allegiance has typically been to the school, doing the best I can with the children and for the principal. The single most distressing change has been the loss of personal freedom I feel I have as a teacher in my own classroom with my group of children. A principal who believes in you and your program may act as a "buffer," but you are still responsible to the larger school system.

The curriculum consultants, in consultation with others, write the grade-level objectives teachers are expected to carry out. When a program audit is carried out at your school, the observer is looking to see that the program objectives *are* met—in the papers among the work folders, in the lesson plans, and in the charts and systems the teacher employs. Given this, it is easy to see why the workbook format is used in many kindergartens today. It is already sequenced, includes grade-level objectives, meets goals and is simple to use (particularly when it includes a teacher guide). Likewise, paper-and-pencil activities are common because they can be saved to demonstrate that a skill was taught and mastered.

Although it may have been apparent in the 1960s that the good kindergarten day is not blocked out into subject-matter periods (Headley, p. 49), it is hard today to find anyone interested in the issue. Today most educators view kindergarten as a necessary downward extension of elementary school (Spodek, 1972, p. 26). That includes subject-matter periods for the teaching of reading, writing and mathematics. Many 1st-grade teachers actually ask kindergarten teachers to have the children become adept in using workbooks (Davis, 1980). It is alarming to see kindergarten take on more and more of the characteristics of 1st grade.

Parents offer another kind of challenge in this process. As James Hymes, Jr., stated in his book, parents "cannot look on their youngsters as being 3- or 4- or 5-year-olds. They see them only as pre-1st graders" (Hymes, 1981, pp. 8-9). Parents whose children have attended nursery school add to the demands for a more formalized kindergarten program (Davis, p. 76). Their children have already spent time playing, and they want them to move ahead as fast as they can. There is so much knowledge to acquire today that no time seems to be too early to begin a somewhat formalized reading program. I think the following quote should receive greater exposure:

Research has indicated no significant differences between programs using reading readiness workbooks and programs using normal kindergarten play activities. Such leading experts in teaching reading as Nila Banton Smith and George D. Spache have stated that formal reading readiness is contraindicated in the Kindergarten, and that the Kindergarten should be a place for the child to have formal language experiences, a position reminiscent of the original Froebelians (Ross, 1976, p. 94).

Where Are We Now?

To revisit Sheehy's book is to enter another era. Where have we gone in 30 years? We seem to be a long way from play, although it *is* still a part of the 5s and 6s' day. But then life in general has changed too: divorce rates are up; one-parent families are common; in two-parent families, both are likely to be working; the television is a large part of our lives; early schooling is quite common. Frost and Rowland even state it is a dream realized that early childhood education seems to be so universal (Frost and Rowland, 1969, p. 431).

The children come every year with fresh, eager faces, and with an honesty and directness that propel them into a whole world of learning. They want to know! Even though we are now held responsible for a more formalized cognitive program, children still need to be treated with dignity. They can still bring something of their own to the curriculum. They still have unique needs to be met; they still have a developmental level that must be reckoned with—or, as the Gesell Institute re-

fers to it, "a behavior age" (Ilg, Ames, Haines and Gillespie, 1978). This fact has remained unchanged through the years: the children are just 5 and still have the basic needs of their age group whether or not they have been in nursery school for three years or know how to read.

Sheehy's book continues to carry a special and important message for kindergarten teachers today. The challenge is to support the kindergarten child's intellectual growth as part of the child's total being, remembering the child is a *whole* person. And every kindergarten teacher needs to care enough to say to those who will listen, "I teach the child, not the subject!"

Bibliography

Almy, Millie. *The Early Childhood Educator at Work.* New York: McGraw-Hill, 1975.

Bereiter, Carl, and Siegfried Englemann. *Teaching Disadvantaged Children in the Preschool.* Englewood Cliffs, NJ: Prentice-Hall, 1966.

Bloom, Benjamin. *All Our Children Learning.* New York: McGraw-Hill, 1981.

_____. *Stability and Change in Human Characteristics.* New York: Wiley, 1964.

Bruner, Jerome. *The Process of Education.* Cambridge, MA: Harvard University Press, 1960.

Dade County Public School System. "Balanced Curriculum—Minimal Criteria." 1980.

_____. "Summary Report on History of Dade County Kindergarten Program." 1969.

Davis, Hazel G. "Reading Pressures in the Kindergarten." *Childhood Education* 57, 2 (Nov./Dec. 1980):76-79.

Frost, Joe L., and G. Thomas Rowland. *Curricula for the Seventies.* Boston: Houghton Mifflin, 1969.

Headley, Neith. *The Kindergarten: Its Place in the Program of Education.* New York: The Center for Applied Research in Education, 1965.

Hymes, James L., Jr. *Teaching the Child Under Six.* Columbus, OH: Charles E. Merrill, 1981.

Ilg, Frances L.; Louise Ames; Jacqueline Haines and Clyde Gillespie. *School Readiness: Behavior Tests Used at the Gesell Institute.* New York: Harper and Row, 1978.

Mussen, Paul H.; John J. Conger and Jerome Kagan. *Child Development and Personality.* New York: Harper and Row, 1974.

Nimnicht, Glen P., and Edna Brown. "The Toy Library: Parents and Children Learning with Toys." *Young Children* (Dec. 1972):110-16.

Pratt, David. *Curriculum Design and Development.* New York: Harcourt Brace Jovanovich, 1980.

Robinson, Sandra L. "Educational Opportunities for Young Children in America." *Childhood Education* 59, 1 (1982):42-45.

Robison, Helen, and Bernard Spodek. *New Directions in Kindergarten.* New York: Teachers College Press, Columbia University, 1965.

Ross, Elizabeth Dale. *The Kindergarten Crusade: The Establishment of Preschool Education in the United States.* Athens, OH: Ohio University Press, 1976.

Sheehy, Emma. *The 5s and 6s Go to School.* New York: Henry Holt, 1954.

Spodek, Bernard. *Teaching in the Early Years.* Englewood Cliffs, NJ: Prentice-Hall, 1972.

Weikart, David. "Preschool Programs: Preliminary Findings." *Journal of Special Education* 1(1967):163-82.

When Parents of Kindergartners Ask "Why?"

Barbara Simmons and JoAnn Brewer

Barbara Simmons in an Associate Dean and Professor of Education in the Graduate School, Texas Tech University, Lubbock. JoAnn Brewer is Assistant Superintendent for Instruction, Hesperia Elementary District, California.

Teachers and principals regularly encounter the task of answering parents' questions about early childhood education. Motivated by genuine concern, parents sometimes ask questions that reveal misconceptions about the goals of a kindergarten program which cause them to focus only on cursory academic skills like knowing the alphabet and reciting numerals. When a principal or teacher answers their questions adequately, however, with emphasis on all areas of a child's development, their concerns diminish and their knowledge increases. Typical questions are addressed here and references provided for parents who want further information.

1. When will my child begin to read?

Reading is a continuum that began when your child first started to use language; it will continue well into adult life. Even though our culture presently dictates that formal reading should begin early, much research tells us that an informal beginning eventually produces more skilled and willing readers. The most important component of the reading process is *learning to love and appreciate books*. Recognition of individual words follows—but must never precede—this step. Another vital ingredient in reading successfully is *the reader's background of experience*. One of the important functions of the early childhood teacher is to build children's non-visual experiences so that meaning can be attached to print. *Oral language development* is the third major area of reading instruction for young children. Phonetically decoding words is of no value to children when the words have no meaning.

In addition to all of these areas of reading, children in an early childhood classroom have many opportunities to practice perceptual skills necessary for reading. Reciting and writing the alphabet are not prerequisites for learning to read; but a love of

From *Childhood Education*, Vol. 61, No. 3, (January/February 1985): pp. 177-184. Reprinted by permission of Barbara Simmons, JoAnn Brewer and the Association for Childhood Education International, 11141 Georgia Avenue, Suite 200, Wheaton, MD. Copyright © 1985 by the Association.

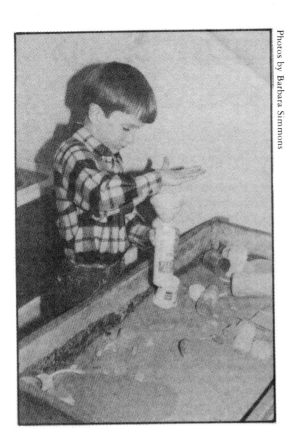

Photos by Barbara Simmons

books, a broad experiential background and oral language skills are essential (Durkin, 1983; Clay, 1981).

2. Is the kindergarten teacher really getting my child ready for 1st grade?

Your child's teacher is working very hard to help each student make the transition from home to school. Activities are planned that will develop independence, enhance motor skills, encourage creative thinking and promote the ability to cooperate with others. Students do learn many skills that will help them to be successful 1st-graders, but pushing them into academic areas too soon has a negative effect on learning. David Elkind explains the problem in his book *The Hurried Child* (1982).

3. Why is it so noisy in my child's classroom?

Promoting children's language development is one of the primary goals of early childhood education. Research clearly indicates that classrooms that do not stimulate talking retard language development (Petty and Starkey, 1967). Teachers who encourage verbal interaction make it possible for children to improve their communication skills. Also, a good early childhood environment is active. Hammering, singing, building, cooking, manipulating and role-playing are the child's work. Teachers who are aware of young children's need for involvement provide a variety of activities, resulting in a room that is filled with the busy sound of students working (ACEI et al., 1979).

4. Why does the teacher encourage the children to play with sand, water and blocks? Aren't these activities a waste of time if the child is old enough to be in school?

Play is the way a young child learns most efficiently. Rather than waste time telling young children about concepts such as texture and weight, high and low, liquid and solid, the teacher lets the children learn the concepts through manipulation of real materials. Working with open-ended materials such as sand, water and blocks is particularly effective as children strive to solve problems and attain social skills.

A child working with sand, for example, wants to mold the sand to hold the shape of a container. To achieve this goal, the child experiments with various ratios of sand and water until exactly the right formula is achieved. Because there are no "right" and "wrong" answers, the child is free to learn without pressure or fear of making an error. The freedom to be in control of the situation helps the child achieve a sense of competency and self-worth. The child is usually compelled to share the sand table with other children and has an opportunity to practice the social skills of joining a group — learning to ask for needed materials in ways that produce desired results and learning how others perceive his/her actions. Playing with sand, water and blocks can help a child learn in the most efficient manner possible (Hirsch, 1974).

5. When will my child learn to count to a hundred?

Many children can count when they enter an early childhood program; however, they do not really understand a number's meaning. Working with manipulatives promotes the ability to conceptualize numbers. Students who can relate the numeral *five* to five objects have a more important skill than those who can count by rote to one hundred (Kamii, 1982).

6. If we had some math problems to work at home, wouldn't my child learn to add and subtract more quickly?

The paper-and-pencil math we learned as children is not really an indication of understanding or learning. In our programs, we are much more concerned with the development of concepts than paper-and-pencil skills. Children playing games, for example, must learn to divide the pieces so that the amounts are equal for each player. They learn number concepts and operations with real materials that can be manipulated. Children work often with blocks, beans, sticks and other appropriate materials to help them truly understand math.

If you would like your child to be involved in homework that will be meaningful, suggest that she/he 1) keep score in family games, 2) set the table (counting correct number of plates, glasses, silverware), 3) help cook (measure ingredients), 4) fold laundry, 5) play shape-search around the house, 6) grow flowers and record vital information, or 7) decide how to apportion materials fairly. All of these activities and others that imaginative parents invent help the child achieve a real understanding of mathematical concepts without the pressure of memorizing and recording symbolically.

Writing problems not only fails to indicate levels of knowledge, but puts excessive pressure on the child who does not have the fine motor control necessary for making numerals correctly. Many children do not achieve this control for a few years after they begin school, but their mathematical progress should not be delayed because of poor motor control (Kamii, 1982).

7. Why hasn't my child learned to write the alphabet?

Many children do not have the fine motor skills necessary to write letters correctly. When forced to try too early, the result is frustration. Your child is learning songs and finger plays about the sounds of letters. The ability to hear these sounds is much more closely related to beginning reading than writing the alphabet. Fine motor skills are

being developed as students handle tools, manipulate clay and work puzzles (Tway, 1983).

8. How can the teacher possibly teach my child to pay attention to instructions when there are so many activities going on at once?

Teachers of young children know that whole-group instruction is rarely productive. They deliberately schedule small groups and often engage in one-to-one instruction for brief periods throughout the day. Small-group instruction and individual instruction have been found to be more effective for young children. For example, you may notice the teacher asking a few children to recall the events of a story while other children work around the room in various learning areas. Such an activity would lose much of its effectiveness if the whole group tried to respond at once: for some, the activity would be too complex and for others, too easy; for the shy child, there is no chance to answer. Teaching is taking place even when the teacher is not standing in front of the class. One of the important functions of teachers of young children is setting up the learning environment so that predetermined goals can be achieved. If you observe closely, you will find that new materials are being added, physical arrangements are being modified, and people and communities are being utilized as resources for the children.

Providing multiple activities for children 1) allows the teacher to match the child's individual needs with a learning activity; 2) encourages children to develop self-direction; and 3) gives children the chance to rely on their own initiative in solving problems through using resources such as books, peers and other adults, rather than assuming only the teacher has the answers. Children who work in a learning environment where choices are encouraged will learn independent work habits and cooperative attitudes (Almy, 1966; Labinowicz, 1980).

9. Why aren't grades given? How will I know that my child is making progress?

Grades are inadequate for evaluating many aspects of your child's development. Socialization skills, physical ability and emotional maturity are easier for your child's teacher to analyze in a conference with you. A folder of work, checklists, anecdotal records and answers to your specific questions will provide you much more information about your child's achievements than a simple grade (Manning and Manning, 1981).

10. Why doesn't the teacher put more emphasis on being obedient, sitting still and walking in straight lines?

Teachers of young children are not encouraging unruly behavior or disobedience. They are attempting to provide a learning atmosphere in which children will be able to develop self-control rather than merely conform to the autocratic control of the teacher. This means that the adult is very much in control, but children are allowed to make choices when they have the maturity and experience to do so. To illustrate, children might be asked if they prefer to listen to a story or play quietly with clay. The choice of listening to a story carries with it the obligation not to disturb the reader or other listeners.

Teachers attempt to require from children only those developmentally appropriate behaviors which enhance learning. Young

children learn best when actively involved; therefore, requiring them to sit still for long periods of time may be detrimental to their learning as well as physically inappropriate. Children can learn to be thoughtful of others as they move from place to place without the requirement of walking in a straight line. The goal of self-discipline is well worth the time and effort required for achievement (Gilstrap, 1981; Stone, 1980).

11. Why doesn't the teacher spend more time teaching the children to read and less time reading them stories?

Children who are introduced to a large number of outstanding books are likely to develop a love for literature that will last throughout their entire lives. Books provide a vehicle for developing comprehension when students are asked to retell stories or engage in dramatic play. When books are read to them frequently, children learn to predict words and sentence patterns of books that they will read. These skills are an integral component of the reading process (Butler and Clay, 1982; Trelease, 1982).

12. My child seems to waste a lot of time in cooking and playing in the house-keeping center. Shouldn't school time be devoted to academic learning?

Cooking is an activity that involves many subject matter areas. As an example, when the children participated in making tortillas they learned more than you might guess. They bought the ingredients at the supermarket and learned classification skills as they discovered why ingredients were grouped together on the shelves. They learned reading skills as they chose a brand of flour and math as they computed the price of groceries and calculated change. They also learned about roles of various store employees.

Math skills continued as the children measured ingredients, and new vocabulary developed as they labeled utensils and tools required in the cooking. Changes were observed when ingredients were combined and heat applied. They began to develop an understanding of similarities in two cultures when tortillas and bread were compared. They also practiced table manners and the social skills of using appropriate dinner-table conversation while eating. A teacher planning to teach anthropology, mathematics, social studies, reading, language arts and science could not have planned a more efficient lesson.

Play in a dramatic play or housekeeping center can be valuable in teaching academic skills, as well as social skills. Academically, children learn reading skills when they match labels. They learn math as they group, quantify, classify and seriate. Social concepts are gained when pupils pretend to be members of groups, such as families, or various occupations such as baker or salesperson. Science is learned by mixing water and soap, trying to make dishes float, and getting doll clothes dry.

Socially, dramatic play offers children the unique opportunity to practice various life roles and actions required in that role. They can try out a role as they perceive it and get feedback from their peers to test the accuracy of their perceptions without the threat of being "corrected" by the teacher. A child grows socially as behaviors are tried in the safe environment of the dramatic play center. A child may need to experience being the bully and can do so safely in a play situation. The child learns how others react to being bullied and can stop the behavior when it becomes threatening. Other learning areas often fail to provide the child with these opportunities for social development (Markun, 1974; McAfee et al., 1974).

13. What is my son doing playing with dolls in the housekeeping center? (or) Why is my daughter pretending to be a firefighter in the dramatic play area?

In early childhood classrooms both boys and girls are encouraged to think divergently about future careers and are given many opportunities to test their aptitudes. A variety of manipulative tasks, nurturing experiences and artistic activities are offered to both boys and girls (Cohen, 1976; Sprung, 1975).

14. Isn't there a great deal of time spent playing games?

Playing games is a very effective way of getting children to listen and follow directions. Fingerplays, for example, enlarge children's vocabularies, enable them to demonstrate physically that they are listening carefully and lengthen attention spans. Many games that are played during recess,

math and music require children to organize their thoughts and sequence their actions (Kamii and DeVries, 1980).

15. Why don't they play baseball in kindergarten?

When children engage in highly organized sports too soon, a few students will experience success and others, lowered self-esteem. Physical development is stressed daily, but teachers try to avoid games that make it necessary for children to stand quietly and wait their turn. Children learn by doing, not by watching (Lundsteen and Tarrow, 1981).

16. Why wasn't my gifted child placed in 1st grade and allowed to skip kindergarten?

Even children who are gifted academically often need to develop physical and social skills. Cooperating and competing with peers make it possible for young children to nurture healthy self-concepts. Also, the long-term results of skipping need to be considered. How will being the youngest affect your child during puberty, in athletics and at college entrance age? The teacher will endeavor to improve your child's ability to solve problems and think critically. The focus will be on the processes of learning, not just content (Elkind, 1982).

17. As a parent, what can I do at home to help my child?

Parents make valuable contributions to their child's progress in several ways. First, read to your child frequently. Children need to hear the language of books and to know that their parents value reading. Second, talk to your child. Discuss what you see, hear, smell, think, remember and feel. Children need to know that their parents are genuinely interested in what they say. Writing with your child is another means of encouraging growth: 1) write stories as your child dictates them and bind them into simple books; 2) let your child participate in writing letters and thank-you notes; 3) allow your child to help write shopping lists or fill out orders for merchandise; and 4) write notes to communicate tasks.

Broaden your children's experiences by taking them to various stores. Numerous learning experiences are possible in barber shops, hardware stores and plant nurseries, as well as in grocery stores, zoos and airports. Libraries and museums are other community resources not to be overlooked. Many of these activities cost nothing, yet they provide children with important real-life experiences.

You can help your child achieve by helping him/her learn to solve problems and be responsible. Finally, please don't pressure your child to express all knowledge with pencil and paper. Accept other means of expression: movement, drama, music and art are valid and worthwhile. Be a thinking parent who gets involved in your child's learning; you will then be able to find many activities to help your child learn at home (Baron et al., 1983; Olmsted et al., 1980).

When teachers and principals give knowledgeable answers to questions about early childhood and teaching strategies, parents gain more confidence in the school and its personnel. Investing time during these first contacts promotes positive communication and creates long-time rewards for all—children, parents, teachers and administrators.

Bibliography

Almy, Millie. *Young Children's Thinking.* New York: Teachers College Press, 1966.

Association for Childhood Education International et al. "Reading and Pre-First Grade: A Joint Statement of Concerns about Present Practices in Pre-First Grade Reading Instruction and Recommendations for Improvement." *Childhood Education* 55, 5 (Apr./May 1979): 289.

Baker, Donald. *Functions of Folk and Fairy Tales.* Wheaton, MD: Association for Childhood Education International, 1981.

Baron, Bruce; Christie Baron and Bonnie McDonald. *What Did You Learn in School Today?* New York: Warne Books, 1983.

Butler, D., and Marie Clay. *Reading Begins At Home.* Exeter, NH: Heinemann, 1982.

Clay, Marie. *Reading: The Patterning of Complex Behavior.* Exeter, NH: Heinemann, 1981.

Cohen, Monroe, ed. *Growing Free: Ways To Help Children Overcome Sex-Role Stereotypes.* Wheaton, MD: Association for Childhood Education International, 1976.

Davis, Hazel Grubbs. "Reading Pressures in the Kindergarten." *Childhood Education* 57, 2 (Nov./Dec. 1980): 76-79.

Durkin, Delores. *Teaching Them To Read* (4th Edition). Boston: Allyn and Bacon, 1983.

Elkind, David. *The Hurried Child.* Reading, MA: Addison-Wesley, 1982.

Frank, Lawrence K. *Play is Valid.* ACEI Position Paper. Wheaton, MD: Association for Childhood Education International, 1968.

Gilstrap, Robert, ed. *Toward Self-Discipline: A Guide for Parents and Teachers.* Wheaton, MD: Association for Childhood Education International, 1981.

Hirsch, Elisabeth. *The Block Book.* Washington, DC: National Association for the Education of Young Children, 1974.

Jefferson, Blanche. *The Color Book Craze.* Wheaton, MD: Association for Childhood Education International, 1964.

Kamii, Constance. *Numbers in Preschool and Kindergarten.* Washington, DC: National Association for the Education of Young Children, 1982.

Kamii, C., and R. DeVries. *Group Games in Early Education.* Washington, DC: National Association for the Education of Young Children, 1980.

Labinowicz, ed. *The Piaget Primer.* Reading, MA: Addison-Wesley, 1980.

Langstaff, Nancy, and Adelaide Sproul. *Exploring with Clay.* Wheaton, MD: Association for Childhood Education International, 1979.

Lundsteen, S.W., and N.B. Tarrow. *Guiding Young Children's Learning.* New York: McGraw-Hill, 1981.

Manning, Maryann, and Gary Manning. "The School's Assault on Childhood." *Childhood Education* 58, 2 (Nov./Dec. 1981): 84-87.

Markun, Patricia M., ed. *Play: Children's Business.* Wheaton, MD: Association for Childhood Education International, 1974.

McAfee, Oralie, et al. *Cooking and Eating with Children: A Way To Learn.* Wheaton, MD: Association for Childhood Education International, 1974.

Olmsted, Patricia, et al. *Parent Education: The Contributions of Ira J. Gordon.* Wheaton, MD: Association for Childhood Education International, 1980.

Petty, Walter T., and Robert J. Starkey. "Oral Language and Personal and Social Development." In Walter T. Petty, ed., *Research in Oral Language Development.* Champaign, IL: National Council of Teachers of English, 1967.

"Pressures Abolishing Childhood." Special issue. *Childhood Education* 58, 2 (Nov./Dec. 1981).

Sprung, Barbara. *Non-Sexist Education for Young Children.* New York: Citation Press, 1975.

Stone, Jeanette G. *A Guide to Discipline* (2nd Edition). Washington, DC: National Association for the Education of Young Children, 1980.

Strickland, Dorothy S. *On Reading.* ACEI Position Paper. Wheaton, MD: Association for Childhood Education International, 1979.

Sunderlin, Sylvia, ed. *Bibliography of Books for Children* (1983 Edition). Wheaton, MD: Association for Childhood Education International, 1984.

Trelease, Jim. *Read Aloud Handbook.* New York: Penguin Books, 1982.

Tway, Eileen. "When Will My Child Write?" *Childhood Education* 59, 5 (May/June 1983): 332-35.

Webster, Nancy K. "The 5s and 6s Go to School, Revisited." *Childhood Education* 60, 5 (May/June 1984): 325-30.

Nebraska State
Board of Education
POSITION STATEMENT ON
KINDERGARTEN

Adopted October, 1984

Changes in Kindergarten Programs

During the first two-thirds of this century, kindergarten programs were designed expressly for five-year-olds, curriculum decisions were based upon increasing knowledge about child development, and kindergarten teachers used content and methods appropriate for five-year-old children. In recent years a number of conflicting societal pressures and attitudes have caused changes in the focus of kindergarten programs. This shift in emphasis has caused many schools to begin to use content and methods unsuited to the learning needs of most five-year-old children, for whom kindergartens were originally designed. Commonly stated examples of these conflicting pressures include the following:

Five-year-old children are often perceived to be more advanced than they used to be. This perception causes many teachers and administrators to think that the kindergarten program should require mastery of content that was formerly expected in later primary grades. Many people also believe that today's children should be taught more at an earlier age so that they can keep up with expanding knowledge. BUT AT THE SAME TIME.
. . . many five-year-old children are judged to be unready for today's kindergarten program. A growing arm of the testing industry now provides a variety of instruments designed to ascertain whether children are likely to be successful in kindergarten. Ironically, at the same time that such tests are being used to discourage enrolling many "typical" five-year-olds in kindergarten, recent legislation assures that handicapped youngsters receive appropriate educational services, whether they are "ready" or not.

Many preschools and child care centers are now presenting inappropriate concepts and skills that were formerly taught in kindergarten or even first grade. This causes many people to believe that children who have been to preschool will be bored by kindergarten. BUT AT THE SAME TIME . . .

. . . many of the preschools, as well as the educational components of many child care centers, erroneously believe the center must "get children ready" for the more demanding kindergarten programs.

. . . a kindergarten should provide a place where:

•Parents and school personnel work cooperatively to build a partnership between home and school that will support the child throughout the school experience . . .

. . . not a place where the expectations of the parents and the school are in conflict or where parents feel isolated from their child's experience.

•Children experience a planned, child centered environment that encourages learning through exploration and discovery . . . not a sit-down-be-quiet classroom dominated by desks, paper and workbooks.

•Children have access to multilevel experiences and activities of varying degrees of complexity. They should be able to use concrete materials which allow for individual differences and natural variations in each one's ability to perform . . .

. . . not a place where all children are expected to perform the same task, reach the same level of performance, and accomplish the same objectives.

●Children can make choices and decisions within the limits of the materials provided . . .

. . . not a largely teacher-directed room where children seldom choose.

●Children learn there is often more than one right answer. Divergent thinking is developed and encouraged through use of open-ended materials and many informal conversations among the children and with adults . . .

. . . not a place where the day's activities are largely dominated by worksheets and discussions with predetermined answers.

●The children's own language, experiences, and stages of development form the basis of reading and writing activities . . .

. . . not the almost universal use of commercial, formal pre-reading and early-reading programs.

●Children learn to enjoy books and to appreciate literary language through a daily storytime, creative dramatics and repeated opportunities to hear and learn simple rhymes and other poems . . . not a place where the day is too short for storytime and the opportunity to appreciate literature comes only by way of educational television.

●Children participate in daily, planned activities fostering both gross and fine motor development, including such activities as running, jumping, bouncing balls, lacing cards, hammering nails, playing with clay, etc. . . not a place where children are expected to sit quietly for long periods of time and perform the motor skills beyond the current ability of many of them.

●Children develop mathematical understanding through use of familiar materials such as sand, water, unit blocks and counters . . . not a place where children are asked to mark an X on the right answer in a work book.

●Children's curiosity about natural, familiar elements forms the basis of scientific observations, experimentation and conclusions. Both planned and spontaneous interaction with plant, animals, rocks, soil, water, etc., is considered to be essential . . . not a place where science is included only when time permits or where the books tell outcomes and the teachers do the experiments.

●Experimentation, enjoyment and appreciation of varied forms of music are encouraged on a daily basis . . . not a place where music is included only when time permits.

●Art expression is encouraged through the use of a wide assortment of media integrated within the daily curriculum . . . not a place where art usually consists of copying a model, coloring a ditto or cutting and pasting a pattern, and/or where art is delegated to the specialist.

●All the activities are planned to promote a positive self-image and attitude toward school and peers . . . not a place where the child's worth is measured only by his/her ability to conform to expectations.

●Play is respected for its value as an appropriate learning medium for children of this age . . . not a place where play is deemphasized because the child "played enough" in preschool and should be ready for "real" learning.

Families, Child Rearing, and Parent Education

- Families (Articles 26-29)
- Parent Education (Articles 30-31)

In the 1980s about one-half of all American children can be expected to spend part of their childhood in some type of "non-traditional" family; that is, they will live and grow up in a family that has experienced a divorce, has a sole female head, has two working parents, has a teenager as a parent, or has two families blended into a new stepfamily. These families have special needs that require educators to be especially vigilant to potential problems that may interfere with the learning process.

As 25 million stepparents raise 6.5 million stepchildren, early childhood educators need to overcome prejudicial misconceptions so they can be of assistance to these blended, or recoupled, families rather than present another obstacle to be overcome. The inevitable disruptions and complications of new blended family relationships impact on growing children, affecting their interaction with both adults and peers. A unique way early childhood educators can aid all children today, whatever their background, is by providing a program that has a sympathetic and trained staff, consistency, routine, humor, and the expressive arts (art, music, movement, and play). When the arts, including play, are not included in programs, there is an irreplaceable loss of modalities to express inner images, wishes, feelings, and anxieties; to promote identity and confidence; and to provide essential balance for and perspective on one's life.

A century ago educators were deeply concerned with families. As a result, professional organizations such as the Parent-Teachers' Association and the American Association of University Women often undertook extensive programs aimed at providing information on parenting to families. Teachers of kindergarten children in the 1920s and 1930s would teach in the morning and spend the afternoon working with parents so they could better understand their children and their developmental abilities. Also during this period, women who received mother's pensions, or welfare as it is called today, were required to take classes in child-rearing techniques. Proper nutrition, language stimulation, and activities for children were taught.

The nuclear family no longer can depend on the extended family network to provide care, assistance, or daily support. Families relocate often and do not have direct access to family resources. It is therefore necessary for the educational community to assist children and their parents as they strive to work and learn together.

Federal agencies like Head Start provide services to American families in need but only fifteen percent of the children eligible to attend Head Start are in a program. There are thousands of children who would benefit from the medical, nutritional, social-emotional, and cognitive intervention offered at a Head Start center. Educators need to do more to reach these children and their families.

Divorce affects one million children each year. The effects on children's emotional and cognitive development are traumatic in the short-run and may be long lasting for one in three children (Kelly and Wallerstein, 1985). Boys are especially stressed by the loss of a father figure, and their changed behavior is reflected in early childhood programs.

A growing number of parents are dedicating themselves to producing "superkids." They are expecting their children to become pleasingly precocious and proficient in mastering facts and skills in academic, artistic, and athletic areas. Professionals indicate that too much stimulation of the wrong type, at the wrong time, and in the wrong context can be exceedingly harmful to children's emotional health, problem-solving abilities, desire to learn, and relationships with adults.

Many parents feel more comfortable asking teachers for advice than going to representatives of other social agencies. A well-run educational program for young children with an authoritative, sympathetic teacher can be a stabiliz-

ing support system serving both children and parents. Despite their training, experiences, or personal preferences, educators will increasingly be called upon to communicate current information to parents on a wide range of topics.

Professionals who are aware of the enormously varied life circumstances children and parents experience today are mindful not to offer magic formulas, quick remedies, or simplistic suggestions to complicated, longstanding problems of living and growing together. What many parents seem to appreciate is a sense of caring about people in general and up-to-date information about their child that is objectively presented. Practical suggestions and alternative strategies for handling daily situations are usually welcomed.

Issues related to the many changes occurring in the American family such as teenage parenting, divorce, and remarriage, along with helpful suggestions for parents who are deeply committed to their children's education, are covered in this section.

Looking Ahead: Challenge Questions

What are the stressors facing a pregnant adolescent? How does the prenatal care and parenting knowledge and skills of teenage parents affect the development of their children?

As Head Start enters its third decade, how should the program change to meet the needs of American families?

What can school personnel do to help both divorced parents and their children? How does divorce affect children's emotional needs?

Why are parents and teachers depriving children of the joys of childhood in order to prematurely experience the adult world? Are children who learn to read and play instruments as preschoolers better off than children who spend their days building with blocks and listening to stories?

Developmental Effects on Children of Pregnant Adolescents

Alice Sterling Honig

Alice S. Honig is Professor in the Department of Child and Family Studies, College for Human Development, Syracuse University in New York. Dr. Honig teaches, researches, writes and consults on numerous facets of young children and their families.

Those who serve pregnant or parenting teenagers often focus on medical risks and the provision of services to the young mother. The proportion of children currently born to teen parents is so high—one in five births—that we cannot ignore possible developmental hazards to which these children may be particularly vulnerable. Since teen parents often must find outside caregiving services for their children in order to continue schooling or job training, both home and group day care workers as well as outreach home visitors and counselors working with young parents need to be aware of potential risks in the development of children born of children.

Among sexually active teenage females, only one in five uses contraception consistently. Yet young girls who are pregnant are usually totally unprepared for the pregnancy experience. And they are overwhelmingly unprepared in terms of the parenting knowledge and skills required to rear the

children who are born. Adolescents are having sexual relations earlier and more frequently today. Every year, more than one million 15–19 year olds (10% of the young women in this age group) become pregnant, and younger teens are becoming pregnant in increasing numbers. (Finkelstein, 1980) The great majority of teen mothers (9 out of 10) elect to keep their babies. Developmental effects need to be looked at in terms of the prenatal and postnatal environment and conditions for infant growth and development.

Much of the current literature focuses on the physical condition and sociological status of the pregnant teenager. Few studies have dealt with developmental *outcomes* for children or with teen parenting practices. Yet, by focusing on the teen parent one can gather information and insights concerning *potential* difficulties that may arise developmentally for the fetus initially and later for a baby. The reason why assessment of risk for children of

adolescent pregnancies is difficult is that teen pregnancy, per se, at least in the *later* teens, does not bring with it an altogether unique set of problems. Many of the developmental difficulties experienced by the infants involved in teen pregnancy and parenting are much the same as those encountered by some infants of older parents, poor parents, and single parents. Immaturity in parenting can be found at all ages. For example, a reason that some teens give for having a baby is "to have someone to love me." Such a "reason" may of course also motivate an older mother. The extent of care and nurturing that a real (rather than fantasied) infant requires may lead to extreme frustration, depression, or anger on the part of the mother who herself wants and needs nurturing. The important point is that many of the developmental difficulties babies may endure in such cases are *more likely* to occur in conjunction with a more physically and emotionally immature mother. The probabilities of unwelcome developmental sequelae are enhanced by the physical and social youthfulness and lack of life experience and skills of the teen parent. (See Fraiberg (1975) for an excellent description of therapeutic work with young mothers whose inappropriate parenting endangers the physical and emotional health of their babies.)

Five areas relating to risk will be considered here. First, physical risks are higher for pregnant adolescents and for their babies. Second, some child problems stem from the adolescent parent's own struggles with developmental tasks unique to this life stage. Third, lack of information regarding prenatal care and parenting may be more common among teen parents and thus result in more developmental difficulties for the infant. Fourth, some infant and child problems reported are not directly the result of teen pregnancy but result from interference with some life opportunities (such as education advancement for the mother) which have had to be terminated or limited during pregnancy and after childbirth. Finally, the social milieu in which the teenage parent more frequently tends to live may affect the further development of the child.

Physical Risks

As far as physicial risks are concerned, pregnant teenagers run a four-to-five times higher risk of pregnancy complications than a woman in her twenties (Menken, 1972; Oppel & Royston, 1971). Complications such as toxemia, premature birth, and higher infant mortality bring with them increased risks for mental retardation and physical defects for infants. Babies of young mothers are more likely to die during the first year of life. Where the baby is the outcome of a repeat pregnancy for the young mother, there is an even higher risk of death in the first year of life (Whelan & Higgins, 1973).

The percentage of babies who are of low birth weight (under 2,500 grams) is much higher for adolescent mothers (Baldwin & Cain, 1980). Low birth-weight infants have a higher probabil-

ity of neurological defect and developmental delay.

Not only is the infant of a teenage mother at greater risk of death, defect, and illness than the infant born to a mother in her twenties, but the teenage mother herself is more likely to die or to suffer illness or injury. "The death rate from complications of pregnancy, birth and delivery is 60% higher for women who become pregnant before they are 15" (Alan Guttmacher Institute, 1976). Such death and the attendant transfer of infants to other caregivers may endanger the formation of early bonding and attachment between the infant and a primary caregiver. Such attachments have been found to relate strongly to later emotional and mental health of the infant (Blehar, 1980) and to later cognitive and social competency of toddlers and kindergarteners (Arend, R.A., Gove, F.L. & Sroufe, L.A., 1979).

CIGARETTES Cigarette smoking is rising sharply among teenage girls. Smoking has become habitual among 15% of girls between 12 and 18 years of age. Those who start young tend to smoke heavily and the heavy smokers run the greatest risks. For example, women who smoke spend 15% more days sick in bed each year with less serious ailments, as well as increase their chance for developing lung cancer. Also, sick mothers cannot take care of babies as effectively as healthy mothers. Children of smoking mothers run an increased risk for developing respiratory ailments. For the pregnant teenager, the effects of smoking extend to the unborn child. Girls who smoke during pregnancy are more likely to have a stillborn infant or a baby who dies soon after birth (American Cancer Society, 1976). Carbon monoxide (a gas in cigarette smoke) levels are higher in fetal blood than in maternal blood. Nicotine causes the blood vessels of the placenta to narrow and diminishes the supply of food and especially of oxygen to the fetus. Nicotine and carbon monoxide can retard the fetus' growth so that the infant is born below normal weight. Davie et al. (1972) in Great Britain have reported that smoking by pregant mothers is cor-

related with decreased reading scores later on for the children during school years.

STRESS Severe stress of the pregnant mother is associated with complications during pregnancy and with the poor condition of the baby. Stress makes for jumpier babies for months after birth. Teenagers, frightened at discovery of the pregnancy, perhaps experiencing abandonment by the biological father, perhaps undergoing punitive parental response to the pregnancy, may be at higher risk for stress effects on their unborn babies than older women with planned pregnancies. Overwhelmingly, teen pregnancies are unplanned. Younger, least prepared (and presumably therefore more highly stressed) mothers show an extraordinarily high incidence of physical abuse and neglect (Phipps-Jonas, 1980).

ALCOHOLISM More teens are using alcohol today. Moderate drinkers who give birth often deliver babies with lower than expected birth weights. Low birth weight is more likely to be associated with developmental difficulties. Babies of heavy drinkers have been born with higher incidence of facial bone abnormalities and brain damage. Even two drinks per day seems to increase the rate of birth anomaly (Streissguth et al., 1980).

DRUG EFFECTS. Two aspects of drugs need to be considered. One concerns increased use of medication for adolescent deliveries, since such deliveries are more prone to complications. Analgesia and anesthesia during labor and delivery have been shown to have a depressing effect on infant sensorimotor functioning for at least the first four weeks (Bowes et al., 1970). If a mother does not have a very alert or responsive baby, the bonding process which is so important for ensuring adequate maternal love and care may be affected (Honig, 1979).

More babies are being born to heroin and angel-dust addicted mothers. Heroin-affected babies have more rapid eye movements, greater variability in heart rates and no truly quiet sleep (Schulman, 1969). Marked tremors, high-pitched crying, and inconsolability are effects associated with withdrawal symptoms in infants born to drug-addicted mothers on methadone. Again, attachment difficulties are likely to be higher for babies more difficult to soothe, and perhaps more likely to require incubator care and medication for withdrawal symptoms.

Adolescent Developmental Tasks in Relation to Child Development

An important factor in assessing the impact of adolescent pregnancy on infant development is the developmental stage of the pregnant mother. According to Eriksonian theory, the adolescent may be struggling with two major conflicts: identity vs. role diffusion and intimacy vs. isolation. Grappling with such unresolved psychosocial conflicts, the adolescent may be ill prepared (in terms of time, energy and know-how) to give sufficient and sensitive mothering to an infant.

Peter Blos (1979) has summarized the adolescent's tasks as:

1. The loosening of childhood ties to parents and the crystallization of an adult personality.
2. The reworking and reintegration of residues of past trauma and deprivation.
3. The establishment and clarification of sense of oneself as having a unique history.
4. The resolution of sexual identity so that biological sexuality is integrated and coordinated with an adult gender role.

A recent report on a Conference on Adolescent Behavior and Health organized by the Institute of Medicine, National Academy of Science (1978) comments that early adolescents are very responsive to their social environment, especially their youth culture. Pubertal changes predispose an adolescent to preoccupation with her or his body image. Feelings of isolation, purposelessness and boredom may become prominent during adolescence. If these are not constructively handled, they can lead to maladaptive behavior inimical to good health. Solnit (1979) has further observed that as a consequence of such changes and forces "the adolescent is simultaneously pulled by regressive forces and pushed by maturational thrusts. As a result, almost all of an adolescent's felt needs are psychologically conflicted . . . . The search for competence is also a reaction to the unsettling of self esteem . . . . Developmental capacities, during adolescence, proceed rapidly, usually in dissynchrony or disharmony with each other."

It becomes apparent, then, that some of the problems in child development associated with early mothering have to do with the difficult developmental tasks in which the adolescent has become engaged but which are as yet unresolved. Indeed, early mothering may "freeze" many of these tasks at unfinished and conflicted levels. As an example, a young teenager seeking ways to acquire independence from parents may find herself after the birth of the baby in an increasingly dependent role vis a vis her parents.

Research on psychological attributes of adolescent parents increases awareness of the potential risks for their children. There is some evidence that the pregnant adolescent begins her parenting with low self-esteem, and (perhaps normal for any teenager) an inability to respond to the changing reality of her physical and social development (Abernathy et al., 1975; Schiller, 1974). Zongker (1977) has also found, in a comparison of nonpregnant school-age girls with classmates who were pregnant, that the pregnant girls had lower self-esteem, greater feelings of worthlessness, more conflict with family members, and greater evidence of defensiveness. Such parental characteristics may adversely affect the mother–baby relationship and the child's emotional development.

In intensive interviews with teen mothers, the most prominent problem reported after financial difficulties was that of isolation and loneliness (Cannon-Bonventre and Kahn, 1979). For many of the mothers in this study, isolation from former peers and school friends and the inability to link up with a new social network after child bearing were stressful aspects of their lives. This phenomenon was found for married as well as single adolescent mothers. The young mothers themselves reported that "the absence of a network of friends contributed to the probability of child abuse and neglect, depression, suicide, and marital stress." Thus, it would seem, that at the very least, agencies involved in services to teen parents need to help them find a network of friends with whom they can share and talk over problems, among them, child-rearing problems.

The interviews noted that none of the teen parents with paid employment reported such feelings. Such research finds should increase the efforts of professionals to provide job training and employment opportunities plus quality day care facilities for teen mothers in order to prevent developmentally unwelcome disturbances in the child due to maladjustments and tensions in the teen parent and consequently in her relationship with the child.

Lack of Parenting Knowledge and Skills

Perhaps the most extensive study of teenage parents' knowledge of child development has been conducted by de Lissovoy (1973). He studied 48 married teenage couples who had become parents during the high school-age period. All lived in small towns or rural areas. Child-rearing information and practices were determined by asking the teen parents when most infants reach certain developmental milestones, such as sitting up alone, toilet training, and first steps. Secondly, he asked the mothers to give their solutions to common childrearing problems, such as how to get a baby to eat something that s/he does not like. The responses were used to rate the mothers on five-point acceptance and control scales. Informal in-home observations were made by the researcher during administration of interviews and questionnaires. His research led de Lissovoy to conclude that these parents were "impatient, insensitive, irritable and prone to use physical punishment with their children."

One striking find was that the teen parents held very unreasonable expectations as to when children should accomplish important developmental tasks. Both mothers and fathers gave very low age estimates for all nine areas of development on which they were questioned. Sitting alone normally occurs at about 28 weeks. Estimates by the mothers and fathers respectively were 12 weeks and 6 weeks.

Unrealistic parental expectations have also been found to err in the direction of not expecting visual and verbal accomplishments from tiny babies. Epstein (1979) found that in her sample, teen mothers were unaware of the needs of babies for vocal, visual, and cognitive stimulation. Sugar (1979) found that adolescent mothers gave significantly less adequate stimulation to infants during the first six months of life than did adult mothers. Osofsky and Osofsky (1970) rated teen mothers in their study as providing very little verbal stimulation to their infants. Williams (1977) reported a tendency for young mothers to feel that verbal and visual stimulation will spoil a child.

Both early and late expectations based on parental ignorance of child development norms can lead to parenting practices inimical to optimal child development. If a teen mother or any mother has very low expectations for her baby's language and cognitive development, she is unlikely to provide the kind of stimulation associated with most desirable developmental outcomes in the early years. Some support for this argument may be found in a study by Ramey et al. (1979). Longitudinal observations indicated that mothers of infants at risk for intellectual retardation due to sociocultural factors interacted with their babies in ways which predicted lower Stanford–Binet intelligence scores at three years in comparison to general population control groups. Similar findings have been reported by Bradley & Caldwell (1976) for the first five years of life.

Baldwin & Cain (1980) reported on several projects that have found lowered developmental and achievement scores for children of teen mothers. Lowered Bayley scores at eight months, lower Stanford–Binet scores at four years and lower WISC and Wide Range Achievement Test scores in comparison to matched controls, were found in a National Institute of Child Health and Human Development project. Lower mental and motor development scores were found by Sandler for 14-to 19-year-old mothers compared to mothers in their twenties. On the Caldwell Preschool Inventory, Furstenberg found that older preschool children born to black, poor, urban teenagers attained significantly lower scores compared with matched controls. In a longitudinal study of long-range intellectual effects of adolescent pregnancy, Hardy et al. (1978) found that at 12 years children born of adolescent mothers performed generally poorer academically and had repeated a school grade more often than children of older women. Some outcomes, of course, may be related more strongly to socioeconomic disadvantage (Chilman, 1979) and curtailment of education of the adolescent parent.

Teen parents may have little understanding of the needs of infants for close, dependent attachments to parenting persons. The result may be forcible attempts to have the child become more independant earlier and fewer attempts to maintain close attachments with their young children (Gutelius, 1970; Oppel & Royston, 1971) in comparison with older mothers. Such children were found to be more dependent and distractible and exhibit more behavioral problems than controls. In such cases, emotional development of the children is certainly at risk.

Nutritional practices of young mothers may also place their children at risk. A clinical example or two may illuminate this problem. At a workshop for teenage parents, a fifteen-year-old mother took out a baby bottle and shoved it in the mouth of her eight-week-old infant seated in an infant seat on the table in front of her. Sputtering and gulping, the baby finished the bottle very quickly, vomited some, and proceeded to chew ravenously on his fists. The young mother, who had made no attempt to pick up or cuddle the infant during this feeding, reported cheerfully that her mother had told her to make large holes in the nipple so that the feeding could go faster. When asked to notice her baby's fist-sucking, the teenager was not able to see for herself the infant's distress. When asked to think about how she could alleviate his strong need for more sucking, the mother whipped out a bottle of water into which she had poured much sugar (on grandmother's advice, she reported) and proceeded to again feed the baby using a bottle with a large holed nipple.

For the past several years, the author has been conducting research with Dr. Frank Oski at Upstate Medical Center in New York State, on the effects of intra-muscular injection of iron (Imferon) for infants with iron deficiency anemia (1978). Lowered attention span, lowered I.Q. scores, irritability and poorer fine motor skills were found. Iron therapy improved scores markedly within one week for infants randomly chosen, compared to their controls who received therapy one week later. These babies were born to teenage mothers. However, all were also from low-income homes. It may be difficult to untangle effects of social situation and early mothering. However, the chances are higher that younger mothers will be unaware of good infant nutritional practices or, for that matter, of the harmful effects of ingestion of lead-paint chips.

Lack of Options for Teen Parents

The pressure of early parenting sometimes forecloses an adolescent's options for schooling or a stable two-parent family. Furstenberg (1976a; 1976b) compared 331 adolescent mothers with 221 of their classmates in a six-year study in Baltimore. The adolescent mothers were more likely to marry by age 18 and twice as likely to have the marriage break up within three and a half years. Teen mothers had higher fertility rates. One year after delivery, over 80% of them *wanted* to wait at least three years before becoming pregnant again. Yet, by the end of the six year study, two-thirds of them had had at least two pregnancies and nearly one-third had had three or more. Only one-fourth of their classmates had had more than one pregnancy. This is another example of the vulnerability of pregnant adolescents to loss of choice. The average teen mother completed about two years less schooling than her classmates five years after pregnancy. In general, this study established findings typical for pregnant teens: disruption of schooling, economic problems, marital instability, and difficulty in regulating family size. As Russell (1980) has noted, "early and unscheduled parenthood denies the young parent the training, material resources, and social support that she or he might have had if the transition to parenthood had been delayed" (p. 52). Important developmental growth experiences such as finishing schooling, early job experience, and living on one's own prior to assuming parenting responsibilities may be foreclosed options for many teen parents. The loss of options and curtailment of choices may lead to resentment of the infant and inability to deal appropriately or lovingly with infant problems while the parent has so many of her own.

The Social Milieu of the Teen Parent

The social milieu in which teen parents find themselves forced to function is often not guaranteed to help an infant or young child flourish. Gunter and colleagues have concluded in a review of research on the influence of adolescent childbearing on subsequent developmental outcome, "the outlook for offspring of adolescent mothers who come from deprived groups is dismal. To the extent that a large majority of these mothers are unmarried and from deprived backgrounds, (the) risk . . . is increased" (1980, p. 24).

Socioeconomic effects are particularly striking for babies born lagging developmentally in early infancy. In a study of 3,037 infants, those retarded at eight months *and* reared by lower social class families were seven times

more likely to obtain IQs under 80 at age four than if they were reared by families in a higher social class. Thus poverty effects and at-risk birth situations can be offset or compounded by the rearing environment provided for the infant (Willerman, Broman & Fiedler, 1970). Intervention and enrichment projects with low-income teen mothers and their infants have shown how quality day care for infants, toddlers and preschoolers plus in-home support for young families can nourish the learning competence of the children (Lally & Honig, 1977).

Sociologically, the teen parent is at-risk financially and materially compared to older parents. The Guttmacher Institute's (1976) figures reveal that teen mothers face greater risk of unemployment, welfare dependency, poverty, school dropout, and increased numbers of unwanted pregnancies beyond the first. Eight of ten who become mothers at 17 or younger do not complete high school. Yet almost all men and women who did not have children before age 20 receive high school diplomas, when groups are controlled for socioeconomic class and race (Card & Wise, 1977). Sometimes the social network of the family, although providing shelter for the teenage parent, is not conducive to harmonious relationships which can best support a child's emotional stability and future mental health (Honig, 1978). Case histories may give some idea of social distortions that can occur.

Case 1. Mother, age 16, lives with her own mother and her 13-month-old baby. "My baby is real bad," she confides. "She gets into the garbage and I have to slap her all the time. She is so bad." When asked if another arrangement could be made to keep the garbage off the floor and out of reach of a creeping, curious baby, the young mother vigorously denied that there was any other place the garbage could be put. The baby *must*, it seems, remain "bad."

One wonders what life scripts of the young mother have taught her so potently that a young child must be bad!

Case 2. Teenage mother comes to the Pediatric Clinic with her two-and-a-

half-year-old son and small newborn daughter by a different father. During the entire half-hour period in the waiting room before the nurse calls the mother into an examination cubicle, the mother totally ignores the boy child and coos and smiles at the tiny infant. The boy child reminds the mother of a disappointing and broken relationship with his father. The teen mother lavishes attention on the tiny new one. The oldest child receives a totally cold message. He sits with downcast eyes and an unhappy expression several seats away from his mother.

Case 3. A 17 year old, 9 months pregnant, says in a counseling session "Now that I'm pregnant I get anything I want. For the first time my mother and I are close—she treats me like I'm grown up. We never used to talk to each other."

Case 4. Fourteen year old entered a pregnancy program when eight months pregnant. She was scared, tense, and untrusting. She later confided that this was her second pregnancy. A year earlier at age 13, her mother forced her to have an abortion. This time she did not tell her mother until she was seven months pregnant—too late for another abortion. Her anger and hatred for her mother and the doctor permeated everything that this girl said. Now, two years later at age 16, she is living with her baby and boyfriend. No longer in contact with her mother, she is dealing with a whole new set of life problems.

Many and varied are the difficulties that can militate against a secure and loving environment attuned to an infant's needs. Many a teen parent in counseling has commented bitterly that the grandmother "acts like it's her baby." It may be helpful for counselors with teen mothers to consider writing contracts when working with the total family. Who will look after the baby while the mother is at school? after school? What if the young father wants to take the baby out of the mother's home and keep it at his mother's for a weekend?

We have scarcely begun to examine the possible issues that arise in teen parenting situations, let alone have research data to help us offer more appropriate choices for handling some of these situations. Suffice it to say that some of the situations, such as when the young girl bitterly rejects any further contact with the father, or vise-versa, do not suggest a good prognosis for psychosexual development of the child if the bitterness is transmitted over a long period of time to the child.

Conclusions

The impact of early child-bearing and child-rearing on the child has to be considered in the light of the impact on the whole family (Furstenberg, 1980). Where there are a number of supportive caregivers "collaborative childcare arrangements protect the infant, but they also shelter a young mother from assuming the full brunt of parental responsibilities precipitously" (p. 78). The delicate balance between *overprotecting* the adolescent from assuming too many new responsibilities that may be overwhelming and, on the other hand, *overwhelming* her with so much responsibility plus isolation so that she neglects and/or abuses her baby requires us to pay individual attention to each pregnant teenager. If we wish to ensure more favorable outcomes for children, we will need to take family context into account, as well as the mother's fund of knowledge about child development and her own family history as it may or may not have prepared her to nurture with sensitive responses as well as delight in her infant.

Professionals cannot afford to move narrowly on one front. Perhaps the wider the variety of support services and practical information and help that can be offered, the greater the chance for the child to have a normal socioemotional and intellective development. Easy-to-read parenting materials, such as those provided by New Readers Press, or the Gordon & Wollin book for young parents (1983), should be part of community resources. Programs that care for pregnant teens after delivery should consider the mother's educational needs, parenting skill needs, and infant care needs in planning services. For example, the Kalamazoo program (Sung & Rothrock, 1980) provides four components—an education unit, child/day care unit, health unit, and social services unit.

Child care workers can do much to provide a secure environment for youngsters to grow while their parents return to schooling. Day care workers can also serve as loving, responsive, language-expressive models for young parents to learn appropriate child-rearing skills. Planned parenthood facilities in a community can be involved in programs to focus on the goal of prevention of repeat pregnancies among the students. Primary care physicians who care for pregnant adolescents need to become alert to the potential developmental risks for babies born to and reared by young mothers.

Optimally, long-term public policy goals should focus on building enough community components into the system for serving pregnant and parenting teenagers so that the potential for child abuse and neglect is decreased, adolescent school completion is promoted, and nurturing skills with infants and young children are developed and supported among teen parents.

Child care workers may need to give an extra measure of attention and loving to little children whose very young parents are not yet adequate to the task of parenting optimally. Teachers will need to guard against the trap of being caught in cycles of reacting impatiently, punitively, or angrily to child "misbehaviors" in the child care center. Such children may have aversive and neglectful or punitive interactions as their only models. Teachers will need to break that pattern by being particularly accepting and warm. Wisely, they will not respond to child provocations by rejection or hostility, which the young child may not only have come to "expect" but will know how to elicit!

For the outreach worker or home visitor, the task of providing child developmental knowledge and skills to the family may have another dimension. The young parent may need more skills and more understanding of how babies and children grow. Such information and materials are available with ideas for enhancing young children's learning provided in the context of everyday chores, routines and daily home activi-

ties of parents (Honig, 1982). In addition, the home visitor may need to provide a climate of trust-building and nurturing for the teen parent to support the young parent's sense of self-competence and self-worth. Then, in turn, the child can benefit from the adolescent's increased sense of confidence and well-being as a parent and as a person.

References

Abernathy, V., et al. Identification of women at risk for unwanted pregnancy. *American Journal of Psychiatry,* 1975, *132,* 1027-1030.

Alan Guttmacher Institute. *11 million teenagers: what can be done about the epidemic of adolescent pregnancies in the United States.* New York: Planned Parenthood Federation of America, 1976.

American Cancer Society. *When A Woman Smokes,* December, 1976.

Arend, R., Gove, F.L. & Sroufe, L.A., Continuity of individual adaptations from infancy to kindergarten. A predictive study of ego-resiliency and curiosity in preschoolers. *Child Development,* 1979, *50,* 950-959.

Baldwin. W. & Cain, V.S.. The Children of Teenage Parents. *Family Planning Perspectives,* 1980, *12,* 34-43.

Blehar, M. Development of Mental Health in Infancy. *National Institute of Mental Health Science Monographs, No. 37,* 1980. DHHS Publication No. (ADM) 80-962.

Blos, P. *The Adolescent Passage: Developmental Issues.* New York: International Universities Press, 1979.

Bowes, W.A., Brackbill, Y., Conway, E. & Steinschneider, A. The effects of obstetrical medication on fetus and infant. *Monographs of the Society for Research in Child Development,* 1970, *35,* (No. 4).

Bradley, R.H. & Caldwell, B.M. The relation of infant's home environments to mental test performance at fifty-four months: A follow-up study. *Child Development,* 1976, *47,* 1172-1174.

Cannon-Bonventre, K. & Kahn, J. *The ecology of help-seeking behavior among adolescent parents. Executive Summary.* Cambridge, Mass.: American Institutes for Research, 1979.

Card, J.J. & Wise, L.L. Teenage mothers and teenage fathers: The impact of early child-bearing on the parents' personal and professional lives. *Family Planning Perspectives,* 1977, *10,* 199-207.

Chilman, C., Adolescent sexuality in a changing society: Social and psychological perspectives. U.S. Department of Health, Education and Welfare, D.H.E.W. Publication No. (NIH) 79-1426, Washington, D.C.: U.S. Government Printing Office, 1979.

4. FAMILIES, CHILD REARING, AND PARENT EDUCATION: Families

Davie, R., Butler, N. & Goldstein, H. *From birth to seven: A report of the National Child Development Study.* London, England: Longman, 1972.

DeLissovoy, V. Child care by adolescent parents. *Children Today,* 1973, *2,* 22-25.

Epstein, Ann S. *Pregnant Teenagers' Knowledge of Infant Development.* Paper presented at the Biennial Meeting of the Society for Research in Child Development, San Francisco, March, 1979.

Finkelstein, J.W. *Teenage pregnancy and parenthood. I. Review of the literature,* Unpublished manuscript, 1980.

Fraiberg, S., Adelson, E. & Shapiro, V. Ghosts in the nursery: A psychoanalytic approach to the problem of impaired infant-mother relationships. *Journal of the American Academy of Child Psychiatry,* 1975, *14,* 387-421.

Furstenberg, F.F., Jr. The social consequences of teenage pregnancy. *Family Planning Perspectives,* 1976, *8,* (No. 4), 148-164 (a)

Furstenberg, F.F., Jr. *Unplanned parenthood: The social consequences of teenage childbearing.* New York: Free Press, 1976. (b)

Furstenberg, F.F. Burdens and benefits: The impact of early childbearing on the family. *Journal of Social Issues: Teenage Parenting: Social Determinants and Consequences,* 1980, *36* (No. 1), 64-87.

Gordon, S. & Wollin, M.M. *Parenting: A Guide for Young People.* New York: Oxford Book Company, 1983.

Gunter, N.C. & Labarba, R.C. The consequences of adolescent childbearing on postnatal development, *International Journal of Behavioral Development,* 1980, *3,* 191-214.

Gutelius, M. Child-rearing attitudes of teenage Negro girls. *American Journal of Public Health,* 1970, *60,* (1), 93-104.

Hardy, J.B., Welcher, D.W., Stanley, J. & Dallas, J.R. Long-range outcome of adolescent pregnancy. *Clinical Obstetrics and Gynecology,* 1978, *21,* (No. 4). 1215-1232.

Honig, A.S. What you need to know to help the teenage parent. *Family Coordinator,* 1978, *27,* 113-119.

Honig, A.S. Recent infancy research. In B. Weissbourd & J. Musick (Eds.), *Infants: Their social environments,* Washington, D.C.: National Association for the Education of Young Children, 1981.

Honig, A.S. *Playtime learning games for young children.* Syracuse, New York: Syracuse University Press, 1982.

Honig, A.S. & Oski, F. Developmental scores of iron deficient infants and effects of therapy. *Infant Behavior and Development,* 1978, *1,* 168-176.

Institute of Medicine, National Academy of Sciences Conference Workshop on Family and Social Environment. (Co-chaired by B. Hamburg and A.J. Solnit), Washington, D.C., October, 1978.

Lally, J.R. & Honig, A.S. *Final report, family development research program* (ERIC Document No. ED 143 458). Syracuse, New York: Syracuse University Children's Center, July, 1977.

Menken, J. The health and social consequences of teenage childbearing. *Family Planning Perspectives,* 1972, *4,* 45-53.

Oppel, W.C. & Royston, A.B. Teenage births: Some social, psychological and physical sequelae. *American Journal of Orthopsychiatry,* 1970, *40,* 751-756.

Osofsky, H. J., & Osofsky, J.D. Adolescents as mothers: Results of a program for low-income pregnant teenagers with some emphasis upon infant's development. *American Journal of Orthopsychiatry,* 1970, *40,* 825-834.

Phipps-Yonas, S. Teenage pregnancy and motherhood: A review of the literature. *American Journal of Orthopsychiatry.* 1980, *50* (3), 403-431.

Ramey, C.T., Favian, D.C. & Campbell, F.A. Predicting IQ from mother infant interactions. *Child Development,* 1979, *50,* 804-814.

Russell, C.S. Unscheduled parenthood: Transition to 'Parent' for the teenager, *Journal of Social Issues,* 1980, *36,* (No. 1), 45-63.

Schiller, P.A. Sex attitude modification process for adolescents. *Journal of Clinical Child Psychology,* 1974, *3,* 50-51.

Schulman, C.A. *Sleep patterns in newborn infants as a function of suspected neurological impairment of maternal heroin addiction.* Paper presented at the meeting of the Society of Research in Child Development, Santa Monica, California, March, 1977.

Solnit, A.J. The adolescent's search for competence. *Children Today,* 1979, *8,* 13-15.

Streissguth, A.P. Landesman-Dwyer, S., Martin, J.C. & Smith, D.W. Teratogenic effects of alcohol in humans and laboratory animals. *Science,* 1980, *209,* 353-361.

Sugar, M. Developmental issues in adolescent motherhood. In M. Sugar (Ed.), *Female Adolescent Development.* New York: Brunner/Mazel, 1979.

Sung, K. & Rothrock, D. An alternate school for pregnant teenagers and teenage mothers. *Child Welfare,* 1980, *59,* 427-436.

Whelan, E. & Higgins, G. *Teenage childrearing: Extent and consequences.* Washington, D.C.: Child Welfare League of America, Inc./Consortium on Early Childbearing and Childrearing, 1973.

Willerman, L., Broman, S.H. & Fiedler, M. Infant development, preschool IQ and social class. *Child Development,* 1970, *41,* (1), 69-77.

Williams, T.M. Childrearing practices of young mothers. *American Journal of Orthopsychiatry,* 1974, *44,* 70-75.

Zongker, C.E. The self concept of pregnant adolescent girls. *Adolescence,* 1977, *12,* 477-488.

The Teacher's Role in Facilitating a Child's Adjustment to Divorce

Patsy Skeen and Patrick C. McKenry

Patsy Skeen, Ed. D., is Assistant Professor, Child and Family Development, University of Georgia, Athens, Georgia.

Patrick C. McKenry, Ph.D., is Assistant Professor, Family Relations and Human Development, School of Home Economics, Ohio State University, Columbus, Ohio.

"At first it's so terrible you could really die, but then it gets better." (Andy—age 9)

"If I'd only kept my room clean [like Daddy asked], he wouldn't have left me." (Alice—age 4)

"Silence." (Becky—age 5)

These actual responses of children involved in divorce are typical of those observed by teachers. Such observations are increasing as the lives of an alarming number of children are being disrupted—at least temporarily—by divorce. The divorce rate has more than doubled in the past ten years. Currently almost four out of ten marriages end in divorce (United States Bureau of the Census 1976). More than 60 percent of these divorcing couples have children at home. Because almost 50 percent of all divorces occur in the first seven years of marriage, the children involved in divorce are usually quite young (Norton and Glick 1976). It is estimated that 20 percent of the children enrolled in elementary school have divorced parents. In some of the kindergarten and first grade classes, this figure is closer to the 40 to 50 percent level (Wilkinson and Beck 1977).

The period of disorganization following divorce is usually extended. The family living standard is likely to change and a nonworking mother often goes to work. One parent generally leaves the home and siblings can be lost as well (Derdeyn 1977). Because divorce is a crisis involving disruption of the family structure, the

Revision of a paper presented at the 1978 National Association for the Education of Young Children Annual Conference.

role of the school and the teacher are of particular importance. A child's sense of continuity and stability is likely to be dependent upon the availability of extra-familial supports such as the school, as well as upon what protection and concern can be mobilized in the parent-child relationship during this time (Kelly and Wallerstein 1977).

The purpose of this article is to provide information that will enable the teacher to be a positive support to children and families during divorce. Research and theory concerning the effects of divorce on children, parenting through divorce, and the role of the school is summarized. Practical suggestions for the classroom teacher are presented.

Children and Divorce

Without exception divorce is a significant event in the life of any child. For the child, divorce may represent a sense of loss, a sense of failure in interpersonal relationships, and the beginning of a difficult transition to new life patterns (Magrab 1978). It cannot be assumed, however, that children will all react to divorce in the same way. For the most part, they are healthy, normal children who are confronted with an extremely stressful situation (Wilkinson and Beck 1977). Research findings indicate that the experience of divorce itself is less harmful than the nature of the parents' personalities and relationships with their children (Despert 1962; McDermott 1968; Westman and Cline 1970). The child's reactions also depend upon such factors as the extent and nature of family disharmony prior to divorce, emotional availability of important people to the child during the divorce period, and the child's age, sex, and personality strengths (Anthony 1974; McDermott 1968).

Some evidence indicates that children of divorce may be better adjusted than children remaining in two-parent homes where there is ongoing tension, conflict, and stress (Nye 1957; Landis 1960; Hetherington, Cox, and Cox 1978). Hetherington et al. (1978) suggest that divorce is often the most positive solution to destructive family functioning. Divorce can have a positive influence. For example, some children of divorce exhibit more empathy for others, increased helping behavior, and greater independence than children from intact families. However, the ease and rapidity with which divorce may be obtained and the recent emphasis on "creative" and "positive" divorce may mask the pain, stress, and adjustment problems inherent in divorce.

Available research findings on children of divorce tend to agree that divorce is to an extent a developmental crisis for children (Jones 1977; Magrab 1978; Wilkinson and Beck 1977). Wallerstein and Kelly (1977) comment that they drew heavily from crisis intervention theory in their research, and Hetherington, Cox and Cox (1976) use the term *critical event* to describe divorce as it affects families. Cantor's (1977) review of the literature revealed that in a period of parental divorce, children often show marked changes in behavior, particularly in school, and the changes are likely to be in the direction of acting-out behaviors.

Kelly and Wallerstein (1976) and Wallerstein and Kelly (1975, 1976) have researched the impact of the divorce process on children. In their preschool sample, they found that the children's self-concept was particularly affected. The children's views of the dependability and predictability of relationships were threatened, and their sense of order regarding the world was disrupted. Some suffered feelings of responsibility for driving the father away. Older preschoolers were better able to experience family turbulence and divorce without breaking developmental stride. The older preschoolers were also better able to find gratification outside the home and to place some psychological and social distance between themselves and their parents. However, heightened anxiety and aggression were noted in this group. Almost half of the children in this preschool group were found to be in a significantly deteriorated psychological condition at the followup study one year later.

Kelly and Wallerstein (1976) reported that young schoolage children respond to divorce with pervasive sadness, fear, feelings of deprivation, and some anger. At the end of one year, many still struggled with the task of integrating divorce-related changes in their lives. For older schoolage children, Wallerstein and Kelly (1976) found that divorce affected the freedom of children to keep major attention focused outside the family, particularly on school-related tasks. These children displayed conscious and intense anger, fears and phobias, and a shaken sense of identity and loneliness. At the end of one year, the anger and hostility lingered, and half the children evidenced troubled, conflictual, and depressed behavior patterns.

Hetherington et al. (1976) characterized behaviors of children of divorce as more dependent, aggressive, whiny, demanding, unaffectionate, and disobedient than behavior of children from intact families. Hether-

ington et al. (1976) noted three areas of anxiety: fear of abandonment, loss of love, and bodily harm. Anthony (1974) noted other behaviors of low vitality, restlessness, guilt, shame, anxiety, depression, low self-esteem, failure to develop as a separate person, a preoccupation with death and disease, inability to be alone, regression to immature behavior, separation and phobia anxiety, and an intense attachment to one parent. With certain groups of children—i.e., handicapped, adopted, and chronic illness cases such as asthmatics, epileptics, and diabetics—the divorce process might precipitate a psychosomatic crisis requiring hospitalization. Jacobson (1978) found the more the amount of time spent with the father was reduced during a 12-month period following divorce, the more a child was likely to show signs of maladjustment. Anthony (1974) concluded that the major reaction *during* divorce is grief associated with guilt, while the major reaction *after* divorce is shame coupled with strong resentment.

Hozman and Froiland (1977) suggested that the experience of losing a parent through divorce is similar to that of losing a parent through death. They adopted the Kubler-Ross model for dealing with loss. In this model, children go through five stages as they learn to accept loss of a parent. Initially, children deny the reality of the divorce. Denial is followed by anger and then bargaining in which children try to get parents back together. When they realize that their efforts cannot persuade parents to live together again, they become depressed. The final stage is acceptance of the divorce situation.

Anthony (1974) and Hetherington et al. (1978) cautioned against expecting all children and parents to react the same way in divorce. Each individual's behavior depends upon his or her unique personality, experiences, and the support system available.

Parenting During Divorce

For parents, divorce is a time of marked stress in everyday living and emotional as well as interpersonal adjustment. Feelings of loneliness, lowered self-esteem, depression, and helplessness interfere with parenting abilities (Hetherington et al. 1978). Several studies have noted a serious deterioration in the quality of the mother-child relationship in divorced families because of the mother's emotional neediness and her ambivalence about her new role as single parent (McDermott 1968; Hetherington et al. 1976; Wallerstein and Kelly 1976). After divorce, some fathers may become freer and less authoritarian. However, other fathers who are absent from the household may become less nurturant and more detached from their children with time (Hetherington et al. 1976; Weiss 1975).

During divorce, specific developmental needs of children are often unmet because of parental preoccupation with their own needs and parental role conflicts. When compared to parents in intact families, Hetherington et al. (1976) found that divorced parents of preschoolers were less consistent and effective in discipline, less nurturant, and generally less appropriately behaved with their children because of the preoccupation with the divorce process. When compared to parents in intact families, divorced parents communicated less well and made fewer demands for mature behavior of their children (Hetherington et al. 1976).

In summary, parent-child relationships are altered as a result of divorce. Parenting becomes difficult as the structure of the family breaks down and parents must make interpersonal adjustments such as dealing with stress, loneliness, and lowered self-esteem. However, there are many unanswered questions concerning parenting capabilities and behaviors during divorce. A great deal more research needs to be done before we can draw definitive conclusions in this area.

Schools and Divorce

The important role that schools can play in facilitating children's adjustment has not been clearly addressed in the divorce literature. Because children spend a great number of hours in school, as compared to time with parents, it is reasonable to assume that schools may be providing emotional support and continuity to a large number of children from divorcing parents. In other words, schools as a major socializing institution for children may play a more vital role in offsetting some of the negative impact of family disruption that accompanies divorce than previously thought (Jones 1977).

Key relationships in the family are often disrupted in part because of the geographic inaccessibility of the noncustodial parent. In addition, the custodial parent may be emotionally unavailable in the usual role to the child. Therefore, it has been argued that the school has an obligation to intervene with children of divorce to prevent reactions from being repressed and thus to prevent future disorders. Because parents are often involved in conflicts over financial support, visitation rights, and a battle for the children's loyalties, the teacher may be forcibly thrust into the role of an interim parent substitute (McDermott 1968).

Many children find some support within the school setting because their attitudes and performance in school provide gratification which is sustaining to them in the face of divorce stress. Kelly and Wallerstein (1977) found that the attention, sympathy, and tolerance demonstrated by teachers who had been informed about the divorce were supportive to a number of children who were feeling emotionally undernourished at home. In their study, teachers became a central stable figure in the lives of several children in the months following the separation, in some cases the only stable figure in these children's lives.

School personnel should be interested and involved in providing developmental assistance to individuals faced with critical life situations such as divorce. To date, few strategies have been published concerning ways that teachers can provide specific assistance to the child involved in divorce (Wilkinson and Beck 1977). Existing strategies that have been developed have been directed primarily to the school psychologist and guidance counselor. The following specific techniques are suggested for the classroom teacher who perhaps first notices behavioral changes and is in a position to help the child on a long-term basis. The teacher's role is discussed in three sections: working in the classroom, working with parents, and working with counselors.

What Can the Teacher Do?

In the Classroom

Team teachers, Harriet Sykes and George Brown, have just discovered that over one-half of the families of their kindergarten children have been involved in divorce. They decide that they want to help the children in their classroom grow through the divorce experience. What can they do?

Be A Careful Observer
1. Look for behavioral cues that help you understand how a child is feeling and what problems and strengths the child might have. Free play, art activities, puppet shows, and individual tasks with the child are particularly good opportunities for observation.
2. Observe the child frequently, over a period of time, and in several types of situations such as at quiet time, in group work, alone, in active play, in free play, and at home. Such varied observations allow the teacher to construct a more complete picture of the total child and reduce the likelihood that judgments will be made on the basis of a "bad day."
3. Be a good listener to both verbalization and body language.

Make a Plan
1. When teachers are attempting to understand, predict, and intervene with behavior, it is important to first determine the child's physical, social, emotional, and cognitive developmental levels. A plan can then be developed to meet the child's individual needs. Direct observation, parents, counselors, and relevant literature are good sources of information to use when planning.

Provide Opportunities for Working Through Feelings
1. Help the child recognize and acceptably express feelings and resolve conflict through the use of curriculum activities such as painting, flannel board, clay, drawing pictures, writing experience, stories about the

child's family, dramatic play, doll play, books about alternate family styles, free play, woodworking, music, and movement.

2. If the child appears to be going through the Kubler-Ross stages, prepare to help the child deal with the feelings in each stage. Give the child time for a resolution in each stage.

3. Allow children the solitude and privacy they sometimes need.

4. Support the establishment of divorce discussion and/or therapy groups for children led by trained leaders or counselors.

Help the Child Understand Cognitively

1. Help the child understand cognitively what his or her situation is, how and why he or she feels, how feelings can be expressed, and the consequences of such expression. Many discussions over an extended period of time will be necessary before such cognitive understanding is established.

2. Provide opportunities for the child to be successful in controlling his or her life. For example, make sure equipment and learning materials are matched to the child's abilities. Tell the child about the sequence of the day's events and notify the child about changes in schedule well ahead of time. Give the child opportunities to make as many choices as he or she can handle.

3. Books and discussions can be used to give information about divorce in general and promote peer acceptance and support for a child from a divorced family. (See Relevant Books, p.   .)

Maintain a Stable Environment

1. Remain consistent in expectations for the child. This may be the only area of consistency in a rapidly changing and difficult period of the child's life.

2. Although children must be dealt with patiently and might regress to immature forms of behavior at times, avoid overprotecting the child.

3. Even though the child might have problems, he or she should not be allowed to "run wild." Because parents may be having difficulty setting limits for the child, it is extremely important for the classroom teacher to lovingly, but firmly, set reasonable limits for the child's behavior.

4. Make a special effort to love the child. Let the child know that he or she is important and worthwhile through smiles, hugs, praise, and attention to appropriate behaviors. However, avoid "being a mother or father" or allowing the child to become overly dependent upon you since you and the child will separate at the end of the year.

5. Prepare the child for separation from you at the end of the year (or an extended absence from you during the year) by telling the child ahead of time about the separation, why it will occur, and what will happen to the child. A visit to the new teacher and room can be very helpful. The child must be reassured that you are not leaving because he or she is "bad" or because you have stopped loving the child.

6. Encourage the child to work through stressful situations (e.g., a move to a new house) by talking about and role playing the situation in advance.

Examine Your Attitude

1. Avoid expecting the child to manifest certain kinds of problems simply because parents are divorcing. Children are skillful in "reading" adult expectations and often will behave accordingly. Adults might also assume that divorce is the reason for a behavior problem when in actuality other factors are the causes. Children have different reactions to divorce just as they do to all other aspects of life.

2. Examine personal feelings and values about divorce. Feelings and values consciously and unconsciously affect the way teachers interact with children and parents.

3. Try to help each child grow through divorce. Remember that divorce can have the positive effects of ending a highly dysfunctional family and providing growth opportunities for family members.

Working with Parents

Andy Robinson's mother has just told Andy's teacher, Mr. Wang, that she and her husband are going to get a divorce. She is worried about how this will affect Andy and wants to do whatever she can to assist her son. How can Mr. Wang help?

1. Realize that since divorce is a stressful time, teacher-parent communication should be especially supportive and positive.

2. Understand that parents are in a crisis situation and may not be able to attend to parenting as well as you or they would like.

3. Support the parent as an important person about whom you are concerned.

4. Provide books written for both children and adults for the parent to read concerning divorce. (See Relevant Books.)

5. Encourage parents to be as open and honest as possible with the child about the divorce and their related feelings.

6. Urge parents to assure their children that divorce occurs because of problems the parents have. The children did not cause the divorce and cannot bring the parents back together.

7. Encourage parents to elicit their children's feelings.

8. Assure parents that children will need time to adjust to divorce and that difficulties in the child's behavior do not mean that the child has become permanently psychologically disturbed.

9. Encourage parents to work together as much as possible in their parenting roles even though they are dissolving their couple role. The attitudes that parents

display toward each other and their divorce are vital factors in the child's adjustment. The use of the child as a messenger or a "pawn" in the couple relationship is particularly harmful to the child.

10. Help alleviate parental guilt by telling parents that their child is not alone. Indicate to parents that there is also evidence that children from stable one-parent families are better off emotionally than children in unstable, conflictual two-parent families.

11. Encourage parents to take time to establish a meaningful personal life both as a parent and as an important person apart from the child. This can be their best gift to their children.

12. Provide an informal atmosphere in which parents can share their problems and solutions.

13. Correctly address notes to parents. "Dear Parent" can be used when you are not sure if the child's parents are divorced or if the mother might have remarried and have a different name from the child.

Working with Counselors

Becky's teacher, Ms. Jones, has been patiently listening for two hours to Becky's father talk about the pain he feels and how hard it is to cope with life as a single man after 15 years of marriage. Ms. Jones wants to help but is at her wits end. What can she do?

1. Refer children and parents to competent counselors in the community instead of trying to assume the role of counselor. A great deal of harm can be done by well-meaning listeners who "get in over their heads" and do not know how to handle a situation.

2. The American Association of Marriage and Family Therapists (225 Yale Ave., Claremont, CA 91711) and the American Psychological Association (1200 17th ST., N.W., Washington, DC 20036) maintain lists of qualified counselors. Counselors belonging to these organizations also generally indicate such membership in yellow page phonebook listings. However, the teacher should find out firsthand about the effectiveness of a counselor before referrals are made. Former clients, other teachers, and a personal visit to the counselor are good sources of information.

3. Work with the counselor when appropriate. The teacher can provide a great deal of information as a result of daily observation and interaction with the child. The teacher might also help carry out treatment strategies in the classroom.

In summary, divorce is a time of crisis for parents and children. The role of the school becomes particularly important during divorce since the family support system is under stress. Teachers are especially significant to the family since they probably spend as much or more time with the child than any other adult outside the family. When teachers are skilled and concerned, they can help parents and children grow through divorce.

References

Anthony, E.J. "Children at Risk from Divorce: A Review." In *The Child in His Family,* ed. E.T. Anthony and C. Koupernils. New York: Wiley, 1974.

Cantor, D.W. "School-Based Groups for Children of Divorce." *Journal of Divorce* 1 (1977): 183-187.

Derdeyn, A.P. "Children in Divorce: Intervention in the Phase of Separation." *Pediatrics* 60 (1977): 20-27.

Despert, L. *Children of Divorce.* Garden City, N.J.: Dolphin Books, 1962.

Hetherington, E.M.; Cox, M.; and Cox, R. "The Aftermath of Divorce." In *Mother/Child, Father/Child Relationships,* ed. J.H. Stevens and M. Mathews. Washington, D.C.: National Association for the Education of Young Children, 1978.

Hetherington, E.M.; Cox, M.; and Cox, R. "Divorced Fathers." *The Family Coordinator* (1976): 417-429.

Hozman, T.L., and Froiland, D.J. "Children: Forgotten in Divorce." *Personnel and Guidance Journal* 5 (1977): 530-533.

Jacobson, D.S. "The Impact of Marital Separation/Divorce on Children: Parent-Child Separation and Child Adjustment." *Journal of Divorce* 1 (1978): 341-360.

Jones, F.N. "The Impact of Divorce on Children." *Conciliation Courts Review* 15 (1977): 25-29.

Kelly, J.B., and Wallerstein, J.S. "Brief Interventions with Children in Divorcing Families." *American Journal of Orthopsychiatry* 47 (1977): 23-39.

Kelly, J.B., and Wallerstein, J.S. "The Effects of Parental Divorce: Experiences of the Child in Early Latency." *American Journal of Orthopsychiatry* 46 (1976): 20-32.

Landis, J. "The Trauma of Children when Parents Divorce." *Marriage and Family Living* 22 (1960): 7-13.

Magrab, P.R. "For the Sake of the Children: A Review of the Psychological Effects of Divorce." *Journal of Divorce* 1 (1978): 233-245.

McDermott, J.F. "Parental Divorce in Early Childhood." *American Journal of Psychiatry* 124 (1968): 1424-1432.

Norton, A.J., and Glick, P.C. "Marital Instability: Past, Present and Future." *Journal of Social Issues* 32 (1976): 5-20

Nye, F.I. "Child Adjustment in Broken and in Unhappy Unbroken Homes." *Marriage and Family Living* 19 (1957): 356-361.

United States Bureau of the Census. *Current Population Reports,* Series P-20, No. 297. Washington, D.C.: U.S. Government Printing Office, 1976.

Wallerstein, J.S., and Kelly, J.B. "Divorce Counseling: A Community Service for Families in the Midst of Divorce." *American Journal of Orthopsychiatry* 47 (1977): 4-22.

Wallerstein, J.S., and Kelly, J.B. "The Effects of Parental Divorce: Experience of the Child in Later Latency." *American Journal of Orthopsychiatry* 46 (1976): 256-269.

Wallerstein J.S., and Kelly, J.B. "The Effects of Parental Divorce: Experience of the Preschool Child." *Journal of Child Psychiatry* 14 (1975): 600-616.

Weiss, R. *Marital Separation.* New York: Basic Books, 1975.

Westman, J.C., and Cline, D.W. "Role of Child Psychiatry in Divorce." *Archives of General Psychiatry,* 23 (1970): 416-420.

Wilkinson, G.S., and Beck, R.T. "Children's Divorce Groups." *Elementary School Guidance and Counseling* 16 (1977): 204-213.

Relevant Books

Books for Children

Picture Books

Adams, F. *Mushy Eggs.* New York: C.P. Putnam's Sons, 1973.
Caines, J. *Daddy.* New York: Harper & Row, 1977.

4. FAMILIES, CHILD REARING, AND PARENT EDUCATION: Families

Kindred, W. *Lucky Wilma.* New York: Dial Press, 1973.

Lexau, J. *Emily and the Klunky Baby and the Next-Door Dog.* New York: Dial Press, 1972.

Lexau, J. *Me Day.* New York: Dial Press, 1971.

Perry, P., and Lynch, M. *Mommy and Daddy Are Divorced.* New York: Dial Press, 1978.

Stein, S.B. *On Divorce.* New York: Walker & Co., 1979.

Elementary and Middle School

Alexander, A. *To Live a Lie.* West Hanover, Mass.: McClelland & Stewart, 1975.

Bach, A. *A Father Every Few Years.* New York: Harper & Row, 1977.

Blue, R. *A Month of Sundays.* New York: Franklin Watts, 1972.

Blume, J. *It's Not the End of the World.* New York: Bradbury Press, 1972.

Corcoran, B. *Hey, That's My Soul You're Stomping On.* New York: Atheneum, 1978.

Donovan, J. *I'll Get There. It Better Be Worth the Trip.* New York: Harper & Row, 1969.

Duncan, L. *A Gift of Magic.* Boston: Little, Brown & Co., 1971.

Fox, P. *Blowfish Live in the Sea.* Scarsdale, N.Y.: Bradbury Press, 1970.

Gardner, R. *The Boys and Girls Book about Divorce.* New York: Bantam Books, 1977.

Goff, B. *Where Is Daddy?* Boston: Beacon Press, 1969.

Greene, C. *A Girl Called Al.* New York: Viking Press, 1969.

Hoban, L. *I Met a Traveller.* New York: Harper & Row, 1977.

Johnson, A., and Johnson, E. *The Grizzly.* New York: Harper & Row, 1964.

Klein, N. *Taking Sides.* New York: Pantheon Books, 1974.

LeShan, E. *What's Going to Happen to Me? When Parents Separate or Divorce.* New York: Four Winds Press, 1978.

Nahn, P. *My Dad Lives in a Downtown Motel.* Garden City, N.J.: Doubleday, 1973.

Mazer, H. *Guy Lenny.* New York: Delacorte Press, 1971.

Mazer, N. *I, Trissy.* New York: Dell Publishing Co., 1971.

Newfield, M. *A Book for Jodan.* New York: Atheneum, 1975.

Rogers, H. *Morris and His Brave Lion.* New York: McGraw-Hill, 1975.

Simon, N. *All Kinds of Families.* Chicago: Whitman, 1976.

Steptoe, J. *My Special Best Words.* New York: Viking Press, 1974.

Stolz, M. *Leap Before You Look.* New York: Harper & Row, 1972.

Talbot, C. *The Great Rat Island Adventure.* New York: Atheneum, 1977.

Walker, M. *A Piece of the World.* New York: Atheneum, 1972.

Books for Teachers and Parents

Gardner, R. *The Parents Book about Divorce.* Garden City, N.J.: Doubleday, 1977.

Grollman, E. *Explaining Divorce to Children.* Boston: Beacon Press, 1969.

Hunt, M., and Hunt, B. *The Divorce Experience.* New York: McGraw-Hill, 1977.

Kessler, S. *The American Way of Divorce: Prescriptions for Change.* Chicago: Nelson-Hall, 1975.

Krantzler, M. *Creative Divorce.* New York: M. Evans & Co., 1974.

Salk, L. *What Every Child Would Like Parents to Know about Divorce.* New York: Harper & Row, 1978.

Sinberg, J. *Divorce Is a Grown Up Problem: A Book about Divorce for Young Children and Their Parents.* New York: Avon, 1978.

Stein, S.B. *On Divorce.* New York: Walker & Co., 1979.

Stevens, J., and Mathews, M., eds. *Mother/Child, Father/Child Relationships.* Washington, D.C.: National Association for the Education of Young Children, 1978.

Turow, R. *Daddy Doesn't Live Here Anymore.* Garden City, N.J.: Anchor Books, 1978.

Weiss, R. *Marital Separation.* New York: Basic Books, 1975.

Journals

Journal of Divorce. Editor: Esther O. Fisher. Haworth Press, 174 Fifth Ave., New York, NY 10010.

The Single Parent: The Journal of Parents Without Partners, Inc. Editor: Barbara Chase. Parents Without Partners, Inc., International Headquarters, 7910 Woodmont Ave., Bethesda, MD 20014.

Blended Families
Overcoming the Cinderella Myth

Young children are familiar with stories of wicked stepmothers—Cinderella's stepmother gave her the vilest household tasks and competed with her for the prince's attention. Hansel and Gretel were abandoned in the woods by their stepmother. Snow White's jealous stepmother tried to poison her. Today's stepfamily relationships are quite different from these portrayals, but they do also differ from intact family relationships. Teachers of young children can be a positive support to children and their stepfamilies if we are better informed.

Patsy Skeen, Bryan E. Robinson,
and Carol Flake-Hobson

Patsy Skeen, Ed.D., is Assistant Professor of Child and Family Development at the University of Georgia, Athens, Georgia.

Bryan E. Robinson, Ph.D., is Associate Professor of Human Development and Learning at the University of North Carolina, Charlotte, North Carolina.

Carol Flake-Hobson, Ph.D., is Associate Professor of Education at the University of South Carolina, Columbia, South Carolina.

Demographic information

The high incidence of stepfamilies in this country is *not* a myth. There are an estimated 25 million stepparents (Visher and Visher 1979), and 6.5 million children live in stepfamilies (Francke and Reese 1980; Jacobson 1980). Sometimes called reconstituted, recoupled, or blended families, such families may be a widow with one child marrying a bachelor, or as complex as four divorced individuals, all with joint custody of their children trying to form two new households. Children may visit rather than live with stepparents (Visher and Visher 1978b). Most blended families are formed through divorce and remarriage (Jacobson 1980), a phenomenon which is expected to continue.

Stepfamily research

Empirical research on stepfamilies is limited. Duberman (1973) studied remarried parents using a Parent-Child Relationship Rating Scale. Her results showed that 64 percent of the blended families had "excellent" relationships, although steprelations were more successful when previous marriages ended in death rather than divorce. Furthermore, stepparent-child relationships were better among families of higher social classes, and among Protestants as compared to Catholics.

Findings from a study of junior and senior high school students contrasted with Duberman's positive report on blended family relationships. Bowerman and Irish (1962) contrasted adjustments of children residing in three family conditions—with natural parents, with a mother and stepfather, and with a father and stepmother. They reported that homes involving steprelations were more characterized by stress, ambivalence, and low cohesiveness than natural parent homes. Stepparents also had more trouble establishing the same degree of affection and closeness with the children than did biological parents. Children in stepfamilies said they felt more rejected than those in nonstepfamilies. In contrast to Duberman's findings, Bowerman and Irish found that children adjusted better toward stepparents when previous marriages were broken by divorce rather than death.

One explanation for these conflicting reports is the differences in research methodology. Duberman surveyed only the husbands and wives involved in stepfamilies, asking spouses to evaluate their own children's relationship with the stepparent. In contrast, Bowerman and Irish's data are based on questionnaires completed by stepchildren, who might evaluate relationships differently from their parents. Changing social attitudes about divorce may also account for some differences.

Touliatos and Lindholm (1980) asked teachers to rate the behavior of children of kindergarten age through eighth grade. Compared to children in intact homes, children in homes with stepparents were rated as having more conduct problems (e.g., negativism, aggression), and children living with a mother and stepfather also had socialized delinquency (e.g., bad companions, cooperative stealing).

Bohannan and Erickson (1978) studied stepchildren and children raised by natural parents. Ratings of stepfathers made by both stepchildren and mothers were as positive as those of biological fathers made by their natural children and by the children's mothers. Lending additional support to this view, two national surveys found no social-psychological differences between high school students brought up in stepfather families and those raised in natural-parent families (Wilson et al. 1975). In addition, Burchinal (1964) assessed the questionnaire responses of adolescents and parents from unbroken, broken, and reconstituted families. He found no significant differences in the personality and social relationships among the three groups. Santrock et al. (1982) also observed unbroken, broken, and stepfamilies. They concluded that the social behavior of children in stepfamilies is not necessarily less competent than that of children in intact or broken families. Nye (1957) did find more adjustment problems in stepfamilies than in unbroken families, but he noted that the greatest adjustment difficulties exist in unhappy intact families. Other reports (Bernard 1956; Bohannan 1970; Goode 1956; Landis 1962; Stinnett and Walters 1977) indicate that stepfamilies had no more difficulty than nonstepfamilies. Instead, children from stepfamilies could have mostly positive, mostly negative, or mixed experiences—the same as children from unbroken families (Wilson et al. 1975).

Stepfathers

I was really turned on by her—then I met her kids. . . . I began to look at them in a very different way after I got serious. . . . Everybody warned me not to marry a woman with children. They said there'd be problems: There were. But the youngest goes off to college next month and I think we've won. (Bohannan and Erickson 1978, p. 53)

More than one-half of families formed by divorce and remarriage include stepfathers (Rallings 1976), but we know very little about stepfatherhood. What we do know is that stepfathers face a real challenge trying to fit into a new family.

Stepfathers tend to be either inattentive and disengaged, giving the mother little childrearing support, or very actively involved. The highly active stepfathers are often restrictive, especially to sons. However, if the stepfather is able to set consistent limits and communicate warmly and well with the children and if the mother welcomes the stepfather's support, the stepchildren, especially boys, generally function better than children in single-parent families or conflicted nondivorced families (Hetherington, Cox, and Cox 1981). Oshman and Manosevitz (1976) also found that stepfathers have a positive effect on stepsons. However, children aged 9 to 15 are less likely to accept an effective stepparent than are younger or older children (Hetherington, Cox, and Cox 1981). Stern (1978) suggests that fathers are likely to be more successful disciplinarians when they adopt a slow, gentle, flexible approach built on friendship which includes the child's participation rather than authoritarian controls over the child.

As mentioned earlier, mothers and children thought stepfathers were just as good parents as biological fathers (Bohannan and Erickson 1978), but stepfathers had lower opinions of their own performance. Some stepfathers whose children lived with their mothers felt pain and regretted the time spent with stepchildren when they could spend so little time with their own children (Brooks 1981). Stepfathers viewed their stepchildren as less happy and they felt less effective in the fathering role than natural fathers. Stepfathers, wanting to do a good job, seemed more self-conscious about their effectiveness and more self-critical, so they set their standards high—measuring themselves against what they thought an ideal father should be (Bohannan and Erickson 1978).

Lending additional support to these findings, Duberman (1973) found that stepfathers had better relationships with stepchildren than did stepmothers. Moreover, better parent-child steprelations existed among never-before-married stepfathers than with never-before-married stepmothers. Although stepfathers may not believe it, other stepfamily members view them to be just as competent in their role as biological fathers are with their children.

Stepmothers

> At the beginning you would find my husband's four children off playing in one corner and my two playing in another corner. But now they don't do that. There's no open hostility, and we handle it by trying hard to be fair. Time and adjustment have brought an improvement in the relationships among them all (Duberman 1975, p. 69)

Stepmothers have been portrayed as wicked or evil in folklore and literature, much more than stepfathers. There is evidence that stepmothers do have a harder time adjusting to stepparenting than stepfathers (Bowerman and Irish 1962; Jones 1978). Perhaps the Cinderella myth of the cruel stepmother lingers, causing more problems for stepmothers and children. Also, society is more apt to give assistance and social support to stepfathers (Bowerman and Irish 1962).

Duberman (1973) reported that younger mothers had better steprelations with children than older mothers, and that stepmothers had better steprelations with children younger than 13 than with teenage children. Draughton (1975) suggested that stepmothers can expect better success by being the child's friend than by trying to become a second mother.

Stepchildren

> Fifteen-year-old child: The main change is getting used to the new parent. Our family has become more closely knit, even though we are separated because my stepfather is a student at a university and I am also. I

find him to be a good man and a fine parent. (Bernard 1956, p. 323)

The plight of children in blended families is not as dismal as it is often portrayed. Generally, research shows that stepchildren are just as happy and just as socially and academically successful as children in unbroken families (Bohannan and Erickson 1978), although one study indicated that children from unbroken families reached a higher level of education than children from stepfamilies (Wilson et al. 1975).

One of the problems that usually arises in blended families is the question of "turf." For example, "Why do I have to share my toys with you?" or "He's *my* dad, not yours" (Johnson 1980). Duberman (1973) found that positive stepsibling relationships are crucial to the success of stepfamilies. The better the relations between stepsiblings, the better the total family integration. When remarried couples had a child together, their children from former marriages were more likely to have harmonious relations. On the other hand, sometimes children from the former marriages feel left out or not as important as the new child which belongs to both the natural parent and the stepparent (Brooks 1981).

Complexities of blended families

> The twins and my stepdaughter hate each other. . . . They always pull this bit about "your mommie" and "my daddy" jazz. There's lots of jealousy among them. The kids drive us crazy with fighting. (Duberman 1975, p. 68)

Living in a blended family is different from simply moving from one primary family into another! There are clear structural differences in how intact nuclear families and stepfamilies interact (Draughton 1975; Nelson and Nelson 1982; Perkins and Kahan 1979; Sager et al. 1981; Schulman 1972; Visher and Visher 1979).

Stepfamilies face a special dilemma because of the difficulty in acquiring stepparenting skills (Fast and Cain 1966; Kompara 1980). Most adults have not had previous experience having a stepchild or living in a stepfamily. Kompara (1980) further points out that "in a remarriage . . . the children have been partially socialized by the first parents'' (p. 69). Stepfamily members have separate histories, memories, and habits. These factors pose difficulties in the socialization process of stepfamilies. Solidarity must be reestablished, and status, duties, and privileges must be redefined in the context of the new family system (Duberman 1973).

The challenge of the blended family involves dealing with the past as well as the present and future. The loss of the initial family must be mourned (Thies 1977). Parents must work through their relationships with the former spouse as well as help their children deal successfully with the divorce (Kleinman, Rosenberg, and Whiteside 1979). Former spouses and their relatives may be part of the new stepfamily's interactions. These interactions can be destructive if former spouses use the children to continue the battle which was not ended with divorce (Brooks 1981).

Children in blended families are faced with adjusting to more complex family interaction than before:

> The child has to adjust to one and sometimes two stepparents (one of whom is visited) and still retain relationships with the biological parent out of the home, biological siblings in and/or out of the home and develop a relationship with stepsiblings who may be in and/or out of the home. (Jacobson 1980, p. 2)

As a result of such complex interaction children may experience divided loyalties (Visher and Visher 1979). Stepchildren may feel twice defeated—first for not preventing the divorce and second for not preventing the remarriage. They may direct anger for the absent parent toward the new stepparent (Francke and Reese 1980). These situations are compounded when relationships are recast in such a way that stepparents and children are thrown into

The transition from unbroken to blended families is not an easy one, but when blended families have realistic expectations and support, it is possible for most to manage their lives with reasonable success.

instant, intimate relationships with strangers for which they are not ready (Kompara 1980). Belief in the myth that blended families should instantly love each other because they are now a family sets families up for failure (Visher and Visher 1978a).

Messinger (1976) identified the stepfamily as a high-risk group for which there are no societal norms. Lack of clear role expectations or guidelines for acceptable stepfamily behavior causes role uncertainty and stress in stepfamily relationships (Fast and Cain 1966; Messinger 1967; Rallings 1976). Some stepparents spend too much time and energy trying to work out their stepparent roles at the expense of working on the couple relationship (Hetherington, Cox, and Cox 1981). The higher divorce rate in second marriages—40 percent compared to 33 percent in first marriages—attests to the difficulty of working out the complex problems typical of stepfamilies (Francke and Reese 1980).

Summary of research findings

Research findings on the effects of children living in blended families are mixed. Some studies indicate the presence of more difficulty for children in stepfamilies than children living with both biological parents, while others suggest no major differences in difficulties in either family type. The nature of the blended family network, however, is strikingly different from the unbroken family network, so stepfamilies experience some complications which unbroken families do not.

Despite the potential difficulties in blended family relationships, there are positive outlooks. Messinger (1976) suggests that stepfamily stress can be prevented or reduced through remarriage preparation courses. Before embarking upon remarriage, Jacobson (1980) recommends "a rehearsal for reality" in which soon-to-be blended family members express their feelings and anticipate potential problems which might arise after the marriage.

Family counselors can help the couple work out their inevitable differences in values, develop faith in their parent-child relationships, and accept rejection by step-

children (Visher and Visher 1978b). Counselors can also help family members mourn the loss of the initial family and develop productive methods of communication. Stepchildren, having observed the break of adult relationships through death or divorce, are given a renewed opportunity to see a couple work together in a positive way (Visher and Visher 1979). The transition from unbroken to blended families is not an easy one, but when blended families have realistic expectations and support, it is possible for most to manage their lives with reasonable success (Schulman 1972). In the next section we will discuss the teacher's unique role in facilitating a stepchild's adjustment after a parent's remarriage.

What can the teacher do?

Because adjustment to divorce and to being a member of a blended family both involve considerable change and stress, some of the techniques teachers can use in facilitating a child's adjustment to divorce are also appropriate for use with children in stepfamilies. Some of the suggestions in this section are modified from those developed by Skeen and McKenry (1982, pp. 232–237) for use with children of divorce.

In the classroom

You and your colleagues know that several children in your groups are members of blended families. You want to help the children grow through this experience. What can you do?

Observe carefully
1. Look for behavioral cues that help you understand how a child is feeling and what problems and strengths the child might have. Free play, art activities, puppet shows, and individual talks with the child are particularly good opportunities for observation.
2. Observe the child frequently, over a period of time, and in several types of situations such as at quiet time, in group work, alone, in active play, in free play, and at home. Such varied observations allow the teacher to construct a more complete picture of the total child and reduce

the likelihood that judgments will be made on the basis of a "bad day."

3. Be a good listener to both verbal and body language.

Make a plan

1. When teachers are attempting to understand, predict, and intervene with behavior, it is important to first determine the child's physical, social, emotional, and cognitive developmental levels. A plan can then be developed to meet the child's individual needs. Direct observation, parents, counselors, and relevant literature are good sources of information to use when planning.

Provide opportunities for working through feelings

1. Help the child recognize and acceptably express feelings and resolve conflict through the use of curriculum activities such as painting, flannel board, clay, drawing pictures, writing experience stories about the child's family, dramatic play, doll play, books about alternate family styles, free play, woodworking, music, and movement.

2. Allow children the solitude and privacy they sometimes need.

3. Support the establishment of blended family discussion and/or therapy groups for children led by counselors.

Help children understand

1. Help children understand what their situation is, how and why they feel, how feelings can be expressed, and the consequences of such expression. Many discussions over an extended period of time will be necessary before such understanding is established.

2. Provide opportunities for the children to be successful in controlling their lives. For example, make sure equipment and learning materials are matched to the children's abilities. Tell them about the sequence of the day's events and notify children about changes in schedule well ahead of time. Give children opportunities to make as many choices as they can handle.

3. Books and discussions can be used to give information about blended family relationships and to promote peer acceptance and support for a child in such a family. (See the Additional resources at the end of the article.)

Maintain a stable environment

1. Remain consistent in expectations for the child. This may be the only area of consistency in a rapidly changing and difficult period of the child's life.

2. Although children must be dealt with patiently and may regress to immature forms of behavior at times, avoid overprotecting the child.

3. Even though children may have problems, they should not be allowed to "run wild." Because parents may be having difficulty setting limits for the child, it is extremely important for the classroom teacher to lovingly, but firmly, set reasonable limits for the child's behavior at school.

4. Make a special effort to love children in blended families. Let them know that they are important and worthwhile through smiles, hugs, praise, and attention to appropriate behaviors. However, avoid taking on the role of a mother or father or allowing children to become overly dependent upon you since you will separate at the end of the year.

5. Prepare children for separation from you at the end of the year (or an extended absence from you during the year) by telling them ahead of time about the separation, why it will occur, and what will happen to the children. A visit to the next teacher and room can be very helpful. Children must be reassured that you are not leaving because they are bad or because you have stopped loving them.

6. Encourage children to work through stressful situations (e.g., a move to a new house) by talking about and role playing the situation in advance.

Examine your attitude

1. Avoid expecting children to manifest certain kinds of problems simply because they are members of blended families. Children are skillful in "reading" adult expectations and often will behave accordingly. Adults might also assume that the stepfamily is the reason for a behavior problem when in actuality other factors may be the causes. Children have different reactions to life in a blended family, just as they do to all other aspects of life.

2. Examine your personal feelings and values about blended families. Feelings and values consciously and unconsciously affect the way teachers interact with children and parents.

3. Remember that blended families must deal with issues that do not come up in natural families. Although life can be stressful, especially at first, family members can grow through the experience and benefit from membership in a family situation that has struggled and made it.

Working with parents

Gillian Price's father has just told her teacher that he is marrying a woman who has two children. He is concerned about how this will affect four-year-old Gillian and wants to do whatever he can to assist his new family. How can a teacher help?

1. Realize that since the establishment of a stepfamily is a stressful time, teacher-parent and teacher-stepparent communication should be especially supportive.

2. Understand that parents and stepparents are involved in a difficult situation requiring adjustments different from those in a natural family. They may not yet feel comfortable in their new stepparenting role.

3. Support parents and stepparents as important persons apart from their parenting role about which you are concerned.

4. Provide information for parents and stepparents. For example, lend the school's copies of books for parents and children suggested at the end of this article or ask the local library to order them. Use the films mentioned at the end of this article. Have parent meetings concerning child discipline and guidance.

5. Encourage stepparents and parents to prepare for their marriage by honestly sharing feelings, defining roles for all family members, discussing changes the new family arrangements will necessitate, and discussing finances.

6. Assure parents and stepparents that they and their children will need considerable time to adjust. Also, stepfamilies that have realistic expectations about typical problems are more likely to deal with them successfully than those who expect instant love and a happily-ever-after life following marriage of the stepparent and parent.

7. Encourage the parent and stepparent to work together in deciding how to parent and interact in their day-to-day relationships with their children. However, parents and stepparents should also be free to disagree as well as include children so that children do not feel it is "us against them."

8. Encourage stepparents to take time and use patience in building relationships with stepchildren. Anger, guilt, jealousy, testing, confusion, comparison with the natural parent, and rejection are typical stepchild responses, especially in the early stages, but can be overcome with time and understanding.

9. Urge parents and stepparents to keep open channels of communication and to involve their children in making family decisions, defining roles of family members, and working out living arrangements.

10. Help stepparents develop realistic expectations regarding their parenting roles. For example, they cannot replace the natural parent, but they can be a vital friend and supporter of the stepchild.

11. Help stepparents to treat both their natural and stepchildren fairly and honestly.

12. Encourage the parent and stepparent to develop new projects and traditions in which the stepfamily can be involved. For example, during holidays new blended family traditions can be begun while previous traditional activities are maintained.

13. Encourage the stepparent and child to spend some time alone together. For example, sharing a hobby or walking might be enjoyable activities which can help build a relationship.

14. Encourage parents and stepparents to elicit their children's feelings.

15. Encourage stepparents to maintain as good a relationship as possible with their former spouses and to avoid making derogatory comments about the other parent which could anger children and force them to be defensive.

16. Encourage parents and stepparents to build a strong couple relationship apart from parenting by sharing feelings, listening to each other, and taking time for themselves as individuals and as a couple. A loving couple relationship which works can be the best gift to children.

17. Encourage parents to make special efforts to help the visiting stepchild feel comfortable and a part of the family by involving the child in planning activities, providing a permanent drawer or toys, or inviting the stepchild's friend along.

18. Correctly address notes to stepparents, remembering that parental surnames may be different from the child's.

19. Provide an informal atmosphere or help establish support groups in which stepparents can share their problems and solutions.

Working with counselors

John's teacher, Mr. Wilson, has been patiently listening to John's mother talk about the serious problems in her stepfamily for an hour. Mr. Wilson wants to help but feels lost. What can he do?

1. Refer stepfamilies to a competent counselor who works with whole families (Visher and Visher 1978b). Well-meaning listeners can do a great deal of harm.

A note of caution: Teachers' roles in working with parents vary. Teachers should be aware of legal restrictions and school policy concerning the degree and type of parental involvement considered appropriate for teachers.

2. Counselors belonging to professional organizations generally indicate their membership in the Yellow Pages telephone listings (see Additional resources). The local Mental Health Association, Human Resources Department of local or state government, or pastoral counseling services may also be good sources of information. However, the teacher should find out about the counselor firsthand from former clients, other teachers, or a personal visit before referrals are made.

3. Work with the counselor when appropriate. Teachers can provide helpful information based on their daily interaction and observation of the child. The teacher might also help carry out treatment strategies in the classroom.

Life in a blended family is different from life in a natural family. Establishing a blended family is a particularly stressful time. Teachers are especially significant since they spend as much or more time with the child than any other adult outside the family. When teachers are skilled and concerned, they can help parents and children grow and create healthy blended families.

References

Bernard, J. *Remarriage: A Study of Marriage.* New York: Dryden, 1956.

Bohannan, P., ed. *Divorce and After.* New York: Doubleday, 1970.

Bohannan, P., and Erickson, R. "Stepping In." *Psychology Today* 11 (1978): 53–59.

Bowerman, C. E., and Irish, D. P. "Some Relationships of Stepchildren to Their Parents." *Marriage and Family Living* 24 (1962): 113–121.

Brooks, J. B. *The Process of Parenting.* Palo Alto, Calif.: Mayfield, 1981.

Burchinal, G. "Characteristics of Adolescents from Unbroken, Broken, and Reconstituted Families." *Journal of Marriage and the Family* 26 (1964): 44–50.

Draughton, M. "Step-Mother's Model of Identification in Relation to Mourning in the Child." *Psychological Reports* 36 (1975): 183–189.

Duberman, L. "Step-Kin Relationships." *Journal of Marriage and the Family* 35 (1973): 283–292.

Duberman, L. *The Reconstituted Family: A Study of Remarried Couples and Their Children.* Chicago: Nelson-Hall, 1975.

Fast, I., and Cain, A. C. "The Stepparent Role: Potential for Disturbances in Family Functioning." *American Journal of Orthopsychiatry* 36 (1966): 485–491.

Francke, L. B., and Reese, M. "After Remarriage." *Newsweek* 11, no. 6 (February 11, 1980): 66.

Goode, W. J. *Women in Divorce,* Glencoe, Ill.: Free Press, 1956.

Hetherington, M. E.; Cox, M.; and Cox, R. "Divorce and Remarriage." Paper presented at the annual meeting of the Society for Research in Child Development, Boston, Massachusetts, April 1981.

Jacobson, D. S. "Stepfamilies." *Children Today* 9 (1980): 2–6.

Johnson, H. C. "Working with Stepfamilies: Principles of Practice." *Social Work* 25 (1980): 304–308.

Jones, S. M. "Divorce and Remarriage: A New Beginning, a New Set of Problems." *Journal of Divorce* 2 (1978): 217–227.

Kleinman, J.; Rosenberg, E.; and Whiteside, M. "Common Developmental Tasks in Forming Reconstituted Families." *Journal of Marriage and Family Therapy* 5 (1979): 79–86.

Kompara, D. R. "Difficulties in the Socialization Process of Stepparenting." *Family Relations* 29 (1980): 69–73.

Landis, J. T. "A Comparison of Children from Divorced and Non-Divorced Unhappy Marriages." *Family Life Coordinator* 11 (1962): 61–65.

Messinger, L. "Remarriage Between Divorced People with Children from Previous Marriages: A Proposal for Preparation for Remarriage." *Journal of Marriage and Family Counseling* 2 (1976): 193–200.

Nelson, M., and Nelson, G. "Problems of Equity in Reconstituted Family: A Social Exchange Analysis." *Family Relations* 31 (1982): 223–231.

Nye, F. I. "Child Adjustment in Broken and in Unhappy Unbroken Homes." *Marriage and Family Living* 19 (1957): 356–361.

Oshman, H. P., and Manosevitz, M. "Father

Absence: Effects of Stepfathers on Psychosocial Development in Males." *Developmental Psychology* 12 (1976): 479–480.

Perkins, T. F., and Kahan, J. P. "An Empirical Comparison of Natural-Father and Stepfather Family Systems." *Family Process* 18 (1979): 175–183.

Rallings, E. M. "The Special Role of Stepfather." *The Family Coordinator* 25 (1976): 445–449.

Sager, C. J.; Walker, E.; Brown, H. S.; Crohn, H. M.; and Rodstein, E. "Improving Functioning of the Remarried Family System." *Journal of Marital and Family Therapy* 1 (1981): 3–13.

Santrock, J.; Warshak, R.; Lindbergh, C.; and Meadows, L. "Children's and Parents' Observed Social Behavior in Stepfather Families." *Child Development* 53 (1982): 472–480.

Schulman, G. L. "Myths That Intrude on the Adaption of the Stepfamily." *Social Casework* 53 (1972): 131–139.

Skeen, P., and McKenry, P. C. "The Teacher's Role in Facilitating a Child's Adjustment to Divorce." In *Curriculum Planning for Young Children*, ed. J. F. Brown. Washington, D.C.: National Association for the Education of Young Children, 1982.

Stern, P. N. "Stepfather Families: Integration Around Child Discipline." *Issues in Mental Health Nursing* 1 (1978): 326–332.

Stinnett, N., and Walters, J. *Relationships in Marriage and Family.* New York: Macmillan, 1977.

Thies, J. M. "Beyond Divorce: The Impact of Remarriage on Children." *Journal of Clinical Child Psychology* 5 (Summer 1977): 59–61.

Touliatos, J., and Lindholm, B. W. "Teachers' Perceptions of Behavior Problems in Children from Intact, Single-Parent and Stepparent Families." *Psychology in the Schools* 17 (1980): 264–269.

Visher, E. B., and Visher, J. S. "Common Problems of Stepparents and Their Spouses." *American Journal of Orthopsychiatry* 48 (1978a): 252–262.

Visher, E. B., and Visher, J. S. "Major Areas of Difficulty for Stepparent Couples." *International Journal of Family Counseling* 6 (1978b): 70–80.

Visher, E. B., and Visher, J. S. *Stepfamilies: A Guide to Working with Stepparents and Stepchildren.* New York: Brunner/Mazel, 1979.

Wilson, K. L.; Zurcher, L. A.; McAdams, D. C.; and Curtis, R. L. "Stepfathers and Stepchildren: An Exploratory Analysis from Two National Surveys." *Journal of Marriage and the Family* 37 (1975): 526–536.

Additional resources

Books for children

Picture books

Drescher, J. *Your Family My Family.* New York: Walker, 1980.

Green, P. *A New Mother for Martha.* New York: Human Sciences Press, 1978.

Lewis, H. *All about Families the Second Time Around.* Atlanta: Peachtree, 1980.

Stenson, J. *Now I Have a Stepparent and It's Kind of Confusing.* New York: Avon, 1979.

Books for young readers

Burt, M., and Burt, R. *What's Special About Our Stepfamily?* Garden City, N.Y.: Doubleday, 1983.

Byars, B. *The Animal, The Vegetable and John D. Jones.* New York: Delacorte, 1982.

Clifton, L. *Everett Anderson's Nine Months Long.* New York: Holt, Rinehart & Winston, 1978.

Gardner, R. *The Boys and Girls Book about Stepfamilies.* New York: Bantam, 1982.

Phillips, C. *Our Family Got a Stepparent.* Ventura, Calif.: Regal Books, 1981.

Sobol, H. *My Other Mother, My Other Father.* New York: Macmillan, 1979.

Books for teachers, parents, and stepparents

Atkin, E., and Rubin, E. *Part-Time Father.* New York: Signet, 1977.

Berman, C. *Making It As a Stepparent.* Garden City, N.J.: Doubleday, 1980.

Capaldi, F., and McRae, B. *Stepfamilies.* New York: New Viewpoints/Vision Books, 1979.

Duberman, L. *The Reconstituted Family.* Chicago: Nelson-Hall, 1975.

Duffin, S. *Yours, Mine, and Ours: Tips for Stepparents.* DHEW Pub. No. (ADM) 78-676, 1978. National Institute of Mental Health, Public Inquiries, 5600 Fishers Ln., Rockville, MD 20857.

Einstein, E. *The Stepfamily: Living, Loving, and Learning.* New York: Macmillan, 1982.

Espinoza, R., and Newman, Y. *Step-Parenting.* DHEW Pub. No. (ADM) 78-579, 1979. National Institute of Mental Health, Public Inquiries, 5600 Fishers Ln., Rockville, MD 20857.

Gardner, R. *The Parents Book about Divorce.* Garden City, N.J.: Doubleday, 1977.

Jensen, L., and Jensen, J. *Stepping into Stepparenting: A Practical Guide.* Palo Alto, Calif.: R & E Research Asso., 1981.

Maddox, B. *The Half-Parent: Living with Other People's Children.* New York: Evans, 1975.

Noble, J., and Noble, W. *How to Live with Other People's Children.* New York: Hawthorn, 1977.

Ricci, I. *Mom's House, Dad's House: Making Shared Custody Work.* New York: Macmillan, 1980.

Roosevelt, R., and Lofas, J. *Living in Step.* New York: Stein & Day, 1976.

Rosenbaum, J., and Rosenbaum, V. *Stepparenting.* Corte Madera, Calif.: Chandler & Share, 1977.

Simon, A. W. *Stepchild in the Family: A View of Children in Remarriage.* New York: Odyssey, 1964.

Thayer, N. *Stepping.* New York: Playbook Paperbooks, 1980.

Troyer, W. *Divorced Kids.* New York: Harcourt Brace Jovanovich, 1979.

Visher, E. B., and Visher, J. S. *Stepfamilies.* New York: Brunner/Mazel, 1979.

Visher, E. B., and Visher, J. S. *How to Win As a Stepfamily.* New York: Dembner Books, 1982.

4. FAMILIES, CHILD REARING, AND PARENT EDUCATION: Families

Newsletter

Stepparent News. Newsletter for parents and professionals. $9–$15 yearly. Listening Inc., 8716 Pine Ave., Gary, IN 46403.

Filmstrip and film for adults

"Daddy Doesn't Live Here Anymore": The Single-Parent Family. Written by Robert Weiss. Four parts of the filmstrip include The Changing Family, When Parents Divorce, One Day at a Time, The Stepparent Family. Sound filmstrip, 52 min., color. Rental: unavailable. Purchase: $145. Human Relations Media, 175 Tompkins Ave., Pleasantville, NY 10570.

Stepparenting: New Families, Old Ties. Film, 25 min., color. Rental: $35. Purchase: $345. Polymorph Films, 118 South St., Boston, MA 02111.

Organizations

American Association of Marriage and Family Therapists. 225 Yale Ave., Claremont, CA 91711.

American Psychological Association. 1200 17th St., N.W., Washington, DC 20036.

National Registry of Clinical Social Workers. 7981 Eastern Ave., Silver Spring, MD 20910.

The Stepfamily Foundation. 333 West End Ave., New York, NY 10023.

Changing Family Trends

HEAD START Must Respond

Valora Washington and Ura Jean Oyemade

Valora Washington, *Ph.D., is Assistant Dean and Associate Professor, Department of Human Development, at Howard University, Washington, DC.*

Ura Jean Oyemade, *Ph.D., is Associate Professor and Chairperson, Department of Human Development, at Howard University, Washington, DC.*

Ellis Herwig

Changes in family structures have altered the ability of many families to achieve or to maintain self-sufficiency. These changes in families indicate an urgent need for complementary changes in Head Start services.

Head Start, now celebrating its 20th year, is the most successful and enduring program from President Johnson's War on Poverty. Head Start continues to be a comprehensive program that provides health, educational, and social services and aims to move preschool children *and* their families toward self-sufficiency.

Who does Head Start serve?

The widely heralded effectiveness of Head Start is particularly important in light of the project's focus on low socioeconomic groups. More than 90% of Head Start families have incomes below the poverty line. Minority children comprise at least two-thirds of Head Start's enrollment: Approximately 42% of Head Start children are Black; 33% White; 20% Hispanic; 4% Native American; and 1% Asian. A study by Royster et al. (1977) suggests that 75% of all Head Start children are members of minority groups. About 11% of Head Start children are handicapped.

Nevertheless, only a fraction of eligible participants are served by Head Start. The 450,000 children now enrolled represent only about 15% of all qualified children (Children's Defense Fund [CDF], 1983). More than 1,000 counties in the country do not offer Head Start.

Not only are just a fraction of the families eligible being served, but the need for Head Start services is increasing. This decade has ushered in a new wave of crises for America's families. In 1983, domestic poverty reached its highest level since Head Start began in 1965. More than 35 million families, or 15% of the population, fell below the official poverty level (U.S. Bureau of the Census, 1983).

Among minorities, the news is even more startling. Almost 36% of Blacks, and 30% of Hispanics, fell below the poverty

Reprinted by permission from *Young Children*, Vol. 40, No. 6 (September 1985), pp. 12-15, 17-19. © 1985 by the National Association for the Education of Young Children, 1834 Connecticut Avenue, N.W., Washington, DC 20009.

level in 1982. Millions of dependent children are affected—in 1982, 22% of our nation's children were members of low-income families.

Changes in families

American public policy generally assumes that families are responsible for their own children, but changes in family structures have altered the ability of many families to achieve or to maintain self-sufficiency. Programs serving low-income families, such as Head Start, are particularly affected by these four trends in family life:

1. the feminization of poverty
2. the rise in teen parenting
3. the surge in the number of mothers of preschool children in the workforce, and
4. the increasing challenge for low-income families to attain economic self-sufficiency.

These trends are often interrelated: The female poor are frequently teen mothers who, in an attempt to attain economic self-sufficiency, seek employment while their children are young. These changes in families indicate an urgent need for complementary changes in the services Head Start provides.

The feminization of poverty

In recent years, the ideal concept of the American family was that of a male worker with a homemaker wife and two children. However, only 11% of families now fit this form. Indeed, about 20% of all children live in female-headed households (U.S. Bureau of the Census, 1984).

This change in family structure has serious economic implications. Female-headed families are 3 times as likely to be in poverty as two-parent families (Auletta, 1982). In fact, 1 in 3 families headed by women is in poverty, compared with only 1 in 10 headed by men, and only 1 in 19 headed by two parents.

Not surprisingly, a disproportionate share of families receiving public assistance are female headed. Four out of five AFDC (Aid to Families with Dependent Children) families are headed by single women. More than one-half have at least one child under the age of 6, the Head Start eligible population (CDF, 1984). The most common reason recipients need assistance is the break up of a marriage. About 45% of AFDC children become eligible due to parental separation or divorce (CDF, 1984).

The feminization of poverty is cause for alarm. Hill (1979) states that if he were forced to choose what group to target to reduce poverty, he would focus on female-headed families, which in his view are the main cause of the underclass. Indeed, there do appear to be at least two distinct minority communities—one consisting mainly of female-headed households who slip more deeply into poverty, and the other of two-parent families who move toward the middle class (Auletta, 1982).

Teenage parenting

The feminization of poverty has particularly severe consequences for teenage mothers. Even a decade ago, more than one-half of all AFDC assistance was paid to women who were or had been teenage mothers (Auletta, 1982).

A dramatic increase in the incidence of teenage pregnancy has occurred in the last 20 years (Chilman, 1979). In 1979, one in six babies was born to a teenage mother; among Blacks, the figure was one in four, and 85% of Black teenage mothers were unmarried (Auletta, 1982). Two facts make this a problem of epidemic proportion when the incidence of poverty among Black- and female-headed families is considered. 1) Black female adolescents are more likely to have more children out of wedlock while still teenagers (Ventura, 1969). 2) Children of teenage parents are at greater risk for adolescent pregnancy (Chilman, 1979).

The social and economic consequences of being a teenage parent are usually tragic, particularly for young mothers. Of-

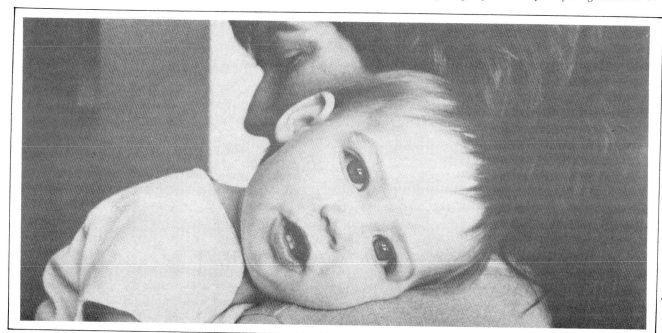

Cathy Nelson

The social and economic consequences of teenage parenting lead to the poverty cycle that Head Start was designed to address.

ten they are forced to drop out of school, so they have inadequate education or skills to find employment, and this leads to dependence on welfare. The children of these teenagers are also at risk in many ways: low birthweight, educa-

tional lags, and generally poor health and nutrition (Washington & Glimps, 1983).

Employed mothers

For the first time in history, more than one-half of all children younger than 18 have an employed mother (Kahn & Kammerman, 1982). Mothers of preschool children constitute the fastest growing segment of the labor force (U.S. Bureau of the Census, 1983; 1982; Burud, Collins, & Divine-Hawkins, 1983; Friedman, 1983). Mothers with young children are almost as likely to be employed full time as are mothers with older children (Kammerman & Hayes, 1982).

Many of these women seek jobs out of economic necessity: 43% of working women are single, widowed, divorced, or separated (U.S. Department of Labor, 1977).

Many low-income mothers are also employed or seeking employment. Of every 10 mothers on AFDC, 4 are caring for preschool children; 3 are employed, seeking employment, or in training; 1 is disabled; and 2 are not currently seeking employment. Of this latter group, more than half are either older than 45 or have never been employed (CDF, 1984).

Economic self-sufficiency

Many low-income families are rooted in economic distress. As many as 45% of these families continue on welfare for at least 5 out of every 7 years. Many individuals mired in poverty are the unemployed who are either discouraged in their efforts to find a job, or who are among the nearly 20% unemployed people from ages 16 to 19. Still others trapped in poverty are school dropouts who lack the skills to match the available jobs (see Auletta, 1982).

In explaining long-term proverty, Bernstein (1982) argues that welfare has fostered dependency instead of reducing it, has encouraged the break up of families, has weakened the sense of family responsibility, has led to a rejection of the work ethic, and has caused children raised in welfare-dependent homes to become dependent, to lack a work ethic, to fail to take responsibility for their own children, and to engage in antisocial behavior.

Challenging this "welfare dependence theory," Hill and Ponza (1983) found that children from low-income homes exhibit substantial income mobility: 57% were not impoverished as young adults. Further, Levy (1980) found that about four out of five new households formed by people from low-income families had incomes well above the poverty line.

We contend that low-income people may fail to achieve due to barriers usually manifested in the form of racial and sexual discrimination, particularly in the job market. Moreover, behaviors such as poor work habits or low self-confidence may be an effect of poverty rather than a cause.

Challenges for Head Start

These four changing conditions in American families create new demands on individuals and on the programs that serve them. Many observers agree that these dramatic changes are neither short term nor likely to be reversed (Cherlin, 1981). New family structures and roles are not automatically accommodated in federal programs, but the implications of these changes for Head Start must be explored by all professionals who are concerned about this nation's children. It is imperative that we consider possible changes because of Head Start's "recognition of the importance of the family, rather

Compared to White children, Black children are

2 times as likely to
- die in the first year of life
- be born prematurely
- suffer low birthweight
- have mothers who received late or no prenatal care
- be born to a teenage or single-parent family
- see a parent die
- live in substandard housing
- be suspended from school or suffer corporal punishment
- be unemployed as teenagers
- have no employed parent
- live in institutions

3 times as likely to
- be poor
- have their mothers die in childbirth
- live with a parent who has separated
- live in a female-headed family
- be placed in an educable mentally retarded class
- be murdered between 5 and 9 years of age
- be in foster care
- die of known child abuse

4 times as likely to
- live with neither parent and be supervised by a child welfare agency
- be murdered before 1 year of age or as a teenager
- be incarcerated between 15 and 19 years of age

5 times as likely to
- be dependent on welfare
- become pregnant as teenagers

12 times as likely to
- live with a parent who never married

From *Black and White Children in America: Key Facts*, a 128-page report available from the Children's Defense Fund, 122 C Street, N.W., Washington, DC 20001-2194. Single copy price is $9.95.

than the school, as the ultimate source of a child's values and behavior" (Zigler & Anderson, 1979, p. 14).

Address the feminization of poverty

Clearly, the families served by Head Start are likely to be headed by women and even more likely to be headed by minority women. The only income support program for low-income families, AFDC, presumes that mothers of young children are homemakers. On the other hand, Head Start's comprehensive design has historically included parent involvement and career development for adults. How can Head Start build on this approach?

1) **Head Start must strengthen its focus on parental employability and preparation to enter the workforce** to help women and their children emerge from poverty.

2) **Head Start can present both boys and girls with positive male images** through curriculum, staffing patterns, and involvement in community activities, since the feminization of poverty infers an absence of male role models in the home.

3) **Head Start can promote positive family relationships** through workshops and seminars. Indeed, the philosophical basis of Head Start emphasizes the role of family and community (Harmon & Hanley, 1979). Head Start has

---

Steps Head Start can take to address the changing needs of American families

1 Strengthen its resolve to be a comprehensive program.

2 Broaden the parent involvement component.

3 Reconsider changes in program models and transportation.

4 Implement new economic self-sufficiency projects.

5 Conduct periodic family needs assessments.

---

already been shown to have a positive effect on parent attitudes toward, and interactions with, their children (Mann, Harrell, & Hurt, 1977). These efforts can be increased.

4) In addition, **Head Start programs should focus on adult male-female relationships.** There should be a renewed emphasis on strengthening family structures and functions through improved marital interaction with a view toward reduction of the divorce rate and hence the number of female-headed households. Head Start programs can also help individuals understand the stresses which impinge upon family life such as the disproportionate number of Black females to Black males and the high unemployment or underemployment of Black males.

Work with adolescents

The social and economic consequences of teenage parenting lead to the poverty cycle that Head Start was designed to address. Since the Head Start eligible population consists primarily of AFDC families, it can be projected that at least 50% of the Head Start families would include, or be at risk for, teenage parenting. Thus, a primary focus of the parent

component of Head Start should be a) to prevent adolescent pregnancy and b) to realize that Head Start is likely to provide services to young mothers.

5) **Effective sex education models can be adapted to the Head Start Parent Involvement Program.** Several studies have focused on causes, treatment, and prevention of teenage pregnancy in the Black community (Washington, 1982; Westney, et al., 1983; Oyemade, et al., 1983). Some of the strategies suggested to reduce the incidence of teenage pregnancies have included sex education with an emphasis on traditional morality which discourages teenage pregnancy, and involvement of all the teenager's network (family, neighbors, peers, and school mates) in programs of pregnancy prevention.

6) **Head Start could influence the quality of social services** through its social change and community action model that has traditionally been a part of the Parent Involvement Program. Black teenagers fail to take advantage of contraceptive services because of the clash in values between the Black clients and social agencies (Washington, 1982).

7) **Head Start programs can seek to increase parental knowledge about childrearing and parenting skills.** As programs work intensively with teenage parents and their children, it is likely that fewer of these children will be at risk developmentally or educationally (Washington & Glimps, 1983).

8) **Head Start must continue to develop leadership potential among low-income families.** Zigler (1979) contends that this effort in Head Start can be an important factor in helping parents recognize that they influence their own destiny. Based on social-learning theory, children too would develop similar attitudes about control over their lives.

Serve employed mothers

9) **Head Start must extend hours and services that accommodate the need for full-day care for infants, toddlers, preschool, and school-age children.** The increase in employment of mothers of young children, coupled with the rise in single-parent households, has created unprecedented demands for all-day child care. Head Start has always had a full-day feature for prekindergarten, but the need for infant- and after-school care has been given less priority.

In a step that further ignores the needs of employed mothers, some Head Start programs are moving toward split sessions, or variation-in-center attendance models. Parents who work full time may not be able to take advantage of a part-time Head Start program.

10) **Head Start mothers who are employed may require increased support for their children's transportation to the program.**

11) **The parent involvement component of Head Start must be restructured to accommodate the schedules of working parents.**

12) **Head Start should increase its focus on the affective and social development of children** due to the rise in the number of employed and/or single parents. Programs can foster skills in independence, self-care, and interpersonal relations to help these children cope with the demands necessitated by the life style of the low-income, employed parent.

13) **Greater emphasis should be placed on maintaining a stable staff** in an effort to enhance the feelings of security and attachment in the Head Start child.

Improve economic self-sufficiency

One of the initial stated purposes of Head Start was to marshal and coordinate federal, state, and local resources to involve low-income families in the process of finding solutions to their own problems (Office of Economic Opportunity, 1967). Head Start jobs and services contribute to the economic vitality of communities and encourage the coordination of community social services (Hubbell, 1983).

From the beginning of Head Start, there has been controversy over whether Head Start sought to empower low-income people politically and economically or to simply provide services (Shriver, 1979). A two-pronged approach that provides services to empower Head Start families would clearly be more effective.

14) **Head Start can develop a program to help families conserve their resources and raise their standard of living.** The Program for Family Resource Development is based on the idea that if families are to break from the poverty cycle and leave AFDC, their ability to see themselves as powerful in their own progress must be strengthened (Edwards, 1982). In successful programs in Washington, D.C. and East St. Louis, Illinois, parents are gaining skills in the basic techniques of wise marketing, budgeting, planning, infant and child care, conservation of resources, stress management, and the knowledge of nutrition, food preparation, sanitation, and health practices.

The overall solution to poverty is jobs that pay a decent income. There are several areas that society must address to reach the goal of increased employment: a) identify available jobs, b) improve access and reduce barriers (such as discrimination) that affect hiring and employment practices; c) develop job search and interview skills to enhance the probability of being hired; d) improve training in skills necessary for specific jobs; and e) develop positive work habits and attitudes necessary to improve productivity on the job.

Further, Keniston & Carnegie Council on Children (1977) suggest that employment of minorities and women can be increased, without preferential treatment, by measures designed to ensure minority and female applications, by eliminating unnecessary requirements, and by requiring employers who have not traditionally employed minorities or women in particular job categories to make training opportunities available.

15) **Head Start programs can emphasize human resource development programs for parents to improve their employability.** These programs, if they are systematic and well-planned, could be incorporated into Head Start with very little disruption of services. They could address some of the efforts outlined above.

Summary

Head Start has always been a popular "effort to interrupt the cycle of poverty" (Cooke, 1979). We contend that, as Head Start services continue to address this goal, attention must be given to changes in families since the inception of the project. In summary, we recommend that Head Start take these steps to meet the changing needs of American families.

First, Head Start must strengthen its resolve to be a **comprehensive** program. While Head Start has not suffered direct budget cuts in support services, the program still serves fewer than one out of five eligible children. Efforts should be

HEAD START Succeeds!

Esther Hernandez
Head Start Parent

Esther Hernandez began her association with Head Start in its first year, 1965, as a parent volunteer. Four of her daughters are Head Start graduates. During her 20 years with Head Start, Esther has worked as a teacher assistant, teacher, head teacher, center administrator, education coordinator, assistant director, and director. In the process, she completed her Bachelor's degree in Education and Master's degree in Bilingual Education at Wayne State University.

Esther, the first Head Start staff member in Michigan to become a trainer for the bilingual curriculum "Un Marco Abierto," now directs the Vista Nuevas Head Start program in Detroit, Michigan.

HEAD START Succeeds!

Keith Pettigrew
Head Start Graduate

Three years after Head Start began, Keith Pettigrew completed the program. Since 1968, Keith has been a good student, and he now attends the University of the District of Columbia.

Keith's concern for the well-being of others led him to counsel alcohol- and drug-abusing youth in Washington, D.C. As a result of his work, Keith was the first young person to serve on the Alcohol, Drug Abuse, and Mental Health Administration Board. He was appointed by Secretary Margaret Heckler of the U.S. Department on Health and Human Services.

Keith has also received a Proclamation from Washington, D.C. Mayor Marion Barry for his work with drug-free youth activities. He has met twice with First Lady Nancy Reagan and received a Teens in Action Award from the White House.

Young Children wishes to express appreciation to Malkia Brantuo of The National Head Start Association for providing these success stories. Photographs by Roffi Kelly.

increased to expand the program and ensure that administrative changes do not dilute parent participation or communication across services.

Secondly, the parent involvement component of Head Start

should a) focus on presenting positive male role models to children, b) heighten understanding of adult male-female relationships, c) promote positive family relationships, d) develop strategies to prevent teenage pregnancy, and e) address the concerns of employed mothers.

Head Start planners should also reconsider changes in program models and transportation to determine whether there might be better ways to serve employed parents.

Economic self-sufficiency projects can be implemented through Head Start to prepare adults for work and to coordinate opportunities for skill development and employment beyond Head Start programs.

Family needs assessments should be conducted periodically by Head Start programs to stay attuned to changing trends in family life and to identify new areas for emphasis. Successful learning experiences for children have accounted for much of Head Start's popularity. However, the family focus of the program must be retained because children's futures are clearly tied to the strength and resiliency of their families.

Head Start was authorized with a huge mandate: to move children and their families toward self-sufficiency. It has been relatively successful in achieving this goal. However, if the proposals outlined here are embraced along with the other successful areas in Head Start, the program can be even more instrumental in reducing the enormous harm to the next generation that poverty can cause.

Head Start advocates can capitalize upon the momentum of support for the program, and ensure the adequacy of America's most successful "social safety net," by informing members of Congress of these and other recommendations which realistically respond to family trends.

Suggestions can also be sent to
Mr. Clennie Murphy
Acting Associate Commissioner
Project Head Start
P.O. Box 1182
Room 5163
Donohoe Building
400 6th St., S.W.
Washington, DC 20201-2706
202-755-7782

References

Auletta, K. (1982). *The underclass.* New York: Random House.

Bernstein, B. (1982). *The politics of welfare: The New York City experience.* Cambridge: Abt Associates.

Burud, S. L., Collins, R. C., & Divine-Hawkins, P. (1983, May/June). Employer sponsored child care: Everybody benefits. *Children Today, 12* (3), 2–7.

Cherlin, A. J. (1981). *Marriage, divorce, remarriage.* Cambridge: Harvard University Press.

Children's Defense Fund. (1983). *Give more children a Head Start: it pays.* Washington, DC: Author.

Children's Defense Fund. (1984). *A children's defense budget: An analysis of the President's FY 1985 budget and children.* Washington, DC: Author.

Children's Defense Fund. (1985). *Black and white children in America: Key facts.* Washington, DC: Children's Defense Fund.

Chilman, C. (1979). *Adolescent sexuality in a changing American society* (DHEW Publication No. 79-1426). Washington, DC: U.S. Department of Health, Education and Welfare.

Cooke, R. E. (1969). Introduction. In E. Zigler & J. Valentine (Eds.), *Project Head Start: A legacy of the War on Poverty* (pp. XXIII–XXVI). New York: Free Press.

Edwards, C. H. (1982). *Training program for prospective residents of renovated public housing.* Proposal submitted to the District of Columbia Department of Housing and Community Development. Washington, DC: Howard University.

Friedman, D. E. (1983). *Encouraging employer support to working parents.* New York: Center for Public Advocacy Research.

Harmon, C., & Hanley, E. (1979). Administrative aspects of the Head Start program. In E. Zigler & J. Valentine (Eds.), *Project Head Start: A legacy of the War on Poverty* (pp. 379–398). New York: Free Press.

Hill, M. S., & Ponza, M. (1983, Summer). Poverty and welfare dependence across generations. *Economic Outlook USA, 10* (3), 61–64.

Hill, M. S. (1983). Trends in the economic situation of U.S. families and children: 1970–1980. In R. Nerson (Ed.), *The high costs of living: Economic and demographic conditions of American families.* Washington, DC: National Academy of Sciences.

Hill, R. (1979). *The widening economic gap.* Washington, DC: National Urban League Research Department.

Hubbell, R. (1983). *A review of Head Start research since 1970.* (Contract No. 105-81-C-026). Washington, DC: CSR, Inc.

Kahn, A. H., & Kammerman, S. B. (1982). *Helping America's families.* Philadelphia: Temple University Press.

Kammerman, S. B., & Hayes, C. (Eds.). (1982). *Families that work: Children in a changing world.* Washington, DC: National Academy Press.

Keniston, K., & Carnegie Council on Children. (1977). *All Our Children: The American family under pressure.* New York: Harcourt Brace Jovanovich.

Levy, F. (1980). *The intergenerational transfer of poverty* (Working paper No. 1241-102). Washington, DC: The Urban Institute.

Mann, A. J., Harrell, A., & Hurt, M. (1977). *A review of the Head Start research since 1969 and an annotated bibliography* (DHEW Publication No. 78-31102). Washington, DC: U.S. Department of Health, Education and Welfare.

Office of Economic Opportunity. (1967, June 1). *Catalog of federal assistance programs* (No. 554). Washington, DC: Author.

Oyemade, U. J., Kane, E., Dejoie-Smith, M., & Laryea, H. (1983). *Black family coping styles and adolescent behaviors: Final report.* (No. 90-C-1763). Washington, DC: Department of Health and Human Services.

Rivlin, A. M., & Timpane, P. M. (Eds.). (1975). *Planned variation in education.* Washington, DC: Brookings Institution.

Royster, E. C., Larson, J. C., Fer, T., Fosburg, S., Nauta, M., Nelson, B., & Takata, G. (1977). *A national survey of Head Start graduates and their peers* (Report No. AAI-77-54). Cambridge: Abt Associates.

Shriver, S. (1979). The origins of Head Start: In E. Zigler & J. Valentine (Eds.) *Project Head Start: A legacy of the War on Poverty* (pp. 49–67). New York: Free Press.

U.S. Bureau of the Census. (1981, March). *Marital status and living arrangements. Current population report* (Series P-20, No. 52). Washington, DC: Author.

U.S. Bureau of the Census. (1982). *Trends in child care arrangements of working mothers. Current population report* (Series P-23, No. 117). Washington, DC: Author.

U.S. Bureau of the Census. (1983). *Statistical abstract of the United States: 1982–1983.* Washington, DC: Author.

U.S. Bureau of the Census. (1983). *Money income and poverty status of families and persons in the United States: 1983* (Series P-60, No. 145). Washington, DC: Author.

U.S. Department of Labor. (1977). *U.S. working women: A data book.* Washington, DC: Author.

Ventura, S. J. (1969). Recent trends and differentials in illegitimacy. *Journal of Marriage and the Family, 31* (2), 447–450.

Washington, A. C. (1982). A cultural and historical perspective on pregnancy-related activity among U.S. teenagers. *Journal of Black Psychology, 9,* 1–28.

Washington, V., & Glimps, B. (1983). Developmental issues for adolescent parents and their children. *Educational Horizons, 61*(4), 195–199.

Westney, O. E., Jenkins, R. R., Williams, I. C., & Butts, J. D. (1984). Sexual development and behavior in Black preadolescents. *Adolescence, 19* (75), 557–568.

Zigler, E. (1979). Project Head Start: Success or failure? In E. Zigler & J. Valentine (Eds.), *Project Head Start: A legacy of the War on Poverty* (pp. 495–507). New York: Free Press.

Zigler, E., & Anderson, K. (1979). An idea whose time had come: The intellectual and political climate. In E. Zigler & J. Valentine (Eds.), *Project Head Start: A Legacy of the War on Poverty.* New York: Free Press.

Practical Parenting with Piaget

Jonelle Pieti Thibault
and Judy Spitler McKee

Jonelle Pieti Thibault, M.A., is presently working with handicapped high-risk youth as a counselor and trainer and is a former public school teacher.

Judy Spitler McKee, Ed.D., is a Professor of Educational Psychology and Early Childhood Education at Eastern Michigan University, Ypsilanti, Michigan.

What play materials and activities are most appropriate for adults to provide children? All adults who work with children from birth through adolescence will enjoy these helpful hints about what to expect and how to capitalize upon children's understanding and interests.

Four-year-old Kris listens very carefully to his mother's explanation of why the goldfish needs to live in the fish tank and will die if removed from the water. However, Kris is soon found holding the goldfish, "to see what it feels like." To the mother, the child's actions are exasperating, but to those familiar with the work of Piaget, the child's actions are representative of a typical preoperational child seeking knowledge through curiosity and experience. If you ask parents why they allow a ten-month-old child to play with pots and pans; a sixteen-month-old to play with a dishpan of water; or a six-year-old to collect bags of treasures, they answer, "Because they want to do it—they are having fun." Such parents are responding intuitively to the natural needs and desires of their children at various developmental stages.

Parents and teachers who pick up on children's cues and curiosity by reinforcing the children's growing interests and by using appropriate language to expand the experience (White 1975) are well on their way to a practical application of

Piaget's theory, which primarily describes how knowledge develops during childhood. The child develops through personal action upon, interaction with, and reaction to objects, events, people, and ideas. The child is an explorer, a scientist, an inquirer, and an artist, who pursues, constructs, and organizes the environment. Intelligence, according to Piaget, is the adaptation of the child to the physical, social, and intellectual world. Although it is not possible to speed up a child's rate of development through instruction or drill, parents and teachers with a basic understanding of Piaget's theory can be ready to act on children's cues and enrich the environment.

Basic concepts and their implications

Piaget believed intelligence develops through a process of construction and organization that begins at birth and continues throughout life. This continuous process is divided into four major invariant stages: *sensorimotor* (birth to two years); *preoperational* (two to seven years); *concrete operational* (seven to eleven years); and *formal operational* (eleven to fifteen years or older).

During these stages, children form new schemata, or patterns of behavior, through *assimilation* and *accommodation*. Assimilation refers to activities during which children take in information and bend it to fit their own patterns, knowledge, and skills.

Thus very young children will usually try to assimilate anything new to their familiar pattern of eating, whether the object is edible or not. Accommodation requires discrimination on the child's part, occurring when previously held ideas are changed to fit new concepts. When Rebecca is given

"Practical Parenting with Piaget," Jonelle Pieti Thibault and Judy Spitler McKee, *Young Children*, November 1982, pp. 18-27. Reprinted by permission of the authors.

151

a rubber ball for the first time and discovers that it cannot be eaten, she is likely to drop or throw it. Watching what the ball does several times, she will begin to accommodate the concept that the ball will bounce. Through each of the four stages of development, the dual processes of assimilation and accommodation are expanded, each time at a higher level, as children form new schemata or constructs of behavior. The approximate age levels for each stage represent the child's mental age, not chronological age. The sequence of development from stage to stage is unchanging and universal; transitions between are gradual, not abrupt. These stages, the child's activities, and suggestions for adults to expand children's learning are presented in Table 1. Additional explanations of these stages can be found in Piaget (1963; 1965; 1968), and in Piaget and Inhelder (1969).

Sensorimotor stage

The sensorimotor stage spans the years from birth to about age two. The term sensorimotor refers to the child's response to the environment through the use of muscles and senses present at birth. In order to take into account the vast changes during this period, Piaget distinguished six substages.

The first substage is that of *reflex activity* (birth to one month), during which the infant uses and refines innate reflex responses. For example, infants will begin a sucking motion when the cheek or lips are touched, and will turn in the direction of a sound.

To many parents, the first month of an infant's life may seem like an endless monotony of sleeping, eating, and diaper changing. However, even the newborn prefers the sight of a human face to that of a head-shaped outline, responds to sound by synchronizing body movements to the human voice, and to some degree recognizes the mother.

Because all five senses are functioning, the parents should attend to them. Taste is the most basic and easiest to satisfy through bottle or breast. Keeping newborns warm, dry, content, and cuddled satisfies touch. Infants can differentiate between the odors of licorice and onions, so a diaper pail of soiled diapers near the crib could be quite offensive to the baby.

Sight can be stimulated by bright colors rather than sterile, neutral tones in children's sleeping and play areas. Infants also prefer colors to black and white, and patterns to line drawings. Because babies prefer human sounds to nonhuman ones, adults should not feel silly in singing, speaking, or reciting poetry to babies (Lake 1976). While infants cannot comprehend meaning, the sounds stimulate the senses and babies enjoy the attention.

During the period of *primary circular reactions* (one to four months), infants become more active. They repeat and modify actions which previously occurred by chance. For example, three-month-old Gabriel may kick and stretch while lying in the crib, and notice that at the same time the mobile above the bed moves. Soon Gabriel will associate the movement of the mobile with his action. Children also begin to enjoy toys that shake or bells that ring when the child moves and bounces. The infant's body movements begin to coordinate with the sense responses of the previous substage, so mother's vocalizations and smiles at baby's movements become even more productive. Recognition of these cause and effect actions may be marked by a change in the infant's expression, such as a smile.

Infants at this age do not recognize the existence of objects unless they are seen or touched. Objects out of sight are also out of mind, so that if the baby's mother leaves the room, to the child the mother is nonexistent until she reappears. It would, therefore, be more stimulating for infants to spend waking hours in the visual and auditory presence of the family or group, instead of being tucked away in a crib in another room.

The third period, *secondary circular reactions* (four to ten months), marks the phase when infants manipulate and explore. Stuffed toys, rattles, and other safe items (not necessarily toys) that children can grasp and hold are now appropriate. Children can now act upon these items for desired responses, such as reaching for and shaking a rattle or bell. At the end of this substage, babies begin to develop *object permanence*. They will follow a dropped toy with their eyes, or retrieve a toy partially concealed by a blanket, because they now know the toy still exists.

Table 1. Highlights of Piaget's stages of development

Stage	Child's activity	Adult's activity
Sensorimotor (birth to 2 years)		
Reflex activity (birth to 1 month)	Refines innate responses	Respond to and stimulate the child's senses (sight, sound, taste, touch, and smell)
Primary circular reaction (1 to 4 months)	Repeats and refines actions which once occurred by chance	Stimulate the senses through objects the child can interact with—rattles, bells, or mobiles
Secondary circular reactions (4 to 10 months)	Manipulates objects Repeats actions by choice Develops object permanence	Provide toys to handle with various shapes, textures, and colors Partially hide a toy while child watches
Coordination of secondary schemata (10 to 12 months)	Combines previous activities for new results Imitation begins	Provide toys: familiar dolls, balls, or boxes Encourage imitation
Tertiary circular reactions (12 to 18 months)	Experiments with objects to discover new uses Locates an object with eyes and tracks it	Provide experience with water, sand, textures Include toys which can be manipulated to turn, nest, roll, open, or close
Invention through mental combination (18 to 24 months)	Practices deferred imitation Applies old skills in new situations	Provide opportunities to apply old skills to new experiences Provide peer contact and interaction
Preoperational (2 to 7 years)	Language appears Imaginative player, deferred imitation, egocentrism prevalent Can complete simple operations, but cannot explain why	Provide dolls, cars, blocks, crayons, paste, paper, scissors, books, musical instruments, etc. Communicate at child's level or above Provide experience with liquid, mass, and length informally Encourage decision making (red shirt or yellow, apple or orange, bath before dinner or after)
Concrete operational (7 to 11 years)	Applies simple logic to arrive at conclusions Reasons deductively Performs simple operations with physical objects Conserves	Provide opportunity to pursue areas of interest Use questions to understand child's reasoning processes but do not question too much
Formal operational (11 to 15 years)	Reasons abstractly Solves problems through inductive reasoning Employs logical thought	Propose hypothetical problems for the child to solve Discuss ethical questions Encourage personal decision making and problem solving

Between ten and twelve months, infants are in the phase of *coordination of secondary schemata*, a stage of major transitions. They combine previous schemata to gain an end, can generalize information, and are beginning to imitate. Children can push one toy aside in order to reach a second toy. Adults can take a movement of the child, such as the hand in the air, and by repeating it with "bye-bye," the child will soon imitate. Such a seemingly simple repetition is usually cause for great delight for both the child and the parent. Play becomes apparent during this period, and toys which the child can assimilate to existing behaviors are useful, such as the rag doll which can be rocked and hugged, or the ball which can be rolled back and forth. The child at this stage is mobile, creeping, crawling, and occasionally walking.

During the substage of *tertiary circular reactions* (twelve to eighteen months), children begin to actively use trial and error to learn more about objects and their relationships. At this phase, children can follow an object with their eyes and retrieve it when it is hidden. They no longer repeat actions seemingly only for the sake of repetition. Stacy no longer opens and closes a cupboard door solely for pleasure now that she has discovered that behind the door are hinges, pots and pans, shoes, or towels, each with unique qualities which open new worlds.

In the final substage of the sensorimotor stage, children enter the period of *invention of means through mental combinations*. By the age of two, children have the beginnings of symbolic thought and have fully developed object permanence. Children can now imitate a behavior seen previously *(deferred imitation)*. Alexander watches his parents planting a garden, and then three days later he decides to plant his own garden.

Children at the age of two can solve problems through mental manipulation, rather than only by physical manipulation. They can think about a toy on a shelf, and can get a stool to stand on in order to reach the toy. Internalization of concepts begins to appear, so that once a problem has been solved, the solution is usually remembered. Once children learn to use a stool to reach a toy, the activity will be repeated when necessary.

These last two sensorimotor substages mark a major transformation. The child's curiosity leads to creative discoveries in the environment. Through deferred imitation, children will find the cat food in the cupboard and feed the cat, comb the dog's hair, and rock the doll or perhaps tell it, "No, no." They will put objects in a box and have even more fun taking them out, and then sit on the box or in it. Children will listen to the different sounds that shoes make on the linoleum and carpeting, or in the dry cereal spilled on the linoleum, and repeat the activity for the enjoyment of the sound and feeling. They know where things are located, and can find them at will. Language begins to appear as simple labels, words, or phrases, such as *kitty, ball,* or *no.* Because these children comprehend more complex language, adult conversation with them is extremely important for sensory stimulation and also as a model for imitation.

Preoperational stage

Like the sensorimotor stage, the *preoperational stage* (approximately two to seven years) covers a time of vast growth and change. During the *preconceptual* or *egocentric period* (two to four years) language emerges as the main system of representation. Once language is attained, children's problem-solving abilities broaden and they can learn through verbalization with others. Both imaginative play (through assimilation) and deferred imitation (through accommodation) are markedly increased during this phase.

In the *intuitive phase* (four to seven years) children can complete mental operations such as simple classifying, although children usually cannot explain the process. Children in the intuitive phase cannot practice *reversibility*, either logically or through physical manipulation, as in the well-known example with water in different beakers. These children are unable to grasp the idea that the same amount of water exists in a low, shallow bowl as it does in a tall, narrow beaker. They are also unable to focus on more than one aspect of a problem, a trait called *centration*. A child grouping buttons by size will probably be unable to simultaneously group the same buttons by color. *Egocentricism*, another aspect of this stage, does not mean the selfish, self-centered attitude often attributed to an egotistic adult. Egocentric preoperational children think that everyone has the same thoughts, experiences, actions, and reactions that they do. As pointed out by Singer (1972), the characters of A. A. Milne's stories are very egocentric. Winnie-the-Pooh knows that the only reason for bees is to make honey, and the only reason for making honey is that he, Pooh, can eat it.

There are many spontaneous opportunities throughout the day when preoperational children can act upon and react to their environment. For example, discrimination of size can be demonstrated in many ways. At the grocery store, the parents can ask the child to get a large loaf of bread, or a small jar of peanut butter. Opportunities for classification by color are readily available: red and yellow apples, orange oranges, various colored blocks, fish in the fish tank, or kittens in a new litter. Spontaneous grouping by physical characteristics occurs naturally while putting groceries away since eggs, fruits, vegetables, bottles, and cans each have distinctive colors, shapes, and sizes.

While preoperational children cannot conserve liquid or mass, there are many occasions for the child to physically experiment with these materials in the kitchen. Milk might be poured into identical clear glasses to an equal level, then one glass can be emptied into a clear, shallow bowl. Through repeated experimenting, children will begin to develop the concept of conservation of liquid. Meanwhile a glass of milk is ready to drink or to make pudding. Dry spaghetti, pretzels, or bread sticks can be used for comparing length, and once again, the results can be eaten. Seriation (arranging items from largest to smallest or smallest to largest) can be explored with various utensils, plates, or glasses.

Many games can be integrated into everyday situations. Sharp (1969) suggests using colored paper shapes and asking that the child make a face using the paper shapes. This same process can be carried out with crackers, cheese, or fruit slices quite casually during a snack break. Classification skills can be sharpened by assigning specific locations. For example, the blocks go into the laundry basket, and the toy cars go on the shelf. Children can also sort silverware, socks, and towels.

Children love to help when there is someone to talk with about the task at hand.

Numbers become important during this stage. Children may want two crackers or to show that they are three years old. Rote counting is relatively easy because no understanding is required, but number concepts in everyday life are more complex. The three fingers a three-year-old holds up do not indicate an understanding of the connection between each finger and year. To give a three-year-old two crackers, one for each hand, has more meaning. To a five-year-old, one hundred is an enormous amount, which she or he may refer to as "e-hundred."

One-to-one correspondence can easily be encouraged in the home. Children can match one napkin, fork, knife, and spoon to each plate on the table. The concept of left and right can be introduced as the situation arises. As the concept of number improves, children can count out the necessary number of each item required to set the table. These concepts and activities are valuable only when the child is in a receptive mood. If they are forced tasks, children may lose interest and the natural curiosity necessary for active and personal participation to build intelligence. See Kamii (1982) for further details about children and number activities.

Language at this preconceptual level can be deceptive. Children may have a large oral vocabulary, but the meanings of the words and phrases are unique to the child's life and experiences. When viewing the "Wizard of Oz" for the first time, a five-year-old kept referring to it as the "Lizard of Oz." He did not know anything about wizards, but was very familiar with lizards. Children know that the sun and the moon exist, but believe that both are alive and are following them, an example of their egocentrism. Adults should ask questions such as: "Why?", "How do you know?", "Why do you think so?", or "What will happen next?" The responses the child gives will reveal thought processes that can be taken into consideration in the future.

Preoperational children cannot understand a period of time such as a week, month, or year, unless the time factor is within the child's immediate experience: "Right after lunch, we will go to the park."

Children who are egocentric likewise cannot understand any approach or manner of thinking other than their own. Just because the parent says something is so will not change the child's belief. The child may nod and agree with a forceful parent, but the child remains unconvinced. Only after children have explored many objects, people, and ideas, and talked about them, will the egocentrism begin to subside.

Concrete operational and formal operational stages

In the *concrete operational* stage (from about seven to eleven years) children can use logic to arrive at concrete conclusions, although abstract thinking is still elusive. These children can think deductively and classify objects if the objects are present, although they cannot solve such a problem mentally. If given a set of pictures of ducks, birds, and animals, the concrete operational child will be able to classify the pictures into the three groups. The child will also understand class inclusion, that is, ducks are birds and birds are animals. When asked, "If all the animals were sent to the moon, would there be any ducks left on earth?" the concrete operational child would be able to rearrange the hierarchy of ducks to animals, and know there would not be any ducks left on earth. The concrete operational child, unlike the preoperational child, can *conserve* (change in shape or position does not change amount). These children no longer need to break crackers into several smaller pieces so there will be more to eat (as does the preoperational child).

Parents of children at this stage can ask questions of a more complex nature, asking the child to analyze, combine, separate, multiply, and substitute with physical aids. Parents can listen carefully to what the child says, and then ask questions to help the child think and reason.

Central to Piaget's developmental view of learning by discovery is the premise that learning involves the active participation of the learner, whether in relation to objects or to social relationships. In other words, knowledge is not something that is transmitted verbally or otherwise; it has to be constructed and reconstructed by the individual learner. Each individual must discover his or her own knowledge. (Morris and Pai 1976, p. 371)

Parents must allow their children to determine the paths of pursuits of knowledge and be prepared to augment these pursuits in such a way that they continue to be the child's construction of knowledge, not what the parents think it should be. In posing questions to evaluate the child's cognitive process and delve deeper into an activity at hand, parents must be careful not to ask too many questions or to make the child feel compelled to give a response that pleases the adult.

About age eleven or twelve, the *formal operational* stage begins. Teenagers become more logical in mental processes. In a problem-solving situation, they can consider more than one factor and deal with an abstract aspect of the problem. At this stage, people can usually accept contrary information, develop a hypothesis, and support a viewpoint. It is now possible to deal with questions such as "What if snow were green?" Some teenagers and adults are able to develop ethical beliefs through consensus of the group rather than unquestioned acceptance of an authority figure. Although formal operations is the ultimate stage of Piaget's developmental continuum, it is one stage which is not necessarily completely achieved by all children or adults.

Moral development

A Piagetian approach must also consider children's social development. In addition to interaction with parents and other adults, children must have the opportunity for contact and interaction with peers, either siblings, neighbors, or a group. Through such relationships the child begins to formulate moral attitudes in a series of invariant stages similar to the stages of intellectual development (Piaget 1965).

Young children's first moral feelings are affected by respect for their parents and other adults. They will do things or make moral judgments in view of approval or disapproval of the parents or other respected adults. With the acquisition of language, children have a more precise tool with which to communicate with peers. Although young children show an interest in peers, egocentrism still prevails and interferes with these children taking the viewpoint of a peer. Asking two- or three-year-olds to share a toy is inappropriate because they see the toy as a personal extension which they are not quite ready to give up. The child is not being selfish, good, or bad; sharing is often not yet understood by the young egocentric child.

For preoperational children, *moral absolutism* prevails (Hetherington and Parke 1975). Rules are viewed as being beyond their control, never to be altered. To break the rules is to invite inevitable punishment from adults. Children at this stage also have difficulty in determining the seriousness of an act. If a rule is broken, the reasoning is not as important to the child as are the consequences. In a classic example, a preoperational child will feel that it is much worse to break fifteen teacups accidentally, than to break one teacup while sneaking a cookie.

At the age of about nine years, children attain the *morality of reciprocity*. They realize that rules are arbitrary and can be altered without resulting punishment from adults. Since these children are no longer controlled by egocentrism, they can more easily consider and appreciate the viewpoint and feelings of a peer. If a friend has been hurt, the child at this stage can feel compassion for that friend, whether it is emotional pain or physical pain. In order for the child to be able to share and understand the feelings of others frequently, the child must have access to a peer group. As the child's intellectual abilities develop, so does the ability to understand the feelings, actions, and reactions of others. Through interaction with peers, the child can experience and reinforce changing ideas about the moral world.

Parents who wish to be a more positive influence on their children's moral development will step down from the traditional authoritarian parental role. In an authoritarian home, the parent is always right, and the child is not allowed a voice in decision making. A democratic home requires more freedom of choice for the child, and more time for the parent to discuss, when necessary, the choices made and to evaluate the consequences with the child. By living in accordance with the same basic rules that are expected of the child, and by allowing the child a reasonable role in decision making, the parent can be an example of reciprocal morality. The parent is also a model of reciprocity in dealings with a spouse, older children, or other adults, to which the child may be an audience.

Conclusion

Parents who attempt a Piagetian approach should remember that "children have real understanding only of that which they invent themselves, and each time we try to teach them something too quickly, we keep them from reinventing it themselves" (Piaget, in Almy, Chittenden, and Miller 1966). Enjoying children does not come from seeing how quickly they can comprehend a task, but in seeing that they have really made their knowledge personal. When children can appropriately apply their knowledge to a situation removed from the original experience, true comprehension has been achieved. What is taken in by the child through personal experience, action, interaction, and reaction, becomes knowledge and truth for that child. To rush a child through any aspect of the developmental continuum is to risk overlooking an important concept needed by the individual.

While play materials, games, and other activities to promote Piagetian cognitive tasks at all levels have been devised for use in the home and classroom, they may not accurately reflect Piagetian theory. Parents and other teachers who are interested in a Piagetian approach can follow it without resorting to fancy equipment, tests, or formal drills. Parents can best aid their children's development by providing an enriched and diverse environment. This environment must include the opportunity to explore and act upon the physical surroundings, the opportunity for social and moral interaction with a peer group, and the opportunity to intellectually construct and reconstruct the world. Through understanding of developmental paths, and by providing the appropriate environment, parents can relax and enjoy listening to and talking with their children as they discover the world in their individual ways.

4. FAMILIES, CHILD REARING, AND PARENT EDUCATION: Parent Education

Bibliography

Almy, M.; Chittenden, E.; and Miller, P. *Young Children's Thinking.* New York: Teachers College Press, 1966.

Elkind, D. *A Sympathetic Understanding of the Child: Birth to Sixteen,* 2nd ed. Boston: Allyn & Bacon, 1978.

Elkind, D. "Piaget." *Human Behavior* 4, no. 8 (August, 1975): 24–39.

Gruber, H. W., and Vonèche, J. J., eds. *The Essential Piaget.* New York: Basic Books, 1977.

Hess, R. D., and Croft, D. J. *Teachers of Young Children.* Boston: Houghton-Mifflin, 1972.

Hetherington, E. M., and Parke, R. D. *Child Psychology: A Contemporary Viewpoint.* New York: McGraw-Hill, 1975.

Hunt, J. McV. *Intelligence and Experience.* New York: Ronald Press, 1961.

Kamii, C. *Number in Preschool and Kindergarten: Educational Implications of Piaget's Theory.* Washington, D. C.: National Association for the Education of Young Children, 1982.

Lake, A. "New Babies Are Smarter Than You Think," *Woman's Day* 9 (June 1976): 22+.

Morris, V. C., and Pai, Y. *Philosophy and the American School,* 2nd ed. Boston: Houghton-Mifflin, 1976.

Piaget, J. *The Origins of Intelligence in Children.* New York: Norton, 1963.

Piaget, J. *The Moral Judgment of the Child.* New York: The Free Press, 1965.

Piaget, J. *Six Psychological Studies.* New York: Vintage, 1968.

Piaget, J., and Inhelder, B. *The Psychology of the Child.* New York: Basic Books, 1969.

Sharp, E. *Thinking Is Child's Play.* New York: Avon, 1969.

Singer, D. G. "Piglet, Pooh, and Piaget." *Psychology Today* 6, no. 1 (June 1972): 71–74, 96.

Sund, R. B. *Piaget for Educators.* Columbus, Ohio: Merrill, 1976.

Wadsworth, B. J. *Piaget for the Classroom Teacher.* New York: Longman, 1978.

White, B. L. *The First Three Years of Life.* Englewood Cliffs, N.J.: Prentice-Hall, 1975.

I'm Worried About Our Kids

Mimi Brodsky Chenfeld

Mimi Brodsky Chenfeld is a teacher and author. Her books include Teaching Language Arts Creatively *and* Creative Activities for Young Children.

Joe Cunningham

There's a new fad sweeping the country. Don't buy into it!

"New Age" adults, under the ABC's of Anxiety, Betterment, and Competition, are practicing a kind of push-comes-to-shove child-rearing philosophy that starts programming children for success at birth and, sometimes, even in the womb.

"To everything there is a season and a time . . . " has even greater relevance as we view this frightening educational approach that boasts of four year olds naming the characters from Shakespeare before they learn to love the rhymes and rhythms of Mother Goose; that encourages children to skip by "Twinkle Twinkle Little Star" and

move directly to Beethoven's Ninth. These well-intentioned but misguided parents and teachers forget that children find their own ten toes without the aid of cards flashing pictures of ten toes, crawl without crawling lessons, and babble, imitate, sing, and talk without the assistance of computer games.

Those who advocate this speeded-up, adult-directed curriculum look to the lives of such geniuses as Michelangelo, Einstein, and Leonardo. Let's take another look at those lives: Michelangelo's parents never encouraged his artistic abilities. Einstein was considered a "slow learner" with learning disabilities. Leonardo spent his life looking for the mother he never knew. Now, I am NOT recommending discouragement, desertion, or misunderstanding as guarantees of high-achieving offspring! I am just reminding us that children are complex, total beings (in the state of becoming, as we all are). They begin the world anew with their own unique combination of strengths, interests, originality, courage, imagination, and determination. They are NOT "little sponges" as one of the "new age" parents described in a recent magazine article.

The most distressing aspect of this rapidly emerging (and fading quickly, I hope) system is that it conveys a *closed-up* notion of the world. Parents and teachers who advocate this high-pressure educational philosophy are really telling their children:

—We will provide you with all the answers.

—Learn them and you will succeed.

—Better still, learn them faster and you will make it sooner than everyone else.

(Why, these kids may even hit puberty before kindergarten!)

We constantly clarify values. We teach what we believe. In this unnatural, high-anxiety setting, there is no room for questions, no slot reserved for spontaneous discovery, for the surprise of exploration, for the excitement of learning. In this scheme of things, it's the product that's emphasized. The process is devalued. Plato believed that *the only beginning of learning is wonder.* Where does *wonder* fit into this accelerated, pressure-cooker scheme?

Remember, children are the greatest learners on earth. They can learn anything, anyway, from anyone. (Hitler vividly taught us that fact.) *But, just what is it that they are learning?*

I'm afraid that many of these "super-babies" are learning how *not* to be children. They are learning before they need to, more than they need to about tension, competition, failure, disappointment, and frustration. Most importantly, they might be learning that somehow love is connected with successfully performing for parents and teachers. Children who lose their spirit of adventure, their willingness to risk in new experiences, their ability to play with ideas and concepts can be considered "deprived." Maybe even "handicapped."

The Talmud teaches: "The lesson that is not enjoyed is not learned."

I am worried about our children caught in this newest craze. Here are two incidents chosen from a too ample supply:

Do you think Robbie enjoys his lessons? As his fellow kindergarteners practice writing their names with feelings of exuberance and pride, he freezes at the touch of a pencil in his hand, terrified to write even his own name because, "What if I make a mistake?"

Does first-grader Sherry "rejoice in her own works"? Everyday, she shreds her school papers, calling herself "dumb and stupid." Instead of heeding A.A. Milne's glorious proclamation, "Now I am six and I'm clever as clever/I think I'll be six now forever and ever!" she stares with deep, sorrowful, defeated six-year-old eyes of failure and says, "I wish I was dead . . . ."

I have seen kindergarten children sitting in "silent reading" groups working on dittos. I have seen three year olds told to redo their Thanksgiving pictures and "do it right! Pilgrims' hats are *black.* Don't use any other color. Watch Nancy. She's doing the BEST job!"

Ah, yes, Graham Nash's song, "Teach your children well . . . ."

When teachers and parents discuss ways of enriching the lives of young children, ways of helping them to *learn to love learning*, the best suggestions are the oldest, most natural, most obvious, most simple. They are so easy that we forget that we already know them:

• Hang loose. Relax.
• Talk with your children. Share and compare observations, questions, experiences, wishes, wonderings. Laugh together.
• Listen to music of all kinds. Enjoy the music. Let it inspire movement, art, stories, quiet times.
• Read to and with your children. Surround them with stories, poems, riddles, plays. Read to yourself. (What books do YOU love? If you want children to love reading, show them by your example.) Discover the delight of creating your own stories, your own writings. Children already know about this. Keep the flame burning.
• Walk with the children. Walk with awareness. Stop! Look! Listen! Be a person on whom "nothing is lost." Martin Buber believed that everything is waiting to be hallowed by you. For this, your beginning, God created the world. What do you hallow? A walk around the street with an aware, responsive, sensitive, involved adult is more enjoyable and valuable to a child than a trip around the world with a rigid, closed-minded, authoritarian tour leader.
• Encourage imaginative responses, original thinking, freedom of expression, new experiences. Don't be a critic, a judge. Be a person who rejoices in your own works and the works of others.
• Use the resources at your fingertips: libraries, museums, art galleries, parks, playgrounds, construction sites, gardens, zoos, bakeries, fruit stands, orchards, street signs, parking lots . . . . The word "boring" should not be permitted in the vocabulary of any child.

Our kids don't need expensive gimmicks, shiny educational tools, designer jigsaw puzzles, video games and heavy-handed adult intervention in their daily education. Let's not rely on the machines, no matter how valuable their potential in the learning process. An apple is still more incredible than a Apple Computer!

Our kids need an environment sweetened with TLC, encouragement, inspiration, role models, and time. Time to play, pretend, explore, experiment, and wonder. Time to develop at their own pace, in their own special rhythms. When children learn in such safe, supportive settings under the gentle, constant guidance of loving adults, they prove over and over again that they are among the most creative members of this gifted and talented family of ours.

Be ready for astonishment. Those of us who have spent most of our lives working with children know that, when we let them, *they teach us* about looking at everyday, ordinary miracles with fresh eyesight and insight. They take us on a journey to our own beginnings when the world was new and waiting to be discovered again.

We have a lot to learn. Maybe, *we're* the slow learners.

Behavior, Stressors, and Guidance

- **Discipline (Articles 32-33)**
- **Stressors and Stress-Reduction (Articles 34-35)**

Many Americans feel there has been a widespread societal breakdown in disciplined behavior in both children and adults. Discipline, guidance, and behavior problems, therefore, continue to be common discussion topics for adults who live and work with young children.

Specific identification of the causes of children's undesirable behavior, however, are not so widely agreed upon by either experts or laypeople. Opposing positions are often expressed that the root causes of misbehavior stem from permissiveness, economic upheavals, family disrup-

tions, media messages, improper diets, abuse or neglect, general frustrations caused by an era of rapid changes, or normal problems of growing and growing up.

Heated, unproductive arguments may occur if adults do not realize that the broad concept of discipline suggests varied meanings, purposes, and strategies for differing groups of people. For some adults, discipline means *punishment*—swift, painful, and controlled through fear and coercion. But researchers and observers of young children have shown that punished and overly-coerced children feel humiliated, lose self-esteem, and fail to develop coping strategies to handle future problems. For other adults, especially in Early Childhood Education, discipline means *guidance* in the form of modifying undesirable behavior and modeling or explaining about more acceptable, satisfying, or mature behavior. Discipline, in addition, means building self-control so children can develop positive self-esteem, respect the needs of others and gradually move toward healthy independence and problem-solving skills that will be used in future situations. Experienced and humane adults can modify their personal interaction style with children, the learning environment and schedule, and their expectations for individual children.

Key understandings for educators include knowing when to intervene in a situation, when to observe from afar, when to curb behavior immediately or wait and discuss it later, when to establish an inviolable rule, and when to permit cooperative establishment of rules. When assessing behavior, educators must consider what individual children are capable of doing relative to their age or stage, what special needs and skills they possess, and what opportunities could be provided to promote emotional growth and interpersonal competence.

Power struggles and contests between children's expanding willpower and adults' tolerance levels are inevitable in early childhood programs as they are in home settings. Caregivers and teachers can objectively understand and accurately interpret children's behavior and emotional reactions from the framework of developmental levels and context variables.

Childhood is a time of growing and striving, learning and struggling. Stress and stressors are part of that childhood picture around the world. Positive stress, or eustress, and negative stress, or distress, are experienced in the same way by the physiological and physical structures of the body: the person is energized for a "fight" or "flight" reaction. The rapidly accelerating changes of this era sometimes bewilder even the most mature and stable of adults, but professionals are in a crucial position to help children cope with the stressors of growing and growing up. The first entry into an early childhood program may engender "separation anxiety," and children's reactions can be both physical and psychological. Observant caregivers and teachers can provide curricular opportunities for children to rebuild their security base and self-confidence. An activity-based program where young children can play, make choices, take reasonable risks, and listen to children's literature on the theme of separation can affect healthy feelings of competence.

In addition to the normal, expected developmental stressors of childhood, millions of young children are daily experiencing distress from family disruptions—conflict, separation, divorce, custody battles, or remarriage—neglect or abuse, illness or hospitalization, death of a special person or pet, moving, family economic problems, and even anxieties about abduction or nuclear war. In recognition of these distressful events and their tremendous impact on children's behavior and learning, many educators are incorporating stress-management and relaxation activities into their programs. Growth in positive coping skills, self-control, and social competence are typical results of these stress-management exercises.

This section examines the ways in which humane educators can discipline children, provide guidance, and help them in dealing with stressors in their lives.

Looking Ahead: Challenge Questions

Are there techniques for disciplining young children that are both effective and humane? How can teachers model acceptable attitudes and habits for growing children?

What are the differences between punishment and discipline? How can young children be taught to rely on problem-solving skills so they can gradually move toward self-control? What's ineffective about spanking children when they have been physically aggressive?

What are the behavioral signs of "separation anxiety"? How can an activity-based curriculum help young children deal with their separation problems in a healthy manner? How can play and children's literature help children deal with separation fears?

What are the major causes of stress for today's children? What are some relaxation techniques teachers can use to help children deal with these stressors? Are today's children under more stress than ever before? What differentiates the "capable kids" from the "vulnerable kids"?

Classroom Discipline Problems? Fifteen Humane Solutions

Marjorie L. Hipple

Marjorie Hipple is a Preschool Teacher at Bent Twig School, Gainesville, Florida.

Concern about how to guide children effectively and humanely is common to all teachers whether they are veterans or beginners, young or old, male or female. Some teachers, however, seem to have less difficulty with child guidance or "discipline," as it is often called, than do others. The reasons for the differences are no doubt varied; the personality of the teacher or the size and composition of the class, for example, can readily affect the choice of approaches used and the success of these methods. Yet there are approaches that seem to work well for many teachers and that are based upon knowledge of child development, learning theories and sound pedagogy. The purpose of this article is to suggest some of these for your consideration.

The approaches are grounded upon some basic assumptions. One is that *it is preferable to try to identify causation whenever possible in guiding child behavior rather than to treat the behavior in isolation*. We know all behavior is caused—by internal needs of the child, by external factors, or by an interaction of these forces.[1] An awareness of causation can enable us to respond more effectively and intelligently to specific behaviors. For example, if we realize that the aggression children display is the result of frustration they feel because a task is too difficult for them, we might want to modify the task

rather than simply treat the symptom, aggression.

Second, it is assumed that *the use of positive or at least neutral techniques is more productive when guiding children than the use of negative methods*. Although various schools of psychology diverge on other points, most agree about the value of positive responses in maintaining productive human interaction. Self theorists claim that as we deal in positive ways with children, we bolster their self-concepts and thereby enable them to develop emotionally in growth-promoting ways. Behaviorists assert that positive reinforcement of behavior tends to increase the occurrence of that behavior. On the other hand, when we resort to *negative* techniques, including not only punishment but also the threat of punishment, we may create a mood of hostility that can transform classrooms into battlegrounds. And, once this pattern begins, we may be unable to turn it around as easily as we would like. Stated more simply, the difference between the use of positive and negative approaches often accounts for "the teacher who never scolds, but has such a good class" and "the teacher who has to yell and scream at her children, who still do not behave."

A third assumption is that *versatility in the use of guidance approaches is more effective than reliance upon any single technique*. No doubt you have experienced the frustration of using a method that works well one day only to note its ineffectiveness the next time it is tried. This inconsistency is not difficult to understand when we consider the variations of mood, motives, personality and situational factors that enter every human interaction. What works one day may fail another. What works with one child may fail with another. What works for one teacher may fail for another. Versatility—or

---

[1] For reasons of clarity and brevity, this article will deal specifically with ways to guide children. The analysis and modification of situational factors that affect behavior are also necessary when we deal with the ecology of the classroom. That aspect of management is, however, beyond the scope of this article.

From *Childhood Education*, February 1978, pp. 183-187. Reprinted by permission of Marjorie L. Hipple and the Association for Childhood Education International, 11141 Georgia Avenue, Suite 200, Wheaton, MD 20902. Copyright © 1978 by the Association.

eclecticism if you wish—is vital if we are to be responsive facilitators.

Finally, it is assumed that, over the long haul, *approaches that foster the development of internal behavioral controls and problem solving are more productive than those that rely upon external controls or authoritarianism to keep the immediate peace.* Said another way, our goal is to foster self-discipline.

The following approaches and illustrative scenarios are offered as suggestions rather than as prescriptive cure-alls. They are a tiny part of the universe of guidance approaches that can make teaching and learning more humane and enjoyable.

1. Accentuate the positive. If a child's behavior is unacceptable, suggest appropriate alternatives—positive substitutes—rather than focus negative attention on the inappropriate behavior.

Scenario: A child is throwing building blocks. Intervene by suggesting that the blocks are for building but that, if the child wishes to throw, he may work with bean bags or balls. Two positive alternatives are offered the child: either to build with the blocks or to throw with other objects.

2. Be a "model" model. As a teacher you are assuredly a significant model for your students—yet quite inadvertently you may model the very behavior you wish to modify. Still, it is rather encouraging to also realize that when you model desired behavior that, too, is emulated. Note how much more effective Scenario 2 is likely to be.

Scenario 1: A child pushes another child in order to cut into line. You shake her violently while exclaiming, "I won't have you pushing other children around."

Scenario 2: Having in hand a leaking paint container, you need to use the classroom sink. You ask if you may *please* use the sink out of turn rather than simply cut in front of the children who patiently await their turns. They agree to your request, and you remember to thank them.

3. Spotlight behavioral consequences. Young children are egocentric. And their egocentrism can prevent them from being able to put themselves in another person's place. You can help children move from egocentrism to socialized behavior by having them analyze the consequences of their actions. In spotlighting consequences, try to discuss the child's behavior in a nonjudgmental way and encourage him to think about its impact on people, objects and events with the intent of developing his consideration of cause/effect relationships.

Scenario: A child continually damages equipment . . . take him aside for a probing discussion about "What will happen if all of the toys get broken?" Encourage him to think about the various effects of his behavior and to suggest alternate behaviors himself.

4. Send "I-messages." The use of I-messages is an approach developed by Thomas Gordon (1974) to deal with behavior that is causing problems for the teacher.[2] An "I-message" is a personal statement by you, the teacher, that has three components: your nonjudgmental description of the problem, its tangible effects upon you, and your feelings about it. The sending of "I-messages" is an intimate form of communication in that it bares your feelings in order to raise the child's consciousness about the effects of his behavior. For this reason, you may feel uncomfortable about using this technique and, if so, you may be better advised not to use it. Like the rationale for spotlighting consequences, this approach is based upon the belief that many children are unaware of the impact their behavior has upon others.

Scenario: Discuss a problem with your class concerning, say, clean-up behaviors: "When you leave the clay uncovered, it dries out and I have to mix a new batch which takes a lot of time. I really hate having to make new clay every day." Then facilitate a discussion of how the problem might be worked out.

5. Help children hurdle. Sometimes you can help a child avoid frustration or the loss of his or her self-control by simply offering a suggestion, a question or a gesture at the right time. This approach may sound alien to ears that have long received the message that teachers should encourage autonomy. Assuredly you do want to support this attribute. But you also need to foster interdependence when the situation calls for it. Everyone needs a helping hand sometime.

Scenario: A child stamps his feet in exasperation as he tries for the umpteenth time to pull on an unwieldy boot. Sensitive to his plight, give him a reassuring start with a pull on the stubborn footwear.

---

[2] Gordon espouses this technique for dealing *only* with behavior that causes the teacher problems. Behavior that is causing problems for the child (e.g., fear, worry) are more effectively dealt with in other ways which he outlines. Readers interested in learning more about Gordon's approach are urged to consult the references that follow this article.

6. Instruct. Children often behave inappropriately because they do not know what is expected of them. Even that which appears to be obvious or simple to you may not be at all apparent to the children. A good dictum is: When in doubt, teach them how.

Scenario: A new set of manipulative math materials arrives. In introducing the equipment, demonstrate a few of the many possibilities for its use, and then observe children using the materials to determine whether further instruction is necessary.

7. Limit options. Sometimes children are overstimulated by the number of choices available to them or, once they have made a choice, they may not handle it well. They may have too much time, too much space, too many materials, or too many activities on their hands. This overload is often the case with children who enter school for the first time. Ultimately children must learn to make choices and, as they mature, they do. But their immediate problems may require the limiting of those choices.

Scenario: A child has great difficulty staying with a task. He moves from one learning center to another, staying only long enough to take out materials, then moving on. Request that he choose one activity, help him get started with it, and, if necessary, monitor his behavior until the activity is underway.

8. Divert behavior. Some unacceptable behaviors are fleeting or situation-specific. In these instances it is often most effective to alter the social environment by diverting the child to another activity.

Scenario: Two children, best friends, sometimes rub each other the wrong way. On these occasions, step in before their conflict gets out of hand, directing each child to different activities.

9. Ignore behavior. Sometimes the best thing you can do is to ignore inappropriate behavior. Although this can be difficult to do, ignoring some behaviors has positive outcomes worth considering. First, behavior that is ignored is *not* reinforced. And behavior that is not reinforced tends to subside or stop. (At least one exception to this generalization should be noted: Aggressive behavior does not necessarily lessen when it is ignored. It may, in fact, increase. For this reason, it often must be dealt with directly by other methods.)[3] A second value to ignoring some behaviors is that children will often solve their own problems when left to do so, utiliz-

---

[3] See Restraining Behavior (Point No. 15).

ing worthwhile personal or interpersonal skills in the process.

Scenario: Two children argue over the use of a toy. Silently observe them and decide not to intervene when they work out a method of taking turns that is satisfactory to them.

10. Reinforce appropriate behavior. Teachers continually reinforce behavior, either consciously or unconsciously, for good or ill. An important task for you is to become conscious about reinforcing behaviors you wish to see repeated. Unfortunately, if you are not aware of your impact as a reinforcing agent, you may reward the wrong kinds of behavior.

Scenario: A child who usually "acts out" during group activities interacts productively today. Immediately reinforce his long-desired behavior with either tangible or intangible rewards.

11. Reinforce adjacent behavior. Sometimes it is exceedingly difficult to reinforce desirable behavior because it appears so seldom. The next best approach may be to reinforce acceptable behavior of adjacent peers in the hope that the misbehaving child will imitate those peers so as to obtain similar reinforcement. This technique should *never* involve a direct comparison of one child with another (e.g., "Why can't you sit like John?")!

Scenario: Although a few children behave disruptively during a class activity, most of the children participate well. Praise the group of "good workers," commenting on the businesslike way most of them are working today. (Possibly suggest that those who complete their work might utilize the extra time to pursue activities of their own choosing.)

12. Cue behavior. Young children need and want a sense of order in their lives. Routines can provide the security that enables children to adapt with confidence to new situations. Everyone responds, often unconsciously, to environmental cues. Cues can be helpful in signalling fairly regular events such as transition periods between classes or activities. A flick of a light switch, a chord on the piano, or an upraised hand communicates messages in an effortless way.

Scenario: It is time to clean up materials used during the activity period. The children finish their work as they hear a familiar "Clean Up" tune on the piano.

13. Monitor behavior. Teachers monitor behavior in a number of ways, many of which take the form of body language or other nonverbal communication. An uplifted

eyebrow or a surprised glance can sometimes relay messages to children more effectively than words. Physical proximity—placing a hand on a child's shoulder, moving about among the students, standing quietly in a potential problem area—can say, "I am here if you need my support."

Scenario: Two girls enjoy each other's company so much that they sometimes forget the task at hand in their happy socialization. A glance in their direction may clearly say, "It's time to get back to work, girls."

14. Give a breather. Occasionally it is necessary to remove a child from a provoking situation. The removal or breather is a neutralizing, temporary event—a time out—that is ended when the child indicates that he has the desire and control needed to reenter the group. Giving a breather is *NOT* punishing a child, placing him in a dark or otherwise frightening situation, or demeaning him. Instead it is providing him with an unprovoking alternative activity which he pursues by himself.

Scenario: Coming to school charged up with frustration, a child continually aggresses against her peers until adult intervention is imperative. Guide her to a quiet part of the room where she can work at an activity of her choice until she feels better about herself and can work productively with the group.

15. Restrain behavior. It is sometimes necessary to restrain children from continuing their behavior. When children are in the throes of anger that can make their actions potentially dangerous to themselves or others, restraint may be the only workable approach. Verbal restraints are simple, nonjudgmental statements that say, in effect, "I can't let you harm yourself or another child.

You are angry now, but once you calm down, you will be better able to handle the situation." It may be necessary to accompany the verbalization by physically restraining the child. Physical restraint should never be a punitive or aggressive response: It is NOT hitting, shaking or pushing a child about. Instead the child is calmly but firmly held in a neutral way until regaining self-control.

Scenario: A playground altercation quickly escalates to a fight between two boys. Part them, but hold the one who will not stop until he calms down.

A FINAL WORD— WHEN ALL ELSE FAILS . . .

It is so easy to take ourselves too seriously, to get lost in the welter of problems, to lose our sense of humor—and our sense of perspective—especially on those days when everything goes wrong, our mood is a bit rocky, and we *know* the barometric pressure is affecting both ourselves and the children. Why not accept those days with humor rather than fighting them? Why not revise those plans so carefully made, laugh a bit, and find ways, with the input of the children, to salvage the day? After all, some days *are* like that, aren't they?

References

Galambos, Jeannette. *A Guide to Discipline.* Washington, DC: National Association for the Education of Young Children, 1969.

Gordon, Thomas. *Teacher Effectiveness Training.* New York: Wyden, 1974.

Greer, Mary, & Bonnie Rubenstein. *Will the Real Teacher Please Stand Up?* Pacific Palisades, CA: Goodyear, 1972.

Hipple, Marjorie. *Early Childhood Education: Problems and Methods.* Pacific Palisades, CA: Goodyear, 1975.

Pringle, Mia Kellmer. *The Needs of Children.* New York: Schocken, 1975.

Building Self-Control

Discipline for Young Children

Cheri Sterman Miller

Cheri Sterman Miller, M.A., is Director of the Office of Child Care Services for the state of Ohio.

What happened the last time you were faced with a child's misbehavior? Was the child punished—or disciplined?

Children are *punished* when . . . their behavior is controlled through fear . . . they behave to avoid a penalty imposed by an adult . . . the adult stresses what *not* to do. Children who are punished . . . feel humiliated . . . hide their mistakes . . . have a poor self-concept . . . fail to develop inner controls to handle future problems.

Children are *disciplined* when . . . they see the possible consequences of their actions . . . alternative behaviors are proposed . . . they learn to control themselves. Children who are disciplined . . . learn to balance their needs with those of other people . . . feel good about themselves . . . become increasingly independent.

When we look toward the future, discipline accomplishes the goals we have for children. How, then, do we help children build self-control?

Prevention

Broken rules, disruptive behavior, lack of cooperation—all are real problems for parents and teachers. However, effective discipline begins long before such behaviors erupt. Your personal interaction style, the environment, the schedule, and your expectations all have an effect on children.

Interaction style

Start by examining your own teaching or parenting style, and your tolerance levels. You may be giving subtle messages to your children. Your responses to these questions will help you identify some of your strengths and weaknesses.

- What behaviors do you consider to be inappropriate?
- What levels of noise and confusion do you consider normal? When does the level become intolerable?
- Do you identify who really has the problem in a conflict?
- When a child's anger is directed toward you, do you feel hurt or threatened?
- Do you need to make most of the decisions or do you share control with the children?
- Do you model the behavior you expect from children? What contradictions are there between what you say or expect and what you do?

Environment

Sit on a child-size chair and take a good look at your home or classroom. Your observations may give you some ideas about how to improve the arrangement of furniture or learning materials. Be sure to consider children's abilities and interests.

- Are there tempting items on display that are off-limits to children?
- Are toys and supplies on low, open shelves where children can reach and return them, thus encouraging independence?
- How does the arrangement of materials or furniture encourage appropriate behavior? (Are paints or water located away from the books? Can children build with blocks in a protected area?)
- How do you limit access to areas with limited materials?

Reprinted by permission from *Young Children*, Vol. 40, No. 1 (November 1984), pp. 15-19. © 1984 by the National Association for the Education of Young Children, 1834 Connecticut Avenue, N.W., Washington, DC 20009.

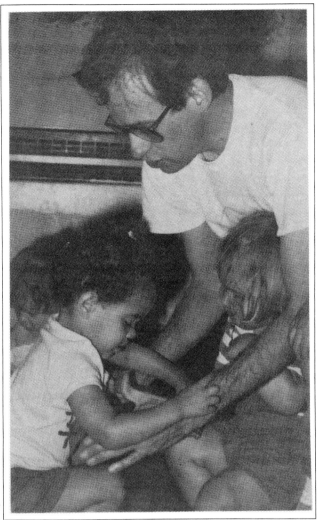

Discipline problems can be expected when children are bored or rushed, when they have to wait, or when they are over-stimulated without time to unwind.

When groups are expected to participate in an activity, are there sufficient items for everyone to remain involved?

Schedule

Discipline problems can be expected when children are bored or rushed, when they have to wait, or when they are over-stimulated without time to unwind. Children are learning every minute of the day, so your schedule may contain opportunities to encourage more self-control.

• Are most of the day's activities child selected? Are those determined by adults appropriate and interesting for the children? Can children move between activities at their own pace?

• Is the length of time for an activity based on growing attention spans? For example, group times should be limited to 10–20 minutes for preschoolers, and then only if children are actively involved.

• How are children prepared for changes in activity/place throughout the day? Children need to know in advance what to expect. Ample time to complete projects and clean up make transitions move more smoothly.

• Do you use creative or dramatic activities to help children move between areas or wait for an unexpected delay?

• Have you established a sense of rhythm to the day—a routine that can be counted on to give children a sense of security? Even children who cannot tell time gain a sense of how the day evolves.

Expectations

Consistent and fair limits help children control their own behavior—if they know what the limits are. Review your expectations for possible sources of difficulties.

• Are limits clear? Is the real reason for the rule stated?

• Are limits appropriate? Do they show understanding of children's needs and abilities?

• Are the limits truly necessary? Too many rules are confusing and easily forgotten. Some adults have only one basic rule: You may not hurt yourself, others or things. *Hurt* can be explained as either physical or feelings.

• Have the children helped form the rules? All of us are more inclined to adhere to limits that we have contributed to. For example, if a pet is introduced, children might suggest rules that an adult can record. Then together review the suggestions and choose those that seem best.

• Are children's rights protected? Do they feel assured that if another child grabs their marker that an adult will help them preserve their right to finish using it? Do children feel confident that they will get a turn later?

• Do you help children interpret each other's feelings? Are children encouraged to verbalize their frustrations, hurts, and disappointments?

The way in which you prepare the environment and how you treat children when all is well form the basis for your actions when the inevitable problems arise.

No magic solutions

When discipline is viewed as a teaching opportunity we can see that there are no magic techniques which work for every problem or every child. Our approach must relate to the problem. Any consequence must logically follow the child's action if the child is to learn from the experience. The techniques I recommend are positive and tend to rely on problem-solving skills—essential factors if children are to become self-disciplined.

Natural consequence

In many instances, children may already have found the consequences of their actions when the problem becomes evident. The child may already have learned from the experience, although sometimes it may be appropriate to point out what happened and why.

Two children who both yank on their favorite doll and break it can be encouraged to discuss how they could prevent this next time. A child who forgets to put a treasured painting in her or his cubby and then searches in vain for it will be likely to store items more carefully in the future.

Direct toward consequence

Some situations call for the adult to positively direct the child to a logical consequence without being punitive. This approach helps children become more responsible for their own actions. For example, toddlers can wipe up spilled

The best discipline method is to encourage children to think of alternative solutions and their possible effects.

drinks. An older child who writes on the wall can be expected to wash it off.

Problem solving

Whenever possible, the best discipline method is to encourage children to think of alternative solutions and possible effects of taking those alternatives. Through problem solving, children develop a sense of responsibility for their actions, begin to understand others' needs, and strengthen their decision-making skills. Just as in setting limits, children who participate in the decision-making process are more likely to adhere to their decisions.

Younger or inexperienced children probably will need adult assistance to think of alternatives that are potentially agreeable. You might ask "How can you . . .?" Or "What could we do to . . .?" Children soon learn to generate their own solutions. One preschooler who had just collided with another paused for a moment and then demanded, "Well, aren't you going to kiss it?"

Problems between children and adults, or between two adults, can also be resolved with this technique—it is called negotiation!

Redirection

Infants about to engage in an unwanted activity can be easily distracted. Older children may have their activity redirected or replaced with an acceptable substitute. Combined with other approaches, it is an effective technique because the circumstances are changed, albeit by an adult. When reasons are stated, children can soon learn to redirect themselves.

When you want to redirect an activity, you first need to think about why the child is involved. For instance, if two children are fighting for a scoop in the sandbox, you can find another way or item or place to resolve the difficulty—a cup might work just as well. A child climbing on the table may be encouraged to climb trees or climbers instead.

A similar but more acceptable substitute can nearly always be found, but if not, another enticing activity may work equally well. What can you do during a long trip when a bored toddler begins kicking the safety seat? Unveil a soft new toy, or play a tape of children's songs for the whole family to sing along. Wise parents and teachers are always prepared!

Time out

This technique is one of the most misunderstood and misused disciplinary methods. While time out is more behavioristic than the other approaches suggested here, it can be especially effective in situations when children have lost control and are unable to reason. However, the following principles must be observed for time out to be a positive learning experience leading toward self-discipline.

Peter Waugh

When discipline is viewed as a teaching opportunity we can see that there are no magic techniques which work for every problem or every child.

- Time out is not a punishment. Children should not be threatened with or fearful of a time out.
- Time out should not be humiliating. Consequently, there should not be a predetermined time out chair or place.
- Time out should last as long as the *child* feels is needed to calm down. If children underestimate the length of time they need, they can be asked to try to calm down again in time out.
- Time out can be a time for the adult and child to talk about feelings—after the child has calmed down. An adult's presence can help calm an angry child, but only after calm has been restored will it be productive to talk.

How you apply these techniques is just as essential as knowing *what* to do.

Sometimes children will become overly excited and behave inappropriately. Such children can be asked to remove themselves from the situation to take an opportunity to calm down. Another appropriate use of time out is for an aggressive child to gain self-control away from the other children. One such child in time out was reminded that he could decide when he was ready to return to play. He responded, "I know, but I'm not ready yet . . . if I go over now, I'll hit him." In a short while, with the help of the adult, the aggressor talked out his anger and felt ready to resume play.

Restraint/holding

In some situations a child will be so upset and so intense that he or she is unable to talk. An adult can hold the child with just sufficient strength to protect the child or other children and help restore calm. A child screaming and thrashing may need to be soothed in this manner before discussing the incident.

Ignoring inappropriate behavior

Children who behave inappropriately often receive the most attention from adults. This can encourage negative behavior from others. While not all inappropriate behavior can or should be ignored, situations that are simply annoying rather than harmful may be handled best in this way. For example, preschool children often find that foul language gains them immediate attention, although they probably have no idea what it means. If you ignore the cursing, however, the child will eventually see there is no gain in using that language, and the words may not be repeated.

Other factors besides the need for attention may account for the disruption of quiet times such as naps or stories. Try to determine the cause for disruptions and take appropriate action. When children are cuddled, talked with, and made to feel important throughout the day, they will be less likely to demand attention by disrupting such activities. During naptime or storytime, however, because these behaviors are generally not harmful, ignoring them may lead to fewer disruptions.

This technique usually takes longer to be effective than other methods, and at first the inappropriate behavior may increase as children diligently try to attract your attention. These behaviors will also escalate if you sometimes ignore and sometimes criticize the children. Be consistent.

Before you try these techniques

In offering these suggestions about ways to discipline children, I take the risk that the style you use to implement them may be inappropriate or punative. *How* you apply these techniques is just as essential as knowing *what* to do. Otherwise, discipline may not be consistent with our goals for the healthy growth and development of children.

As you use these ideas, keep these principles about effective discipline in mind.

• The goal of discipline is to help children build their own self-control, not to have them behave through adult-imposed control.

• Any discipline technique will be most effective if it is applied in a way that maintains or enhances the child's self-esteem.

• Discipline must immediately follow the behavior. Children cannot be expected to relate future consequences to their current actions.

• Match the technique you use to the behavior and the child. No technique will be effective in every situation.

• Help the child understand why she or he is being disciplined—after the child has gained self-control.

Spanking stimulates children to fight and hit because children copy adult behavior.

• Effective discipline requires follow through. Idle or impossible threats encourage children to test rules and push limits. When you use a disciplinary action, make sure the problem-solving solution works, that a redirected child becomes involved elsewhere, or that a child in time out has an adult with whom to talk.

• Progress may be slow. If either you or the children are accustomed to other techniques, time and patience are required for these ideas to be effective. It takes time for children to understand self-control instead of adult-imposed discipline. And it may take you a while to be consistent and in control of yourself.

• Help others understand the positive approach to discipline. Emphasize why helping children learn to control themselves is an essential part of becoming an independent and caring person. When adults see that spanking stimulates children to fight and hit because children copy adult behavior, they may be more inclined to adopt other more effective methods.

Take a minute now to think through what you will do when the inevitable difficulties arise between children. How will you use discipline to help children balance their needs with those of others, to feel good about themselves, and to become increasingly independent?

Bibliography

Ackerman, P., and M. Kappleman, M. *Signals—What Your Child Is Really Telling You.* New York: Dial, 1978.

Brophy, J., and Everston, C. *Learning From Teaching: A Developmental Perspective.* Boston: Allyn & Bacon, 1976.

Dodson, F. *How To Discipline with Love.* New York: Rawson Associates, 1977.

Dodson, F. *How To Parent.* Los Angeles: Nash Publishing Corp., 1970.

Dreikurs, R., and Cassel, P. *Discipline Without Tears: What To Do With Children Who Misbehave.* New York: Hawthorn Books, 1972.

Ginott, H. *Between Parent and Child.* New York: Macmillan, 1967.

Gordon, T. *Parent Effectiveness Training.* New York: Wyden, 1970.

Gordon, T. *Teacher Effectiveness Training.* New York: Wyden, 1974.

Marion, M. *Guidance of Young Children.* St. Louis, Mo.: Mosby, 1981.

Purkey, W. *Inviting School Success: A Self-Concept Approach to Teaching and Learning.* Belmont, Calif.: Wadsworth, 1978.

Riley, S. S. *How to Generate Values in Young Children.* Washington, D.C.: National Association for the Education of Young Children, 1984.

Shure, M. B., and Spivak, G. "Interpersonal Cognitive Problem Solving and Primary Prevention Programming for Preschool and Kindergarten Children." *Journal of Clinical Child Psychology* 2 (1979): 89–94.

Stone, J. G. *A Guide to Discipline.* Washington, D.C.: National Association for the Education of Young Children, 1978.

The name of the game is confidence

Separation anxiety can cheat young children out of school fun and learning. Here's how to help kids overcome it.

Nancy Balaban

Nancy Balaban is director of the Infant and Parent Development Program at Bank Street College of Education, New York. She has taught children in preschool and first grade.

Diana still seems not quite in school. She has a faraway expression and roams around, touching a puzzle, a book, but can't seem to settle anywhere....She enjoys the attention of the other children, but she's not ready to interact with them....Today Diana is playing with puppets, and they're helping her out of her withdrawn state. An affectionate demonstration between a momma and a baby puppet helped Diana deal with her separation feelings. She brought momma into the classroom when she needed her. A giant step for Diana....Diana drew a girl with crayons. With much effort,

From *Instructor*, September 1985, pp. 108-110, 112. Excerpted from STARTING SCHOOL: FROM SEPARATION TO INDEPENDENCE/ A GUIDE FOR EARLY CHILDHOOD TEACHERS by Nancy Balaban. Reprinted by permission of Teachers College Press.

she began to tie her shoe. Diana is growing in confidence....Diana is walking her mother to the door. It gives her more control over the separation....Today Diana made a girl from clay, complete with "arms, legs, eyes, nose, and a tushie," she explained. I have the feeling Diana now has a greater sense of herself as a separate person. She has all of those parts....Diana is beginning to play with the other children....Diana is blooming. She seems to experience herself as a separate person. She has gained confidence and strength....

These excerpts from a teacher's log chronicle how one child overcame a problem that affects many youngsters when they enter preschool or kindergarten—separation anxiety. When the moment of separation from a parent is traumatic, children react in different ways. Some kick, scream, cry, bite; their sense of abandonment is obvious.

You can focus immediately on these children, helping them make the adjustment from home to school.

Other children like Diana may hide their feelings. They appear quiet and unassertive. They seem to be oblivious to the life of the classroom. Yet because they are unassuming, they are often overlooked. A closer examination may reveal that they are not involved with other children or with classroom materials to any significant degree. Such children may be physically at school but psychologically at home.

Even more puzzling, some children walk into the classroom as though they belong there. They play with the toys and make friendly gestures toward other children. They blithely wave good-bye to their parents. "Great kids!" you say. "No problems here." Then two weeks into school, one of these "no-problem" children collapses into tears when the parent leaves.

Not every child comes into the classroom affected in these adverse ways. For many the first day of school is the culmination of a summer of anticipation, the reality of a longed-for adventure. Yet because separation anxiety is a problem for some young children, teachers of this age level must be prepared to help them gain the self-confidence they will need to function independently.

Why is separation so difficult for some kids? One reason is that children enter school with preconceived notions about adults. Consequently, they may become uncomfortable when they perceive that the teacher does not behave like their mother, father, or grandmother. They need time to learn about the teacher, to learn what certain tones of voice mean, and to learn what to expect in various situations. They need time to differentiate between what goes on at home and what goes on at school. If the teacher is a benign and caring person, a child who is ready for school or group care will be able to transfer feelings of "basic trust" from home to school.

Until children come to feel this sense of trust, the teacher and the classroom remain strange. You can help alleviate some of that strangeness through careful planning. Use these strategies and activities to help all students, but especially those for whom separation is very difficult, cope with insecurity and move on to competence.

First-day strategies

A list of children's names on a wall chart will attract the attention

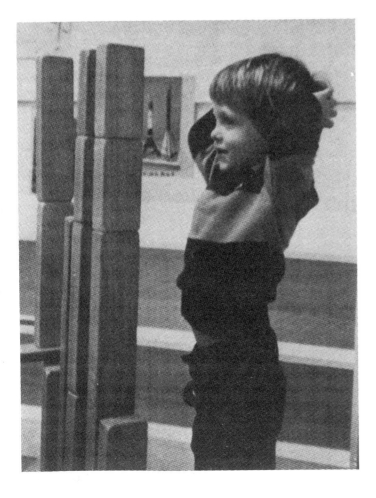

"*The early childhood classroom offers many opportunities for children to build self-confidence...in choosing materials...taking risks....*"

of children and parents. What a sure message to children that the teacher really wants them! Print the names with a large felt-tip marker so that children who can recognize their own names will be better able to do so. Children who do not read will be equally delighted when parents point out their names.

Encourage children to participate fully in saying good-bye to their parents. Hugging, kissing, crying, waving, and saying "I'll miss you" are all ways to bring feelings out into the open. Once in the open, they are easier to deal with. Never allow a parent to sneak out. The child's anxiety will only be increased.

Help parents and children plan together for the next day's parting. Through such planning children gain security and experience self-confidence.

Provide an opportunity for children to watch their parents leave. Perhaps there is a window in the classroom where a child can stand if he or she desires to. Provide a step-stool if it's a high window.

Talk with children about their feelings. This enables them to take steps toward mastery of their emotions and control of their actions.

Regard regressive behavior, such as thumb-sucking or wetting pants, without a fuss. The less attention you pay to such behavior, the sooner children will get control.

Follow-up strategies

Try having children say good-bye to parents when you take the group outdoors. If parents stay in the room until you're on the playground, then the children are the ones who are doing the "leaving."

Have children dictate or write letters to their parents, detailing what they are doing in school. Putting "I miss you," "I love you," "Come back soon" on paper can be very reassuring to a young child. Give kids the option of sharing the letter or not sharing it with the parent.

Encourage children to bring a favorite toy or blanket to school

each day, or something belonging to their parents. These are not meant to be shared with other children. They are meant to represent a bit of home for those who need the tie.

Photographs of children's families, including pets, posted at eye-level in an accessible spot, help young children remember that their families do exist, even though they may not be with them. Laminate the photos so that they'll withstand lots of loving attention.

A book of photographs of life at home may also ease the transition from home to school and provide a good opportunity for parent involvement. Or the children could draw a series of pictures of life at home—eating, playing, bedtime—either at home or in school. Add

---

"Separation is a developmental necessity. It underlies all children's discovery of themselves as builders."

---

covers and bind the pictures into books for children to look at and to show to others.

Be aware of transition times in your daily schedule, such as clean-up periods or moving from one activity to another. Sometimes those moments are especially difficult for children who are coping with separation. Involve these children in an activity right away.

Evaluate the appropriateness of the materials you have made available to the children. Are the number of block shapes overwhelming or too few? Are there enough colors of paint to satisfy everyone? Are the puzzles too easy or too difficult? Are you spending too much time teaching pupils how to use the paste? Would it be better

to put it away for a while? Do the children have the control needed for felt-tip markers or would they be less frustrated with crayons? An array of attractive playthings that are developmentally "right" for your students will show them (and their parents) that you are aware of, and prepared to meet, their needs.

Curriculum ties

Cooking Cooking activities link school to home for young children in a very concrete way. Nothing could be more familiar than food and its preparation, except perhaps its consumption! Shaping cookies, mixing batter, cutting vegetables for soup, or dipping bread for French toast are all activities that conjure up memories of home; reading recipes, calculating quantities, measuring and predicting (What will happen to the flour when we add milk?) introduce reading, math, and science concepts.

Play Play can be good therapy for children. For example, puppets help children express their feelings of longing for their parents. While young children generally prefer animal puppets, they will still label them "mommy," "daddy," "grandma." Lead into the role-playing by asking questions of the puppets: Do you go to school? Where is your mommy (daddy, grandma)? Do you have a baby puppet? Who takes care of your baby? You may find yourself included in the play, and perhaps assigned a role.

Games of peekaboo and hide-and-seek can be played at the sand and water tables where toys can be hidden and found easily. Such games give children control over the process of letting go and of retrieving. It's a way of "practicing" being left and being reunited.

Provide for, and observe, children's natural dramatic play. This will give you consistent clues as to how children are doing in their attempts to cope with separation reactions. Children may play baby or nurturing parent many times over in their attempts to come to terms with their feelings. They may choose themes of moving or going away. They may play monster as they begin to face their fears of being on their own at school. You can provide for this play by supplying props such as suitcases, dolls, a doll bed or cot large enough for a child to lie in, and space and privacy for play.

Art Provide nonstructured materials such as paints, blocks, clay, crayons, felt-tip markers, and clean drawing paper. These allow children to spontaneously represent their feelings about themselves, their families, and their entry into the new world of school.

Books Picture books and stories about school or how it feels to be separated from a loved one can open the way for you and the children to talk about separation. Naturally, such books should be chosen with care. The first consideration should always be that the book be good literature. It should be a pleasure to read and a pleasure to listen to. Are there interesting characters and appealing illustrations? Is the story related to the children's own experiences? Check resources for books on school and on separation.

Encouraging self-confidence

Through a curriculum that has an understructure of support for children who are coping with separation, teachers can provide the means for them to develop and exercise competence. Helping children build self-confidence can make them feel comfortable and safe when they are away from the protection of their parents.

The desire to be capable comes from within. Encouraging this innate motivation will build competence in the young. There are many opportunities in the early childhood classroom for this confidence-building; let pupils dress and undress themselves, choose foods to eat, pour juice, select toys to play with or art materials to use, choose books to read or to listen to, make friends, and take risks. (How many blocks can I add without the tower falling?)

Your most valuable contribution to your students' development may be the recognition that separation reactions are valid and to be expected. Your knowledge and understanding of this will help children in your care develop a strong sense of themselves as individuals who can feel sad, angry, or grieving. They will be able to develop the ability to cope with those feelings without being overwhelmed.

The steps children take in school to achieve self-confidence will help them practice the skills they will use in many different separation experiences all through their lives.

Achievement fills a child with pride and self-gratification. It is fed by the comfort and trust generated in a secure classroom environment. Separation is the "developmental necessity" underlying all children's discovery of themselves as builders.

Resources

Amos & Boris by William Steig. Farrar, Straus & Giroux, 1971.

Are You My Mother? by Philip Eastman. Random House, 1960.

Betsy's First Day at Nursery School by Gunilla Wolde. Random House, 1976.

Don't Forget to Come Back by Robie Harris. Knopf, 1978.

Frog, Where Are You? by Mercer Mayer. Dial, 1969.

I Don't Want to Go to School by Elizabeth Bram. Greenwillow, 1977.

I'm Busy, Too by Norma Simon. Albert Whitman, 1980.

Maybe Tomorrow I'll Have a Good Time by Mary Soderstrom. Human Sciences Press, 1981.

Moose, Goose & Little Nobody by Ellen Raskin. Scholastic, 1980.

My Nursery School by Harlow Rockwell. Greenwillow, 1976.

Timothy Goes to School by Rosemary Wells. Dial, 1981.

Will I Have a Friend? by Miriam Cohen. Macmillan, 1967.

Willy Bear by Mildred Kantrowitz. Parents Magazine Press, 1978.

You Go Away by Dorothy Corey. Albert Whitman, 1975.

STRESS
what makes kids vulnerable?

Sally Reed

Sally Reed, a former senior editor for INSTRUCTOR, is a freelance education writer in Chicago.

Overhearing her parents discuss her while she gets ready for school shakes Ronni. After that happens in the morning, she can't seem to handle anything—from a class starting late to one cross word from anyone. Her reactions range from belligerence to pouting.

Jeremy is distracted by *his* stress; his stomach is queasy and his concentration nil. It's hard to say why he's so tied up in knots all the time.

You could understand it if Kevin would show symptoms of stress. He's had to endure many difficult situations this past year, including the death of his grandfather, the birth of a sister, and a move 1,500 miles away brought on by his father's new job. Kevin, however, seems relatively stress-free and could be described as a "capable kid," coping with life's punches.

Just like today's executives, some children today seem to thrive despite stress, others are extremely vulnerable to it. Reactions to stress can include headaches, stomach problems, mood swings, belligerent behavior, and poor attention spans. Teachers have always seen these symptoms in their classes,

but it is not merely in their imaginations that more children today exhibit them.

Until recently teachers haven't had the training nor the resources to address the issue of stress. That's where child psychologist Antoinette Saunders steps in. Drawing upon her experience in the University of Illinois Medical School, Department of Pediatric and Child Psychiatry, Dr. Saunders opened her own Stress Clinic for Children five years ago in Evanston, Illinois, and has recently completed a book with Bonnie Remsberg, called *The Capable Kid: Raising Children to Handle Stress.* Dr. Saunders has taken her program to the schools with an eight-week training session to help elementary students better manage the stress in their lives by using relaxation techniques, improved listening skills, and better problem-solving abilities. Here she talks with former INSTRUCTOR editor Sally Reed about why and how teachers can make children more stress-resistant.

Reed: *What exactly do you mean by stress?*
Saunders: In simple terms, it is that extra demand made on our bodies. Stress may be negative, but it may be positive, too. Having a new baby brother can be positive, for example. But it also causes

stress. No matter the source, we have the same automatic physiological reaction. The body prepares itself for "fight or flight."

What are the major causes of stress for children?
Saunders: For some children stress stems from problems at home: divorce, chronic illnesses, racial differences in a neighborhood. Other children feel a pressure to perform, and this has everything to do with the shocking increase in suicide in some communities.

At the lower elementary level the major cause of stress in children is separating from their families. With older children it is peer pressure. In adolescence it gets more complicated because bodies are changing and sexual identities are beginning.

But are children today really under more stress than ever before?
Saunders: The stress today is different. Children today lack support. Their families are more mobile and spread out. Many families are simply falling apart. Sixty percent of all children will live in a single-parent home before they reach the age of 18. The other 40 percent are concerned that a divorce will affect their families soon. Also, more children today are unattended at home and are pushed to grow up sooner in

order to be less troublesome to their parents.

While some children thrive on this pressure, most kids don't; children today are frightened, threatened, and alienated. They are so needy and emotionally hungry inside that they can't concentrate on their schoolwork or they look for attention any way they can. That's why stress education is so important for schools today.

Is this why you are training children to manage their own stress?
Saunders: Yes, plus we now know that stress plays a role in serious illnesses such as cancer and heart disease. If we believe that attitudes and our ability to solve problems affect our health as adults, then the prevention should start with the children.

There are other benefits to schools. Once students learn to manage their own stress, illness will be reduced, resulting in less absenteeism in school. This is, if nothing else, cost effective. Students will spend more time on task, less time in trouble. They will learn how to calm themselves down. Once they feel like capable kids, they will be more responsible, cooperative, helpful.

What are capable kids?
Saunders: What every kid should be. Capable kids are resourceful, relaxed, responsive, able to express their feelings easily and get excited about good things. They are reflective and thoughtful. They are also spontaneous, active, energetic, happy, opinionated but open to new ideas and sensitive to others. They have a sense of direction.

By contrast then, who are the vulnerable kids?
Saunders: Children who do not handle stress well. They are preoccupied, frequently sick, noncommunicative, uncooperative, isolated. They lie and distort things.

Teachers know them. They overuse the phrase "I don't know," are lonely but unable to seek the resources of others for company, dependent, frightened, worried about animals and storms. They keep their feelings inside, they are defensive and easily angered, stubborn, subject to frequent unexplained aches and pains, unable to concentrate, constantly complaining, and impatient. They are generally negative in attitude.

How can teachers build capable kids?
Saunders: By believing in "wellness" themselves first. That means getting exercise, practicing good nutrition, and taking charge of their lives. Teachers are, after all, models first.

Where do they go from there?
Saunders: Stress education can be taught formally in health, as a separate course, or informally, in the way a teacher deals with problems.

But students should learn to identify stress and learn the different ways of handling it. They can learn to listen and express their feelings. They should reframe or switch negative thoughts to positive ones. And they should realize the importance of exercise, sleep, and nutrition.

What strategies do you use with children at your clinic?
Saunders: Students draw pictures of what stress is and how it affects them. They keep journals about their feel-

The stress scale for children

You may have seen the Holmes and Rahe Stress Scale for adults. The scale below, based on that scale, ranks the life events that cause stress in children.

Life Event	Value
Death of a parent	100
Parent's new relationship (new siblings involved)	90
Divorce of parents	73
Parent's new relationship	70
Separation of parents	65
Parent's jail term	63
Death of a close family member (i.e., grandparent)	63
Personal injury or illness	53
Parent's remarriage	50
Suspension or expulsion from school	47
Parents' reconciliation	45
Summer vacation	45
Parent or sibling illness	44
Mother's pregnancy	40
Anxiety over sex	39
Birth of a new baby (or adoption)	39
New school or new classroom or new teacher	39
Money problems at home	38
Death (or moving away) of a close friend	37
Death of valued pet	37
Change in school work	36
More quarrels with parents (or parents quarreling more)	35
Change in school responsibilities	29
Sibling going away to school	29
Family arguments with grandparents	29
Winning school or community awards	28
Mother going to work or stopping work	26
School beginning or ending	26
Family's living standard changing	25
Change in personal habits—(bedtime, homework)	24
Trouble with parents— lack of communication, hostility	23
Change in school hours, schedule of courses	23
Family's moving	20
A new school—high school	20
New sports, hobbies, family recreation activities	20
Change in church activities—more involvement or less	19
Change in social activities—new friends, loss of old ones, peer pressures, teasing	18
Change in sleeping habits (giving up naps)	16
Change in number of family get-togethers	15
Change in eating habits—going on or off diet, new way of family cooking	15
Vacation, other than summer	13
Christmas	12
Breaking home, school, or community rules	11

Mark the items that happened in the last 12 months and add up the points. If the score exceeds 300 points, the child may be (but not necessarily is) more vulnerable to stress-related problems.

How to calm down tense kids
Robert Ritson

How many times have you made comments like, "When my students return from PE, they can't sit still for one minute," or "It takes the children 20 minutes of my teaching time to settle down after recess"? These and other comments have often been made after a session in the gym or on the field. And they are valid. But the PE teacher is not to blame.

Children need to learn how to relax in order to get rid of excess stress and tension, but they especially need a chance to calm down after a period of physical activity. Everyone fluctuates within a range of calmness to excitement, from the state of being totally relaxed to being overly tense. When muscles are repeatedly contracted, the activation level is raised; an active session of prolonged and repetitive muscular contractions can produce a higher excitement level in students than is necessary for classroom work. They may not even be able to pay attention to what the teacher is saying or wants to do. But if children are given two- or three-minute relaxation lessons after PE or recess, the transition to a sedentary class will be much smoother and less time-consuming.

Each of the following techniques and activities focuses on a single element related to physical activity—muscle tension, heartbeat, and so on. They all will help produce the effects of relaxation. Try to keep your classroom quiet and still while doing them, with dim lights if possible. You will also need to direct each activity yourself to achieve the greatest effect. Some exercises are more appropriate for the gym; see if you can team up with the PE teacher for these. Some are suitable in the classroom after PE, the walk back down the hall, the trip to the restroom, and the proverbial drink of water.

Recognizing tension Have children walk around the room like tin soldiers, concentrating on the feeling of stiffness or tenseness in their joints. Now have them lie on their backs with eyes closed and raise alternate arms and legs at the same time, while keeping this same stiffness in knees and elbows. After students have done this several times, ask them to make their arms and legs feel stiff and tense without lifting

them. Once children have learned to recognize tension and how to acquire it without moving, they will be better able to relax these muscles, also without moving.

Arm pendulum swing This exercise will help relax the upper part of the body. Stand with feet spread apart and knees straight. Raise arms forward to shoulder level, then let them drop and swing easily until they come to rest. Repeat this several times. Now do the same thing, but when arms swing forward, raise them somewhat higher with each swing, until they go straight up and behind the head. Now let the head relax and drop as the arms drop down, then lift the head as the arms go forward and up. Gradually let the upper back and trunk relax with the head and arms until the entire trunk drops down as the arms swing down, and up as the arms are raised.

Checking relaxation Have children choose partners for this exercise. One child lies down, face up. You say, "Relax the arms (or legs, left arm, and so on)." The partner checks the arms by lifting or moving them; if there is no resistance or assistance, they are relaxed. If there is resistance, the partner should say so and continue lifting the arms until the child has succeeded in relaxing them. (Be sure the partner understands not to drop an arm or leg, or jerk or pull roughly.) Continue calling out parts of the body for the partner to check. After being checked, the prone child should relax his or her whole body for 30 seconds and then switch positions with his or her partner.

Blank time After excess tension in the body has been eliminated, tell students they can also reduce "thinking tension." Start with a quick verbal check of body parts, then ask everyone to be silent for two or three minutes and try to keep their minds perfectly blank. Careful—someone may fall asleep!

Palming Here's one students can do sitting or lying down. Tell them to rub hands together until they are warm. Now tell pupils to close both eyes and cover them with the palms of their hands, the fingers crossed over each other on the forehead. Let the eyes enjoy the warmth of the hands. Breathe deeply and slowly. Relax.

Discover your heart Tell students that by lying very still they can feel their heart beat. Give them these directions: Take one hand and move it slowly across your stomach to cover your heart. Feel it beating? Now place your fingertips on your neck under the chin and move them slowly toward your ear until your fingers feel the beating. This is the pulse. Each of us has a different rhythm. Watch the second hand on the clock, and count the number of beats you feel in three minutes. Compare this number with your neighbor's.

Recording recovery When students come back from PE or recess, have them count the number of beats in their pulse for a 15-second interval. Then let them spend two minutes of blank time or three minutes in a progressive relaxation lesson. Now have them check the pulse rate again. Is there a difference? Discuss with children what caused this difference. If you do this for a week, you can make a math lesson out of the exercise by having students graph their entry and recovery pulse rates for the five days.

Differential relaxation Have children do the following different exercises, focusing on what isn't moving instead of what is.

1. Jump up and down gently and relax the upper body.
2. Run around the room or in place and let the arms relax.
3. Relax the lower limbs and pull your body to the other side of the room, lying down or sitting.
4. Relax the torso while sitting on the floor, and catch yourself before you tilt too far.
5. Try to get a friend pretending to be a rag doll to stand up. It's hard. One person relaxes sitting down, and two people try to stand him or her up. Careful! Don't drop. Now have 10 students try to stand their teacher up. This activity really demonstrates what muscles and bones do . . . and don't do!

Relaxation activities take only a short period of time, but you will see their results very quickly—a classful of calm, alert students. □

Robert Ritson is assistant professor at the College of Human Development and Performance of the University of Oregon, Eugene.

"Children always worry about whether their teacher likes them."

ings. We do psychodramas or role play about problems at home and school with parents, friends, or their brothers and sisters. We make a game out of turning negative statements into positive ones. If something disturbing happens, we talk about it, study the options, and learn to be reflective. Once students get used to thinking this way, it becomes second nature.

How can we train children to relax?
Saunders: Use the simple "Quick Relax" or "Breathing Feet" technique. It takes six minutes. There are four steps.

1. Be aware that you are upset. Everyone gets upset, nervous, and scared sometimes. When that happens, we don't do as well in whatever we are trying to do. Recognize when this is happening.

2. Smile inwardly and tell yourself "I can calm myself down." We can learn to be more in control of our lives, and calming down is one way to do so.

3. Breathe slowly and easily through imaginary holes in your feet. (Imagine cool air flowing up your feet through your legs to your stomach. Now, hold it there for a second. Let that stressful air out of your legs through the holes in your feet.)

4. As you imagine that cool air coming in and that stressful air going out, imagine you are going to a place where you are fully relaxed and happy (lying in the sun or curled up on your bed with a blanket). Once students have mastered this techique, they can use it whenever they feel upset.

How can teachers improve communication skills?
Saunders: Try "The Caring Formula." Begin the exercise by stating out loud the first three steps of the formula below. Ask your listener to repeat exactly what you said, then state the first three steps of the formula again. Continue stating and repeating the formula until the listener can recite it perfectly. Now reverse roles. Then exchange hugs and kisses and say, "I love you."

1. Say something you like about the other person.

2. Tell the other person something you did that day that made you feel especially good about yourself.

3. Tell the other person about something you are planning to do tomorrow that you are really looking forward to.

4. Say "I love you" with hugs.

What else can adults do for children?
Saunders: Validate children. We validate children by giving them a feeling that they are doing their best and they are acceptable and lovable.

One of the things I hear over and over from children is not whether or not they like a teacher but whether the teacher likes them. Teachers need to make children feel they care, that they are taken seriously. Every child is potentially likable and lovable, but a lot of children are good at setting themselves up. They don't put their best foot forward because they expect to be rejected. They need to be validated by an adult.

One technique you can use to suggest you are on the side of an especially vulnerable child is to "Close the Door and Open Your Heart."

At the beginning of the day or end, or during a break, close the classroom door and put a "Please Do Not Disturb" sign on it. Get rid of all distractions. Clear all other children out of the way. Don't accept interruptions.

The child needs to know he or she has your undivided attention. Often, teachers pretend to be listening while looking at tomorrow's lesson plans. Children, however, usually know the difference.

Then talk to the child in a nonjudgmental atmosphere. See if you can get the child to open up. This can be done in 10 minutes. Compare that to the time spent disciplining a difficult child.

Think about the time in your life when you genuinely opened up to another person. You had that person's undivided attention. The other person listened. Students are no different. They respond to situations the same way adults do.

For more information, contact Dr. Antoinette Saunders, Stress Education for Children, Dept. IN, 1603 Orrington Ave., Evanston, IL 60201.

Children with Special Needs

The fields of Early Childhood Education and Special Education have certain theoretical and practical similarities and have included collaborative efforts over the years. Programs for children under six years of age have selectively accepted special children. Such placements were seen as providing "normalizing" opportunities for the special children and sensitizing opportunities for the staff and other children.

Since 1972, federal guidelines have stipulated that ten percent of Head Start participants must be children with handicaps. The Education for All Handicapped Children Act of 1975 (PL 94-142) mandated that a "free and appropriate public education will be available for all handicapped children between the ages of three and eighteen. . . ." This act and subsequent legislation on state levels produced major modifications in existing early childhood programs. Recently, however, some state agencies have reduced funding for programs and services for children with special needs, changing from mandatory (required) programs to permissive (may or may not provide) policies. When an accurate assessment of need is determined, the intervention phase begins. This involves the development of an individualized education program (IEP) that is to be harmonious with each child's needs and as free of stigma as possible.

Many early childhood teachers have had little or no special training and only spotty experiences in dealing with the range and diversity of children with special needs or with community agencies serving the children's families. Yet, they are being asked to assist in various aspects of the intervention program. Those teachers who have been prepared or have received special assistance during their IEP work generally express greater satisfaction than do teachers who have been expected to acquire the necessary attitudes, information, and skills entirely on their own.

Young gifted children pose a special problem for early childhood educators for several reasons. They are not covered under PL 94-142, despite the fact that they are indeed "special." Many of the estimated two and a half million gifted American children go unrecognized, especially when they are under six years of age, due to the difficulties of identification. While general enrichment through teacher modification of the existing program, academic acceleration, or tutorial help may be used with older gifted children, those children in Head Start and other preschool programs will benefit from individualization, discovery learning, and encouragement. Teachers who value initiative and inquiry, understand child development, possess flexibility, and avoid detailed structuring of assignments that inhibit creativity will greatly assist the young gifted child's progress.

Play is an area that has been infrequently used by special educators. Most programs serving handicapped children have focused exclusively on a teacher-centered, skill and drill, objectives and evaluation approach. More recently, researchers have demonstrated that children who have certain handicaps or are severely impaired may be trained in learning how to play, thus producing special "normalizing" and unique therapeutic benefits.

Teachers may also have other special children in their classrooms—those with medical problems. These may include allergies, diabetes, epilepsy, hyperactivity, or otitis media (chronic ear infections). Knowing how to recognize the symptoms of each of these physical disorders, when medication is necessary, and how to deal with a medical emergency is a part of teaching these children who generally do not receive any special programming from specialists.

Despite the differing traits, disabilities, or talents special children may display, it is helpful to keep in mind that early childhood educators have historically viewed all young children under their care, first and foremost, as children, and as special children, second. The label of "special" can be put into perspective if it is viewed as a designation for a type of educational program a child may benefit from but not as a label for the child's personality. Further, all children can be helped if varied methods and modalities are provided by skilled, flexible, tolerant educators.

This section examines intervention in Special Education, with particular emphasis on gifted children, using play with handicapped children, and helping the child with special medical problems.

Looking Ahead: Challenge Questions

How can objective parent reports and teacher observations be effectively used to identify the gifted child under six years of age? What are the problems associated with the use of intelligence tests to determine giftedness in the preschooler? How can early childhood curriculum be designed to meet the very special needs of the young gifted child with special developmental needs?

What are the special contributions of play to handicapped children's social and emotional development? When is special play intervention necessary for this population of children? What special benefits can be derived from play activity with peers for handicapped children?

How can classroom teachers accurately recognize and deal with the medically special child? How can children who suffer from allergies, diabetes, hyperactivity, epilepsy, or recurring ear infections be helped by knowledgeable teachers?

Meeting the Needs

of Gifted Preschoolers

Three-year-old Chris takes a book from the shelf and begins reading aloud. Four-year-old Michelle has been working several days building an intricate block-machine she says can be used to make "spaghetti ice cream." Daniel is playing a tune on the piano as he sings along. Susie has organized other children on the block to construct a "time machine."

Ann E. Lupkowski and Elizabeth A. Lupkowski

Ann E. Lupkowski is a doctoral student in educational psychology at Texas A & M University, College Station. Elizabeth A. Lupkowski is a teacher with the Bradford/Tioga Head Start Program, Mansfield, Pa.

Children like these may be part of the three to five percent of the population that can be classified as "gifted" or "talented." It is likely that Head Start and other preschool teachers will have at least one of these gifted children in their classrooms during their careers. In order to adequately meet their needs, it is necessary for teachers to be aware of characteristics of gifted children and to develop strategies for meeting their needs.

Generally, a child is characterized as "gifted" if he or she shows above-average ability or potential in one or more of the following areas: 1) general intellectual ability, 2) specific academic aptitude, 3) leadership ability, 4) creative or productive thinking, 5) visual and performing arts, or 6) psychomotor ability.

Identification

Gifted children, who come from all socioeconomic backgrounds, can be identified by using traditional intelligence tests and parent reports or through observation of behaviors exhibited in the classroom and at home.

Gifted children can be identified at a young age. The Seattle Project at the University of Washington, which was one of the few programs in the country established to serve gifted young children (and is no longer in operation), identified young children through age five who demonstrated intellectual superiority.[1] Project researchers identified young children who were able to perform extraordinary intellectual feats but did not necessarily score at the highest ranges on general intelligence tests. Children were selected on the basis of intelligence, spatial reasoning, reading and mathematics skills and memory.

Gifted young children may show "peaks" of extraordinarily high performance in some areas—but not necessarily in all cognitive ability areas—when they are tested using standardized intelligence tests.[2] A child may not do well on parts of an intelligence test because of a short attention span, discomfort with unfamiliar people or strange surroundings, or because the child plays games with the test materials. Because many intelligence tests require verbal responses to items, children who have difficulty expressing themselves verbally may not score as high as they could on a non-verbal test.

Standardized intelligence tests have been fairly unsuccessful in the identification of young gifted children since IQ tests are only partially reliable before the child reaches the age of five or six.[3] Data from the Seattle Project suggest that scores in the areas of best performance may be the best indicators of a child's capabilities. Those concerned should look at what the child can do instead of what he or she cannot do. A profile of the child—composed of a variety of test scores and teacher and parent reports—could be compiled. Those involved with identification of gifted children could then examine the profiles and focus on the areas of highest performance as possible indicators of giftedness.

Since even the most complete battery of tests may not provide a good estimate of children's abilities, it is necessary to include parent reports detailing children's capabilities.

Parent Reports

Parents can be used as an immediate

From *Children Today*, March/April 1985, pp. 10-14. Reprinted by permission of the authors and Children Today.

screening device in the identification of preschool gifted children. Parents do know their own children: There is evidence from previous research that parents are reasonably accurate when it comes to estimating their own child's intellectual abilities.[4] Questionnaire and interview formats can be used to elicit information. Information from parents is especially useful if they provide examples of the children's behavior rather than simply estimating their ability level. Trained judges can then rate the parents' information to assess the extent of the child's intellectural precocity.

Parents may tend to over-estimate their children's abilities. However, the Seattle Project collected several years of evidence demonstrating that parental ratings compare positively with a child's later test performance. Researchers found several children who earned average test scores at age two but had extraordinary test scores two years later. Parent reports obtained when these children were two years old did predict their later extraordinary performance.

Observations

If they participate in the screening process, parents and preschool teachers must be aware of the characteristics of young gifted children. It is important to remember that the gifted child may show peaks of high performance in some areas, but not necessarily in all cognitive areas. However, isolated incidents cannot confirm a child's giftedness; it is necessary to look for trends and patterns in the child's development. Following are some of the behaviors, which we and others have observed, that may be displayed by young gifted children.

● **Long attention span.** The attention span of gifted children is often longer than that of their peers. For example, when asked to count the elephants on a book cover, 3-year-old Chris persisted until she had counted all 103 elephants. Michelle, also 3, would continue "projects" from one day to the next. Some young gifted children are able to work on projects for blocks of time as long as 45 minutes to 2½ hours.

● **Creativity and imagination.** Gifted children may have unique and innovative ideas for the use of common materials or unique names for possessions. Young Joey for instance, named his toy car "Tweety Stem." These children may also design unusual dramatic play situations, such as astronauts landing on the moon, and they often have imaginary friends or companions.

● **Social relationships.** All children have varied social skills, and gifted children are no exception. They may be leaders of other children, with advanced social skills for their age, or they may prefer to be alone to work on their own interests. For example, other children seemed to recognize that Judy had good ideas and were enthusiastic in following her lead. Some gifted children may find innovative ways to settle disputes. Also, young gifted children may prefer to interact with older children and adults rather than with their same-age peers.

● **Number concepts.** Some gifted children seem to be fascinated with numbers before they begin formal schooling. Peter could tell time at a young age and often calculated the minutes left until a specific time (such as snack time). He also showed the ability to use numbers in adding, subtracting, multiplying and dividing before he entered kindergarten.

● **Verbal skills.** Gifted preschoolers may recognize letters early and show an early interest in printed matter. They may be interested in foreign languages and also exhibit correct pronunciation and sentence structure in their native language. Young gifted children may show an advanced vocabulary and may begin reading before they start school, although the significance of early reading as an indicator of giftedness has not been established.[5]

● **Memory.** Gifted children may show exceptional memories—2-year-old Bobby would sit at the window for long periods of time and recite the makes of cars as they drove past.

● **Specific interests.** The young gifted child may show an in-depth interest in one or more areas and spend a great deal of time developing a collection of a class of objects, such as rocks or plastic animals.

● **Attention to detail.** Gifted children often notice "insignificant" details in pictures and situations. They also enjoy making things more complex—elaborating on rules for games, for example.

● **High energy level.** Some gifted children have been called hyperactive because of the high level of energy they show. These children also seem to need little sleep.

● **Reasoning ability.** The ability to form analogies at a young age and to justify those responses may be another indicator of giftedness. In one study, 4- and 5-year-olds were given colored blocks—a yellow triangle, a red triangle and a yellow circle—and asked to choose the fourth block (a red circle) to complete the analogy.[6] The children were also asked to justify their responses. Perhaps the ability to successfully complete and justify this type of task is an indicator of advanced cognitive development.

● **Insight ability.** Exceptional insight ability has been postulated as another characteristic of the intellectually gifted.[7] They may be superior in insight ability because of the ability to sift out relevant information, blend those pieces of information and add new information to appropriate information acquired in the past. These children have the ability to find solutions to complex problems.

Programs

Early identification of preschool gifted children creates the opportunity for early intervention. Gifted programs with an early childhood focus should challenge the children's strengths and counteract weak areas.

Individualization should be the rule for preschool curricula for the gifted. While this does not have to mean a constant one-to-one ratio for teacher and student, the curriculum content is closely linked to the quality of the relationship between the child and adult.

An ideal preschool gifted program would help children develop independence in learning to prepare them for the expectations teachers will have for them as they grow older. Its format would combine the informal style of kindergarten with advanced content matched to the child's advanced intellectual and academic skills. Appropriate acceleration in subject matter would be made without expecting equally accelerated skills in other areas. The program should emphasize discovery learning, open-endedness, group process and interaction, and encourage independence and self-direction.

"Systematic nurturance" is a technique that was used in the Seattle Project to match learning experiences with children's competence levels in each subject area and allow the children to progress at their own rate. Since preschool children—including those who are gifted—have a shorter attention span than older children, advanced materials can be adapted to shorter time periods of presentation. The development of large and small motor skills and social skills are also emphasized.

Preschool classrooms often use the unit approach, studying a topic such as animals or the seasons for a week or more. This practice is easily adapted to education for the gifted preschooler because the amount of instruction planned at each level depends on individual needs and interests. Programs for gifted children should be developed for the child's actual level, not just by age level.

The Ideal Teacher

An important person in a young child's life is the preschool teacher. Ideally, teachers of young gifted children should accept all children and appreciate each child's uniqueness. They should demonstrate flexibility and a willingness to change lesson plans to accommodate special interests and abilities. The ideal teacher values initiative and inquiry on the part of the children and avoids initial detailed structuring of assignments to encourage creativity. We recommend that teachers also have a background in child development and the ability to recognize when a child performs above or below norms.

Teachers must create a comfortable learning environment for all children in the classroom. They should answer children's questions and give them individual attention but also allow them time alone. Teachers should communi-

cate the understanding that it is OK to be different. They should also hold frequent parent conferences to tell parents what the child is doing in school and to learn about what is happening at home.

An important thing to remember when dealing with gifted children is that they are first of all children, with the same social, physical and emotional needs as all children. Thus, curricula should be designed to meet the needs of the whole child.

Curriculum

Not only should basic skills development be included in the educational plan for gifted children, but as much enrichment as possible should be provided by the teacher. In class, teachers can respond to gifted preschoolers (and other children) by structuring, modeling and using positive reinforcement to sustain prosocial behaviors already present. Discussion, creative movement, field trips, role play, collections, drawings, music and stories can all be used effectively by teachers.

Such resource people as a father who speaks French or a mother who demonstrates the uses of a calculator may visit the classroom. A piano with color-coded keys and color-coded music may be provided for children who show an interest in music. Children also enjoy dramatic play and science experiments.

In addition to field trips to usual places such as the fire station, the children might visit art museums and interesting buildings to study architecture. After the trips, children may want to make "experience charts."

The unit approach, which can be used with all children, is especially appropriate for use with gifted preschoolers. These children, however may want to go into more detail than the rest of the class. In a unit on transportation, for example, the gifted children may be interested in hydroplanes and balloons as forms of transportation, and the teacher could have them look through magazines for pictures and words about different types of transportation. A unit on likenesses and differences in people could be expanded to include people in different geographic areas as well as those of different races.

Conclusions

While traditional standardized intelligence tests may be useful in identifying gifted children, these tests have been fairly unsuccessful in the identification of *young* gifted children. The option of using parent and teacher observations of the children is a more dependable and effective means of identification. Characteristics associated with the "ideal" teacher of young gifted children—such as flexibility and acceptance—play a crucial role in the development of the gifted child. Finally, programs for young gifted children should emphasize individualization and foster independence in learning.

Resources

National Association for Gifted Children (NAGC)
5100 N. Edgewood Dr.
St. Paul, Minn. 55112

The Association for the Gifted (TAG)
Council for Exceptional Children
1920 Association Dr.
Reston, Va. 22091

World Council for Gifted and Talented Children
HMS 414
University of South Florida
Tampa, Fla. 33620

[1] H.B. Robinson, W.C. Roedell, and N.E. Jackson, "Early Identification and Intervention," in W.B. Barbe and J.S. Renzulli (Eds.), *The Psychology and Education of the Gifted*, (3rd. ed.), New York, Irvington Publishers, Inc., 1981.

[2] W.C. Roedell, *The Development of Giftedness in Young Children*, paper presented at the 1982 Annual Meeting of the American Educational Research Association, New York.

[3] A. Roeper, "The Young Gifted Child," *Gifted Child Quarterly*, 21, 1977.

[4] T.E. Ciha, R. Harris, C. Hoffman and M. Potter, "Parents As Identifiers of Giftedness, Ignored But Accurate," *Gifted Child Quarterly*, 18, 1974.

[5] S.C. Perino and J. Perino, *Parenting the Gifted*, New York, R.R. Bowker Co., 1981 and Robinson, Roedell and Jackson, op. cit.

[6] C.S. White, P.A. Alexander and J.D. Fuqua. "Reasoning Ability in Young Children," in M.T. Riley, J. Tucker and R. Swearengen (Eds.), *Research in Action III: Conference Proceedings* (in press).

[7] J.E. Davidson and R.J. Sternberg, "The Role of Insight in Intellectual Giftedness," *Roeper Review*, 28, 1984.

How Important Is Play for Handicapped Children?

Whether or not spontaneous free play is appropriate for handicapped pre-schoolers is the issue of this review. The research would seem to favor the view of developmentalists; namely, that play enhances learning for all children. The author points out that because differing handicapping conditions influence the quality of play for those children, specific play training interventions may be needed.—**John R. Cryan**

Anne Widerstrom, Assistant Professor, Early Childhood/Special Education, School of Education, University of Colorado at Denver

Play has traditionally been considered an important part of the preschool curriculum. In the contemporary nursery school, for example, a large part of each day's schedule is given over to play activities. This is because the benefits of play for optimal child development are well established by research, and so teachers can allow children to engage in spontaneous play, knowing that to do so is in the children's best interest. Preschool teachers also know that they don't have to teach children to play, since play is something most children do spontaneously. Moreover, the learnings to be gained from play activities seem to be somewhat indirect and therefore not very "teachable."

But the situation for young handicapped children is somewhat different. As programs for handicapped children have become more numerous at the preschool level due to the increasingly widespread philosophy of early intervention, emphasis has come to be placed on the direct teaching of skills to the young child. Teachers are perhaps less willing to trust in the seemingly haphazard benefits of play to promote learning.

The purpose of many early intervention programs is to help the at-risk or handicapped child to "catch up" with his/her peers; direct instruction has seemed a faster, surer method of ensuring progress. In addition, early intervention programs have generally been funded through federal grants and many are experimental in nature, so there is a strong emphasis placed on testable results. Teaching of specific skills, therefore, has been and continues to be the major focus of most preschool programs for the handicapped. The emphasis on play that is at the core of the traditional nursery school has been rejected as too non-directive and too haphazard an approach.

As a result of this directive teaching trend, the benefits of spontaneous play as a means for cognitive, social, language and motor development have been temporarily lost to many preschool programs or at least underemphasized. There is nevertheless a strong case to be made for the inclusion of play in the curriculum of the handicapped child, for there is compelling evidence that play is necessary for every child's optimal development.

Here we will examine some issues related to play and learning in general, with special emphasis on the implications of research. Then we will relate these issues to what we know about the play of handicapped children. Finally, we will discuss whether handicapped children can be helped to optimal development through play.

Let us begin with a definition of play. Sylva (1977, p. 62), drawing on several other writers, defines it as active, persistent manipulative or locomotor experimentation with objects, with the environment, with one's own body and/or with other organisms. It is self-initiated and apparently lacks immediate survival purpose. Bower (1974) adds that it is enjoyable, serious and voluntary. According to Tizard and Harvey (1977), it is orderly and not goal-oriented. The lack of a goal in play distinguishes it from problem-solving (Sylva, 1977).

In summary, we may say that play is an enjoyable activity in which children engage voluntarily for the fun of it, that they have no particular goal in mind but nevertheless pursue the activity in an orderly fashion because they are quite serious about it. And there seem to be serious consequences of a child's play experiences, as we shall see in the following section.

Play and Learning

In studies of other animals, play has been found to be biologically useful (Lorenz, 1972). Many animals have an inborn curiosity that encourages them to explore their environment. Through play they learn about new objects, a greater variety of events, and become more adaptable to new situations. As a result, they are at home in a variety of environments and therefore better survivors.

From their research on rhesus monkeys, Suomi and Harlow (1975) have concluded that play among monkey infants serves two important purposes. First, play with peers gives young monkeys a chance to practice adult behaviors. Second, it provides them a safe outlet for the aggression all rhesus monkeys begin displaying when they are about 7 months old. Young monkeys deprived of play opportunities grow into helpless adults, according to Suomi and Harlow, suffering both cognitive and social negative effects.

Through play animals learn flexibility, too (Sylva, 1977). The playing animal uses behaviors from survival patterns such as feeding or fleeing and combines them into novel approaches. This combinatory aspect is considered by some researchers to be the very essence of play; it trains the animals to string together bits of previously acquired behavior to form novel solutions to problems. In this sense it represents important training for problem-solving.

In a similar fashion, play emerges in children as a result of curiosity about their environment. Because it is self-initiated and because it is relatively tension-free (one can't "fail" in play because there really isn't any goal), it is an excellent means for a child to practice problem-solving.

Studies on children's play and its effect on learning have demonstrated that there is indeed a close relationship. A classic study by Smilansky (1968) found deficits in dramatic play to be associated with cognitive deficiencies in disadvantaged preschoolers. Smilansky developed definitions of cognitive play for her study, which she arranged in a hierarchy of increasing complexity. Her four categories follow:

1. *Functional play* involves simple, repetitive muscle movements with or without objects.
2. *Constructive play* is goal-directed and consists of educational activities like building with blocks or tinker toys and working with puzzles. Objects are necessary.
3. *Dramatic play* involves make-believe activities, role-playing and symbolic play. Dressing up, dramatizing stories, playing house are examples.
4. *Games* are formal, usually highly organized and rule-bound. They vary from simple circle games or chase games to more complex team games.

Since Smilansky developed these categories in 1968, other researchers have used them to analyze children's play. Rubin, Maioni and Hornung (1976), for example, found that non-handicapped middle-class children displayed more constructive and dramatic play whereas lower-class children displayed more functional play.

In an experiment with 3-, 4- and 5-year-old nonhandicapped children involving a problem-solving task, Sylva (1977) found that children who played with test materials solved the problem as well as those who observed an adult solve the problem and then attempted it themselves. The "play" group progressed from simple to complex means in completing the task, showing they learned as they progressed. By contrast, the "observer" group immediately used the most complex means, demonstrated by the adult, to solve the problem. They didn't try to work it out gradually and so less learning took place. In another study, Feitelson and Ross (1973) reported increases in originality and exploration as measured by a test of creativity for 5-year-olds who were trained in symbolic play.

Another study of the relationship between play and problem-solving involved groups of disadvantaged children who were taught to expand their play into more symbolic activities through adult modeling (Rosen 1974). These children showed significant improvement in post-test problem-solving behavior. In a similar experiment, Dansky (1980) examined three groups of low SES children on their performance of cognitive tasks following experiences in (1) sociodramatic play, (2) exploration and (3) free play. The first two groups received training; the third acted as controls. Only those trained in sociodramatic (symbolic) play demonstrated improvement in cognitive performance. Finally, Saltz, Dixon and Johnson (1977) found that fantasy play (e.g., acting out fairy tales) increased the cognitive performance of disadvantaged preschoolers whereas activities such as cutting, pasting or listening to stories had no such measurable effect.

Studies conducted with young handicapped children have yielded similar results. Newcomer and Morrison (1974) used play therapy with institutionalized mentally retarded children and found increases in their scores on the Denver Developmental Screening Test. Both group and individual play therapy seemed to promote cognitive and social development. Fraiberg and Adelson (1973) found that play helps the blind child in developing the capacity for symbolic representation evidenced, for example, in use of pronouns "me" and "I."

In summary, it would appear that there is indeed a strong link between the type of play variously described as symbolic, sociodramatic or fantasy and the development of cognitive abilities.

Play and Social Development

In addition to promoting a child's cognitive development, play has important implications for social development. While early forms of play are solitary or centered on the infant's interactions with his/her mother (Widerstrom, 1982; Bruner, 1972; Trevarthen, 1976), much of a child's later play depends on interactions with other children. Earlier solitary play behaviors are important to social development because they help the child to differentiate self from other. It is only as the child's cognitive development becomes less egocentric that the child can begin to play cooperatively with others. Cooperative play relies upon a child's ability to take the perspective of the playmate and thus sets the stage for the development of prosocial behaviors like sharing, helping and cooperation.

Researchers have identified several types of play based on interactions with people. The best known and most widely used category system for social play is probably that of Parten (1932). By observing normal nursery school children during free play, she identified six categories of play that children typically engage in. These are presented below as Parten (1932) defined them, but in summarized form.

1. *Unoccupied behavior:* Child engages in random behavior such as watching something of momentary interest, following the

teacher or engaging in play limited to child's own body.

2. *Onlooker:* Child spends most of the time watching others play; often talks to the children, making suggestions or asking questions, but doesn't enter into their play.

3. *Solitary independent play:* Child plays alone and independently with toys different from those used by children within speaking distance and makes no effort to get close to other children.

4. *Parallel activity:* Child plays independently but the activity chosen naturally brings child among other children. Child is *beside* rather than *with* other children; uses toys similar to those of children nearby, however.

5. *Associative play:* Child plays with other children in a common activity, forming a group that excludes other children. Each child acts as he/she wishes; there is no subordination to the needs of the group. All children engage in similar if not identical activity; there is no division of labor.

6. *Cooperative or organized play:* Child plays in a group organized for some play purpose (product, drama, competition or game). Labor is divided, with children taking different roles. One or two children dominate, become leaders, exclude some other children from the group.

Parten found that all the children she observed, who ranged in age from 2 to 5 years, participated in all the types of play described except *onlooker behavior,* which was observed only in children younger than 3 years, and *cooperative play,* which was not seen in the youngest children. She noted that onlookers were most common at 2½ to 3½ years of age, solitary play at 2½ years, parallel play at 2 years. Associative play was observed mostly among the 4- and 5-year-olds, and cooperative play was most common among older children who had the highest IQ levels. There was also a positive correlation found between group play and IQ level in 3-year-olds; that is, only the 3-year-olds with higher IQ level engaged in group play. By 4 years of age all the children were observed in associative or cooperative play. Parten speculated that language development facilitated group play.

Concerning solitary play, which Parten considered to be a lower or younger form of play, it should be noted that her purpose was to measure social (group) participation. This would automatically relegate solitary play to a less-favored position. Nevertheless,

that is not necessarily so. Rubin et al. (1976) suggest in their study of middle and lower SES preschoolers that parallel, and not solitary play, is indicative of the least mature level of a social play hierarchy for 3- and 4-year-olds. Children who play by themselves may simply wish to "get away from it all," they suggest, and their activities—such as painting, clay-modeling or writing a story—may be at a very high level indeed. On the other hand, children who exhibit parallel play (playing beside other children rather than with them) may actually desire the company of the other children but may not be able to successfully take their points of view in order to play in a cooperative manner. Capobianco and Cole (1960), in their study of the play of educable and trainable mentally retarded children based on Parten's categories, felt that those children assigned to Parten's *solitary* category had their play ability underestimated.

The Play of Handicapped Children

How does the play of handicapped children differ from that of nonhandicapped children? Or does it? Do handicapped children play in a manner expected for their mental age? Or are their play habits qualitatively different from those of other children? The answers to these questions are important in helping us to understand the educational needs of handicapped children. In addition, we need to know whether handicapped children play spontaneously or whether they need to be taught to do so. Can or should they be taught to play at higher levels than they play spontaneously?

Fortunately, a great deal of research has been done to attempt to answer these questions. Although the results are mixed, there are some definite trends. Let us examine the evidence.

As Rogers (1982) and Li (1981) have pointed out, many studies of handicapped children's play involve institutionalized children. This makes it difficult to separate the effects of institutional life from the effects of the handicapping condition on the children's play abilities. Another confounding variable is socioeconomic status, and a third is the subject's

degree of emotional adjustment. These three variables sometimes affect the child's play more than the handicapping condition. Taking these variables into consideration, we find few differences between handicapped children's play and the play of nonhandicapped children.

For example, Tizard (1964) found that mentally retarded children play at a level commensurate with mental age, and that they engage in spontaneous free play. Hulme and Lunzer (1966) found in a study involving relatively well-adjusted, non-institutionalized mentally retarded children that their play behavior was not easily distinguishable from that of normal children of comparable mental age. In a similar study, Weiner and Weiner (1974) analyzed the toy-play behavior of mentally retarded noninstitutionalized children and compared it to that of normal children. They found that certain types of play seemed to be primarily related to chronological age, certain types to be associated with mental age, and a few play behaviors to be found exclusively in normal children. Throwing and pounding of toys, for example, were observed only in a group of 3-year-old normal children but not in 6-year-old mentally retarded children whose mental age was 3 years. Using push-pull toys, manipulating toy parts, and oral exploration of toys, on the other hand, seemed associated with mental age; both normal 3-year-olds and mentally retarded 6-year-olds (MA of 3 years) demonstrated these. And only the normal 3-year-olds were observed to combine toys into more complex forms. The mentally retarded children, even though of similar mental age, didn't demonstrate combinatory abilities.

All the studies reported below involving institutionalized children suffer from the problem described above. Nevertheless, they provide evidence that young handicapped children can be taught to play in more symbolic and/or cooperative ways. Strain's (1975) study is an example. In this project severely retarded 4-year-olds were involved in sociodramatic activities such as listening to a story and taking roles of the story's characters;

their subsequent free play was found to be more social and less solitary than previously. Similarly, Knapczyk and Yoppi (1975) successfully trained young mentally retarded children with behavior and communication disorders, using behavior modification techniques, to play more cooperatively.

In a study of the symbolic play of severely retarded and autistic children, Wing, Gould, Yeates and Brierley (1977) found that both the type of handicap and the environmental setting (home, school, residential care) affected the child's level of play. Autistic children were not observed to engage in symbolic play, even when their mental ages were greater than 2 years, the time when normal children emerge from the sensorimotor period and begin to engage in symbolic activities. Wing et al. (1977) further noted that children without any symbolic play were more likely to be in residential care than living at home. Many of these institutionalized children had mental ages above 2 years but still did not play symbolically. On the other hand, children with Down's syndrome tended to play symbolically most often.

Not all studies of young handicapped children have been limited to the mentally retarded. Mogford (1977) examined the play of children with other handicapping conditions. She reports that deaf children engage in imaginative play and play involving representation as much as hearing children. Deaf children, even though they experienced serious expressive and receptive language deficits, were observed by Gregory (1976, reported in Mogford 1977) to have imaginary playmates. The play of these children was less social and more solitary in nature. Aphasic children engaged in make-believe play and produced symbolic drawings, according to Mogford, whereas autistic children did not.

Mogford also reported that children with cerebral palsy do not play as spontaneously as nonhandicapped children and need both encouragement and some assistance with toys. This is true of blind children as well (Fraiberg and Adelson, 1973).

The research appears to state, in summary, that some handicapped children are very much like other children in the quality and spontaneity of their play. These children should not be denied the pleasures of spontaneous play which preschool programs for the handicapped usually offer. Others who are more severely impaired need encouragement, assistance or training. Sheridan (1975) expresses the consensus of several authors (Li, 1981; Wehman, 1977; Mogford, 1977) when she states that some handicapped children are slow learners, sometimes lacking in drive and powers of concentration. Having once achieved a basic skill, they may not elaborate on it but become stuck at an elementary level. To progress they need "prolonged patient individual step-by-step instruction and must be stimulated to constant practice" (p. 118).

Some models of preschool education rely heavily on the child's basic ability to play and natural curiosity to explore the environment. Such programs may not be optimal for handicapped children who need encouragement or training in play. Evidently children who are deaf, blind or aphasic can engage in symbolic play but do not always do so spontaneously. This is true of Down's children and children with cerebral palsy, too. It is necessary to arrange the learning environments of these children to maximize their opportunities to interact with adults and other children. Such children may also benefit from directed play experiences (Lerner, Mardell-Czudnowski and Goldenberg, 1981) which encourage them to play at higher levels (i.e., cooperative play, dramatic play, constructive play).

It is through play that children try out new roles, experiment with their environment, and test their limits in physical and mental activity. Play also provides a safe forum in which a child may experiment with aggression and sexual arousal as a means of learning how to handle these feelings, without fear of adult antagonism. Hartup (1978) points out that play is a uniquely child-child activity and that peer interaction is therefore a better means of eliciting play behavior than adult-child interaction. In play activity with peers children encounter an equalitarian environment with fewer constraints than

adult-child relationships typically encompass, and this environment facilitates many kinds of learning: social, cognitive, moral, language and motor. Indeed, inadequate peer relations are prognostic indicators of social and emotional trouble in young children, for loners more often end up as delinquents or develop adjustment difficulties in adulthood. For these reasons play should be an integral part of any program designed to maximize the development of handicapped children.

References

Bower, E.; K. Bersamin, A. Fine and J. Carlson. *Learning To Play, Playing To Learn.* New York: Human Sciences Press, 1974.

Bruner, J. "The Nature and Uses of Immaturity." *American Psychologist* 27 (1972): 687-708.

Capobianco, R.J., and D.A. Cole. "Social Behavior of Mentally Retarded Children." *American Journal of Mental Deficiency* 64(1960): 638-51.

Dansky, J.L. "Cognitive Consequences of Sociodramatic Play and Exploration Training for Economically Disadvantaged Preschoolers." *Journal of Child Psychology and Psychiatry and Allied Disciplines* 21(1980): 47-58.

Feitelson, D., and G.A. Ross. "The Neglected Factor—Play." *Human Development* 16(1973): 202-223.

Fraiberg, S., and E. Adelson. "Self Representation in Language and Play: Observations of Blind Children." *Psychoanalytic Quarterly* 42(1973): 539.

Hartup, W.W. "Peer Interaction and the Process of Socialization." In *Early Intervention and the Integration of Handicapped and Nonhandicapped Children,* edited by M.J. Guralnick. Baltimore: University Park Press, 1978.

Hulme, I., and E.A. Lunzer. "Play, Language and Reasoning in Subnormal Children." *Journal of Child Psychology and Psychiatry* 7(1966): 107.

Knapczyk, D.R., and J.O. Yoppi. "Development of Cooperative and Competitive Play Responses in Developmentally Disabled Children." *American Journal of Mental Deficiency* 80(1975): 245-55.

Lerner, J.; C. Mardell-Czudnowski and D. Goldenberg. *Special Education for the Early Childhood Years.* Englewood Cliffs, NJ: Prentice-Hall, 1981.

Li, A.K.F. "Play and the Mentally Retarded Child." *Mental Retardation* 19(1981): 121-26.

Lorenz, K. "Psychology and Phylogeny." In *Studies in Animal and Human Behavior,* translated by R. Martin. Cambridge: Harvard University Press, 1972.

Mogford, K. "The Play of Handicapped Children." In *Biology of Play,* edited by B. Tizard and D. Harvey. Philadelphia: Lippincott, 1977.

Newcomer, B.L., and T.L. Morrison. "Play Therapy with Institutionalized Mentally Retarded Children." *American Journal of Mental Deficiency* 78(1974): 727-33.

Parten, M.B. "Social Participation Among Preschool Children." *Journal of Abnormal and Social Psychology* 27(1932): 243-69.

Rogers, S. "Developmental Characteristics of Children's Play." In *Psychological Assessment of Handicapped Infants and Young Children,* edited by G. Ulrey and S. Rogers. New York: Thieme-Stratton, 1982.

Rosen, C.E. "The Effects of Sociodramatic Play on Problem-Solving Behaviors Among Culturally Disadvantaged Preschool Children." *Child Development* 45(1974): 920-27.

Rubin, K.H.; T.L. Maioni and M. Hornung. "Free Play Behavior in Middle- and Lower-Class Preschoolers: Parten and Piaget Revisited." *Child Development* 47(1976): 414-19.

Saltz, E.; D. Dixon and J. Johnson. "Training Disadvantaged Preschoolers on Various Fantasy Activities: Effects on Cognitive Functioning and Impulse Control." *Child Development* 48(1977): 367-80.

Sheridan, M. "The Importance of Spontaneous Play in the Fundamental Learning of Handicapped Children." *Child Care, Health and Development* 1(1975): 118-22.

Smilansky, S. *The Effects of Sociodramatic Play on Disadvantaged Preschool Children.* New York: Wiley, 1968.

Strain, P. "Increasing Social Play of Severely Retarded Preschoolers with Sociodramatic Activities." *Mental Retardation* 13(1975): 7-9.

Suomi, S.J., and H.F. Harlow. "The Role and Reason of Peer Relationships in Rhesus Monkeys." In *Friendship and Peer Relations,* edited by M. Lewis and L. Rosenblum. New York: Wiley, 1975.

Sylva, K. "Play and Learning." In *Biology of Play,* edited by B. Tizard and D. Harvey. Philadelphia: Lippincott, 1977.

Tizard, B., and D. Harvey, editors. *Biology of Play.* Philadelphia: Lippincott, 1977.

Tizard, J. *Community Services for the Mentally Handicapped.* Oxford: Oxford University Press, 1964.

Trevarthen, C. "Conversations with a Two-Month-Old." *New Scientist* 16(1976): 230-35.

Wehman, P. *Helping the Mentally Retarded Acquire Play Skills.* Springfield, IL: C.C. Thomas, 1977.

Weiner, E.A., and B.J. Weiner. "Differentiation of Retarded and Normal Children Through Toy-Play Analysis." *Multivariate Behavioral Research* 9(1974): 245-52.

Widerstrom, A.H. "Mother's Language and Infant Sensorimotor Development: Is There a Relationship?" *Language Learning* 32(1982): 145-66.

Wing, L.; J. Gould; S.R. Yeates and L.M. Brierley. "Symbolic Play in Severely Mentally Retarded and in Autistic Children." *Journal of Child Psychology and Psychiatry* 18(1977): 167-78.

The medically special child

What every teacher should know about five physical disorders that affect some children in every school

The odds are that at some point in your teaching career you will have a medically special child in your classroom. And the chances are good that you also will need to recognize symptoms, be aware of a child's medical needs, and even be confronted with a medical emergency involving a child with a special medical problem.

In this article, a pediatrician and qualified teachers explain the causes, symptoms, and treatments of five physical disorders: allergies (including asthma), diabetes, epilepsy, hyperactivity, and otitis media (ear infections). Knowing who these special kids are and how to help them is part of every teacher's job.

the allergic child

Michael's eyes water and his nose is red from continual blowing and wiping. Melinda coughs incessantly and complains of stomach pains. Bruce cannot seem to stay awake and drifts off to sleep during the morning. Each of these children may be suffering from an allergic reaction or from a side effect of a medication used in treating an allergy.

In simple terms, an allergy is an acquired, abnormal sensitivity of the body to a substance found in the environment. Different people have developed allergies to almost every substance imaginable. Some common allergens or antigens (the substance that causes a reaction) are dust (including chalk dust), flowers, pets, foods of every kind, perfume, pollen, feathers, medicines, and insect venom.

Ten percent of all Americans are allergic enough to something to require medical attention. These people are allergic to a substance that is impossible to avoid, or they have extreme reactions such as vomiting, breaking out in a rash, or having trouble breathing. The most common treatment is a pro-

gram of desensitization in which gradually increasing amounts of the antigen are injected into the body. The length of time a person remains on these allergy shots varies, but he or she is usually required to take them for two to three years.

Many more people experience less severe allergic reactions such as sneezing, coughing, and a runny nose. Children are sometimes treated for these reactions with antihistamines or decongestants. Antihistamines cause drowsiness and should be given to children only after school hours. Decongestants should be used to control symptoms during the school day.

Children with suspected allergy problems are often referred by a pediatrician to an allergist who makes a diagnosis through a look at a complete family medical history (75 percent of allergic children come from families with a history of allergies), a review of symptoms, and diagnostic allergy tests. The allergy test most often used with children is the scratch test. A series of small scratches is made on the child's back, and solutions containing com-

mon antigens are applied to each scratch. If the reaction is positive, a small hive will appear. By observing its size and color, the allergist can determine the severity of the allergy. The scratch test is most useful in identifying allergens that are inhaled. If the suspected allergens are eaten, the patient is put on a diet without the suspected foods. These are later added, one by one, and the reaction to them noted.

A common and sometimes serious allergy in children is asthma, a chronic lung disorder that causes attacks of coughing and wheezing. Many asthmatic children require around-the-clock medication (every six hours is a common dosage), which means they must take medicine at school. Treatments may be in the form of tablets, liquids, or sprays, and they are all necessary to keep the child from having a serious attack.

Teachers should ask every student's parents to supply a list of each child's known allergies and the treatment, if any, that the child receives. Allergic children can be seated away from the chalkboard, and the teacher can remind them to avoid close contact with allergens. Teachers should also know that people can develop new allergies at any age and should be on the lookout for children who start to show persistent symptoms of allergies.

For more information on allergies, write the Asthma and Allergies Foundation of America, 1302 18th St. N.W., Suite 303, Washington, D.C. 20036.

the diabetic child

You have led your class in warm-up exercises, and everyone is now enjoying a fast-paced relay race. Someone touches your arm and tells you Jenny is not feeling well. You investigate and find that Jenny is dizzy and has a headache. Her speech is slurred and her skin feels clammy. Her eyes close and she slumps to the floor. Jenny is diabetic and could be sinking into a diabetic coma. You should know how to help the diabetic children in your class to avoid such emergencies and you should also know what to do if they occur.

Diabetes occurs in almost two out of every 1,000 school children. It develops when the body's cells are unable to obtain or utilize sufficient amounts of the hormone insulin. Insulin, which is produced in the pancreas, enables the body to metabolize and reduce the levels of sugar in the blood. Without insulin, sugar accumulates in the blood to the point where the body becomes unable to use this source of energy. Alternate sources of energy must be found, so fat is broken down into fatty acids, and vastly increased amounts of fat are transported to the liver. This excessive metabolism of fat produces ketones, which are highly acidic and toxic.

Practically all diabetic children require insulin treatment. Insulin must be injected under the skin because intestinal enzymes destroy its effect when taken orally. Shots are given once or twice a day. Children are usually taught by the age of six or seven to check their own sugar levels and give themselves insulin shots. Normally, shots are given in the early morning and late afternoon, before the child's dinner.

Diabetic children must also follow a specified diet that they eat at very regular times. They will probably need a midmorning and afternoon snack. If lunch is delayed for any reason, such as a field trip, plans must be made so a protein snack is available to these students. Diabetics must avoid eating sugar, so ice cream, candy, fruit juices, and many processed foods are usually forbidden.

The diabetic is subject to two types of diabetic coma. The first is a result of *hyperglycemia,* an excess of sugar and ketones in the blood. The child will first feel warm, nauseous, and lethargic. Breathing will become difficult and the child's breath will have a sweet smell from the ketones. Hyperglycemia occurs when insulin injections are omitted, when the child is ill, and if the child overeats, eats too much sugar, or does not eat at the proper time. There are no emergency procedures a teacher can use other than to recognize the symptoms and immediately call for medical help. Sugar should never be given to a child with these symptoms.

The second type of diabetic coma is caused by low blood sugar level, a condition called *hypoglycemia.* This condition develops very rapidly as in the case of Jenny. The child will have one or more of these symptoms: clammy, sweaty feeling skin; slurred speech; headache; uncoordinated muscle movement; mental confusion; and vertigo. Hypoglycemia is brought on by a mistake in insulin dosage, meal irregularity, or vigorous exercise. Each diabetic child should have a plan for such emergencies and should let the teacher know what to do. Generally, orange juice with sugar added is a good source of sugar in such cases, but, of course, should never be given if the child is unconscious. Should the child's normal sugar source be unavailable, any available candy or soda pop should be used. Always alert parents if a child should experience such symptoms.

A teacher should be aware of the psychological pressures facing a diabetic child. Because he or she may be overprotected at home, school may be the only place where the child has a chance to be treated as "normal." The best therapy, then, that a teacher can give is to make the diabetic child subject to the same classroom standards observed by all the other students. One very important exception is be sure to plan ahead and have special sugar-free treats set aside when the class is having a party.

You can obtain more information on diabetes from the American Diabetes Association, 2 Park Avenue, New York, NY 10016.

the epileptic child

Melanie suddenly falls to the floor from her seat as you are in the middle of a reading group session. By the time you reach her she appears to be unconscious. A few minutes later she awakens in a confused state and complains of a headache. Melanie may have just had an epileptic seizure.

Epilepsy is a malfunction of the electrical activity of the brain. It is usually caused by some kind of damage to a part of the brain. This does not mean, however, that epileptics are "slow" or any more prone to have learning disabilities than nonepileptics. Sometimes epilepsy is passed from parent to child. No one is quite sure how, but studies show that a parent with epilepsy has a 1 in 50 chance of having an epileptic child, and a person who does not have epilepsy has a 1 in 200 chance that his or her child will have epilepsy.

There are three general types of epileptic seizures. The most common type with children is the *tonic-clonic* or *grand mal seizure.* Seizures of this type cause generalized convulsions along with rigidity and involuntary muscle movement. The onset of the attack is dramatically abrupt, with the first spasm usually occurring simultaneously with loss of consciousness. If sitting or standing when the seizure begins, the child will fall to the floor. The face becomes pale, pupils dilate, eyes roll, the face is distorted, the glottis (mouth of the windpipe) closes, the head may be thrown to the side or backwards, abdominal and chest muscles become

rigid, and limbs stiffen or contract irregularly. This phase usually will last only 20 seconds to a minute, and another "clonic" or jerking phase may follow. The child will then fall asleep for a short period of time and may awaken with a severe headache and confusion.

Absence or *petit mal seizures* involve only a momentary loss of consciousness and are characterized by brief periods of staring or blinking. There may be an upward rolling of the eyes, rhythmic nodding of the head, or slight quivering of the limb muscles. Attacks can last from 5 to 30 seconds and may be so minor that they go unnoticed for months. Parents and children may sometimes dismiss these seizures as "lapses" or "dizzy spells."

The last type of epileptic seizure, called *psychomotor seizures,* is the most difficult to recognize and control. It takes the form of purposeful but inappropriate movements that are repetitive and often complicated. For instance, a child might turn around in circles or run to the teacher for no apparent reason. After a one- to five-minute period of unconsciousness, the

child will return to his or her normal activity and feel slightly drowsy.

Epileptic attacks are usually treated with anticonvulsant drugs, with phenobarbital the first choice for children and Dilantin as the second-line therapy. A single dose at bedtime is usually enough. The petit mal and psychomotor seizures are often hard to detect, but a teacher's familiarity with the signs of these seizures may help a physician make the correct diagnosis.

If a child suffers a grand mal seizure, the teacher should help the child lie down; open the child's airway by tilting the head slightly backward; clear away other children, furniture, and sharp objects; loosen the child's clothing; allow the child to sleep afterward if drowsy; explain to the other children what a seizure is, that it is not contagious, and that there is no reason for alarm; and notify parents of the seizure so any necessary changes in medication can be made.

To obtain more information about epilepsy in children or in adults, write the Epilepsy Foundation of America, 4351 Garden City Drive, Landover, MD 20785.

the hyperactive child

Sean is out of his seat more than he is in it. He is distracted by small noises and movements of his classmates. He cannot pay attention long enough to understand concepts being taught and distracts others from learning. Sean has been diagnosed as hyperactive.

This diagnosis alone won't help Sean's teacher very much because there is no standard method of controlling and helping a hyperactive child. The term *hyperactive* (some use hyperkinetic) is applied to the estimated 5 to 10 percent of all elementary school children (75 percent are boys) who display any combination of the following behaviors: impulsiveness, excitability, frequent crying, sulking, low tolerance to frustration, tendency to deny mistakes or blame others, temper outbursts, and difficulty learning.

The term *minimal brain damage* has

been applied by the medical profession to the learning and behavior problems associated with hyperactivity. But what causes that brain damage is unknown. Some of the factors that have been suggested are birth defects, early infection or injury, diet, environmental and social factors, and even fluorescent lighting.

The problem generally becomes evident after the child enters first grade, with classroom teachers often the first to suggest that the child seek medical help. The teacher remains an important source of information when a pediatrician considers various options for treatment. It is not unusual for a doctor to request a behavioral observation by the teacher based on a comparison to the student's peers.

If a doctor diagnoses hyperactivity, parents of the child are given various

options for treatment: putting the child on a diet of reduced artificial food additives and sugar; reduction of classroom stimuli; a short-term memory program designed to help the child "chain" information together to remain on task; and most commonly, drug therapy.

Children are most often treated with drugs called psychoactive stimulants. Currently, Ritalin is the most popular of these drugs. Cylert is a newer drug that seems to have similar effects and must be taken only once a day instead of the two doses of Ritalin required. Paradoxically, all of the drugs used to slow down hyperactive kids are stimulants. These drugs seem to increase the activity in the brain called *neurotransmitters.* These chemicals make the connections among the different neurons in the brain—in other words, they are the substances that complete the messages that the brain sends to, and receives from, other parts of the body. So doctors who prescribe these drugs for children believe that the stimulants increase the child's attention span and concentration by increasing the production of neurotransmitters. Other hyperactive children sometimes benefit from taking drugs such as Thorazine that are most often prescribed to lessen anxiety.

The teacher's role in helping the hyperactive child is, first, to provide parents and pediatricians with information so that the physician is able to diagnose and treat the student. The teacher then supports the recommended treatment by helping to enforce a diet, reducing classroom stimuli for the child, or monitoring the child's drug intake during school hours and noting his or her performance while on the medication.

the child with otitis media

Jason cannot answer a simple question lately. He's always been attentive but recently he's begun asking you to repeat things and is likely to give some answer totally unrelated to your question. Jason may suffer from otitis media—an infection of the middle ear, which impairs hearing.

Otitis media is most common in children six years old and younger. It does, however, strike older schoolchildren, as well. Otitis media affects the part of the middle ear called the *eustachian tube*. This tube connects the ear with the back of the throat and serves three important roles: it equalizes pressure on the inside and outside of the eardrum by acting as an air passageway; it drains fluids from the middle ear to the throat; and it serves to protect the middle ear from germs that may enter through the throat.

When the eustachian tube gets blocked for any reason, fluid accumulates and can no longer drain into the throat. Sometimes this buildup becomes infected, resulting in pain and redness. Any redness will not, however, be visible in the outer ear. This infection can eventually lead to partial hearing loss. And, should the eustachian tube close, the buildup of fluid or pressure can become so severe that the eardrum ruptures.

The most common sequence of events leading to otitis media is an upper respiratory infection followed by an earache. Certain children seem to be more susceptible to otitis media because of a tendency to have frequent colds and infections that start the blockage of the eustachian tube. The angle, size, and shape of the tube may also predispose children to this disease.

Antibiotics are used to combat the infection. Otitis media is almost never treated with eardrops alone. When a child repeatedly suffers from the infection, a physician will sometimes recommend implanting plastic tubes in the eardrums to equalize pressure, decrease temporary hearing loss, and reduce the danger of permanent auditory damage. These tubes usually remain in the ear for several months.

The hearing loss from otitis media may occur only within a certain range of sound, causing the child to seemingly hear only what he or she wants to hear. Without knowledge of the disorder, a teacher may become irritated at a child for not paying attention or for daydreaming when the child is really not able to hear adequately.

The teacher's role in helping children with any of the five physiological problems discussed here is, first, to know and be on the lookout for their symptoms. Teachers must also be prepared to help in any medical emergency that arises from these disorders. Finally, teachers should be aware of which children in their classes suffer from any physical problem and do all they can to help those kids be accepted by their peers as equals.

Contributors to this article include **Dr. Elizabeth Dedman,** assistant professor of family medicine, University of Louisville; **Betty Lindsey,** a doctoral student in education, University of Louisville; and **Dr. Bernard Strenecky,** associate professor of education and family medicine, University of Louisville. **Larry Lewin,** a fourth grade teacher at the Adams School in Eugene, Oregon, contributed to the section on hyperactivity.

Curricular Applications

Curricular applications can be studied according to the *type of content* provided, such as language arts or computation; the *type of learning processes* supported; and the *amount of time* spent on verbal or discovery methods, competitive or cooperative learning with peers, and self-expression, group efforts, or copying of prescribed work. Let us examine two curricular approaches to Early Childhood Education.

In Program 1000, the children spend twenty minutes each on consonants, addition, and cursive writing under direct teacher instruction and correction. They are provided with and expected to finish many worksheets and workbooks. They are told to "move on" to another subject for another twenty minutes, even though they may be unable to "regroup" intellectually as quickly as adults. The academic focus is clear, the 3Rs are emphasized, and children copy numerals, alphabets, and words from either the chalkboard or commercial charts. The classroom is generally quiet; many children sit with their shoulders almost touching the desktops. Many children are observed hurrying through their paper work and guessing at answers. Occasionally, some scribble or copy from peers so they can have a few minutes to "play" in a corner of the room. Practice, drill, and recitation are part of the daily activities. The teacher keeps order and circulates between the desks to help individual children. Many adults remember Program 1000 from their own schooling days. It is often based on sentiment and tradition.

In Program 2000, many types of materials are arranged in centers around the room, and several activities occur simultaneously. There is a noise of busyness, but it is not distracting. Children are observed sitting, standing, or moving to various areas and conversing with peers or adults. Some children are copying favorite songs or poetry from books; others are working on a group mural; some are building a space shuttle using three types of blocks; several are preparing imaginary pizza from play dough for their Care Bears. Four children are playing UNO, while three play Chutes and Ladders. The teacher visits each child during the morning to enforce rules, assist with problems, check on learnings, or offer vocabulary, props, or ideas for continued activities. Program 2000 is based on scientific knowledge about motor, language, social-affective, cognitive, and moral development.

Contrary to popular opinion, greater professional expertise and effort are required to plan, monitor, and evaluate Program 2000—an activity based, play, games, cooperative learning approach—than is required to conduct Program 1000—a teacher-directed, sit-and-listen, paper and pencil task. The beneficial effects on later reading, compositional writing, and arithmetic achievements are well documented by researchers for Program 2000. Also documented by clinicians and observed in many later elementary students are the damaging effects on motivational, affective, and cognitive development of too much formal, sedentary, group work found in Program 1000.

Playing with materials and media is the way the young child conquers the world of objects and constructs knowledge about their properties. Thus equipping an early childhood program like 2000, requires, in addition to time and money, a thorough knowledge of how to select play materials and media for children of differing ages, abilities, and backgrounds.

During the second and third years of life, healthy children engage in symbolic play where something is used to stand for something else—e.g., a paper bag becomes a tent for a doll. These interiorized mental representations are especially apparent in dramatic play enactments. Cen-tered on the themes of home and family relationships, "school" programs and teachers, medical settings, and Super Heroes and Heroines, these dramatic play episodes represent the way the child participates in wish-fulfillment and links inner fantasies and desires with perceptions of outer reality and demands. Caregivers and teachers who can knowledgeably assist children by stimulating and extending their dramatic play are helping them expand their abilities to visualize, verbalize, sequence events, and order material and human relationships. All of these are vital to children's later achievements in reading, compositional writing, and arithmetic.

Play with language as both a sensory and symbolic medium enables the child to construct two important learnings: First, language has delightful properties of sound and rhythm (e.g., hocus pocus; Timbuctu and Kalamazoo; abracadabra). Second, language can be varied in meaning (e.g., Fuzzy Wuzzy was a bear; knock-knock jokes). Both of these learnings are only internalized through personal experimentation with, investigative playing with, and manipulation of sounds, words, phrases, and meanings. This results in fluency, flexibility, and competence in oral language, which researchers have found to be essential for later literacy enjoyment and production in elementary school.

This section addresses conflicting philosophies and practices in early childhood programs, curriculum content and processes, criteria for selecting play materials, and facilitating and expanding dramatic play engagements.

Looking Ahead: Challenge Questions

How can early childhood educators lead elementary education toward excellence using a knowledge base of cognitive and moral development? Why is play superior to worksheets in helping children learn arithmetic?

In what ways are the common sense notions that teaching means telling and using rewards and/or punishments totally erroneous for early childhood programs?

What do young children actually learn by playing? How can play materials be evaluated for their contribution to children's development? How can teachers promote and extend children's dramatic play engagements?

Why are normal six-year-old children so often confused about the properties of numbers, addition, and subtraction? How does an understanding of Piaget's stages help the teacher "see" what first-graders are unable to "see" in arithmetic?

Leading Primary Education Toward Excellence

Beyond Worksheets and Drill

Constance Kamii

Constance Kamii, Ph.D., is Professor of Early Childhood Education, University of Alabama at Birmingham, Birmingham, Alabama.

It is almost impossible today to talk with teachers of young children, especially those in the primary grades, without hearing some complaints about having to produce higher test scores. Most teachers trained in the child development tradition believe, for example, that some of their children are not yet ready to learn how to read. Yet these teachers feel compelled to give phonics lessons simply because they are expected to produce acceptable test scores, and this pressure is working downward even to some classrooms of 4-year-old children. In arithmetic, too, many teachers believe that first graders cannot possibly understand missing addends (the $\square$ in $4 + \square = 6$) and place value (the fact that the first *3* in *33* means 30, while the second *3* means 3). Yet, they feel compelled to teach this content simply because it is on the achievement test.

Education is an amazing profession in which professionals can be forced to do things against their conscience. Physicians are not forced to give treatments that only make the symptoms disappear, but many teachers give phonics lessons and worksheets, knowing perfectly well that the imposition of the 3 R's may make children dislike school and lose confidence in their own ability to figure things out. Why is it that such harmful practices are going on in early childhood education from coast to coast?

One explanation is that administrators in education, who have the power to make decisions, are ignorant of child development. Many of them are politically motivated and go along with the pressure to produce higher test scores. While these statements may be true, they do not fully explain why those of us within the profession who believe in child development are not winning the battle against those who believe in force-feeding the 3 R's. I would like to offer an additional explanation of why we are not winning the battle and then propose some suggestions about what we might do to lead primary education forward toward excellence rather than backwards to worksheets and drill.

Common sense notions of instruction and development

Let me clarify first what is generally understood by the term *development*. To most people, development means a long-term process of unfolding or maturation from inside the child, like the unfolding of a flower that develops out of a bud. Child development is a loosely related field in psychology consisting of a variety of theories about the child that are not directly applicable to education. For example, Sigmund and Anna Freud are big names in child development, and so are Erik Erikson and Jane Loevinger. But their theories cannot be applied to instruction because they do not deal with children's cognitive development, and social and emotional development is only indirectly related to the 3 R's and other academic subjects. The work of Arnold Gesell and L. S. Vygotsky comes closer to education because it deals with children's cognitive development. However, their ideas are too diverse to unite into a theory of instruction, and each is too sketchy to select one of them for curriculum development.

When early childhood educators speak of child development, they are referring not to descriptive or explanatory theories but to a philosophy or an approach to education. This philosophy may be excellent, but it represents an intuitive leap from psychological theories to educational practices, without precise theoretical links between the two. In medicine, the objective of the practitioner is always defined in relation to scientific explanation, and if the cause of a disease is not known, physicians know that the cause is not yet known.

In early childhood education, however, if we look in any textbook written in the child development tradition, we do not find objectives based on a precise explanatory theory. We find, instead, vague and broad goals such as emotional, social, and intellectual development and more specific objectives defined along traditional subjects such as language arts, math, and science. With these objectives defined without any foundation in a precise, scientific, explanatory theory, it is not surprising to find a variety of activities—all without precise theoretical links to an explanatory theory—such as pretend play, painting, block building, water play, and games. It is these activities that seem softheaded and worthless to the traditionalists who believe that education consists of the 3 R's, lessons, exercises, and/or drills. When the pressure is on to use worksheets, furthermore, advocates of play can usually not defend play's educational value.

For centuries, education has been based on mere common sense, trial and error, and opinions called philosophies, such as Rousseau's and Dewey's philosophies. When some educators attempted to introduce a scientific foundation into the profession, they found associationism, behaviorism, and psychometric tests. Behaviorism, a more intense and systematic version of associationism, is a scientific theory that has been confirmed all over the world. Psychometric tests yield numbers and printouts that give the impression of being scientific. If we want to win the battle against the force-feeding of the 3 R's and worksheets, we have to have a scientific theory that is powerful enough to disprove associationism, behaviorism, and the desirability of psychometric tests.

I would like to back up and focus more sharply on common sense. According to common sense, teaching consists of *telling* or *presenting* knowledge, and learning takes place by the *internalization* of what is taught. When proponents of child development methods speak of unfolding from the inside, or maturation, these ideas appear in an almost mutually exclusive relationship with the common-sense notion of instruction as can be seen in Figure 1. To people who think in common-sensical and either-or terms, this relationship implies

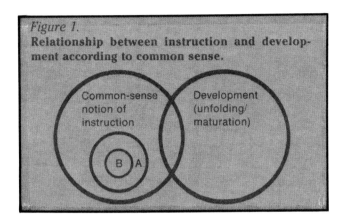

Figure 1.
Relationship between instruction and development according to common sense.

that the development approach necessitates giving up instruction, which is exactly what they want to intensify in going back to basics. Behaviorism, associationism, and psychometric tests are compatible with common sense because they grew out of common sense. This is why I put A for associationism inside the circle on the left. Behaviorism, shown with the B within associationism, is an intensified version of associationism that breaks "correct" behaviors, or answers, down to small components and sequences them to ensure better internalization. Psychometric tests approach evaluation in a similar way, by focusing on "correct" behaviors, or answers, thereby reinforcing the common-sense notion that the child who has acquired more knowledge is the one who can give more correct answers. Now that the common-sense notion of teaching has thus been buttressed by behaviorism, associationism, and psychometric tests, it is even harder for the Educational Establishment to accept the child development philosophy.

Developmentalists, however, are convinced that there is a process of unfolding from inside the child, and that the force-feeding of isolated skills with worksheets is inappropriate for young children. But we need to go beyond saying that worksheets are developmentally inappropriate and explain precisely and scientifically **why** these are inappropriate. We must also go beyond criticizing the undesirable, and advance alternative ways to replace what we criticize. I would now like to show how Piaget's theory can help us accomplish both of these tasks.

Constructivism and the curriculum

Reading and writing. Let me give an example from Ferreiro's (Ferreiro and Teberosky, 1982) research in reading and writing to show the kind of precise scientific explanation that is possible to present against associationists and behaviorists. Ferreiro was a collaborator of Piaget in Geneva until she returned to her native land, Argentina, where she did her research in Spanish. She interviewed 4- to 6-year-old children before they received any instruction in school in reading and writing. She asked them, for example, to write their own name, the name of a friend or a member of their family, and words such as *mamá, papá, oso* (bear), *sapo* (toad), and *pato* (*duck*).

She found developmental levels among these children who had not received any instruction in school. At the first and lowest level, the children wrote essentially the same squiggles for everything. Here is an example:

mamá

papá

oso

Interestingly, at this level, the child often thought that a big animal like a bear had to be written with bigger squiggles or with more squiggles than a small animal like a duck!

At the second level, the child believed that to read different things, there had to be objective differences in the writing. When they had a limited repertoire of letters consisting of only four letters, for instance, they wrote different words such as the following by varying the order of the same four letters:

mamá   oso

papá   sapo

The third level, called the syllabic hypothesis level, is a major achievement because the child thinks that each "letter" stands for one syllable. One child wrote as follows:

sapo

oso

patito

This syllabic level is a major achievement because for the first time children make correspondences between the parts they write and the parts they utter.

At the fourth level, called the alphabetic hypothesis level, the child's analysis goes beyond syllables as can be seen in the following examples:

pato   PAO

Susana   SANA

I simplified all these levels for purposes of clarity, and further details can be found in Ferreiro and Teberosky's book entitled *Literacy before Schooling.* I hope you can see that the conventional alphabetic writing comes next, at the fifth level, and that the children who can benefit most from phonics lessons are those who are already at this high developmental level. Some children learn despite the poor methods!

These levels illustrate what to me is the most important point of Piaget's theory, namely constructivism. No one teaches children that if they write *mamá* with four letters, they can write *papá* simply by changing the order of the same letters. Yet, children construct, or invent, this way of writing when it occurs to them that each word has to look different. The syllabic hypothesis at the next level is also wrong, but it represents enormous progress over the previous level. Such progress is never picked up by achievement tests. For tests, the only thing that counts is correct answers, but according to Piaget children develop by constructing one level after another of being "wrong."

Arithmetic. I would now like to go on to the teaching of arithmetic to illustrate constructivism in another area of the curriculum. A typical worksheet gets children to write *3* next to a picture of three cookies and *4* next to a picture of four bottles. Children who can do these worksheets already know how to do them, and do not learn number concepts by completing them. Those who cannot do them, on the other hand, will not learn number concepts by filling out worksheets. Number is something children construct by thinking, in their heads, and not by pushing pencils.

I would like to clarify children's construction of number by discussing a Piagetian task (Inhelder and Piaget, 1963). The child is given a glass, and the researcher takes an identical glass. The adult then asks the child to drop a bead into his glass each time she drops one into hers. After about six beads have thus been dropped in each glass with one-to-one correspondence, the adult says, "Let's stop now, and I want you to watch what I am going to do." The researcher then drops one bead into her glass and suggests, "Let's get going again." Each person drops about six more beads into his or her glass with one-to-one correspondence, and the child is asked whether the two people have the same amount, or the child has more, or the adult has more.

Four-year-olds usually say that the two glasses have the same amount, and when asked "How do you know?" they explain, "Because I can see they both have the same." Upon being asked to describe how the beads were dropped, they can usually give all the empirical facts correctly ("... Then you told me to stop, and you put one in your glass.... Only you put an extra one in your glass, and I watched 'cause you told me to wait.... Then we got going again... ").

By age five or six, however, the majority of children can deduce logically that the experimenter has one more. When we asked them what will happen "if we continued to drop beads in the same way [one-to-one correspondence] all afternoon," only some of them reply that the adult will always have one more. Others make empirical statements such as "I don't know because we haven't done it yet" or "We don't have enough beads to keep going all afternoon."

The logical nature of number can be clarified by understanding the distinction Piaget made among three kinds of knowledge according to their ultimate sources: physical

Number is something children construct by thinking, in their heads, and not by pushing pencils.

knowledge, logico-mathematical knowledge, and social (conventional) knowledge. *Physical knowledge* is knowledge of objects in external reality. The color and weight of a bead are examples of physical properties that are *in* objects in external reality, and can be known by observation. The knowledge that a bead will go down when we let go of it is also an example of physical, empirical knowledge.

Logico-mathematical knowledge, on the other hand, consists of relationships constructed by each individual. For instance, when we are presented with a red bead and a blue one, and think that they are different, this difference is an example of logico-mathematical knowledge. The beads are indeed observable, but the difference between them is not. The difference is a *relationship* created mentally by the individual who puts the two objects into this relationship. The

---

Worksheets are harmful for first graders' development of arithmetic, while play is highly beneficial.

---

difference is neither *in* the red bead nor *in* the blue one, and if a person did not put the objects into this relationship, the difference would not exist for that person. Other examples of relationships the individual can create between the two beads are "similar," "the same in weight," and "two."

The ultimate source of *social knowledge* is conventions made by people. Examples of social knowledge are the fact that Christmas comes on December 25, that a bead is called *bead,* and that grown-ups sometimes greet each other by shaking hands.

You can see that the spoken words "one, two, three, four ..." and written numerals belong to social knowledge and representation, which are the most superficial parts of arithmetic. The underlying number concepts belong to logico-mathematical knowledge, which has its source in each child's head. The bad news from Piaget's theory is that **number concepts are not teachable,** as they can be constructed only by children, through their own mental activity. The good news, however, is that **we don't have to teach number concepts because children will construct them on their own.**

It is amazing to me that all of math education is based on the empiricist, wrong assumption that number is something that has to be learned by internalization from the environment. Piaget (Piaget and Szeminska, 1941) showed more than 40 years ago that number concepts are constructed by each child, but math education is still going on as if Piaget had never published *The Child's Conception of Number* and many other subsequent volumes.

Based on his theory, I did an experiment in first grade arithmetic. We eliminated all traditional instruction from first grade arithmetic including worksheets and used instead two kinds of activities that emphasized thinking: (a) situations in daily living such as the counting of votes and (b) group games such as dice and card games. I will not go into the details of this study, since a book was recently published entitled *Young Children Reinvent Arithmetic* (Kamii, 1985). I would simply like to make one point from this research, that **worksheets are harmful for first graders' development of arithmetic while play is highly beneficial.**

One of my reasons for saying that worksheets are harmful is that they require children to write answers, and having to write interferes with the possibility of remembering combinations such as "3, 2, 5" and "4, 2, 6." Children can remember sums better when they are free to concentrate on these combinations, without having to write the answers.

My second reason for saying that worksheets are harmful is that they teach children to count mechanically when they don't know a sum. In extending my research into second and third grades, I am amazed that the great majority of traditionally taught second graders are still counting on fingers to do sums such as 5 + 6, and this need to count persists in the third grade. The first graders I had worked with used their heads instead and said, "5 + 5 = 10; so 5 + 6 has to be 11," but the children who had been taught with worksheets in first grade had become counting machines. Since they were required to write answers to satisfy the teacher, they used the most mechanical, surest, deadly technique they were taught to be able to write the correct answer. Children who had thus mindlessly engaged in counting, repeated the same mechanical procedure if 7 + 2 was followed immediately by 2 + 7, or 6 + 4 was followed immediately by 7 + 4.

Going beyond common sense

I would like to return to Figure 1 to point out that constructivist teaching is not maturationist. Piaget clearly differentiated maturation, which is a biological process like the baby's becoming able to walk, from the construction of knowledge through children's own mental activity. While people are passive in biological maturation, they are mentally very active when they construct knowledge. A more precise way to talk about this mental activity is to say that children construct knowledge by putting things into relationships. For example, children are mentally very active when they construct the knowledge that 2 + 3 gives the same result as 4 + 1.

Knowledge is constructed through an active mental process that is far from the maturationist view represented by the Gesellian school. If you believe in maturation, you will wait for the child to mature. If you believe in construction, however, you will promote activities that stimulate the constructive process such as board games with dice in the first grade.

You must have noted that Piaget's scientific theory about how children learn is very different from behaviorism, which is another scientific theory about how children learn. Why is it that two scientific theories can be so diametrically opposed?

The answer is that the same relationship can be found in every other scientific field such as astronomy. While the he-

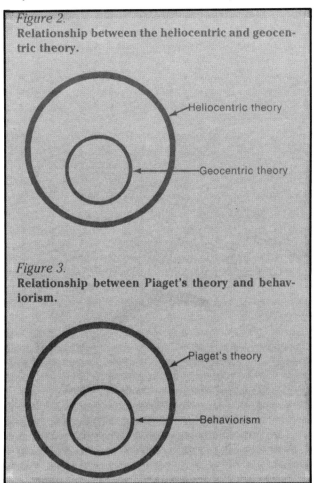

Figure 2.
Relationship between the heliocentric and geocentric theory.

Heliocentric theory

Geocentric theory

Figure 3.
Relationship between Piaget's theory and behaviorism.

Piaget's theory

Behaviorism

liocentric theory disproved the geocentric theory, according to which the sun revolved around the earth, the new theory did not eliminate the old one. The new theory went beyond the old one by encompassing it as can be seen in Figure 2. The proof is that even today, we still talk about the sunrise and sunset, even though no one believes in the geocentric theory anymore. It is still true that the sun rises and sets, when we limit ourselves to a certain perspective.

The relationship between Piaget's theory and behaviorism is similar as can be seen in Figure 3. Piaget's theory went beyond behaviorism by encompassing it. Therefore, his theory can explain the phenomena explained by behaviorism, but the converse is not true. Piaget explained conditioning as an instance of organisms' adaptation to the environment. Worms, rats, and dogs, as well as human beings, adapt to rewards and punishments. But human beings are more complicated than dogs, and behaviorism cannot explain human knowledge.

Piaget's constructivism thus did not eliminate behaviorism. This is why behaviorism remains scientifically true as long as we limit ourselves to surface, observable behaviors. If we view learning only as a change in behavior, we can define

We must define objectives based on precise scientific knowledge of how children construct knowledge.

our objectives behaviorally and use rewards and/or punishments to modify it. The results of such teaching are often higher test scores because psychometric tests in early childhood education are made to evaluate surface skills such as children's ability to count and to recognize numerals. But this kind of teaching is like trying to cure a patient's illness by giving aspirin. Aspirin works on symptoms, but not on the underlying cause of the illness. Many children who can write *8* next to a picture of eight ice cream cones continue to believe that eight chips spread out are more than eight chips pushed close together.

I would like to say one more thing about Piaget's theory in relation to behaviorism and associationism. All sciences begin by studying surface, observable, and limited phenomena, and by explaining them with mere common sense. In astronomy, the geocentric theory came first and was a surface, common-sensical interpretation of the apparent movement of the sun. It is not surprising that psychologists, too, began by studying behavior, which is observable and easier to study than complicated phenomena such as human knowledge and morality. Teaching by telling and rewards and/or punishments makes good common sense, but the time has come for educators to go beyond mere common sense. It is very hard to give up common sense, and this is why it took humanity about 150 years to accept the heliocentric theory (Taylor, 1949).

I hate to say this, but I think educators' acceptance of behaviorism, associationism, and/or psychometric tests constitutes progress in our profession. I say *progress* because it was a big step forward for education to go beyond the primitive stage of making decisions based only on tradition, common sense, and opinions called philosophies. Other professions such as medicine, engineering, and architecture have long had a scientific foundation, but education was entirely in a prescientific stage until it accepted associationism, behaviorism, and psychometric tests.

One of the major points of constructivism, as I said earlier, is that each child has to develop by going through one level after another of being "wrong." Science, too, develops by going through one level after another of being "wrong." The geocentric theory was wrong, but it was a necessary stage without which the heliocentric theory could not have been invented. The heliocentric theory was thus a great achievement, but Kepler later proved Copernicus wrong when he found the planets to move in elliptical orbits rather than circular ones.

Behaviorism was likewise a necessary stage in the history of psychology, and many psychologists are already saying that behaviorism is dead. I have seen many people change from behaviorism and associationism to Piaget's theory as I did, but I have never heard of a Piagetian who later became a behaviorist. Psychometric tests, too, are a stage that psychology is bound to go beyond. Speaking of intelligence tests, Piaget (1965) said 20 years ago, "either we shall one day find

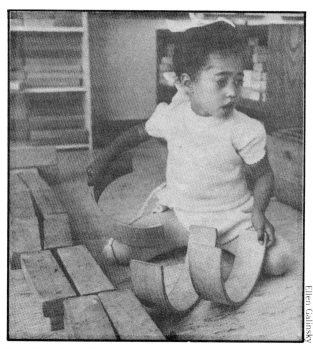

Teaching by telling and rewards and/or punishments makes good common sense, but the time has come for educators to go beyond mere common sense.

good tests, or else intelligence tests will go into history as an example of a fruitful error (p. 150)."

I have no doubt about the eventual victory of the developmental point of view simply because science does not stand still and human intelligence does not stay permanently satisfied with low-level knowledge. But victory will not happen all by itself, without considerable efforts on our part.

As I said earlier, I have not found in a single book written in the child development tradition any rigorous conceptualization of educational objectives based on a scientific, explanatory theory. Physicians know whether their objective is to alleviate only the symptom or to remove the cause of a disease. But educators do not define their objectives with such scientific rigor. We must first be clear about how children construct knowledge because without an explanatory theory about how children construct knowledge, it is impossible to conceptualize specific objectives in relation to long-range goals. [For a clarification of this point, the reader is referred to Kamii (1984).]

I cannot insist enough on the importance of defining objectives based on precise scientific knowledge of how children construct knowledge. In arithmetic, for example, place value is taught not only in first grade but also in second grade, third grade, fourth grade, fifth grade, and sixth grade! It is amazing to me that no one in the Educational Establishment has noticed that there must be something profoundly wrong if the same thing has to be taught every single year in the

There is something profoundly wrong if the same thing has to be taught every single year in the first six grades.

While the public does not tell physicians and engineers to go back to the basics of 40 years ago, it proudly tells *us* to go back . . .

first six grades. Place value ought to be outlawed in the first two grades, along with missing addends, because it is cognitively impossible for most young children to understand them.

Only after defining valid objectives based on children's development does it make sense to debate whether play is superior to worksheets to achieve these goals. Some kinds of play are more educational than others, and the same kind of play, such as the card game of War, is educational only at a certain level of intellectual development. I will not go into the details of these activities, since these have already been published in *Physical Knowledge in Preschool Education* (Kamii and DeVries, 1978), *Group Games in Early Education* (Kamii and DeVries, 1980), *Number in Preschool and Kindergarten* (Kamii, 1982), and *Young Children Reinvent Arithmetic* (Kamii, 1985).

The philosophy of child development may be correct, but we must go beyond philosophies or opinions if we want to stop being dictated to by other philosophies or opinions. I, therefore, plead for educators to construct the next stage of our profession from within by studying Piaget's theory about how human beings construct knowledge and moral values. It is easy to complain about the naiveté of behavioral objectives and the evils of achievement tests. But we must be willing to go beyond complaining and study children's construction of knowledge in the same rigorous way physicians study physiology and pathology, and engineers study physics and mathematics. Rather than being on the defensive and complaining about the pressure downward from the primary grades, we ought to be leading primary education toward excellence based on precise knowledge of cognitive and moral development.

The public knows that today's medicine and engineering are not what they were 30 or 40 years ago because it knows that science does not stand still. While the public does not tell physicians and engineers to go back to the basics of 40 years ago, it proudly tells us to go back to . . . I don't even know when. The reason is that politicians and the public honestly believe that there is no more to education than common sense, and that their common sense is as good as educators' common sense. As long as we continue to teach with worksheets, the public will continue to think of education as an unskilled job because any adult of normal intelligence can give and correct worksheets, with or without a teaching certificate.

The recommendations often espoused for "excellence" are based on mere common sense. It is not by lengthening the school day or the school year, giving more homework, pushing the 3 R's down to kindergarten, and increasing the requirements for high school graduation, that we are going to produce a generation who has the knowledge and originality to build a better world in ways that humanity has not yet imagined.

I am aware that scientific rigor alone will not stop legislators or the Educational Establishment from imposing its quick and simple solutions. But if all the teachers in America knew only parts of ten books by Piaget, the Establishment could not get away with their ignorance anymore.

I am also aware that education will always remain an art, in spite of my insistence on science. As Piaget (1965) said, the practice of medicine, too, is an art, but an art based on scientific knowledge rather than on mere common sense or intuition.

Reform is obviously needed in teacher education and colleges of education, too. Although change is painfully slow in colleges of education, the fact is that not a single course is taught today in educational psychology without some discussion of Piaget's theory. This is an improvement, considering that when I got my Ph.D. 20 years ago, I did not get even 2 minutes of graduate school devoted to Piaget's theory. The theory is usually badly taught and misunderstood, but professors of education, too, must go through one level after another of being wrong.

I apologize for all the negative statements I made about the child development philosophy, and would like to hear about any disagreement anyone may have. I honestly believe that educators must construct the next stage of our own profession from within if we are to stop being dictated by politicians and the public and by the old pendulum that keeps going back to what did not work before. Back to basics is bound to fail because it is based on wrong, outdated assumptions about how human beings construct knowledge. Whether education will then go forward or backward on another bandwagon depends on us and our willingness to be scientifically more rigorous, both about how we define our objectives and about how we try to achieve these objectives.

References

Ferreiro, E., & Teberosky, A. (1982). *Literacy before schooling.* Exeter, NH: Heinemann.

Inhelder, B., & Piaget, J. (1963). De l'itération des actions à la récurrence élémentaire. (From the iteration of actions to elementary recurrence). In P. Gréco, B. Inhelder, B. Matalon, & J. Piaget (Eds.), *La formation des raisonnements recurrentiels* (Etudes d'epistemologie genetique, XVIII). (*The formation of reasoning by recurrence.*) Paris: Presses Universitaires de France.

Kamii, C. (1982). *Number in preschool and kindergarten.* Washington, DC: National Association for the Education of Young Children.

Kamii, C. (1984). Autonomy: The aim of education envisioned by Piaget. *Phi Delta Kappan, 65,* 410–415.

Kamii, C. (1985). *Young children reinvent arithmetic.* New York: Teachers College Press, Columbia University.

Kamii, C., & DeVries, R. (1978). *Physical knowledge in preschool education.* Englewood Cliffs, NJ: Prentice-Hall.

Kamii, C., & DeVries, R. (1980). *Group games in early education.* Washington, DC: National Association for the Education of Young Children.

Piaget, J. (1972). *Science of education and the psychology of the child* (rev. ed.). New York: Viking. (Original work published 1965)

Piaget, J., & Szeminska, A. (1965). *The child's conception of number* (rev. ed.). New York: Norton. (Original work published 1941)

Taylor, F. S. (1949). *A short history of science and scientific thought.* New York: Norton.

This article was originally presented as the keynote address at the annual conference of the California Association for the Education of Young Children, San Diego, March 9, 1985. I am grateful to Professors Roberta Long, Delbert Long, and Bernice Wolfson of the University of Alabama at Birmingham for critically reading earlier drafts.

Choosing Good Toys for Young Children

Parents, grandparents, teachers, and others who buy toys and play materials for young children may be overwhelmed by the selection. You may ask "Why does a child need any of this anyway?" or "How will I choose the right one?" NAEYC's brochure "Choosing Good Toys for Young Children" gives ideas for selecting good toys for children from 2 through 6. Because the holiday season is so near, it is reprinted here!

Stephanie Feeney and Marion Magarick

Why is play important?

Play is vital for every young child—it is the natural activity of childhood! Play provides many ways for children to grow and learn.

Through play children

- figure out how things work and solve problems
- develop their senses
- learn to talk and share ideas
- build strength and control of their bodies
- develop and express imagination and creativity
- learn about themselves, others, and the world
- express their feelings and energy in healthy ways
- increase their ability to concentrate

Many skills and abilities develop at the same time during play. For example, children building with blocks plan, observe size relationships and contruction principles, develop coordination, build their muscles, use language, and cooperate with others.

All young children, boys, girls, and those with special needs and abilities, develop in the same way and have the same need for play and for carefully chosen play materials.

What are good toys?

Children need good toys, just as adults need good tools to do their work well. Good toys need not cost a lot, and children do not need very many. Wonderful toys and play materials can be made from common household items such as plastic containers, magazines, or fabric scraps. Too many toys can overstimulate children and make it hard for them to choose something interesting. Buy only a few toys—but select them carefully.

Good toys for young children are

- attractive and interesting to children
- well constructed, durable, and safe
- matched to children's abilities
- good for children of different ages
- useful in various ways

Safe toys for young children are

- well made (no sharp parts, splinters; will not pinch)
- strong enough to hold the child's weight
- painted with nontoxic, lead-free paint
- shatter–proof
- easily cleaned
- not electric
- checked frequently for safety
- out of reach of younger children

How do adults affect children's play?

Adults set the stage by (1) providing the right toys for children's ages and interests, (2) showing children how to use and care for their toys, and (3) playing with children when invited. Children should decide which toys to use and how to play with them.

Toy selection. What kind of people do you want your children to become? The toys you select affect what children think and learn about themselves and others. For example, many adults try to encourage broad interests and abilities by giving similar toys to both boys and girls. Those who want a peaceful society may prohibit war toys.

Storage. Toys arranged on low, open shelves are easy for young children to reach and return. Toys get lost and broken in toy chests, and falling lids are dangerous.

How do play materials contribute to development?

Sensory materials develop children's senses through experimentation. While playing with water, children begin to understand science and math ideas such as measurement. Children will soon pour without spilling, too! Sand never breaks or wears out—an ideal toy! Whether in a dishpan or at the beach, children become absorbed playing with sand. Clay feels good and can be rolled, pounded, and poked endlessly.

Children's hearing is enhanced as they play *authentic* musical instruments. They also develop their senses and have

Reprinted by permission from *Young Children*, Vol. 40, No. 1 (November 1984), pp. 21-25. © 1984 by the National Association for the Education of Young Children, 1834 Connecticut Avenue, N.W., Washington, DC 20009.

What are some good toys and play materials for young children?

All ages are approximate. Most suggestions for younger children are also appropriate for older children.

	Sensory materials	Active play equipment	Construction materials	Manipulative toys	Dolls and dramatic play	Books and recordings	Art materials
2-year-olds and young 3's	Water and sand toys: cups, shovels Modeling dough Sound-matching games Bells, wood block, triangle, drum Texture matching games, feel box	Low climber Canvas swing Low slide Wagon, cart, or wheelbarrow Large rubber balls Low 3-wheeled, steerable vehicle with pedals	Unit blocks and accessories: animals, people, simple wood cars and trucks Interlocking construction set with large pieces Wood train and track set Hammer (13 oz. steel shanked), soft wood, roofing nails, nailing block	Wooden puzzles with 4–20 large pieces Pegboards Big beads or spools to string Sewing cards Stacking toys Picture lotto, picture dominoes	Washable dolls with a few clothes Doll bed Child-sized table and chairs Dishes, pots and pans Dress-up clothes: hats, shoes, shirts Hand puppets Shopping cart	Clear picture books, stories, and poems about things children know Records or tapes of classical music, folk music, or children's songs	Wide-tip watercolor markers Large sheets of paper, easel Finger or tempura paint, 1/2" brushes Blunt-nose scissors White glue
Older 3's and 4-year-olds	Water toys: measuring cups, egg beaters Sand toys: muffin tins, vehicles Xylophone, maracas, tambourine Potter's clay	Larger 3-wheeled riding vehicle Roller skates Climbing structure Rope or tire swing Plastic bats and balls Various sized rubber balls Balance board Planks, boxes, old tires Bowling pins, ring toss, bean bags and target	More unit blocks, shapes, and accessories Table blocks Realistic model vehicles Construction set with smaller pieces Woodworking bench, saw, sandpaper, nails	Puzzles, pegboard, small beads to string Parquetry blocks Small objects to sort Marbles Magnifying glass Simple card or board games Flannel board with pictures, letters Sturdy letters and numbers	Dolls and accessories Doll carriage Child-sized stove or sink More dress-up clothes Play food, cardboard cartons Airport, doll house, or other settings with accessories Finger or stick puppets	Simple science books More detailed picture and story books Sturdy record or tape player Recordings of wider variety of music Book and recording sets	Easel, narrower brushes Thick crayons, chalk Paste, tape with dispenser Collage materials
5- and 6-year-olds	Water toys: food coloring, pumps, funnels Sand toys: containers, utensils Harmonica, kazoo, guitar, recorder Tools for working with clay	Bicycle Outdoor games: bocce, tetherball, shuffleboard, jumprope, Frisbee	More unit blocks, shapes, and accessories Props for roads, towns Hollow blocks Brace and bits, screwdrivers, screws, metric measure, accessories	More complex puzzles Dominoes More difficult board and card games Yarn, big needles, mesh fabric, weaving materials Magnets, balances Attribute blocks	Cash register, play money, accessories, or props for other dramatic play settings: gas station, construction, office Typewriter	Books on cultures Stories with chapters Favorite stories children can read Children's recipe books	Watercolors, smaller paper, stapler, hole puncher Chalkboard Oil crayons, paint crayons, charcoal Simple camera, film

great fun trying to guess what something is while touching, smelling, tasting, or listening to it with their eyes closed!

Active play equipment allows for vigorous use of many muscles. Children who meet these physical challenges are more sure of their abilities at other times, too. Adults must decide what activities are just difficult enough for each child and then step aside.

Dome-shaped climbing frames, sturdy wooden crates, planks, tires, or trees are good for balancing, climbing, and playing together. Swings, slides, and rocking toys challenge balance, are soothing, and give children a chance to see the world from another angle. Pine bark, sand, or grass cushion children's falls or jumps.

Wagons and riding toys also develop children's muscles. Match the size and type of vehicle to the child.

Construction materials such as blocks or building sets help children develop coordination and creativity. Hardwood unit blocks are expensive but last for generations! Toy people, animals, and vehicles expand the possibilities for block play. Wooden toys don't rust or break.

Woodworking is an excellent construction activity. Children learn about math and science and build skills and coordination. Interest in making objects grows with experience. Choose small-scale, *real* tools, large-headed nails, and soft woods to ensure children's success.

Manipulative toys such as puzzles, beads, pegboards, and lotto games help children develop hand and finger muscles, hand-eye coordination, and concepts. These experiences help prepare them for later reading and writing. Board and card games encourage cooperation and problem solving.

Dolls, stuffed animals, and dramatic play give children the chance to try new behaviors. Children who play house, school, or firefighter are learning what it is like to imitate the adults around them. They are beginning to understand the world and to work together. Pretend play might involve child-sized furniture, dress-up clothing for both sexes, and accessories such as dishes or briefcases. Doll houses, play farms, or other small settings give children a chance to be in charge and to arrange things their way.

Children need a cuddly companion to care for and to laugh and cry with as they grow up. Puppets made from socks or fabric scraps sometimes help children share ideas and talk about their worries.

Books and recordings are sources of joy and learning for children from infancy. Children who are read to generally become better readers. Choose books with pictures and stories that appeal to you and your child. Recordings can be delightful—if they are not too cute and don't talk down to children. Appreciation of good music and literature begins early!

Art materials are ideal for fostering creativity and for developing skills leading to reading and writing. At first, children will explore the materials and enjoy the motion of scribbling. Older children will begin to make more recognizable drawings.

Washable paints (add soap flakes to tempera) assure that children and their clothes will come clean! Children have more control over their work when they use 1/2" brushes, thick paint, bold colors, and large sheets of blank paper. Finger painting is messy but what fun!

Collages and constructions made from paper scraps and white glue help children develop a sense of design, texture, and balance. Adult-made models for copying and coloring books should be avoided. They stifle creativity, frustrate children, and fail to help children feel good about what *they* have done.

What are young children like?

(All ages are approximate.)

Characteristics of 2-year-olds and young 3's

- always on the go—prefer to run or climb
- beginning to develop a sense of danger
- easily frustrated—upset when events do not meet expectations
- developing independence—says "Me do it" or "No," but are still dependent, too
- learning to be more helpful and responsible
- beginning to take care of dolls and act out familiar scenes
- experimenting with art materials
- developing control of finger and hand muscles
- acquiring interest in playing *with* other children
- learning language rapidly
- enjoy learning and using new skills

Characteristics of older 3's and 4-year-olds

- test physical skills and courage—have some sense of caution
- like to play with others
- share and take turns sometimes—cannot wait long
- talk a lot—are silly, boisterous, use shocking language
- very interested in the world—ask lots of questions
- reveal feelings in dramatic play
- enjoy art materials—want to keep projects
- want to be grown up one day and a child the next
- developing a longer attention span
- want real adult things
- do not like to lose—may change rules or quit

Characteristics of 5- and 6-year-olds

- becoming more outgoing, sociable
- like to play cooperatively
- more interested in making final product
- more confident about physical skills
- able to use words to express feelings and cope with situations
- like grown-up activities
- still may need adult help to calm down
- take care of dressing and other personal needs
- prefer realistic working toys
- interested in numbers, letters, reading, and writing
- still need reassurance and affection
- curious about people and how the world works

For more information

Caney, S. *Steven Caney's Toy Book.* New York: Workman, 1972. $5.95.

Cole, A.; Haas, C.; Bushnell, F.; and Weinberger, B. *I Saw a Purple Cow and 100 Other Recipes for Learning.* Boston: Little, Brown, 1972. $5.95.

Isenberg, J. P. and Jacobs, J. E. *Playthings as Learning Tools: A Parents' Guide.* New York: Wiley, 1982.

Kaban, B. *Choosing Toys for Children from Birth to Five.* New York: Schocken, 1979. $9.95.

Lorton, M. B. *Workjobs for Parents.* Reading, Mass.: Addison-Wesley, 1975. $7.50.

McDiarmid, N. J.; Peterson, M. A.; and Sutherland, J. R. *Loving and Learning.* New York: Harcourt Brace Jovanovich, 1977. $7.95

Encouraging Dramatic Play in Early Childhood

What can teachers do to involve children more fully in dramatic play? How might play centers be arranged and equipped? Should you be involved in the children's play? You may want to take a closer look at your classroom and teaching techniques with the principles suggested here for facilitating dramatic play.

Penelope Griffing

Penelope Griffing, Ph.D., is Assistant Professor in the Department of Family Relations and Human Development at The Ohio State University, Columbus, Ohio.

David, Ruth, Shaun, and Ilene are Black kindergarten children playing in a research playroom in their school (Griffing 1980). There are three centers of interest for dramatic play—a home, grocery store, and doctor's office—and props for dramatic play including large boxes, ropes, and other unstructured materials as well as realistic toys.

The girls, wearing hats and carrying purses, shop at the grocery store with pretend money (gestures only) for food to take on a picnic. David, after trying out other roles briefly, crawls beneath the table in the home area with tools in hand. "I'm fixing the car. We got to fix the car before we can go anywhere." He is joined by Shaun, who began play as cashier at the store, and the two boys lie on their backs beneath the car using hammer, pliers, screw driver, and pretend screws on the imaginary vehicle.

Returning home with bags of food from the store, Ruth addresses Shaun and David. "Boys, let's get ready for the picnic." David slides out from under the car. "Time to go now. We can fix the car later. You be the grandfather." He hands grocery bags to Shaun, then turns to Ilene, "I told you not to wear your new hat!" Ilene complies, "OK." She takes off the hat, then directs David to "pick up all the stuff and put it in the car." David picks up the doll, "OK, I'll take the baby."

All four children load things on the table (car), Ilene explaining to some invisible person still at home, "We'll be back tomorrow." David adds, "We're going to Hollywood." Ilene: "Here's a nice spot right here." David: "This is Hollywood." They begin to unload the car. Ruth: "Watch the eggs, they might break." (To David): "Don't put the baby on the table." (The table is now the picnic table.) "We're ready to eat now."

The boys depart for the grocery store, saying, "We'll be back." At the store David sits at the cash register. "I'm typing a letter to my wife." He punches the keys. "I love you."

Eventually the children return home again where the activity centers about another meal (although not everyone agrees to come and eat). They talk about their favorite foods, prepare corn dips for Shaun, to whom they refer as Grandpa, and wrap the food in pretend plastic wrap before storing it in the refrigerator.

Evidence is building that dramatic and sociodramatic play have important benefits for children (Fein 1981). This series of play episodes illustrates some of these benefits. The play was rich in symbolic activity—the transformations of self, objects, and situations into characters, objects, and events that existed in imagination only. The play was cognitively complex in its organization, consisting of sequences of related ideas and events rather than isolated pretend behaviors. There was extensive social interaction and verbal communication with children taking roles and carrying them out cooperatively. In several instances, the children were flexi-

Reprinted by permission from *Young Children*, Vol. 38, No. 2 (January 1983), pp. 13-22. © 1983 by the National Association for the Education of Young Children, 1834 Connecticut Avenue, N.W., Washington, DC 20009.

ble in adapting to the views of others, and thoughts and feelings of the characters were occasionally expressed. The children also displayed a high degree of persistence, interest, and involvement in their enactment of these familiar events in their lives. This type of play certainly provides children valuable opportunities to practice important cognitive, social, and emotional skills. It may do more by contributing *actively* to the development of these skills.

As teachers grow in awareness of the benefits of dramatic play for children, they are increasingly asking how such play can be encouraged. The purpose of this article is to make suggestions concerning ways in which early childhood teachers can enhance children's dramatic and sociodramatic play.

Observe children's play

"The problem of starting . . . is reduced to a minimum if we keep in mind that we are not attempting to add something new and strange—we are simply taking what already exists and working outwards from there" (Way 1966). It is only by observing that we can discover what exists already in children's play. Anecdotal descriptions either written or taped can give you much information about the extent and quality of children's dramatic play and about the roles and themes that interest them the most. In analyzing these observations it is helpful to ask the following questions regarding the play of each child:

1. Which activities and in what settings does the child most frequently use dramatic play?

2. In what types of pretend (types of symbolic transformations) does the child engage? Does the child pretend to be someone else or ascribe roles to toys or animals? Use actions to represent real action? Pretend with objects—substituting toys, other materials, or gestures for real objects? Use words to represent pretend situations or settings? Well-developed dramatic play usually involves all of these types of transformations.

3. How complex is the play? Does the child engage in the single, fleeting pretend acts characteristic of children just beginning to participate in pretend play, or

does she or he combine actions and words into sequences or related make-believe events, or into themes?

4. What is the social context for dramatic play? Is it solitary, parallel, or socially interactive (sociodramatic) play? Sociodramatic play appears later and is more complex than nonsocial dramatic play.

5. To what extent does the child communicate with other children within the context of the pretend play situations? Increasingly, as children develop dramatic play skills, communication involves planning the play as well as engaging in role talk (speaking like an imaginary character).

6. What is the duration of the dramatic play? Does the child maintain play for increasingly longer periods of time? Is she or he persistent in play?

7. What is the content of the play? What themes and roles does the child undertake and how are these developed? Descriptions of the content of play as well as its form will provide clues not only about children's interests but also about their understanding of concepts expressed and of important concerns in their personal social worlds. These may need special understanding if teachers are to help.

Describing children's play in terms of these characteristics can heighten your awareness of patterns or trends in the development of play among children of different ages, and at the same time can provide added appreciation of children's individuality in play styles, interests, abilities, and settings in which dramatic play is most likely to occur. This kind of understanding gives direction for the guidance of play.

For example, four-year-old Craig and Bethany pretended each day to be astronauts. They placed large blocks together to form a space ship, sat side by side on the space ship, but not speaking, for a brief period, then moved on to other activities. These children demonstrated imaginative play by pretending that the blocks were a space ship. However, the teacher had observed these and other four- and five-year-olds in the group develop themes and roles more extensively when the content of play was more familiar. She also wanted to encourage movement from parallel to socially interactive

Elaine M. Ward

Dramatic play provides children valuable opportunities to develop important cognitive, social, and emotional skills.

play. Using books, stories, and discussion to help the children acquire greater understanding of the space theme, making a few suggestions during play as to what astronauts might do next, and adding a few relevant props (special food containers, tools, and radio equipment to facilitate communication between space ships) resulted in enriched play. There was greater variety in types of pretend, more extensive theme development, more social interaction, greater persistence, and more use of language in play. In this instance the play was developed within a block play context. It was highly successful partly because the space ship interest originated with the children themselves.

Set the stage for play

Time for play

Free-play periods indoors and outdoors must, of course, be long enough for chil-

dren to plan and carry out play ideas. Not as well recognized is the possible need, at least occasionally, to reduce the number of activities available during free play in order that there will be less distraction and greater opportunity for involvement in dramatic play. Tizard, Philps, and Plewis (1976a) hypothesized that distraction by the multitude of activities from which to choose was at least partially responsible for the low levels of play they observed. Rubin and Seibel (1979) found that sociodramatic play was inhibited by the presence of sand, water, puzzles, and art activities.

In planning the program, therefore, it might be wise to schedule free-play periods that emphasize dramatic play and related activities at different times from those periods in which activities that appear to cause distraction are the primary focus. Puppets, blocks, books, art, or woodworking projects in which play props are constructed are among the activities that have been found to stimulate or complement dramatic and sociodramatic play.

Another way to reduce distraction is to set up a separate pretend room with a home, store, and/or another play interest area (Griffing 1980). Children's play in this special playroom was found to be at a higher level than play in the classroom (Soiberg 1972), again possibly a result of less distraction from other activities.

Student teachers with whom I have worked have experimented with devoting an entire free-play period to dramatic play. On one such occasion three centers of interest—a home, post office, and airport—were set up. These centers had previously been available one or two at a time. During grouptime preceding the free-play period, the teachers prepared the children through stories and discussion for play and for integration of the home, post office, and airport. When play began the teachers participated in it for a short period of time, modeling family members going to the post office or airport, and taking letters from the post office to the airport. They were soon able to withdraw from active participation and to serve instead as interested resource people. They helped the children procure, for example, a second small wagon when one was needed at home for garbage pick up as well as for carrying luggage and mail to and from the airport. All but one or two children in this group of 16 three- to five-year-old preschoolers responded enthusiastically to this experience. They played actively at varying levels of social and cognitive complexity for a 40-minute period with minimum adult guidance.

Space and basic equipment

Housekeeping and block areas are among the play spaces in which dramatic play is most likely to occur, and both require continual attention and planning (see Hirsch 1974). It is important to examine these areas with a critical eye each week, if not each day. Are children becoming involved in dramatic or constructive play in these areas? If not, what could be done to make them more inviting and more likely to support sustained play?

Location of learning or interest centers also needs attention. Tizard, Philps, and Plewis (1976a) and Field (1980) observed more imaginative play and/or more social interaction among children when rooms were partitioned into smaller play areas than when more open space designs were utilized. On the other hand, some opening up of space may be helpful, as when Kinsman and Berk (1979) joined block and housekeeping areas.

Use of other pretend areas can greatly expand the potential for dramatic play in many classrooms. Wood (1976) arranged dramatic play space in the gymnasium of her school for her class of 11 second graders. Four centers of interest were planned: a home and store, which were present every day for the six weeks of her research; two supplemental areas that varied each week; an occupation area (such as a doctor's office); and an area corresponding to the weekly social studies themes. During the first few sessions the teacher took an active part in play, helping the children to plan themes and roles. Soon, however, the children took charge, rearranging furniture and props according to their plans. The children also introduced new themes and centers of interest that had not been planned in advance.

It is advisable to keep the home center in operation even when dramatic play based upon other themes is planned. Playing house continues to be a preferred theme, and it provides familiar, meaningful roles that children can expand into new roles. In addition, home play increases the number of available roles and themes and makes play possible for several children. Finally, integrating the home center with other themes may help children begin to understand the relationship between home and other community activities. The home center and supplemental areas should be within view of each other and within good communication distance. Telephones in each center also encourage communication.

Outdoor settings offer extremely rich potentials for dramatic play, and provision of outdoor dramatic play opportunities may be especially important for some children. Sanders and Harper (1976) found that imaginative play among boys occurred most often in conjunction with large muscle activity. Working-class British children also engaged more often in imaginative play outdoors than indoors (Tizard, Philps, and Plewis 1976b). Indoor large muscle areas are especially appropriate for physically active, boisterous dramatic play.

Props for play

Many teachers have found collections of props for enacting dramatic play themes to be valuable resources. Bender (1971) suggests constructing light but sturdy cardboard boxes in which props for a variety of themes can be easily carried and stored.

The effectiveness of systematic provision of theme-related props, at least on a short-term basis, was demonstrated by Stacker (1978). She found that preschool children who were provided each week for a five-week period with theme-related play materials doubled the amount of imaginative play in which they engaged and maintained this behavior consistently throughout the remainder of the research period. Control group children who were not regularly provided theme-related props did not develop a consistently high level of play even though they shared the same classroom and had the same teacher as the experimental group. Like the older children of Wood's study, the experimental children appeared to acquire favorable expectations associated with dramatic play, as evidenced by their going first to the dramatic play areas each morning.

In another study Friedrich-Cofer, Huston-Stein, Kipnes, Susman, and Clewett (1979) found that providing relevant materials together with selected fantasy segments from "Mister Rogers' Neighborhood" was a highly successful way of increasing children's imaginative play. Theme-related materials included props for play such as puppets from the program, a mock-up of King Friday's castle, clothes similar to those worn by program characters, and steering wheels placed within taped outlines on the floor representing the plane and rocket ship shown in the program.

The realistic props in these studies were selected because young children seem to need (Fein 1979) and prefer (Stern, Bragdon, and Gordon 1976) fairly realistic props. However, in research by Pulaski (1973), it was found that kindergarten and second grade children enacted a greater variety of themes when provided with unstructured props. The kindergarten children of my research were provided with realistic toys and unstructured materials,

and used both types of materials extensively (Griffing 1980).

Extend and enrich ideas for play

Early childhood teachers have regularly employed field trips, stories, pictures, discussions, and visits of community helpers as learning experiences and as ways of stimulating imaginative play. Smilansky (1968) demonstrated the value of such enrichment. Although these activities alone were not sufficient to increase dramatic and sociodramatic play among Israeli children, enrichment combined with helping children learn dramatic play skills was more effective than teaching skills alone.

Participate in children's play? When and how?

If dramatic play activities are based on children's interests and experiences, and if the stage is set with time, space, and materials for play, relatively little in the way of adult involvement is usually necessary. The teacher's role is primarily that of an interested resource person (Kleiber and Barnett 1980) who can help solve problems or who offers an occasional suggestion or additional prop to extend play. Unobtrusive observation is necessary, of course, to know when such actions are likely to be helpful to the children.

Manolo Guevara, Jr.

Playing house continues to be a preferred theme, and it provides familiar, meaningful roles which children can expand into new roles.

More direct intervention methods may be appropriate if the children are inexperienced with dramatic play (although they may express imagination in other ways), if they appear ready to add new elements to play or themes to their play, or if relatively unfamiliar roles and themes are being enacted. Several researchers have been remarkably successful in increasing the extent and quality of children's play, at least for short periods of time (Smilansky 1968; Feitelson and Ross 1973; Freyberg 1973; Rosen 1974; Singer and Singer 1974; Fink 1976; Wood 1976; Saltz, Dixon, and Johnson 1977; and Dansky 1980). Their research provides clues as to what some of these more direct procedures may be. Although the methodology of these studies varied, they often introduced a play theme for each of several play sessions with small groups of children, encouraging children to take roles and enact themes, and modeling role-playing behavior while taking part in play with the children.

This intervention usually took place in the first few play sessions or in the first few minutes of each session. It was a common finding that the children quickly learned new play skills (or to express already existing skills), and the extent of adult involvement could then be greatly reduced.

The importance of phasing out teacher involvement as soon as children are ready to carry on by themselves is stressed by Kleiber and Barnett (1980) as well as by Singer and Singer (1977). "Your job as an adult should be to set the scene and to help suggest a story line. . . . You may need to provide props or simple costumes . . . but once you have indicated to the child how [she or] he can be the teacher, doctor, carwasher, move away . . . let [her or] him make believe in [her or] his own way with [her or] his own materials and ideas" (p. 97).

Teachers may find it helpful to determine their degree of involvement in play in terms of the following adaptation of Wolfgang's (1977) continuum of open to structured behavior. You may (1) show interest in play through open behavior such as unobtrusively observing the children; (2) ask questions, make relatively nondirective suggestions, or supply an occasional prop; (3) model the behavior by enacting a role with the children; (4) if

necessary, as is sometimes the case with developmentally delayed children, give direct suggestions or an explicit demonstration of how to carry out a particular pretend act or type of social interaction. You will probably want to begin with the less structured approaches, move toward more direct involvement, if it is needed, then gradually, as the children begin to demonstrate the necessary play skills, phase out, using only the more open procedures. Remember that the objective is to foster not only imaginativeness and development of social skills but also independence, self-confidence, and joyful, intrinsically motivated play.

Adapt play facilitation methods to the players

Children's play will vary greatly depending upon factors such as age or developmental level, cultural background, play interests, and styles. For example, the play of four-year-olds will probably not be as advanced as that of the five- and six-year-olds described at the beginning of this article. Instead of carrying out roles using complementary speech and action, four-year-olds are more likely to enact roles independently of other children. Iwanaga (1973) found that four-year-olds playing train took on differentiated roles such as passenger and conductor, made train whistle sounds, and cooperated in getting on and off the train together. Other than that, however, there was little adjustment of behavior to that of a peer.

Teachers should not expect, therefore, a high level of socially interactive play among younger children. You can, however, provide a framework for play that permits children to enact similar roles such as bus, train, or space shuttle passenger; shopper; or homemaker; each in her or his own way. At the same time you can help children move toward more interactive play when they are ready for this step. Modeling interactive behavior in play with the children, or telling a story during grouptime that involves interactive behavior and having the children act out the story as it is being told are among the techniques that may be useful. Mandelbaum (1975) details imaginative activities that can complement and contribute to the development of spontaneous dramatic and sociodramatic play. Books by Sutton-Smith and Sutton-Smith (1974) and Singer and Singer (1977) are also useful resources.

The importance of becoming attuned to children's cultural backgrounds was underscored by Curry (1971), who reported how Navajo children suddenly began to play when housekeeping equipment was pushed back against the walls of their classroom for cleaning purposes. For the first time the furniture arrangement resembled that of their circular hogan homes. How often might the play of other children come to life if play materials and

ideas were well related to their experiences!

Wolf and Gardner (1979) identify another source of variation in children's play—play style. In a study of very young children they observed some who were primarily interested in representing social experience in play. Other children found objects and their relationships more intriguing. When presented with a tea set and several dolls, for example, one child began to enact a feeding scene with the dolls and adults in the playroom. The second child, equally intelligent, became engrossed in stacking and rearranging the

---

Table 1. Dramatic play with a supermarket theme.

Objectives

The children will

1. play imaginatively—enact roles of shoppers, cashier, family members, grocery clerk; use toys and other objects to substitute for real items; use actions and gestures to represent real behavior; use language to describe make-believe situations.

2. demonstrate through their play understanding of what supermarkets sell, how produce is weighed, how purchases are made.

3. use related vocabulary: fruit, vegetables, meat, cleaning supplies, cashier, grocery clerk, family members, etc.

4. interact with each other as shoppers, cashiers, grocery clerk, family members.

Organization of space and equipment

The supermarket will face the housekeeping play space to increase communication between the two areas. Items for sale will be housed on two sets of shelves, one for groceries, one for household supplies. A cash register and bags for purchases will be placed on a table at the entrance. A small table with scales for weighing fruit and vegetables will be located nearby. The home center will be arranged with space and equipment for storing purchases as well as for cooking, eating, and other activities.

Materials

1. empty containers representing a variety of different kinds of groceries;
2. small bags of real potatoes to weigh on the scales;
3. empty detergent and cleaning powder cartons;
4. cash register, scales, grocery bags;
5. telephones for home and supermarket;
6. dress-up clothes, purses, wallets;
7. two wheels mounted on blocks with

chairs behind for children who wish to drive to the store via car or bus.

Procedures

The supermarket theme will be developed over the period of one week with a supermarket field trip, pictures, stories, and poems. During grouptimes the teachers will show and discuss with the children some of the items that can be purchased at the supermarket and will develop role playing games in which groceries are weighed, purchases made, and different roles enacted.

The dramatic play activity will be introduced early in the week with the setting made increasingly complex as the children become ready for new steps such as weighing groceries. Each day the dramatic play will be introduced by means of a story (sometimes an original one) and/or game highlighting the new roles or procedures that children may carry out if they wish. Other activities available will also involve dramatic play or relate well to it. These will include a table top house and store with human figures and other accessories for home and supermarket play, blocks, books, and articles for the home or store to be made from art materials.

During play the teacher will remain near the dramatic play activity, observing with interest, giving an occasional suggestion ("Do your potatoes need to be weighed, Mr. Bachman?") or possibly taking a role if the children need help starting or maintaining the play. The teacher will then withdraw as the children increasingly become involved. The teacher will be alert to and will support new ideas expressed by the children.

Suggestions for parents will be available regarding ways in which they can help children continue to develop the supermarket play at home.

plates. As in the case of other types of individual differences it is probably wise to respect such differences in style and provide ways for children to express their individuality, but at the same time encourage all children to try out several kinds of play.

Make written plans

Quality dramatic play requires careful planning. It will be helpful to many teachers to prepare written plans for this activity. Table 1 illustrates an example of a plan for a supermarket theme that considers learning objectives, equipment and materials, and teaching techniques.

Enjoy the play

Just as play can enhance and enrich the lives of children, so too can our partnership in their play lift our spirits and heighten our own sense of joyfulness in living. Moreover, our own enjoyment of playful activity and our own creativity in developing it with children are probably the most influential factors of all in fostering playfulness, creativity, and learning.

References

Bender, J. "Have You Ever Thought of a Prop Box?" *Young Children* 26, no. 3 (January 1971): 164–169.

Curry, N. "Consideration of Current Basic Issues on Play." In *Play: The Child Strives for Self-Realization,* ed. G. Engstrom. Washington, D.C.: National Association for the Education of Young Children, 1971.

Dansky, J. L. "Cognitive Consequences of Sociodramatic Play and Exploration Training for Economically Disadvantaged Preschoolers." *Journal of Child Psychology and Psychiatry* 21 (1980): 47–58.

Fein, G. "Pretend Play: New Perspectives." *Young Children* 34, no. 5 (July 1979): 61–66.

Fein, G. "Pretend Play: An Integrative Review." *Child Development* 52 (December 1981): 1095–1118.

Feitelson, D., and Ross, G. "The Neglected Factor—Play." *Human Development* 16 (1973): 202–223.

Field, T. M. "Preschool Play: Effects of Teacher/Child Ratio and Organization of Classroom Space." *Child Study Journal* 10 (1980): 191–205.

Fink, R. S. "Role of Imaginative Play in Cognitive Development." *Psychological Reports* 39 (1976): 895–906.

Freyberg, J. T. "Increasing the Imaginative Play of Urban Disadvantaged Kindergarten Children Through Systematic Training." In *The Child's World of Make-Believe,* ed. J. L. Singer. New York: Academic Press, 1973.

Friedrich-Cofer, L. K.; Huston-Stein, A.; Kipnes, D. M.; Susman, E. J.; and Clewett, A. S. "Environmental Enhancement of Prosocial Television Content: Effects on Interpersonal Behavior, Imaginative Play, and Self-Regulation in a Natural Setting." *Developmental Psychology* 15 (1979): 637–646.

Griffing, P. "The Relationship Between Socioeconomic Status and Sociodramatic Play Among Black Kindergarten Children." *Genetic Psychology Monographs* 101 (1980): 3–34.

Hirsch, E. *The Block Book.* Washington, D.C.: National Association for the Education of Young Children, 1974.

Iwanaga, M. "Development of Interpersonal Play Structure in Three, Four, and Five Year Old Children." *Journal of Research and Development in Education* 6 (1973): 71–82.

Kinsman, C. A., and Berk, L. E. "Joining the Block and Housekeeping Areas: Changes in Play and Social Behavior." *Young Children* 35, no. 1 (November 1979): 66–75.

Kleiber, D. A., and Barnett, L. A. "Leisure in Childhood." *Young Children* 35, no. 5 (July 1980): 47–53.

Mandelbaum, J. "Creative Dramatics in Early Childhood." *Young Children* 30, no. 2 (January 1975): 84–92.

Pulaski, M. A. "Toys and Imaginative Play." In *The Child's World of Make-Believe,* ed. J. L. Singer. New York: Academic Press, 1973.

Rosen, C. E. "The Effects of Sociodramatic Play on Problem-Solving Behavior Among Culturally Disadvantaged Preschool Children." *Child Development* 45 (1974): 920–927.

Rubin, K. H., and Seibel, C. "The Effects of Ecological Setting on the Free Play Behaviors of Young Children." Paper presented at the annual meeting of the American Educational Research Association, 1979. (ERIC Document Reproduction Service No. 168 691)

Saltz, E.; Dixon, D.; and Johnson, J. "Training Disadvantaged Preschoolers on Various Fantasy Activities: Effects on Cognitive Functioning and Impulse Control." *Child Development* 48 (1977): 369–380.

Sanders, K. M., and Harper, L. V. "Free-Play Fantasy Behavior in Preschool Children: Relations Among Gender, Age, Season, and Location." *Child Development* 47 (1976): 1182–1185.

Singer, J. L., and Singer, D. G. "Enhancing Imaginative Play in Preschoolers: Television and Live Adult Effects." 1974. (ERIC Document Reproduction Service No. 100 509)

Singer, J. L., and Singer, D. G. *Partners in Play.* New York: Harper & Row, 1977.

Smilansky, S. *The Effects of Sociodramatic Play on Disadvantaged Preschool Children.* New York: Wiley, 1968.

Soiberg, S. "A Comparative Study of the Sociodramatic Play of Black Kindergarten

Children." Master's thesis, The Ohio State University, 1972.

Stacker, J. "The Effects of Altering the Physical Setting for Dramatic Play Upon Cognitive and Social Play Levels of Preschool Children." Master's thesis, The Ohio State University, 1978.

Stern, V.; Bragdon, N.; and Gordon, A. *Cognitive Aspects of Young Children's Symbolic Play. Final Report.* New York: Bank Street College of Education, 1976.

Sutton-Smith, B., and Sutton-Smith, S. *How to Play with Your Children (And When Not To).* New York: Hawthorn Books, 1974.

Tizard, B.; Philps, J.; and Plewis, I. "Play in Preschool Centres I: Play Measures and Their Relation to Age, Sex, and IQ." *Journal of Child Psychology and Psychiatry* 17 (1976a): 251–264.

Tizard, B.; Philps, J.; and Plewis, I. "Play in Preschool Centres II: Effects on Play of the Child's Social Class and Educational Orientation of the Centre." *Journal of Child Psychology and Psychiatry* 17 (1976b): 265–274.

Way, B. *Development Through Drama.* New York: Humanities Press, 1966.

Wolf, D., and Gardner, H. "Style and Sequence in Early Symbolic Play." In *Symbolic Functioning in Childhood*, ed. N. R. Smith and M. B. Franklin. Hillsdale, N.J.: Erlbaum, 1979.

Wolfgang, C. H. *Helping Aggressive and Passive Preschoolers Through Play.* Columbus, Ohio: Merrill, 1977.

Wood, J. K. "An Exploratory Study of the Effects of Intervention in Sociodramatic Play Upon Play Behavior and Upon the Social Structure of a Group of Second Grade Children." Master's thesis, The Ohio State University, 1976.

PIAGET: THE SIX YEAR OLD AND MODERN MATH

ETHEL O'HARA

"When I was a child I spoke like a child, I thought like a child, I reasoned like a child." (St. Paul, First Century, A.D.)

As St. Paul said so long ago and as Piaget has been telling us for 50 years, the thinking (cognition) of children is different from that of adults. Often we adults feel that since we can think things out that children can too if they just pay attention and try or if we just drill enough and repeat enough the concepts we want them to understand. However, if we are to take seriously the theories Piaget has advanced, we must revise our attitudes and the demands we make of children.

Piaget is called a developmental psychologist because he believes that cognition develops in a set pattern and at a somewhat standard rate for all people. He believes that each person must go through each stage of cognition, that no stage can be omitted. Cultural background and intellectual ability may cause variations in the length of stages, but the cognitive development follows patterns with all children, as do teething and walking.

Piaget has described four main stages through which children develop in their thinking:

Stage one is called the sensori-motor period and refers to the way babies learn about their world through their senses and their motor responses to what they sense. It lasts from birth to about age two.

The second stage, which lasts from about ages two to seven, is known as the preoperational stage of concrete operations.

The third, called the concrete operational stage, lasts from approximately ages seven to 11. It is characterized by the ability to deal with two relationships or properties at the same time.

After age 11, most children arrive at the fourth stage, known as formal operational thought. They are then capable of abstract thinking (thoughts about thoughts) and no longer have a great need for the handling and manipulation of concrete materials.

As a first grade teacher, I will concentrate in this article on children in the second stage.

The thinking of stage-two children has many characteristics which make them interesting and delightful. It is really because their thinking is so different from ours that we find them so charming and cute.

Following is a discussion of some characteristics of the thinking of the preoperational child which Piaget has described.

Animism means that the child gives human characteristics to inanimate objects. Often dolls or teddy bears take on very human qualities. Children's books such as *Winnie-the-Pooh* are based on this delightful characteristic of childhood. The difference between children's thinking and adults' is that even if adults enjoy the story they know and accept the reality of what a teddy bear can do—children really do not.

A perfect example of this happened when I read *Ben and Me* to a group of first graders. It is a book

more suited to children a few years older, but since a child had brought the book to me, I attempted to read it with a brief explanation that the story is told by a mouse who lived in Ben Franklin's house and helped Ben with his inventions. One little boy asked, "Did the mouse really write the story?" I explained that Robert Lawson had written the book but had written it *as if* the mouse were telling it.

My little friend again asked, "But did the mouse really do it?" He simply could not think about the mouse in two ways at the same time. The child would have been perfectly well satisfied with a "yes" answer—that the mouse had told the story—but my answer had been quite beyond his understanding at that time.

This inability to see something from two viewpoints at the same time is also the reason young children don't understand any but the most obvious kinds of jokes. At about age seven, the light suddenly dawns and they "get the joke." It is at this stage that they go around telling jokes to everyone and get such a kick out of them. They have discovered the secret of what's funny.

Billy at about age seven told this joke—"What do you do if you break your toe?" When no one knew the answer, he said, "Call a tow truck." Everyone laughed. Later, his little sister (age four) told the same story except that she said, "What do you do if you break a toe?" Her answer was, "Call a truck."

Her preoperational way of thinking had made her miss the point. It seems that a good test of child

Reprinted with permission from *Today's Education*, September/October 1975, pp. 32-36, Journal of the National Education Association and Ethel M. O'Hara, M.A.T. Teacher, Grade 1, Mahopac Public Schools, Mahopac, NY.

development could be made by telling jokes to children and evaluating their responses.

Centering is another characteristic of preoperational thought which emphasizes the child's inability to consider more than one aspect of a situation at a time. An experiment which shows this can be done with two containers, one a short, wide jar, and the other a tall, thin one. If a child takes an even number of beads, puts one bead into each jar, and continues until all the beads are gone, there should be an equal number in each jar. The preoperational child will center on one characteristic, perhaps the height of the beads in the containers and insist that there are more in the tall, thin jar than in the short, wide one. Because the children in stage two do not yet have the concept of equality and the conservation of quantity, their sensory perception (what they see) fools them.

Still another characteristic is *egocentrism*, which refers to the child's inability to take another person's point of view. This quality of egocentrism undoubtedly accounts for the sibling rivalry we have all seen, and the young child's inability to enjoy competitive games. Egocentrism makes it impossible for children to share their parents willingly or to lose a game without tears.

In the nursery school, children play side by side, talking, each in a monologue, paying little attention to the others. This kind of play in the company of other children but not really together is sometimes called *parallel play*. The talking is called the *collective monologue*—each talking in the presence of the others but not really communicating. This type of play and speech is typical of the egocentric preoperational child.

Most of us are aware of how young children confuse time, ages, and relationships. When they see the teacher's husband, they say, "Your Daddy is here." When her daughters visit, they say, "Your sisters are here."

Last year I listened while a group of second graders discussed the ages of the five adults in their room. They decided the 6'2" young man of 25 was the oldest and the 5'10" young lady of 21 next oldest. Apparently they centered on height as their criterion for determining age. They completely ignored the gray hair, glasses, and mature but short figure of the middle-aged teacher who was also there.

Since children grow taller as they grow older, they naturally associate tallness with being older. Their preoccupation with their own growth is probably what leads them to the wrong conclusion.

Their centering on one characteristic at a time is evident. Although second graders are at an age when most of them can consider two characteristics at the same time, they do not always do so.

First graders, six years of age, look like their younger siblings, and their thinking is more like that of younger children than of those older than they. When we see true believers in Santa Claus or the Tooth Fairy, we know what a different view of life they have from ours. Adults see Santa's makeup, his false beard, and the padded red suit, but the child is completely awed and thrilled at seeing Santa himself.

On Halloween, six-year-olds in their costumes are absolutely convinced that people don't recognize them. They are sure they look like pirates, witches, or whatever.

One Halloween two very little boys wearing bunny masks visited their neighbors. One neighbor said, "Why look at these two little rabbits! Put away the candy and let's get some carrots." The older boy, who was about three and a half, quickly told everyone, "We're not really bunnies. We're the boys from next door."

The six-year-olds may not be as naive as those little ones were, but they are easily swayed by appearances and are often not ready for the reasoning expected of them.

Having given some idea of what the child in Piaget's preoperational stage of development is like, I should like to relate all of this to the first graders in our schools, since by reason of age alone most of them are preoperational in their thinking.

It is my belief that many of the things included in first grade programs, particularly in mathematics, are completely unsuited to children of this age. We teachers are trying to help six-year-olds build concepts for which they are not ready.

Among the concepts that first graders find most difficult is the *associative property of number*, known as *regrouping* in first grade. Most children simply cannot follow the reasoning that goes with this example:

$$9 + 4 =$$
$$9 + (1 + 3) =$$
$$(9 + 1) + 3 =$$
$$10 + 3 = 13$$

The idea behind this regrouping is that since it is easier to add a number to 10 than to some other number, we should regroup to make our work easier. It is logical from our adult viewpoint to do this, but first grade children do not yet have the maturity of thought necessary for them to regroup on their own. When we demonstrate, using counters for 9 and 4 and regroup them by moving them to make 10 and 3, they can almost follow our thinking, but I believe that there is very little carry-over to their thinking. The whole concept remains meaningless (perhaps through second grade too) for most children.

Most of the math programs for first graders do not include the associative property concept until near the end of their first grade programs. And even then, only a few of the really bright children get something out of it, so, on the whole, it seems to me unsuited to first grade.

I find that children often understand things on a concrete level but have trouble with the written expression of the same idea. This is especially true with the chevron symbols for "greater than" or "less than." If we show them a counting frame (abacus), they can see that 23 is more than 18 or less than 32. But when it comes to writing or reading the number sentences, they have trouble.

Eventually they get so they can make the chevron point to the smaller number, but then they can't read it without help. They can't remember which way the chevron points when they say "less than" or when they say "more than." It is really a complicated process, and I question its value in first grade.

Frances L. Ilg and Louise Bates Ames tell us in their book, *School Readiness,* that oblique lines are the most difficult ones for children to make. Most children before age seven cannot make the diamond (◊) because of its oblique lines, and yet our math programs ask children to make the arrows (<) for less than and (>) for more than.

Another place that I feel we move too far in first grade is in teaching measurements such as cups, pints, and quarts. It is fine for children to use containers, to play with them, and to hear the measurement vocabulary, but we shouldn't expect them to understand concepts such as four cups to the quart.

On one of the standardized tests we give, I have found that almost all of the six-year-olds are sure they can fill six cups from a quart. When we ask how many cups can be filled from a quart, they always mark *all* of the six cups shown, and I suspect if there were more, they would still mark all of them. Yet so many of our math programs make an attempt to present this concept of changing quarts to pints and cups and so on to these six-year-olds, who, Piaget tells us, *cannot* reverse their thinking; i.e., they cannot see in their minds that four full cups can be transformed into exactly one quart and vice-versa.

I have found it frustrating trying to get these younger first graders to "know" their number facts cold.

We give them much experience in counting, using number lines and folding perception cards (they look like large dominoes). After constant repetition of certain facts such as $3 + 2 = 5$ or $5 - 3 = 2$, I find that many children still must count each time they meet these facts in their work.

Newell C. Kephart, in his book, *Learning Disability: An Educational Adventure,* says, "Drill may be important . . ., but it will become important only after the concept has been developed, not before." Applying this principle to all first graders, perhaps we should expect less of our first graders.

It is startling to see young first graders always start over from one when combining addends even though they have just counted out blocks for each addend. For example, when they meet the number sentence $5 + 3 = \square$, they count out five blocks and then three more. When they are told to put them together, they cannot start from five and then count six, seven, eight. Instead, they count all the way from "one" again, indicating they are not conserving quantity.

One of the tests used to see if children do conserve quantity shows five blocks in an extended row and five in a short row in this fashion.

☐ ☐ ☐ ☐ ☐ ☐☐☐☐☐

Preoperational children will insist the extended row has more blocks. They think the long row has more blocks than the small group even after counting each and finding five in each. If five blocks in a long row are more than five in a small group, then what does *five* mean to these children? Are they ready to work with numbers with any real insight?

Of all the concepts presented in first grade math programs, I believe that the missing addend is the one which children find most difficult.

For example, I gave Paul, a child almost seven years old who had completed first grade in a school where an attempt is made to teach this concept, a sheet of arithmetic

equations of the type used in his mathematics program. Some were very easy and some were more difficult because of what we usually call their abstract quality.

Paul had counters (small blocks) to use. I had given him 10, since no sum was greater than 10. When he met the equation $4 + \square = 9$, he started counting, decided he didn't have enough blocks, and had to get more. After he answered with 13, I asked him to read the equation. As he read $4 + [13] = 9$, he immediately realized it did not make sense. He was quite surprised, and when we reread it as $4 + [\text{how many}] = 9$, he got the right answer.

In each case when he made an error, he was able to see the answer did not make sense when I asked him to read the equation aloud. From experience with younger first graders, I would say that, unlike Paul, almost none of them can see the absurdity of their answers.

The characteristics of preoperative children, which I feel interfere with their dealing with equations, are *centering, transductive reasoning,* and *irreversibility.*

Most six-year-olds can learn to count objects accurately. They can count to 100 by ones, twos, fives, and tens with some understanding and can add and subtract vertically:

$$\begin{array}{cc} 3 & 5 \\ +2 & -3 \\ \hline 5 & 2 \end{array}$$

They can do equations such as $3 + 2 = \square$ and $5 - 3 = \square$, but almost all have great difficulty understanding equations where the unknown is in a different position as in the following:

$3 + \square = 5$ (Here they answer 8.)

$\square + 2 = 5$ (Their answer is 7.)

$3 = \square - 2$ (They answer 1.)

By checking the *wrong* answers (à la Piaget), we can see they are centering on the sign (the + or −) and operating on the numbers without trying to give meaning to the number sentence. I have always called it a reading problem—one of comprehension—and not a math problem. Since studying Piaget, I feel that preoperational children can't understand these so-called abstract equations because they don't yet have the concrete operations of thought necessary to deal with them.

Another characteristic which may prevent six-year-olds from dealing logically with equations is an inability to see things as a whole (*transductive reasoning*). Perhaps they focus on each element of the equation separately and cannot put them together into a coherent thought. Since the elements of the equation remain separate in their thinking, the whole number sentence (a first grade term for equations) remains meaningless. This is also probably the reason six-year-olds cannot understand the associative property of number. They just don't connect the several steps in the regrouping process.

Irreversibility means that if six-year-olds see something one way, they cannot automatically see the reverse, which indicates to me that to six-year-olds it does not follow that since $6 + 1 = 7$, then necessarily $7 - 1 = 6$. Our textbooks usually present subtraction in this fashion. Perhaps, in spite of our best efforts, preoperational children do not understand the reversibility of addition and subtraction but deal with each equation or algorism separately.

Does irreversibility enter into the difficulty six-year-olds have with the equation $4 + \square = 6$? Maybe it does, since they don't understand that they must think "how many more" (an additive approach to subtraction) when the sign $(+)$ tells them to put numbers together.

It has occurred to me that perhaps six-year-olds work on the equations they get right with the same lack of understanding they do on the ones they get wrong. They center in the same fashion on the sign $(+$ or $-)$ and fortuitously get the right answer. Teachers may thus assume they understand the equation when really they do not. This was brought to my attention when I noticed that in subtraction, although the unknown may be in the more abstract position, they get the answer right. For example:

$8 - 7 = \square$ (ordinary position of the unknown)

$8 - \square = 7$ (more abstract position of the unknown)

Here the sign tells them to subtract, and they get the right answer. Is it with understanding or just luck? In the equation $\square - 1 = 7$, the minus sign does not help them, and they usually answer "6."

Some say that the missing addend is included in math programs to teach children that "$+$" does not always mean they should add. While this may be the eventual aim, it seems to me that it is useless to present an idea to children who are unable to understand it because their method of thinking is not yet sufficiently developed.

Some experts in the field of mathematics say that subtraction must be taught as the reverse of addition. Here, again, this is what we hope children will eventually understand when they have had enough experience with the processes of addition and subtraction and have matured sufficiently, but I doubt they can learn it that way in first grade.

The "spiral curriculum," so popular with textbook companies, is built on the premise that we introduce a concept early and then repeat it again and again every six weeks or so, each time building on past experience until eventually the children "get it." Maybe instead of building a concept slowly, we are really introducing children to failure because they are not yet mature enough to learn it. The spiral curriculum for many children may mean failure today, failure six weeks later, failure 12 weeks later, and so on with eventual success at 30 weeks or even in second grade.

Do children need this continual practice and failure? Would they have been more successful and therefore happier if we had waited to introduce these concepts?

At this time, the trend in teaching math is somewhat away from the workbook-textbook approach and toward the mathematics center or workshop with all sorts of games and materials, such as balances, weights, shapes (flat and solid), and containers.

This kind of program seems ideal for first grade, but it is difficult to administer. If the program is too unstructured, some children may try too few things and learn too little. An individual program for each child leaves very little time for each if math time is limited to 30 or 40 minutes a day. A structure that meets minimum needs for most children and allows time for them to experiment and play with mathematical toys and ideas is probably best.

"New Math" came about because educators wanted to put more meaning into math programs. I agree that math with understanding is desirable. It is fun to teach math with Cuisenaire rods and other objects which add a dimension of reality to the abstraction that is number. It is fun to catch the "Aha!" expression when a child discovers a principle. But let's not put into the math program of six-year-olds concepts they are incapable of understanding.

We cannot return to childhood and reason again as children do. We can only do what Piaget has done—observe children and try to understand their thinking. Only then will we devise programs with which they can be comfortable.

Teaching and Evaluation

- Teaching: Possibilities and Problems (Articles 43-45)
- Planning the Environment (Articles 46-47)
- Evaluation of Children (Articles 48-49)

An Early Childhood Education teacher may be enthusiastic, satisfied, apologetic, ambivalent, energized, or fatigued depending upon many overlapping factors at differing times.

Often a teacher of young children shows total self-involvement, hopes for satisfaction and progress, and emerges with both fullfillment and strain, pleasure and pain. There is a deeply embedded societal myth that not much intellectual ability or professional skill are required for those who work with young children. Professionals understand the fallacy, deceptiveness, and dangers of such thinking and are learning to legitimatize their beliefs and articulate their philosophies, policies, and practices to wider audiences.

A persistent problem for the teaching profession is that many very qualified professionals justifiably feel they are overworked and underpaid for the tremendous responsibilities they have. The field of Early Childhood Education is losing many caring and concerned caregivers because they are unable to afford to stay in the profession. Many parents already believe they are paying exorbitantly high fees for child care. In many cases they are unable or unwilling to pay more for the care of their children. Until there is a collaborative effort among the government, corporations, and parents to provide quality child care, staff salaries, which constitute seventy percent of a program's budget, will continue to be low.

An emergent issue concerns the possibility of abuse of children while they are in child-care centers. Although less then two percent of sex abuse cases occurs in child-care situations, media magnification of this devastating problem has caused many parents and children to panic unnecessarily. Teachers are now becoming understandably concerned about their ability to carry out normal teaching duties such as comforting children, assisting with toileting, or providing the much needed physical contact that is a normal part of working with children on a daily basis.

Most early childhood educators understand the tremendous affect different environments have on humans. They have had specific training in providing safe, challenging learning environments and in helping children feel comfortable in them. These settings can be created in vari-ous ways: to be physically inviting or discouraging; to be emotionally open and helpful, or tense and hurtful; to be socially democratic, laissez faire, or autocratic; to be intellectually rich and challenging, or sterile and deadening; to be creatively unstructured, low-structured, or high-structured and flowing, or frozen.

Another critical role teachers play is the systematic observation of children in their programs. A first purpose is to diagnose individual and group abilities, interests, and needs. A second purpose is to use the information gained to plan and monitor diversified and challenging learning opportunities.

This section presents interpretations of what teaching actually involves, evaluation of classroom environments, and ways of observing children.

Looking Ahead: Challenge Questions

Are teachers overly concerned about being sued for committing sexual abuse? Is this concern keeping them from fulfilling their duties as teachers?

What can be done to keep quality teachers from leaving the profession because of low pay and status?

How can an early childhood setting be evaluated for creativity?

What purposes are served by making accurate, systematic observations of children? How can teachers effectively use running records, checklists, and informal interviews?

How can teachers help parents understand their children's test results?

The Satisfactions

James L. Hymes, Jr

Young children want to solve their own problems.

The profession of Early Childhood Education isn't one problem after another. The field offers many deep satisfactions. One solid satisfaction—it has been the theme of much in the earlier pages—is *the chance to work in a still unsettled, expanding field where there is much work to be done.* Early Childhood Education is a good field for activists. It offers everyone the real possibility of contributing to the solution of problems.

A second satisfaction in Early Childhood Education is *the chance to work with parents as well as children.* All teachers in the field—in nursery school, kindergarten, child care, Head Start—need to work closely with parents. These adults can be good friends; they can become true allies. Associating initimately with them can be a rewarding experience. You don't work with children alone.

The main joy, however, will come from your response to the children themselves. Most people, of course, say, "I love little children." If you have worked with older youngsters, you probably "love" them too. Children of all ages are not hard to like. The best way of being sure that early childhood is *your* field is to match yourself up against the strengths that are peculiar to young children. This way you can be more sure that *young* children—not just all children—will bring you special satisfaction.

Young children—from birth—are highly imaginative, for example. Does this thrill you? They are creative, in paint and blocks and language. They are experimental, ever trying something that no one else has thought of doing. Do you get excited by freshness and innovation, or does it seem better to you when people stick to the tried-and-true?

Young children have a biting curiosity. This makes some people a little uncomfortable. How do you feel about children probing all the time? With questions, with their fingers, getting up so very close so they can be sure to see? You have to prize curiosity if you work with the early childhood age range, not want to shut it off and short-cut it.

The whole age range is bursting with ego. This is not surprising, but not everyone likes it. As babies, these children do not know they exist. Later, they have moments when it is hard for them to realize that anyone else exists. They want to try everything (even though you could do the job better and quicker). They want to solve their own problems (even though you could show them how in a jiffy). Some people work with young children because they want to tame them and civilize them and make them like the rest of us. A teacher has to have a due regard for the rights of all, but you won't get any fun out of spending time with young children unless you treasure individuality. The job at this age level is to build children up, to make individuals strong, not to knock them down and keep them in their place.

These are active children, not meant to stay put, not meant to stay seated, not meant to line up. They can work hard but almost never in one great big beautiful group. Five or six or seven or more different activities must be going on at once. Does the thought of this drive you crazy? You always have to have something up your sleeve, a ready suggestion as one small group tires of what it is doing. You can't run out of ideas. You have to think of your feet. And, because there is so much going on all at once, you have to be observant. You need eyes in back of your head, and sometimes you will wish that you had six pairs of hands. All the busyness and movement wears some people down to a frazzle in no time. Their great urge is to stand in front of the class and talk and be TEACHER, with everyone's eyes glued on them. How about you? How do you feel? What do you like?

There is always a lot of emotion in young children's groups. These boys and girls have strong feelings. A child may be hurt, and hate, for the moment. You see glee—it gets loud and noisy, for the moment. You see fear. Many people would rather work with older children who keep their feelings hidden. Some take it as their job to get young children to cover up how they feel or to pretend that they do not have emotions. The good teacher of young children starts on the assumption that youngsters do have feelings, and that the emotions are a real and important part of life.

You have to be smart, and very well-informed to teach young children well. Don't think of working with young children unless you do quite well in English, in science, history, math. . . . If you work with older children you have the textbook to protect you. Three- to eight-year-olds can pop any question at you: about dinosaurs or rockets, about China or twins or what makes a rainbow, or anything under the sun. If school work has always been a chore for you, these curious youngsters will show you up.

Of course, you can't know everything. No one can. But it is the spirit that counts. These children are in love with life. Everything around them looks so appealing and exciting and mysterious and wonderful. If you too are in love with learning, you will get a lot of satisfaction from working with your soulmates. If reading, thinking, puzzling, and asking bore you, then do watch out. A lot of people make the mistake of assuming you don't have to be very academic to work with young children. They really are off base. They probably are fooled because the good teacher of young children does not talk much at the whole group of children. You can't get through to these children with lectures and a lot of words. But these children want to find out, and they want the truth, and they ask very rock-bottom questions. You have to be on your toes to keep up with them.

One last satisfaction: *You will have a lot of freedom teaching in Early Childhood Education.* You are more apt to be your own boss. This is especially true in the nursery school, and this is one of the reasons why so many nursery school teachers truly love their work. But there is freedom in Head Start and in kindergarten and in child care, also. There is less chance of some confining "approved" course of study that has to be covered. Actually, there is also more freedom in the primary grades than most teachers take advantage of.

Often the teacher in early childhood can do almost what s/he pleases. This is very deeply satisfying *if* what you please is significant. The little world, the private world of your children's environment can be a laboratory in democ-

Prize curiosity if you work with young children; don't shut it off and short-cut it.

racy. It can be where young children get their first outside-the-home taste of what it means to live in America.

The way you speak to children, how you conduct yourself, your relationships, the tone and climate and spirit of your group, these can all be expressions of your best dreams for how you wish everyone would live. Guided by reason and with a respect for law. With a devotion to freedom. With a reverence for the right of all to life and liberty and to the pursuit of happiness. Where the majority have their rights but where even the single lone individual has rights, too. A place of decency, of kindliness, of warmth and friendship, a place where a child feels safe.

To teach young children well you must study children. You must study much subject matter. You also have to be a student of how this country of ours lives, and of how it could live and prosper even better. If you use your freedom to help young children grow and develop, teaching can bring great pleasure to you, a good start in life for the children, and a firm base for the future.

OVERWORKED AND UNDERPAID

Everyone agrees that day care
providers should earn more,
but who will foot the bill?

MARY ELLEN SCHOONMAKER

After 19 years on the job, Mary Clark should be making more money than most of the people in her field. That she isn't is no reflection on her abilities or her dedication. Mary Clark is a day care teacher, in a profession where even people with college degrees can be too close for comfort to the minimum wage.

Mary Clark works in the Patricia M. Hassett Day Care Center in a Boston housing project, and she makes about $5 an hour. She started in the 1960s at half that amount, and, with the nickel-and-dime raises she got over the years, she and her husband, a packer in a frozen-food plant, reared eight children. In darker moments, she says, she thought about looking for a better-paying job. But her bottom line was the need of the day care children, many from unstable homes, for something solid.

"It's not very good for the little ones to keep changing teachers," she says, noting that because of the low wages, there has always been high staff turnover at the nonprofit, subsidized center. "Caregivers don't want to leave, but they can't afford to stay," she says. Some of those

who do stay work two jobs to make ends meet. And it's only since joining a union in 1979 that the workers receive health-insurance coverage.

Poor salaries are not limited to financially strapped centers in rundown urban areas. In the brightly painted profit-making day care centers that dot suburban highways and cater to professional couples, in mom-and-pop storefront centers, in church schools and nursery schools, the hourly pay can be even lower, in the worst instances floating just above $3.35, the minimum wage. "The difference is not significant between profit and nonprofit centers," says Roger Neugebauer, editor of the *Day Care Information Exchange,* a Seattle newsletter. "They both pay abominably poor wages."

Neugebauer co-authored a national study, by region, of child care staff wages. People can earn as much money making hamburgers, he found, as they can in a job where they are responsible for the well-being and education of children. "Places like K mart and McDonald's are competing for the same group of people," he says.

In 1983, workers in day care centers

averaged $168 a week, according to the Bureau of Labor Statistics, while garage and service-station workers made an average weekly salary of $202, janitors $242, and cabdrivers $256. Given those numbers, it's no wonder child care work has been among the top 10 of the country's job categories with the highest turnover, along with such occupations as dishwashing and pumping gas, according to the most recent BLS study.

"It's a scary, scary thing, staff turnover," says Marcy Whitebook, one of the founders of the national Child Care Employee Project in Berkeley, California. "My son's main teacher changed three times last year."

Equally scary, day care policy experts believe low salaries are directly related to the competency of workers. While a number of people strongly interested in working with young children, such as older women seeking only to supplement their husbands' income, have not been deterred by the paltry wages, they have also attracted people who can't get any other job. Licensing requirements for day care workers vary from state to state, and are in most cases minimal. The result,

From *Working Mother*, June 1985, pp. 110-112, 114, 115. Copyright © 1985 by McCall's Publishing Company.

says Gwen Morgan, a lecturer on day care policy at Wheelock College in Boston, is a random "mix of dedicated people and incompetent people."

The problem with such a mix is that child care, at least for very young children, is a personal transaction, not a product that any stranger can supply. Clearly, there is a crucial relationship between salaries and the quality of care. Morgan calls it a "tri-lemma," a problem affecting parents, children and workers. If parents cannot, or will not, pay the real cost of child care, she asks, who does? "Either the child pays, by receiving really bad care," she says, or the staff pays, "subsidizing child care by accepting much lower salaries than they should." In any event, Morgan warns, "Somebody has to pay."

Although a peek into any day care center usually reveals what looks like choreographed chaos, there is a structure to the care that's going on, beginning with the titles and responsibilities of the caregivers. They are generally divided up between teachers and assistant teachers, those with more training and experience on the one hand, and aides, with less experience, on the other. Depending on state licensing requirements, a teacher can have anywhere from a few college credits in early-childhood education to a two-year or four-year degree, while an aide may be required only to have a high-school diploma. Teachers are generally paid about one third more than the aides, according to Marcy Whitebook, and have the ultimate responsibility for the children. However, says Whitebook, a former day care teacher herself, the lines of responsibility between caregivers can sometimes blur, and in those cases, "There isn't that much difference as to what they do." At bottom, they are all there for the children.

Day care workers with a college degree, if they are involved with preschoolers in a good program, do much the same work as kindergarten teachers, except day care professionals may put in longer hours. And they are likely to be getting paid a lot less. Whitebook suggests paying day care workers on a comparable level with other teachers. "I'm not so naive as to believe that that's what we're going to realize anytime soon," she admits. "Now we just want to get them above the poverty level."

Donna Lee Scro, a young woman who works at the Leonard Johnson Day Nursery, a nonprofit center in Englewood, New Jersey, is a college graduate certified to teach in New Jersey's public schools. She has 17 four- and five-year-olds eight hours a day, in varied activities from math and reading readiness to art, music and science. "It's anything but babysitting," she says. "And it's as important as teaching kindergarten and first grade. You can really accomplish a lot with this age-group."

Yet Scro's annual salary, about $10,700 in her third year at the center, is at least five or six thousand dollars less than she would make as a kindergarten teacher with the same experience in northeastern New Jersey. So, although she "truly loves" working with small children, Donna Lee Scro does not plan to make it a lifetime career. "I will eventually go into something that pays more money," she says.

Unless she were to become a live-in nanny for a well-to-do couple—one New Jersey nanny working for the executive of a large corporation got a five-room apartment and a Mercedes—Scro would have a hard time finding a child care worker's job that pays much more money. Profit-making centers, whether small and privately owned or large national chains, generally pay no better.

The largest day care chain in the country is Kinder-Care Learning Centers, Inc., which expects to open its thousandth center this year. Headquartered in Montgomery, Alabama, it now has over 900 centers in 40 states and Canada. Kinder-Care is a Wall Street winner—its last fiscal year, it reported record net earnings of more than $16 million, up 49 percent from the year before—and the centers standing under its trademark red bell towers have clean, open classrooms, cheery decor and impressive toys and playground equipment.

Much of Kinder-Care's ability to provide such standardized attractions—and generally moderate fees—comes from keeping its costs, including labor, very low. "We try to be as competitive as we can with salaries," says Edward Gibson, vice president of human resources at Kinder-Care, "and still give a return to stockholders."

A few years ago, Kinder-Care was paying its teachers starting salaries at or near the minimum wage. Today, Gibson emphasizes the fact that no day care teacher employed by Kinder-Care starts at the minimum wage. Teachers start at $3.60 or $3.70, he says, or as high as $4.25 or more. Employees are also entitled to periodic merit raises—they are not automatic—and those who work 20 hours a week or more are eligible for benefits, including health insurance, Gibson says.

The growth of corporate day care—child care associated with a parent's employer—has done little to raise the pay of child care workers either, according to Dana Friedman, senior research fellow at the Conference Board in New York City. That's because the employer usually hires an outside agency to provide the care and does not consider the child care workers its own employees.

In order to keep their parent fees low, all kinds of day care centers are tempted to resort to cost-cutting practices, and that usually means the staff will be affected. "In a labor-intensive industry, such as child care is," says Marcy Whitebook, "the main way to cut costs is to do it through the workers."

These practices can range from not paying caregivers for overtime to fudging state-mandated teacher-child ratios and squeezing in a few extra kids with one teacher, or giving workers the day off without pay if not enough children show up.

Some centers save money by hiring college students who are studying early-childhood education and paying them less than other workers. Whitebrook says that can be a good idea if the students are adequately trained and supervised in a professional atmosphere. "But it takes a lot of energy and resources to do that," she says.

Why are child care workers' wages so low? For one thing, the job is basically considered women's work, and women in general make about 64 cents for every dollar made by men. For another, the only way to meet even tolerable staff-child ratios and still charge fees parents can afford is to trade off wages.

Whose problem is it? The question goes to the heart of the financial fix so many caregivers find themselves in. By working for substandard wages, child care workers are subsidizing an entire industry to the tune of millions of dollars each year.

Certainly, some parents could afford to pay higher fees. Nancy Travis, director of Save the Children in Atlanta, which operates a child care information and referral service, says, "Some of us who could afford more are contributing to exploiting women. But we don't think about it."

However, in a majority of families the cost of child care takes an enormous chunk out of income, running only behind food, housing and taxes. And if parents are single, they are apt to be struggling just to make ends meet.

"The bottom line is who is going to pay," says Dana Friedman. "Parents can't, government won't, and corporations don't know about it yet or aren't doing much about it. But there is no other problem to talk about. All roads lead back to funding. We need a massive infusion of dollars from someplace." Friedman's personal pessimistic thoughts on where the money might come from: "pennies from heaven."

For a very small, but growing, number of child care workers, the answer is to get out, organize, and negotiate with their employers for higher wages and benefits. Workers in New York City have long benefited from the clout of the American Federation of State, County and Municipal Employees. Certified day care teachers in subsidized centers there start at over $15,000, almost on a par with teachers in the city's public schools. Benefits include medical and dental insurance, even a legal-services plan. And District 65 of the United Auto Workers has had some suc-

cess in Massachusetts, in recent years organizing workers at more than 20 day care centers.

Massachusetts is also the site of a landmark effort to help underpaid day care workers and attract qualified people to the field. Early this year, Governor Dukakis asked the state legislature to set aside $7.5 million to increase the salaries of child care workers in centers that receive state aid. The budget proposal, still under consideration, calls for raising those salaries 30 percent in two years.

Most experts believe that there will be a rocketing demand for child care over the next few years. By 1990, the number of

preschoolers is expected to top 19 million, up from 15.6 million in 1977. But while the doors of day care centers may be bursting, the number of qualified people willing to accept meager wages is expected to shrink—which may force salaries to rise, eventually. Self-sacrificing women like Mary Clark are already hard to find, and young women are no longer willing to work even five years just for the intangible rewards. "A friend has been advertising for a day care teacher for three months now," says Gwen Morgan at Wheelock College in Boston. "The pay is good, although it's nowhere near the public-school salary. Not one person has applied."

Can Teachers Touch Children Anymore?

Physical Contact and Its Value in Child Development

Sally Mazur and Carrie Pekor

Sally Mazur, M.S., is Head Teacher at the Cambridge-Somerville Mental Health and Retardation Preschools Unit, and a faculty member at Community Training Resources, Cambridge, Massachusetts.

Carrie Pekor, M.S., is Head Toddler Teacher at the Wellesley Community Children's Center, Wellesley, Massachusetts, and a faculty member at Community Training Resources, Cambridge, Massachusetts.

As free play time comes to an end for a group of 3- and 4-year-olds, one girl darts back and forth across the room instead of sharing in cleanup. A teacher intercepts her with her arms and reminds the child "It's not time for running but for putting toys away." The child wriggles free and firmly states, "Don't touch me. My mommy told me teachers can't touch me anymore!"

On the day that allegations of sexual abuse in a child care program several miles away are reported by the media, all the parents in a university-affiliated center pick up their children early.

A 24-month-old boy is sitting on a potty chair, unsuccessfully attempting to direct his urine into the potty. Although for years his teacher has been guiding toddlers in a hand-over-hand fashion as they learn how to use the toilet, she is suddenly worried that her actions may be misunderstood.

At a child care staff meeting, the male teachers request that staffing patterns be redesigned so they are never alone with children. The men feel they are being scrutinized and see this step as necessary to protect themselves against false accusations.

A child care director suddenly institutes a new center policy which forbids all of the male caregivers in the program to diaper or in any other way have intimate contact with children.

As teachers of young children, we all face the challenge of effectively and sensitively combining the physical nurturance of children, a crucial component of child care, with awareness and respect for children's autonomy and body integrity. Our efforts to appropriately meet this challenge have been complicated by recent investigations of sexual abuse in child care programs.

These examples represent some typical responses to those investigations and typical perceptions about the role of physical contact with young children. Many child care professionals, like those in the examples, are experiencing a heightened sense of vulnerability.

What are some of the factors in our society that influence the public reaction to the sexual abuse of young children? How do these reactions affect the relationships between parents and professionals, teachers and children, and early childhood programs and the community? Because physical contact is so important for children's healthy development, how can professionals and parents work together to assure the best care for young children?

Public perceptions of child care

The public mistrust of programs for young children reflects our society's ambivalence about child care as an institution. While there is certainly more tolerance for family differences today, the mainstream culture still glorifies the stay-at-home mother, despite the economic necessity that most parents work. Therefore, the low prestige of our profession is evident in the inadequate salaries for providers, insufficient public funding, and piecemeal societal support for group care of young children.

Sensationalistic accounts of sexual abuse investigations have unfortunately furthered this public mistrust. For those unfamiliar with high quality programs for young children, the repeated juxtaposition of child care and sexual abuse gives the inaccurate impression that these two entities are necessarily linked.

The combined effect of these factors is that the public, and parents of young children in particular, may not have a true picture of the extent and nature of the problem. In fact, children are much less likely to be sexually abused in child care than in their neighborhoods or homes. Fewer than 1% of all reported child sexual abuse cases occur in child care (Murphy, 1984). The number of recent cases of abuse in child care reflects a general increase in reporting of sexual, physical, and psychological abuse and neglect.

8. TEACHING AND EVALUATION: Teaching

The incidence of abuse in child care remains consistently miniscule in proportion to the number of cases of abuse that occur in other places. However, the statistics in no way diminish the horror of any incident of child sexual abuse in a program for young children, nor do they negate the concerns of both parents and professionals.

Parent and professional concerns

Despite the relative infrequency of incidents of abuse in programs for young children, each case painfully reminds parents that in some instances, the trust they invest in the professionals who care for their children may be violated. This heightened awareness for parents in turn affects the already complicated relationship between parents and caregivers. While parents have always sought programs for their young children in which the staff are loving and supportive, they are increasingly concerned about finding programs that offer appropriate physical nurturing and guidance.

Teachers share in the horror and dismay about the scattered incidents of child abuse in programs for young children. Although as teachers we sympathize with parents' concerns for the safety of their children, it is hard for us not to feel mistrusted and rejected. When all of the parents removed their children from a program early one afternoon, for example, their actions reflected a breakdown, albeit a partial one, of the necessary trust formed between parents and caregivers.

Because teachers' physical affection and guidance of young children may be under special scrutiny and perhaps misunderstood, professionals are seeking additional ways to convey their intentions in a clear and supportive manner to parents. In doing so, we can stress the value of appropriate touch for healthy human development.

Child development implications

Thoughtful, developmentally appropriate physical contact between teachers and children plays an important role in any early childhood program. Cuddles and hugs, physical caretaking, and setting limits are all part of the daily experience shared between infants and toddlers and their caregivers. This nurturance helps to create and sustain the trusting relationships which enable children to feel secure and to become autonomous.

Older preschool children are navigating the transition from more physically dependent toddlerhood to becoming competent and independent. Teachers can provide children at this stage with physical nurturance carefully balanced with opportunities to express their growing autonomy.

Physical contact is also essential when working with special needs children. In addition to aiding children with mobility problems, physical contact can be a valuable part of the learning process. Very aggressive children or those with other behavioral disorders often require physical restraint. It can be scary for young children to feel out of control, so holding a distressed child tells the child that the teacher will keep her or him safe in the classroom.

It is important to examine the role our own feelings play in our relationships with children. Warm moments spent with a child can be personally rewarding for teachers. The loss of spontaneous affection would be a serious detriment for both children and teachers.

Thoughtful, developmentally appropriate physical contact between teachers and children plays an important role in any early childhood program.

David McPherson

Therefore, as professionals, we must continue to develop a clear theoretical understanding of the importance of physical contact for facilitating children's development. Just as we understand any other aspect of the curriculum, we can use our understanding of the importance of physical contact as the basis for thoughtful interactions with children.

In addition to keeping ourselves informed about the value of appropriate physical contact with young children, we need to discuss the issues openly with one another. Professionals can support each other at a time when we are all concerned and are feeling anxious and vulnerable. We can share ideas about appropriate types of physical interactions with children, and acknowledge the particular sense of vulnerability that male teachers are experiencing. Directors can explore ways with each other to support teachers and consider the role that program policies can play in providing this support.

As professionals, all of us can share with each other our experiences and strategies for responding to the concerns of parents. We can continue to base our physical interactions with children upon developmental principles, rather than to fearfully avoid or feel uneasy about physical contact in the classroom. These principles can and should be shared with parents. The difference between the touching that has an important place in an early childhood program and touch which is sexually exploitative can be clearly communicated and understood in this context.

Well-informed parents will continue to expect the warmth and physical nurturance their children deserve in group care. Through open communication, mutual support, and developmental knowledge, we can provide high quality programs for young children.

Bibliography

Biggar, M. L. (1984). Maternal aversion to mother-infant contact. In C. C. Brown (Ed.), *The many facets of touch.* (pp. 66–72). Skillman, NJ: Johnson & Johnson.

Greenfield, M. (1984, September). Child care salaries and working conditions. *Child Care News, 11*(1), pp. 1, 6.

Hnatiuk, P. (1984, October). Child sexual abuse: A worker's response. *Child Care News, 11*(2), pp. 1, 4–5.

Stern, D. (1977). *The first relationship: Infant and mother.* Cambridge, MA: Harvard University Press.

U.S. Department of Commerce, Bureau of the Census. (1984). Statistical abstract of U.S.: National data book and guide to sources (104th ed.). Washington, DC: Author.

Watson, R., Greenberg, N. F., King, P., & Junkin, D. (1984, May 14). A hidden epidemic. *Newsweek, 103,* pp. 30–36.

Whitebook, M. (1984, September 23). Child care. *San Francisco Sunday Examiner & Chronicle.*

15 Ways To Cultivate Creativity in Your Classroom

Pat Timberlake

Pat Timberlake is Adjunct Professor in Child Care Technology and CDA Adviser, Walters State Community College, Morristown, Tennessee.

---

*. . . Be creative teachers,
Teach creativity, and
Teach FOR creativity.*
Taylor and Getzels, 1975

"SOUNDS GREAT! That says exactly what I want to do . . . but how do I go about *being* a creative teacher, *teaching* creatively and teaching *for* creativity?"

Here are 15 suggestions that may work for you or prompt you to think of other ideas.

1. *Strive to have a classroom environment that is neither completely free nor authoritarian* (Lowenfeld, 1967).

The noise level reveals much about the classroom environment. In an authoritarian classroom, the teacher's voice predominates—or else there is a structured hush. On the other hand, a cacophony of noise is likely to be heard in a completely free classroom.

In the ideal "balanced" environment, noise is also heard—but the noise is a nondisruptive hum of verbal interchange and activity inducing growth in creativity.

2. *Allow pupils to work independently* (Torrance 1976).

Wade was particularly interested in spiders. When he went to the library, he often chose a book about spiders. Outdoors, he probed corners looking for spider webs.

Wade's knowledge was helpful the day a spider was seen on the window ledge in our section of the lunchroom. Some of the children discovered the spider and were frightened by it. Our expert "Spider Man" was called in.

Wade looked at it and pronounced it a crab spider—completely harmless, and he taught us about its beauty and worth. Wade's independent study had served the whole class well.

3. *Be flexible and patient when accidents, distractions or interruptions occur in your classroom* (Gordon, 1961).

The familiar adage "plan your work then work your plan" is valid, but there are times to set your plans aside. One of these times came for our class when workmen cut down the dead tree outside our room. The noise of the saws called us to the windows. How exciting to watch the men fell the tree—and then later to study it and play on it!

The first snow is another time when lesson plans are put aside for the order-of-the-day. Black construction paper, magnifying glasses and thermometers are gathered to be taken outside as soon as pupils are buttoned up.

4. *Allow pupils to experience mistakes* (Torrance).

A mistake made in an activity can provide a remembered lesson. If no harm will come to the pupils, let the mistake happen. By actually mixing colors, pupils learn how to make purple—and how not to. By experimenting with magnets, they soon know what kinds of things are attracted to magnets and what kinds are not. Even a broken flower pot provides a lesson, revealing root structures of a plant that would otherwise be unseen.

5. *Encourage children to ask important questions* (Torrance).

One child's curious question may lead the whole class into new learnings. This happened to us when someone asked, "Do kangaroos have pockets just so they can carry their babies?" That was the year I learned many interesting things about kangaroos—and so did my pupils!

6. *Be aware of habitual, stereotyped activities (such as "Show and Tell," roll call, dismissal) and evaluate them in terms of the amount of time they consume, the*

From *Childhood Education*, September/October 1978 pp. 19-21. Reprinted by permission of Pat Timberlake and the Association for Childhood Education International, 11141 Georgia Avenue, Suite 200, Wheaton, MD 20902. Copyright © 1978 by the Association.

quality of ideas presented and the interest of your pupils (Hymes, 1974; Timberlake, 1973).

Such tasks as checking the roll and reporting the lunchroom count must be done daily, but that doesn't mean there is only one way to do them. A "Who's Missing?" game may involve all those pupils present and, at the same time, provide needed information for the attendance report.

Lining up—sometimes necessary—is more fun when you can choose the person to stand in FRONT of you. Pupils soon catch on that the last person chosen is at the front of the line and becomes the leader.

7. *Plan time for play and provide a variety of materials for play and manipulation* (Gordon; Osborne, 1969; Robison, 1971).

The value of play has been proclaimed by educators for many years. A teacher who wants to encourage creativity will provide a variety of materials for use by the pupils and will schedule time for play.

Many unusual play materials have fascinated and involved my pupils, including an old carburetor, a pair of crutches, two real telephones, a cash register, a bag of odd nails and screws, a box of buttons, tires, a camera without film, keys on a key ring. Inexpensive, but valuable for learning!

8. *Furnish plain paper for art activities in place of ditto or printed outline pictures to color; avoid cutouts and patterns* (Lowenfeld and Brittain, 1975; Jefferson, 1964).

The classic research by Russell and Waugaman showed that children who had been motivated by experiences with birds lost their previous creativity in drawing them when they became familiar with workbook drawings, changing their pictures to resemble the common stereotype (Lowenfeld and Brittain). Russell and Waugaman account for this change as a "devastating result of the influence of workbook methods."

Lowenfeld and Brittain have been most outspoken about the effects of stereotyped art work. After years of experience and research, they describe it as "predigested activities that force youngsters into imitative behavior and inhibit their own creative expression."

Teachers who strive to release the creativity of their pupils must put aside their 25 copies of "Mary's Little Lamb," their glue and white cotton puffs. They must provide, instead, a variety of papers, collage materials, paints, crayons and clay. Pupils will produce as wide a variety of lambs as can be seen grazing on a hill and even some brilliant unreal ones that can't be seen grazing on a hill!

9. *Encourage pupils to do (make, paint, write, build) something that has never been done before, and something that is unlike anything done by another* (DiLeo, 1970).

Children should be challenged to experiment and do things that are different. How excited I was to learn that Pam's picture

was an upside-down mountain! The story she later dictated about the picture was imaginative too.

10. *Provide many opportunities for your pupils to have their own stories, poems, songs and letters written down* (Gowan and Torrance, 1979).

One beautiful day John was singing as he worked, "I'm so happy because—it's spring!" Overhearing the song, the teacher wrote the words on a large piece of newsprint; John then illustrated his song. The whole class enjoyed John's spring song.

11. *Share creative products of others with your pupils—art prints, records, literature, sculpture* (Gowan and Torrance).

Appreciating the creative work of others stimulates pupils to have new ideas. The art print "Children's Games," by Pieter Brueghel the Elder (c. 1525-1569), was displayed over the TV screen. It prompted the pupils' scrutiny, interesting conversation and exploratory movement. "I know that game. It's leap frog!" "I can get twisted up like he is—look!" "Oh, a stick horse!" "And stilts!" "What's that thing he has out the window?" Pupils saw children in the picture playing familiar games, and they also discovered new games and stunts. Through Brueghel's work, our class was linked with another culture and another century.

The creative products of your own pupils may also be shared—with their permission. Never take it for granted that pupils wish to share every creation.

12. *Protect creativity of children from evaluation and ridicule of other children* (Torrance).

The teacher's attitude toward creative children sets the tone for the whole class; pupils tend to copy teacher's acceptance of and value of creativity. Respect for one another's expression and work must be genuine.

A colorful page of paint squiggles can be laughed at, or it can be appreciated for its design and imaginativeness.

13. *Use community resources—libraries, industries, classes at art galleries and creative adults in the community* (Vernon, Adamson and Vernon, 1977).

Martha, a high school violinist, visited our class. Not only did we see and hear her play, but we saw how she cared for her instrument and heard how she became interested in learning to play the violin. We were also impressed with the amount of hard work and study that learning to play well requires. Martha was our artist-for-the-day.

14. *Work with parents to help them understand and appreciate their children's creative endeavors* (Torrance; Leeper and others, 1979).

Parents are eager to hear good things about their children from the teacher. A brief note of praise to the child will be seen and appreciated by the parent too.

At lunch one winter day, James dictated this poem:

> I been outside
> Outside on the cold, wintry day.
>   Good ole, hot soup!
>   Good, yummy, hot soup!

That afternoon, James took home a copy of his poem and a note from his teacher: "Dear James, Your winter poem was just right for today. All of us enjoyed it! Love, Mrs. Timberlake."

James' mother read the poem and note also. A poem that might have been quickly discarded was now valued because James' classmates and teacher appreciated his creative endeavor.

15. *Let your own ideas flow as freely as they will. Be courageous! Try some of these ideas* (Lowenfeld and Brittain; Taylor and Getzels, 1975; Allstrom, 1970).

As you accept and use your own creative ideas, you will probably find that teaching is more fun. You may also find other teachers curious and dubious about some of your activities.

Hurrying outside to watch a repairman climbing a telephone pole or a worker in a cherry-picker hanging a new sign on the restaurant across the street—when it's not even recess!—may take courage and explanations.

Allstrom is right: "When creativity is encouraged and nurtured, it grows and increases. No one can rightly predict just where it will go, what it will do . . . surprises and discoveries fill the classroom."

As a result of *your* creativity, other teachers may catch your enthusiasm and cultivate creativity in their own classrooms.

References

Allstrom, Elizabeth. *You Can Teach Creatively.* Nashville, TN: Abingdon, 1970.

DiLeo, Joseph H. *Young Children and Their Drawings.* New York: Brunner Mazel, 1970.

Gordon, W. J. *Synectics: The Development of the Creative Capacity.* New York: Harper & Row, 1961.

Gowan, John Curtis, and E. Paul Torrance, eds. *Educating the Ablest.* Itasca, IL: F. E. Peacock, 1979.

Hymes, James L., Jr. *Teaching the Child Under Six.* Columbus, OH: Charles E. Merrill, 1974.

Jefferson, Blanche. *The Color Book Craze.* Washington, DC: Association for Childhood Education International, 1964.

Leeper, Sarah Hammond, and others. *Good Schools for Young Children.* New York: Macmillan, 1979.

Lowenfeld, Viktor. *Your Child and His Art.* New York: Macmillan, 1967.

Lowenfeld, Viktor, and W. Lambert Brittain. *Creative and Mental Growth.* 6th ed. New York: Macmillan, 1975.

Osborne, Elsie L. *Your Five-Year-Old.* London: Transworld, 1969.

Robison, Helen F. "The Decline of Play in Urban Kindergartens." *Young Children* (Aug. 1971): 333-41.

Taylor, Irving A., and J. W. Getzels, eds. *Perspective in Creativity.* Chicago: Aldine, 1975.

Timberlake, Pat. "I Hate Show and Tell." *Language Arts* (Apr. 1973): 651-52.

Torrance, E. Paul. *Guiding Creative Talent.* New York: Krieger, 1976.

Vernon, P. E.; G. Adamson and Dorothy Vernon. *The Psychology and Education of Gifted Children.* Boulder, CO: Westview, 1977.

See also:

Kellogg, Rhoda. *Analyzing Children's Art.* Palo Alto, CA: Mayfield, 1970.

Nixon, Arne J. *A Child's Right to the Expressive Arts.* Washington, DC: Association for Childhood Education International, 1969.

thoughts on creativity

Dr. Leland B. Jacobs

Dr. Jacobs is Professor Emeritus of Education, Teachers College, Columbia University, New York, NY.

In children's lives environment always plays a significant role, and persons play a major part in the nature of the environment. Children's sensitive assessment of other human beings is to be taken into account in any environment to which they are exposed. They have keen awareness of social distance, sincerity of responses, consistencies and inconsistencies, as well as fairness and unfairness in adult behavior.

While the principal, the custodian, the secretary, the nurse and special teachers all make a difference in the children's perception of the school environment, it is the classroom teacher and the peer group that provide children's basic security at school. A poised, dynamic, teacher and a pleasant relationship with peers make school a desirable place to be and to learn. The teacher, as environment, sets the tone for the learning experiences during the school year, and thus encourages or discourages creativity.

The Teacher As a Personality
A teacher's personality directly affects the school living of girls and boys. Besides preferring a teacher whose classroom behavior reflects social and emotional maturity, children also favor a teacher who genuinely likes people, whose sense of humor adds zest to the school day, and who does not feel a need to dominate the class. Students work best with a teacher who maintains a classroom atmosphere in which their development is not sacrificed to minimum standards, rigid routines, unalterable schedules and all such evidences of inflexibilities.

Children also appreciate intellectual alertness in a teacher, and a willingness to participate in ongoing projects that the teacher has individuals and groups pursuing. They respect a teacher who has remained childlike but is never childish. What all this would seem to add up to is children hope to have a teacher who gives competent guidance in the planning and carrying through of learning tasks, in sympathetic counseling on problems—both those of individuals and groups—and in promoting those kinds of educational outcomes that foster children's satisfaction in being learners and knowers.

The Teacher As Explorer
A teacher with an inquiring mind is quite the opposite of being a pedagogical mechanic who drills on skills, hammers at subject matter, and shapes all learning endeavors to a prescriptive formula. On a personal level, the teacher as explorer is an inquirer into children's out-of-school life, and their backgrounds and capabilities, but not in the sense of being a spy. As an explorer, the teacher experiments in using instructional materials in uncommon ways, and is innovative and inventive in activities that seem conducive to more meaningful learning. Children view such a teacher as a learner among learners, and as a person who—as the anthropologist Margaret Mead, once stated—is an individual who finds "security in adaptability."

There are yet other recognizable characteristics of the teacher-explorer. Such a teacher helps children find joy in discovery, as an exhilarating experience; considers the classroom a laboratory for functional learning and personal-social living; provides opportunities for trying out various media for the creative arts.

The teacher-explorer liberates children from such inhibitions as are built up through fear of criticism, through feelings of inadequacy, or inferiority, or through blockings because of standards that the individual cannot possibly meet. A teacher-explorer knows that all explorations will not be fruitful, but that is no reason to quit being an explorer. It means, only, that the road taken wasn't a good choice. And there are always other ways to go—so up and away!

Teacher exploration begets children's explorations. From the teacher-explorer children are learning that change and new beginnings are inevitable and may call for modes of responses that old answers, old solutions will not furnish. So one must take the search—must seek and explore.

The Teacher As Expert
Here is yet another aspect of children's expectations of the person at school who is central in their environment. In a democratic way of life there is a place for expertness if it is used to foster individual development and group good. In the classroom, expertness is demonstrated not only in terms of being well-informed in subject matter, but also by being a resourceful "social planner" and a competent guide in nurturing learning experiences.

Authorities have often pointed out that when a teacher is expert, the role of being teacher is conceived as a service agent: service in guiding mastery of skills and comprehension of content; in evaluating progress; in interpreting and extending knowledge, skills, and appreciations. This can happen, the teacher-expert knows, by starting with a child as he or she is and thinks of that individual in terms of what he or she can possibly become. This can happen if there are made

Reprinted with permission of the publisher Allen Raymond, Inc., Darien, CT 06820. From the March 1984 issue of *Early Years,* pp. 102, 97.

8. TEACHING AND EVALUATION: Planning the Environment

available many kinds of materials, with various levels of difficulty, that facilitate different children's learnings. It can happen if children are helped to use efficient, effective methods of acquiring skills and techniques. It can happen, if children are guided in making choices that lead to more discriminative levels of thinking.

The teacher-expert, furthermore, is adept at leading children to improved ways to meet obstacles, confusions, or bafflements in dealing with learning activities. Too, children are encouraged to seek and value increasing independence, self-control, adaptability, and "growing up" generally. The teacher's expertness helps children come to better understand how desirable social processes make group living more congenial and more productive.

All this means that the teacher's expertness manifests itself in the useful knowledge contributed to studies that have been undertaken, in the employment of methods of teaching that engage children in what is being learned, and in social interactions that are espoused for the group's welfare. In other words, the expert in teaching is not a "forcer," a "former," and "inquisitor," but rather a "pacesetter," and "integrator," a leader.

The Teacher As Artist This is an area less frequently given attention, and yet it's at the apex in providing a positive learning environment for children. If teaching is a compositional act in which the content to be learned is ordered so that "the medium is the message," then there is clearly an artistry involved in the way work with children is being done.

In *Art as Experience,* John Dewey has made the point that in any type of experience where each phase flows freely and harmoniously into what ensues, without loss of identity of the parts in the achievement of the whole, there are aesthetic overtones. Thus one can see that when the selection of content for study, the methods and techniques of presentation of the content, the planning, doing and evaluating become a harmony of content and form so children "know what they know"—the art of teaching is in evidence. When the teacher makes those "pedagogical moves" that present the facts and information or skills and abilities with finesse so that there is both a knowing and a feeling response from the learners, there is an artistic effect in the teaching, to which children respond in affective ways.

In what ways do teacher-artist's work demonstrate esthetic qualities? Consider these, as examples—

• The activities of a period and a day are so harmonized and move forward with such proportion that a rhythm of time and a sense of continuity in procedures is established.

• Patterns of instructions that keep desires for further learnings strong are used.

• The development of honest, life-oriented motivations replaces artificial inducements.

• Guidance pratices avoid rigidities, coercions, harsh punishments that lead away from amity or cause disintegration.

Listen to what children have said:

"I remember my kindergarten teacher. She knew how to smile, and we made butter, and she wore a beautiful cameo."

"In second grade we tried to do things as many ways as we could. How many ways could we make a paper basket? How many ways could we arrange our room so we could work best? How many ways could we get out of the building if there was a fire?"

"Our teacher knows how to help a fellow feel he's making good choices in what he is trying to make."

"Our teacher tells us interesting things about our town in the old times."

"Did you know there are two ways to subtract? Our teacher taught us both.

"In our classroom you just feel it's a nice place to be."

The teacher is environment? Ask a child. Children know it very well!

Observing Children:
Ideas for Teachers

Jean S. Phinney

Jean S. Phinney, Ph.D., is an Associate Professor of Child Development in the Department of Home Economics at California State University in Los Angeles.

Skill in observing and interpreting children's behavior is essential to success in any career that involves direct, daily contact with children. Observation contributes to our knowledge of children in general and to our understanding of individual children, helping to correct the biases and distortions that enter into many judgments about children. As Mischel (1979) states, people "tend to infer, generalize, and predict too much, while observing too little."

While most textbooks for teachers preparing to work with young children stress the need for learning to observe, there is considerable diversity of opinion on what observation techniques should be learned or how such skills should be developed (Shaplin 1966). This article examines what observational skills are most useful in working with children, and suggests ways in which a student or practicing teacher can develop those skills.

Teachers working with children use observation in a way quite different from people conducting observational research. Researchers seek to identify general principles or relationships that hold for all children or for a given group of children. Practitioners use observation to understand specific children and to gain information on which to base immediate decisions on how to direct, guide, teach, or respond to them. While the purposes are different, the methods used by researchers have much to offer teachers and students who are more informal observers (Moore and Cooper 1982).

Like scientists doing observational studies, informal observers must observe and record accurately to avoid possible bias in their observations. Descriptive terms must be used with precision to communicate clearly about vague concepts such as shyness and aggression. It is important to be able to draw valid generalizations about groups of children, whether it is a single class, all four-year-olds, or children with special needs.

Even so, research methods alone provide an inadequate model for teachers who deal not with five-year-olds in general, but with particular five-year-olds with unique combinations of experiences, abilities, attitudes, and responses. Teachers need to develop a coherent picture of individual children, based on their observations and knowledge of child development, usually without the use of psychological tests or a block of time to devote to the process. They must make use of chance behaviors observed in a natural setting and must continually revise and update their view of each child as new events occur. Doing this well requires the ability to spot significant behaviors that provide clues to a child's underlying traits, attitudes, or abilities. Good informal observers need to have the clinician's sensitivity to significant behavior, without sacrificing the researcher's rigor and objectivity.

Running record or specimen description

The observational technique most widely used by child development students is probably the running record or specimen description, in which the observer simply writes down everything that a particular child does for a given period of time. A number of books have been devoted to this type of observation (Cohen and Stern 1958; Rowan 1973), and it still seems to be the best way to begin observing. Any attempt to record the behavior of a child immediately poses two key questions of observation: How much information should be recorded? What type of information should be noted? Irwin and Bushnell (1980) define the goal of a running record as that of "picturing situations in words that are precise enough and complete enough that we, or anyone else, can use our records for later analysis" (p. 100). Probably the most complete discussion of this technique is that of Wright (1967), who provides a number of useful guidelines. Among them are the following:

1. Describe the setting, the behavior of the child (including how she or he does something), and the behavior of others who interact with the child.
2. Report each event in a separate sentence, and report all events in chronological order.
3. Describe what the child does, rather than what the child does not do.
4. Separate all interpretative comments or inferences from the recorded observations, for example, by parenthesis or the use of a separate column.

Note how a good specimen record (Table 1) avoids inferences and provides precise details to convey a clear picture of what the child does, rather than giving interpretations and vague statements (Table 2). While the guidelines make recording seem easy and obvious, observers making a running record for the first time soon realize the difficulties in doing so. They

Table 1.
Specimen record that is precise and complete

Observations	Comments
Jeremy is sitting in the sandbox, letting sand run through his fingers. He's singing. He puts all the sand toys around him into a milk crate very slowly. He picks up the crate, moves over two feet, and puts it down next to Stephanie. He says, "Want to play?" but gets no response. He sits down, takes out a pail, fills it with sand, dumps it, and puts it back in the crate. He picks up another crate and puts it on top of his crate of toys. He looks up at Matt who is walking across the yard. Jeremy walks over to him, says, "Come on," and leads him by the hand over to his crate of toys. He lifts up the top crate and they both look inside. They replace the top crate and walk together over to the climbing frame. Matt leaves and goes back to the sandbox. Matt starts to lift the lid off the crate of toys. Jeremy runs over, yelling, "No!" Matt leaves and Jeremy goes back to the climbing frame.	enjoys sand sociable, accepts rejection able to amuse self leadership bossy

Table 2.
Specimen record that is vague and makes interpretations

Jeremy is playing in the sandbox. He wants to play with someone, so he moves over next to Stephanie and asks her to play. Since she won't play with him, he goes to get another boy to play with. The two boys look at the toys in the sandbox. They go together over to the climbing frame, but the second boy prefers to play in the sandbox. When he starts playing in the sand, Jeremy yells at him to stop playing with his toys.

discover how many different ways there are of recording the same event. Because it is impossible to record every behavior, running records are necessarily selective. Beginning observers are often unaware of their tendency to focus on certain aspects of a situation and to overlook others (Bruner and Postman 1949). Becoming aware of this tendency is an important step in becoming a skillful observer.

It is also difficult to observe behavior without making inferences. First attempts at running records are often full of statements such as *the child wants, the child enjoys, the child is shy*. While these statements may be true, they are inferences rather than observable behaviors; other observers might make different inferences. Observers learn with practice to separate the behavior (hitting another child) from the inference (the child is aggressive). Accurate inferences cannot be drawn from a few instances of behavior or a single observation, so each bit of behavior observed must be thought of as a clue to understanding a child.

Beginning observers can develop sensitivity to behavioral clues that lead to appropriate inferences in several ways. One technique is to make a ten-minute running record of a child, and then to write down inferences based only on that ten-minute observation. The observer attempts to identify in the running record the behavioral clues that led to the inferences. If the inferences about the child can not be directly derived from the running record, the observer needs to look at the child's behavior with sharpened awareness to try to identify the significant behaviors that conveyed the impression. It may be that the inference is quite false, perhaps based on the child's resemblance to another child the observer has known. On the other hand, the impression may be an accurate reflection of subtle behaviors, such as nervous fidgeting, that were not included in the running record.

Another valuable technique is to have two observers read a running record and independently record their impressions. Identical behaviors often can lead two people to quite different conclusions. Where one sees leadership, the other may see bossiness; a child who is shy and withdrawn to one person may be quiet and well-behaved to another. In order to observe and describe children with preci-sion, we need to make clear exactly what we mean by terms such as shy, aggressive, sociable, or independent.

Checklists using operational definitions

What behaviors will be considered to indicate the presence of the trait or characteristic? For example, does aggression include name-calling and threatening gestures, or only actual physical contact? Such decisions are arbitrary, because there is no universally agreed-upon definition of aggression. However, to observe the behavior and to agree with another observer on its occurrence, an operational definition is needed, that is, a clear statement of how it is to be defined in a particular case. Operational definitions are helpful for running records, but essential for the use of checklists as an observational technique. A checklist is a selected list of behaviors of interest, precisely defined, whose presence or occurrence may be indicated with a check.

Checklists are valuable tools for assessing frequency or patterns of children's behavior. How often do particular children engage in aggressive acts, exhibit prosocial behavior (such as sharing and helping), or make dependency bids? To investigate such questions, behaviors to be included must be defined, and then children are observed to see if the occurrence of the behaviors can be reliably recorded.

The best way to reach agreement on definitions of behaviors is for two observers to work together. By working with another person we become aware of the difficulty of agreeing on exactly what terms mean, and on how to characterize behaviors in terms of general characteristics. One observer may notice behavior the other misses, or overlook behavior the other sees. This can be a result of one observer looking away for a moment, but it can also result from the tendency of the observer to see what is expected and to miss what is unexpected. An observer may expect that a neatly dressed child will be better behaved than a messy one, or that a child who is competent in one area will be competent in other areas. This halo effect can work in either direction; an initial negative impression can affect our subsequent observations of the child, as can a positive one. The importance of reliability between two different observers becomes apparent. If there is low agreement on occurrence of aggression either the two observers have different ideas of what aggression is, or one (or both) of them are biased.

Once an observer has developed precise definitions that permit reliable observations of behavior, information can be collected on the frequency of occurrence of a variety of children's behaviors (see Table 3). By observing the children in turn for an ample period of time and checking on the list each time the defined behaviors occur, the observer can obtain numerical data that can be evaluated for individuals or groups of children, or to make comparisons between two settings. For example, an observer may determine whether children are more helpful indoors or out, whether there is more aggression in the morning or afternoon, or whether a particular child is more dependent when a sibling is present or absent. Although a single observation of any behavior or pattern of behavior is never adequate for drawing a firm conclusion, it does serve as a starting point for ideas or hypotheses that must be continually re-examined in the light of additional information.

In using frequency checklists, observers may well experience difficulty in defining certain types of behavior clearly enough to classify a single occurrence. Particularly troublesome are continuous behaviors like clinging to a teacher, talking with a friend, or social withdrawal, which may last for a few seconds or many minutes. Because a single check cannot convey duration, a useful method for getting an accurate record of continuous behaviors is a time sampling checklist.

Time sampling

Time sampling in some form is probably the technique generally used for observational research with children, although it is more complicated than other methods. When using a time sampling checklist, the total observation period is divided into short time intervals, for example, 30 or 60 seconds (often fewer for research), and one check is made in a given time interval for each occurrence of a category defined on the checklist (see Table 4). For a more detailed description of this technique, see Wright (1960).

Some interesting topics to investigate with this technique are the times a child spends alone, with one peer, in a group, with the teacher, or at different types of activities. Of course, all the guidelines for using frequency checklists—establishing definitions, eliminating sources of bias— apply here as well.

If time samplings are collected over a period of time, or if several observers work together, enough data can be accumulated to draw some valid conclusions. Results are likely to show, for example, that younger children spend more time playing alone, while older children play more in groups. Statistical methods could then be used to evaluate the probability that an observed difference occurred by chance. Equally interesting for most teachers would be whether the behavior of some children is similar to or contrary to what might be expected in development: two-year-old Philip may engage in more social play than the average four-year-old. To understand specific children, the observer needs to be aware of both general developmental milestones and individual variations.

Table 3.
Example frequency checklist for self-help skills

Name \ Behavior	Hangs up jacket/sweater without reminder	Puts equipment away after use
Week of *Nov. 12*		
Meaghan	✓✓	✓ ✓ ✓
Scott	✓	✓ ✓ ✓ ✓

Table 4.
Example of time sampling record of children's playground activities

Week of *June 27*. Fifteen-minute record, sampled once each minute.

Activity Child	Tricycle riding	Swinging	Sandbox	Climbing	Unoccupied/other
Kevin	✓✓✓✓✓		✓✓✓✓✓✓✓		✓✓✓

Selecting an observational method

What are the advantages and disadvantages of these observation methods? In all observation, a compromise must be made between the *qualitative* aspects of the record—the richness, the context, the sequence of events; and the *quantitative* aspects—the rate or frequency of events and the possibility for statistical evaluation. The running record conveys the quality of a child's behavior, but it requires much writing and the voluminous material is often difficult to summarize concisely. Checklists require little writing and yield numerical data that can be easily summarized and used for comparisons, but they lack the richness of the running record, and tell little about the dynamics of behavior or about interactions among children.

Some of the advantages of the running record can be retained without the disadvantages by narrowing the focus of an observation to a particular type of event and recording that event in its entirety. This method is called event sampling or an anecdotal record.

Event sampling or anecdotal record

After observing a group of children for a while, teachers may identify recurring incidents that they would like to understand better. In a situation with a group of very young children, some may have great difficulty in separating from their parents in the morning, while others do it with ease. What are the different ways that parents and children handle separation and why do some children have difficulty? By making brief anecdotal records of a series of separation episodes, we can begin to answer that question.

In other instances, we may notice an unusual amount of quarreling or become aware of several children who are often involved in fights; we then want to know how the quarrels get started and how they are resolved. We may be concerned with the difficulty a particular child has in making friends and want to look at the child's social overtures. We may want to examine how children respond to different types of discipline. In each case, by recording only the events of interest, the observer can collect much information with relatively little writing; an event can generally be recorded in three or four sentences. The observer can watch each event in its entirety, before writing it down (see Table 5).

The results of anecdotal records can yield information on both group and individual differences. An example of the use of event sampling for research is the classic study of children's quarrels by Dawe (1934). After recording 200 incidents, she compared the frequency of quarreling of boys versus girls, younger versus older children, and indoor versus outdoor play. While these differences could have been studied equally well with a checklist, anecdotal records allowed her to look at the causes of quarrels, their duration, the effect of teacher intervention, and the after-effects. Thus anecdotal records are particularly valuable in helping us understand the dynamics of behavior: the way a behavioral sequence begins, unfolds, and is concluded.

Teachers may be more interested in looking at differences among individuals. After collecting a number of incidents involving social overtures, we can begin to see, for example, that one child tends to join into activities in a disruptive way, without asking, and is frequently rejected, whereas another child asks permission or offers to help and is allowed to join in. Information such as this can be useful in helping the rejected child develop better strategies for social contact.

However, in using event sampling, much time may be taken waiting for the behavior to happen. This limitation is not serious for the more obvious, frequently occurring behaviors, such as social interaction or gross motor activity. But for behaviors that are either covert, infrequent, or difficult to observe, such as cognition, language, or fine motor coordination, practitioners can learn more from an informal interview—talking to a child or asking the child to do something—than they can by waiting until they see a sample of the behavior.

Informal interview

An informal interview is a direct but casual method for obtaining information from or about a child which is not available through naturalistic observation. This method is in some respects comparable to standardized tests, but, unlike tests, informal assessments can be conducted as the opportunity arises. Interviews should be presented as games or activities for the children, not as a test. Their aim is not, like a standardized test, to yield a precise score which can be compared with a norm, but rather to give an understanding of a child's strengths and weaknesses.

There are many different activities which can be used for this purpose. Important criteria are that the activities be interesting and enjoyable for the child, and that simple, readily available materials be used, which will yield results easy to interpret. One effective method is to ask children to draw, since this is a familiar

activity. Having them copy simple shapes (square, circle, triangle, cross, cross in circle, etc.) gives us insight into their coordination. We can have them draw themselves or a person; a simple count of the body parts included gives a rough index of maturity (Harris 1963). Without getting involved in the clinical implications of such drawings (e.g., Di Leo 1973), we can see a contrast between a small timid drawing and a bold forceful one. Older children can be asked to draw themselves and their family. Such a drawing can serve as the basis for conversations with children about their home, toys, pets, and favorite activities that help us understand them at school.

Children's language can be assessed as they converse, if we listen for clarity of speech, accuracy of grammar, length and complexity of sentences. We can probe language further by asking children to tell us what they did yesterday, or to retell a familiar story or TV incident. When they feel at ease in a conversation, we can introduce questions drawn from Piaget's work to assess logical thinking. If a boy has one brother, does he realize that his brother has a brother (Piaget 1928)? What is the child's concept of being alive? Does she or he believe the following are alive (and why): a tree, a clock, a bicycle, a car, a flower (Piaget 1929)? Additional ideas are available from Meisels and Wiske (1976). A few simple activities can be of tremendous value in getting a more complete picture of a child.

Interviews are thus good ways to fill in the gap left by the other, more detached, observational techniques. Some children may behave much the same in an interview as in other activities, but often a different side of the child is revealed in an interview. The shy child who usually works alone may be bright and verbal

Table 5.
Examples of event sampling: children's initiation of peer contact

T (girl, 4) walks over to B (boy, 3), takes his hand and they begin running together. B: "No, don't pull me. Let go." T drops hand and runs off.

F (boy, 4) calls across the room to M (girl, 4), "Come on, M. Let's play motorcycles." M runs across room making motorcycle noises and begins to play with F.

J (girl, 3) walks into doll house where L (girl, 3) is playing alone. L says, "Sit down and I'll fix dinner."

when given one-to-one attention with an adult. A child who is boastful and assertive with peers may be insecure and uncomfortable with an adult. Interviews provide further important clues to help make up the total picture of the child. However, an interview, even an informal one, is a somewhat restrictive situation which may limit the child's spontaneity and naturalness. Children may be shy, nervous, uncooperative, or overly eager to please, so that their performance is not typical. A child with poor verbal skills may be at a disadvantage. Like other methods, an interview should be regarded as additional input about the child, but not the whole picture.

For students or teachers to develop new observational skills and increase their competence, they need time to stand back from their day-to-day involvement and look at children and their program with some degree of detachment. Practitioners without extensive resources may need to be creative in finding ways to do this. Aides or parent assistants, with an explanation of the project, might assist a teacher temporarily. The program director may find it valuable to spend time in the classroom to free a teacher for observing, or the director may wish to make systematic observations of the children. Local college or university students may be interested in gaining practical experience with children while freeing teachers for observation. These university students and researchers might also be interested in collaborating with teachers on observational studies of mutual interest. While teachers could profit from the opportunity to work with experienced observers, the researchers could gain from teachers the insights derived from their direct knowledge of children.

Conclusion

The ability to understand children through observation might be compared to the ability to judge fine art. We all respond to art—positively, negatively, indifferently—but the person with experience and training can better assess the aesthetic value of a work of art. Similarly, we all form impressions of children, but for the inexperienced observer, the impression may be inaccurate, biased, or limited in scope. As we gain more skill and experience, we know better how to look at children, what to look for, and how to interpret what we see.

The methods of observation described here are just a beginning. Additional suggestions can be found in Boehm and Weinberg (1977) and Irwin and Bushnell (1980). With practice, the teacher or student will learn to use a variety of observation techniques to gain understanding of the particular combination of attitudes, abilities, and traits that make up the uniqueness of each child.

References

Boehm, A. E., and Weinberg, R. *The Classroom Observer: A Guide for Developing Observation Skills.* New York: Teachers College Press, 1977.

Bruner, J., and Postman, L. "On the Perception of Incongruity: A Paradigm." *Journal of Personality* 18 (1949): 206–223.

Cohen, D., and Stern, V. *Observing and Recording the Behavior of Young Children.* New York: Teachers College Press, 1958.

Dawe, H. "An Analysis of Two Hundred Quarrels of Preschool Children." *Child Development* 5 (1934): 139–157.

Di Leo, J. *Children's Drawings As Diagnostic Aids.* New York: Brunner/Mazel, 1973.

Harris, D. B. *Children's Drawings As Measures of Intellectual Maturity.* New York: Harcourt, Brace & World, 1963.

Irwin, D. M., and Bushnell, M. M. *Observational Strategies for Child Study.* New York: Holt, Rinehart & Winston, 1980.

Meisels, S., and Wiske, M. S. *The Eliot-Pearson Screening Inventory.* Medford, Mass.: Department of Child Study, Tufts University, 1976.

Mischel, W. "On the Interface of Cognition and Personality: Beyond the Person-Situation Debate." *American Psychologist* 34 (1979): 740–754.

Moore, S. G., and Cooper, C. R. "Personal and Scientific Sources of Knowledge about Children." In *The Young Child: Reviews of Research, Volume 3,* ed. S. G. Moore and C. R. Cooper, pp. 1–9. Washington, D.C.: National Association for the Education of Young Children, 1982.

Piaget, J. *Judgement and Reasoning in the Child.* London: Routledge & Kegan Paul, 1928.

Piaget, J. *The Child's Conception of the World.* London: Routledge & Kegan Paul, 1929.

Rowan, B. *The Children We See: An Observational Approach to Child Study.* New York: Holt, Rinehart & Winston, 1973.

Shaplin, J. T. "Practice in Teaching." In *Breakthroughs to Better Teaching.* Montpelier, Vt.: Capitol City Press, 1966.

Wright, H. R. "Observational Child Study." In *Handbook of Research in Child Development,* ed. P. Mussen. New York: Wiley, 1960.

Wright, H. R. *Recording and Analyzing Child Behavior.* New York: Harper & Row, 1967.

TestingTestingTesting TestingTesting

How to make sense out of Achievement Tests

Dr. Lester L. Laminack
and Dr. Patricia J. Anderson

Dr. Laminack is on the staff of the Department of Elementary Education and Reading, Western Carolina University, Cullowhee, NC. Dr. Anderson is in the Department of Elementary Education, East Carolina University, Greenville, NC

C ecil's teacher just phoned to arrange a conference to discuss the results of Cecil's second-grade achievement test. Mrs. Parks immediately began to dread the moment; ''How will I know if he's improving?'' I didn't understand all that 'test talk' last year. He's made good grades. What else do I need to know?''

Like many parents, Mrs. Parks is apprehensive about a situation where her knowledge may be minimal. To aid parents in similar circumstances, here are easy-to-understand explanations of often-asked questions about children's achievement test scores—

QUESTION #1: Last year when Cecil was in first grade, he scored second grade, third month, in reading. I never did understand why they didn't give him a second-grade book.
ANSWER: Second-Grade, third month (2.3) is referred to by educators as a grade equivalent. Most importantly, this score does not indicate that children have mastered material at that grade level. For example, Cecil's score of 2.3 does not indicate that he should be given a second-grade reader. Rather,

this score signifies that the ''average'' child who had been in second-grade for three months would have earned an equivalent score on the *same* test that Cecil took. While second-graders may not have actually taken that specific test, scores such as grade equivalents have been determined by mathematical calculations. At the time of the test, actual second-grade material may have been too difficult for Cecil to experience success. Therefore, Cecil's teacher acted wisely by not advancing him into second-grade material.

QUESTION #2: It seems contradictory that Cecil could score 2.3 in reading but only be in the 60th percentile. When I was in school, 60 wasn't even passing.
ANSWER: The first important point to understand is that percentiles and percentages are two different scores. The *percentage* refers to the *actual* number of correct responses compared to the *possible* number of correct responses. In many cases the actual percentage is not even reported. The *percentile*, on the other hand, refers to a child's relative standing within a group. For example, Cecil's score at the 60th percentile indicates that he scored as well as, or better than, 60% of the norm group (a group of similar students who have taken the same test). A national, state, or local group could be used for comparison. Indentifying the origin of the norm group would be advantageous for Mrs. Parks to understand Cecil's scores.

QUESTION #3: Cecil's teacher showed me a sample of the test that he took. I know he'd never even studied some of those things. Why do they give tests like that to first-graders?
ANSWER #3: Cecil's test is called an achievement test. A variety of them are available from different publishing companies. Most achievement tests have been designed to measure children's present mastery of a given body of knowledge. School personnel feel that it is important to keep yearly records of a child's progress. This enables them to more accurately tailor instruction for individual students. These tests are not written for specific schools or classrooms; therefore, they test general infor-

mation that is considered by test makers to be appropriate for the targeted grade level. Almost all of these tests have been standardized, indicating that a set of unchanging procedures are to be followed in giving children a fair and equal chance for success.

QUESTION #4: How is it possible for Cecil to score 1.7 in comprehension and 2.8 in vocabulary? I thought that he only took one test.

ANSWER: Cecil took a series of subtests known as a battery. This format is typical of achievement tests. Each subtest is designed to measure specific kinds of information. The reading section of an achievement test, for example, may consist of several subtests such as comprehension (understanding what was read), vocabulary (identifying word meanings), or word recognition (using phonics and other word-attack skills). A discrepancy between scores on subtests generally indicates areas of strengths and weaknesses. Such information can be valuable to teachers as they plan instruction for their students.

QUESTION #5: Like most parents, I want Cecil to do his best. What should I do to get him ready for next year's achievement test?

ANSWER: Perhaps the best way to answer this question is to provide a list of guidelines that could be followed throughout the school year.

Positive attitude: It is imperative that parents encourage and support their children's efforts. Generally, when parents perceive school to be important and worthwhile, children will acquire similar attitudes.

Parent-teacher conferences: Although children bring home their school work regularly, it is important for parents and teachers to communicate periodically throughout the school year. Both parents and teachers can benefit from open communication between the home and school.

Homework: Through regular monitoring of homework, parents can determine topics being studied at school. Designed to reinforce skills being learned in the classroom, homework can also help children learn responsibility and develop proper study skills. Parents should realize that children's homework is important; therefore, it is essential that they encourage their children to work as independently as possible.

During the week of the achievement test, it is especially important to consider the following points—

Avoid pressure: It is quite natural for parents to want the best from their children. However, it may be counterproductive to overemphasize the significance of the results of an achievement test. This may indeed establish unrealistic goals for children.

Diet and Rest: Research has shown that children's performance in school (and on achievement tests) is better when they have had adequate sleep and a balanced diet.

By helping parents become better informed about test-taking, and its results, you will surely reduce their tensions—which will have only beneficial spin-off effects on their children. Test scores may even jump a few points!

Index

academic achievement: declining, 18; of latchkey children, 50, 52; effect of television on, 29-31

accountability, and pressure on children, 18

achievement tests: of children of teen-mothers, 125; parents' questions about, 240-241

adolescents: developmental effects on children of pregnant, 122-128; and Head Start, 148-150; and parenting, 145-147

adulthood, children hurried into, 17-19

adoption, questions children ask about, 66

adults: as activists in child advocacy, 14-16; authoritative vs. authoritarian, 12; as role models, 12-13

advocacy, and need for action in early childhood profession, 14-16

after-school child care, role of schools in, 102

aggression, effect of television violence on child, 31-34

Aid to Families with Dependent Children, 146

alcoholism, effect of, on babies, 123

allergic children, 190, 191

anecdotal record, 237-238

angel-dust, and addicted mothers, 123, 124

animism, 214

aphasic children, 188

arithmetic: and Piaget's constructivism, 198, 199; and Piaget's theory of intelligence, 214-217; *see also*, math

art: of children in middle childhood years, 70; as necessary to child's education, 62

arts, value of, in schools, 19

associationism, vs. constructivism, 198, 199,200

attentiveness, and crying in infants, 77authoritative vs. authoritarian adults, 12

autistic children, and symbolic play, 188

babies, *see* infants

basic principles, of child development, 9-16

behavior: of children of divorce, 130; of gifted children, 182-183; solving problems of, 164-167; of stepchildren, 136

behaviorism, vs. Piaget's constructivism, 197-201

birth, questions children ask about, 64-65

birth weight, low, 123, 147

blacks, and Head Start, 145, 146

blended family, *see* stepfamily

body contact: importance of, in early child development, 225-227; need of infants for, 76, 89

brain, at seven years of age, 68

business, day care provided by, 94-95

carbon monoxide, and effect of smoking on fetus, 123

centering, 215, 216

centration, 154, 215

child abuse: in child care programs, 225-227; in day care settings, 94; parental neglect as, 45-48

child care: by adolescents to their infants, 122-128; for infants, 76-79, 88-92; selecting quality, 72-79; by stepparents, 135-144; for toddlers, 88-92; for two-year-olds, 80-87; *see also,* daycare

child development: basic concepts of, 9-16; from birth to twelve, 56-59; importance of body contact to, 225-227; caregiver's awareness of infant stages of, 77-78, 88-92; philosophy vs. educational practices, 196, 197; importance of play in, 185-189; at seven years of age, 68-71; effects of television on, 28; at two years of age, 80-87

childhood: historical view of, 24-27; characteristics of middle, 69; and pressure to hurry into adulthood, 17-19

childrearing: historical practices of, 25-26; teenage, 122-128; *see also,* parenting

children: from birth to 12, 56-59; black vs. white, 147; effects of day care on, 96-100; and discipline in classroom, 164-171; and divorce, 129-134; benefits of dramatic play to, 205-213; gifted preschoolers, 182-184; handicapped, 187-188; hurried into adulthood, 17-19; intrinsic motivation of, 60-63; latchkey, 49-53; medically special, 190-193; minority, and Head Start, 145; neglected, 45-48; Piaget's theory of development of intelligence in, 151-158; importance of play to, 185-187; programming of, for success, 159-161; questions asked by, 64-67; relaxation techniques to teach to, 178; and satisfactions of teaching, 220, 221; self-control in, 168-171; and stepparents, 17, 135-144; and stress, 176-179; effects of television on young, 28-39; choosing good toys for, 202-204

Children's Defense Fund (CDF), 145

cigarette smoking, effect of, on unborn child, 123

classroom: creativity in, 228-232; discipline problems in, 164-167; help for children of divorce in, 131, 132

cognitive development: from birth to twelve years of age, 56-59; of infants, 88-92; of infants and quality care, 76-79; of seven-year-olds, 68-71; of toddlers, 88-92; of two-year-olds, 80-87

collective monologue, 215

commercials, effect of television, on children, 36

common sense, and Piaget's theory of constructivism, 196-201

concrete operational stage of thinking (Piaget), 151, 153, 156, 214

conservation, concept of, and Piaget, 155

Consortium for Longitudinal Studies, 42-44

constructivism: vs. behaviorism, 197-199; vs. maturation, 199; of Piaget, 197-201

construct knowledge, 199, 201

corporate-sponsored day care, 94-95

counselors: and children of divorce, 133; and problems in stepfamilies, 142

creativity: and children's intrinsic motivation, 60-63; in the classroom 228-232; and gifted, 183

curiosity: and common questions children ask, 64-67; importance of nurturing children's, 63

curriculum: for gifted preschoolers, 184; and helping children with separation anxiety, 174

day care: for children of adolescents, 122; America's need for quality, 93-95; centers, 223; check list for quality, 99; effects of, on children, 96-100; corporate-sponsored, 94-95; Kaiser Centers for wartime, 6-8; for latchkey children, 49, 52-53; teachers as underpaid, 222-224

death, questions children ask about, 67

discipline: approaches to classroom problems of, 164-167; and building self-control in young children, 168-171

disinhibitory effect, of television violence, 33

divorce: effect of, on children, 129, 130; questions children ask about, 65-66; remarriage and stepfamilies, 135-144; role of schools with children of, 131, 132

drawing-writing-reading progression, 61-62

drugs: and hyperactive children, 192, 193; effect of, on infants of addicted mothers, 123, 124

early childhood education: 196-201, 220, 221; for infants, 76-79, 88-92; past two decades of, 108-109; characteristics of quality, 72-79; for toddlers, 88-92; for two-year-olds, 80-87; *see also*, child care; day care; early intervention programs; preschool

early childhood professionals: in infant day care, 76-79, 88-92; traits of quality, 72-73; as partners with schools, 101-103; in toddler education, 88-92; and two-year-olds, 80-87

early intervention programs: for gifted children, 183, 184; for handicapped children, 185, 187-189; and Head Start research, 41-44; for neglected children, 46, 47; role of schools in, 101-103; *see also,* child care; day care; early childhood education; preschool

egocentrism, 154, 155, 156, 215

eighties, the, early childhood education in, 109

eight years of age, 59

Elkind, David, 14, 17-19, 52, 70, 105, 113

emotional development: from birth to twelve, 56-59; importance of caregiver to, 88-92; of children hurried into adulthood, 17-19; of infants, 76-79; effect of parental neglect on child's, 45, 46; of seven-year-old, 68-71; of two-year-old, 80-87

enrollment, statistics on preschool, 20-21

epileptic children, 191-192

Erikson, Erik, 69, 77

event sampling, 237-238

expectations, effect of low teenage mother's, on infant development, 125

family: and children of divorce, 129-134; female-headed, 146; effect of trends in, on Head Start programs, 145-150; step-, 135-144; impact of television on, 36-37

family history, 24-27

fears, of latchkey children, 52

Credits/ Acknowledgments

Cover design by Charles Vitelli

1. Perspective
Facing overview—UN photo/John Isaac. 10—United Nations/photo by L. Barns.
2. Childhood and Society
Facing overview—Elaine M. Ward. 51—Anna Kaufman Moon.
3. Development and Educational Opportunities
Facing overview—T. Polumbaum. 108-110—Photographs by Kay Pardee. 113-114—Photos by Barbara Simmons.
4. Families, Child Rearing, and Parent Education
Facing overview—UN photo. 138—photo by Faith Bowlus.

5. Behavior, Stressors, and Guidance
Facing overview—Elaine M. Ward. 172-173—Courtesy of Nancy Balaban.
6. Children and Special Needs
Facing overview—United Nations/photo by S. Dimartini.
7. Curricular Applications
Facing overview—Elaine M. Ward.
8. Teaching and Evaluation
Facing overview—United Nations/photo by M. Pinter. 220—Bruce Grossman. 221—Karyl Gatteno.

ANNUAL EDITIONS:
EARLY CHILDHOOD EDUCATION 86/87
Article Rating Form

Here is an opportunity for you to have direct input into the next revision of this volume. We would like you to rate each of the 49 articles listed below, using the following scale:

1. **Excellent: should definitely be retained**
2. **Above average: should probably be retained**
3. **Below average: should probably be deleted**
4. **Poor: should definitely be deleted**

Your ratings will play a vital part in the next revision. So please mail this prepaid form to us just as soon as you complete it.
Thanks for your help!

Rating	Article	Rating	Article
	1. The Best Day Care There Ever Was		27. The Teacher's Role in Facilitating a Child's Adjustment to Divorce
	2. What Is Basic for Young Children?		28. Blended Families: Overcoming the Cinderella Myth
	3. Who Are We in the Lives of Children?		29. Changing Family Trends: Head Start Must Respond
	4. The Hurried Child		30. Practical Parenting with Piaget
	5. The Statistical Trends		31. I'm Worried About Our Kids
	6. Childhood Through the Ages		32. Classroom Discipline Problems? Fifteen Humane Solutions
	7. Television and Young Children		33. Building Self-Control: Discipline for Young Children
	8. Head Start: How Research Changed Public Policy		34. The Name of the Game Is Confidence
	9. Wednesday's Child		35. Stress: What Makes Kids Vulnerable?
	10. Latchkey Children: The Fastest-Growing Special Interest Group in the Schools		36. Meeting the Needs of Gifted Preschoolers
	11. Your Child—From Birth to Twelve		37. How Important Is Play for Handicapped Children?
	12. What Do Young Children Teach Themselves?		38. The Medically Special Child
	13. Why, Mommy, Why?		39. Leading Primary Education Toward Excellence: Beyond Worksheets and Drill
	14. Is Seven the Perfect Age?		40. Choosing Good Toys for Young Children
	15. How to Choose a Good Early Childhood Program		41. Encouraging Dramatic Play in Early Childhood
	16. Meeting the Needs of Infants		42. Piaget: The Six-Year-Old and Modern Math
	17. The Real World of Teaching Two-Year-Old Children		43. The Satisfactions
	18. Very Early Childhood Education for Infants and Toddlers		44. Overworked and Underpaid
	19. Day Care in America		45. Can Teachers Touch Children Anymore?
	20. The Day-Care Child		46. 15 Ways to Cultivate Creativity in Your Classroom
	21. Early Childhood and the Public Schools		47. Thoughts on Creativity
	22. Readiness: Should We Make Them Ready or Let Them Bloom?		48. Observing Children: Ideas for Teachers
	23. The 5s and 6s Go to School		49. Testing Testing Testing Testing Testing
	24. When Parents of Kindergarteners Ask "Why?"		
	25. Nebraska State Board of Education		
	26. Developmental Effects of Children of Pregnant Adolescents		

(cont. on next page)

ABOUT YOU

Name _____ Date _____

Are you a teacher? ☐ Or student? ☐

Your School Name _____

Department _____

Address _____

City _____ State _____ Zip _____

School Telephone # _____

YOUR COMMENTS ARE IMPORTANT TO US!

Please fill in the following information:

For which course did you use this book? _____

Did you use a text with this Annual Edition?   ☐ yes ☐ no

The title of the text: _____

What are your general reactions to the Annual Editions concept?

Have you read any particular articles recently that you think should be included in the next edition?

Are there any articles you feel should be replaced in the next edition? Why?

Are there other areas that you feel would utilize an Annual Edition?

May we contact you for editorial input?

May we quote you from above?

EARLY CHILDHOOD EDUCATION 86/87